THE REALITY OF CHRISTIANITY

Makers of Modern Theology

Edited by Jaroslav Pelikan

PUBLISHED:

Philip Hefner
FAITH AND THE VITALITIES OF HISTORY
A Theological Study Based on the Work of Albrecht Ritschl

Peter C. Hodgson
THE FORMATION OF HISTORICAL THEOLOGY
A Study of Ferdinand Christian Baur

G. Wayne Glick
THE REALITY OF CHRISTIANITY
A Study of Adolf von Harnack as Historian and Theologian

FORTHCOMING:

Paul Sponheim
KIERKEGAARD

Gerhard Spiegler
SCHLEIERMACHER

Adolf von Harnack

A Study of Adolf von Harnack as Historian and Theologian

THE REALITY OF CHRISTIANITY

G. WAYNE GLICK

HARPER & ROW, PUBLISHERS
NEW YORK, EVANSTON, AND LONDON

FIRST EDITION

LIBRARY OF CONGRESS CATALOG CARD NUMBER: *67–14938*

E-R

TO MY FATHER AND MOTHER

AND

TO BARBARA

*"Das Entscheidende ist nicht,
dass man das Ziel erreicht,
sondern dass man den
richtigen Weg geht."*

—Ernst von Harnack,
son of Adolf, while
awaiting execution
(3 March, 1945).

Contents

Editor's Preface

IF THIS series of monographs on "Makers of Modern Theology" is motivated by any *Tendenz,* that *Tendenz* may be said to lie in two convictions: that theological work needs to be informed by substantial historical scholarship, and that the theology of the nineteenth century needs to be restudied for its relevance to the twentieth century.

On both these counts a book about Adolf von Harnack belongs in the series, for among the theologians of the nineteenth (and, for that matter, the twentieth) century none has done more to enthrone historical scholarship as a theological discipline than he. For half a century his lectures, articles, and books helped to mould generations of students, pastors, and professors in the principles and practice of historical study as a way of making theology meaningful and of keeping it honest. With an erudition that would probably have been attributed to witchcraft in a more supernaturalistic age, Harnack ranged from the New Testament to his own times, bringing to men and ideas the catholicity of a civilized, humanistic spirit and the precision of a trained, inquisitive mind. Chapters from his various books could stand as individual portraits of the great; for example, his summary of Augustine in his *History of Dogma* or his essay on Leibnitz in his *History of the Prussian Academy of Sciences* would deserve to be reprinted by themselves, as models of how the historian who is also a man of letters can meet the past on its own ground.

That historiographical ideal is currently regarded as altogether naïve and unsophisticated. Harnack's very lectures on *The Essence of Christianity* are taken as proof that the historian inevitably superimposes the presuppositions of his own situation upon the historical material, since the questions he asks of the past cannot but come from the present. Shaped as so much of it has been by the various "quests for the historical Jesus," this attitude toward history has become almost a consensus uniting theologians of radically divergent positions in a dismissal of what Collingwood calls "philological history" as a distortion of the historian's assignment. For such theologians, Harnack's occasional forays into the question of contemporary relevance—above all, of course, his lectures of 1899–1900—are far more important than the thousands of pages of patristic texts for whose editing and publication he was responsible or the painstaking historical reconstructions by which he put literary, theological, and administrative data into perspective. Harnack himself recognized that such a shift was going on, and in his later years voiced a foreboding that scientific [*wissenschaftlich*] theology would soon be inundated by a new obscurantism. Some of this was certainly the gloom of an old man and a *laudator temporis acti*, but the decades since the death of Harnack have borne out his fear that a new subjectivism, claiming to be more ruthlessly honest than the old "positivism," would cripple historical theology by demanding that it be theologically concerned and committed in a special way. It is time for the pupils of Harnack's pupils to look more deeply into the work of the master himself.

G. Wayne Glick has helped to make possible such a new and deeper look into Harnack. Although by no means a "Harnackian," he has paid Harnack the compliment of studying both his life and his work as Harnack had studied the life and work of so many others—by industrious research into the primary sources. The very criticisms of Harnack's method and results which Dr. Glick expresses are set into the framework of Harnack's scholarship and therefore are all the more telling. Part Two of this book makes a contribution to historical literature in English that is valuable even apart from Harnack, for it takes the American and British reader into a period of Continental theological development that is little known west of the English Channel. Yet without an awareness of the theological *milieu* at Dorpat and Erlangen, neither Harnack's continuing preoccupation with tradition nor his special version of its history can be understood. The chapter on Adolf Harnack's relation to his father, Theodosius, is a sensitive and instructive essay on that *milieu*. The main body of this monograph is contained in its third and fourth parts, where the three most influential books of Harnack—*History of Dogma*, *Marcion*, and *The Essence of Christianity*—are evaluated for their historical and theological importance. The reductionism of the *Essence* is not spared, and the evidences of it in other works are properly noted. But Harnack's historical work is read as history and not merely as theology, as scholarship and not merely as testimony.

The result is a portrait of Harnack that is both critical and constructive. If Glick is right in his evaluation, no one can identify some "essence" in the Christian faith with Harnack's version of the gospel; nor dare we use that "essence" as a touchstone for differentiating between authentic and inauthentic development in the history of Christian doctrine. But the other implication of Glick's monograph is no less clear. We may presume to criticize Harnack only if our dedication to the hard work of historical study is as single-minded as his was. If Harnack the theologian shaped Harnack the historian, this means that we shall not be able to escape the limitations of our own blick either. It means also that we dare not use this blick as an excuse for scholarly indolence. His questions addressed to *die Verächter der wissenschaftlichen Theologie unter den Theologen* (see p. 223 ff.) are still a summons to do the work of a historian with as much honesty and care as we can organize and not to let the abstract problematics of historical method paralyze the scholarly enterprise. We can bear to learn that lesson, and Adolf von Harnack can teach it effectively through the pages of this monograph.

Yale University JAROSLAV PELIKAN

Author's Preface

HARNACK WAS a dangerous exemplar for anyone who would write about Harnack. The person who fascinated him most continuously in all of the nineteen centuries of the history of Christianity was Marcion. His first "trophy" was a gold medal, won at Dorpat in a competition for the best essay on the subject "Marcionis doctrina e Tertulliani adversus Marcionem libris eruatur et explicetur." It was not until *fifty* years later, on June 27, 1920, that Harnack completed his work entitled *Marcion: das Evangelium vom fremden Gott.*

In 1952, I visited Professor Wilhelm Pauck at the University of Chicago in order to discuss with him the possibility of preparing a dissertation spanning the biblical and theological fields. Specifically, I suggested as a topic "Reinhold Niebuhr's Hermeneutics." Pauck's reaction was definite: "There isn't any thesis there; you can't make up a thesis and impose it on the material. It has to arise out of the material." I tried again: "What about Adolf Harnack's Biblical Interpretation?" The face of this very great teacher—who had already accepted a call to the Union Theological Seminary, as I was to learn later in the day—lit up, and the comment was characteristically forthright: "Now there's a thesis!" Indeed so.

Professors Pelikan and Nichols inherited the not-so-young theologue, and for the next several arduous years admonished, advised, shepherded and stretched him as he increasingly immersed himself in the life and thought of a man for whom theology *was* vocation. No words can express the gratitude which I have felt, continuously since those days, toward these men. Yet, the initial milestone of the "lollypop" having been passed, it appeared that this dissertation also would find its way into that unlamented limbo of the "dissertation room." For a few years following 1957, when the work was completed, there were the inevitable papers and articles which a dissertation breeds. Then there was "college administration," decanal duties—and a bad conscience!

It was again Professor Pelikan who provided the incentive and the occasion for the return to this work. For that also I am deeply grateful. A leave of absence made available to me by the Board of Trustees of Franklin and Marshall College provided the time to rework the material of the dissertation and present it for publication; and I am sensible and appreciative of this favor.

Also, I owe a debt to a wife and three children who, if they do not love Harnack as I have come to, must feel that they know him about as well. No bromide about duty to scholarship can release me from the feeling of guilt toward these four beloved people who have experienced, existentially, the *pater absconditus.* I can only pray that the redemption of that guilt will not have to wait as long as the fulfillment of my duty to scholarship.

It seems appropriate to include here a word regarding the conception which has guided the preparation of this book. It will quickly become apparent that the work is mainly expository; and this is deliberately the case. For those whose theological training has been dominated by the *Nein* of Basel, the *Ja* of Berlin must be heard in all the registers in which it sounded. This can be accomplished only by quotation; and the number and extensiveness of the quotations is therefore definitely *not* a coincidence. I have discovered that Kant, for example, is easier to read than Kant's interpreters; and Harnack's erudite and flashing prose deserves better than barely concealed summary. This may not be, therefore, the book that someone else would have written, but what has been written has been deliberately conceived.

Comment needs to be made also about the inclusion of the work of certain critics of Harnack in this volume. Here, an alternate principle has been followed. I have not attempted anything like a complete cataloguing or analysis of Harnack's critics, but have sought out those whose critiques are "type-criticisms," and have developed only that part of their work which is relevant to Harnack's point of view. That this may have resulted in a lack of a balanced view regarding the critic is a possibility I have felt worth risking.

The inevitable problem of translation may be alluded to here, though the notes will make clear what practice has been followed. Had I believed it worthwhile, I would now be able to say that all the translations are my own, and I am responsible for any faults thereof. Instead, I will say that all of the translations are not my own, and I am responsible for any faults thereof. The translation of the *Dogmengeschichte*, to use the most egregious example, is poor; I have done my own translations. The translations, obversely, by Thomas Bailey Saunders, are good; I have used them. *Und so weiter*. In no case have I failed to collate translation and original, however, and therefore I *am* responsible for any flaws.

That the writer has "fought" Harnack will be obvious. A point of view is not lacking, and though I have tried to be fair, I have also tried to identify my commitments as—my commitments. Harnack would not have approved of such "commitments" in a historical work; but he was one of those who taught the epigons by his example that they are inevitable.

"To know [him] you must love him; to love [him] you must know him": so the old saying goes. The Harnack who emerges from these pages will, doubtless, lack the full and vibrant power of the Dorpat *Uberflüssiger* who became the confidant of emperors and one of the greatest church historians of the nineteenth century. But that will not be due to any lack of esteem. He deserves better than these pages can grant; but there will be others to complete what is here set forth. As a catalyst to that end, at least, may this work serve its purpose.

Keuka College G. Wayne Glick
February, 1967

THE REALITY OF CHRISTIANITY

PART ONE

INTRODUCTORY

I

The Search for Reality

DAS WESEN *des Christentums,* whether or not epochal for theological liberalism, *was* the watershed in the career of Adolf von Harnack. The question to which this work presented an answer was the question that subsumed all of Harnack's historical and theological work. To be sure, one cannot interpret Harnack adequately if, as has often been the case, this work alone is entered into evidence. For what had preceded this series of extemporaneous lectures was a life singularly given to theological scholarship, rich in received influences and capable of capitalizing on them; and what followed the 1899–1900 winter-semester lectures was an increasingly varied and influential activity in a vast number of German scientific and cultural organizations. A watershed is the apex of a range; and one reaches such an apex only after traversing the settled plains and the rising slopes, crossing the timber line, and negotiating the lonely stretches that lead to the summit. What one sees from this vantage-point will, no doubt, depend upon the eye with which he sees: Harnack was no different here from any other man. But what he saw, and what he proclaimed in this "symbolic concatenation of liberalism,"[1] was *won*; it came as no simple gift.

[1] Ernst Troeltsch, *Gesammelte Schriften,* Band III: *Der Historismus und seine Probleme* (Tübingen: Mohr, 1922), p. 42.

Harnack's problem was the problem of meaning. This is not to say that he was *primarily* a philosopher, or that he self-consciously set out to perceive "the meaning in history." The meaning with which he was concerned had to do, so far as his own intention was concerned, with the reality of Christianity. To his marrow he believed that the emancipating studies represented by the vigorous discipline of "historical investigation" would yield an answer to this question. Others had failed, to be sure: the ancients because, among other things, they had been dominated by the Hellenistic categories; Luther because he had been too much a captive of his time to break completely with the encystation of medieval Catholicism; Baur, perhaps, because the science of history had not sufficiently established its domain as its own, and had been too dependent on covert philosophical and theological groundings. But history was now prepared, thanks in no small measure to the army of trained philologists and exegetes he himself had marshaled, to discover this meaning and identify "the reality of Christianity."

Conclusions should be stated at the end, rather than at the beginning of a study. But it is important to make clear at the outset that *this* problem, the *Wesen* (not so much the *essence*, perhaps, as the *reality*[2]) of Christianity, is, above all others, Harnack's problem. The form of statement of the problem may vary. The lines of inquiry that strike off from this center are multiform. But the burning center of a life for which theology was vocation remains always the same: what is that reality of Christianity that has stirred men in all ages and stirs them still today? And how does one discover it?

These are *Harnack's* questions. They are *not* the questions of many who have evaluated his work, bearing tribute to his genius at the same time that they express demurrers as to his identification of the problem and his historical method. From the beginning of his scholarly activity, his concern to relate this activity to one's existential situation (he would have avoided the term) led him to certain viewpoints which his critics regarded as anthropocentric. The sharpest and in many ways the most poignant illustration of this charge came in the exchange, in the early twenties, with Karl Barth. But the charge came often, throughout his career.

Someone once remarked that the most crucial sentence in a book

[2] *Passim*, but particularly in Chap. XIV, the reasons for this alternative statement are presented. The point may indeed appear trifling; but the desirability of shattering the categories and looking at Harnack *de novo* justifies the substitution. More to the point, "reality," as a nonphilosophical term, is more accurate.

is the first sentence, for one is inevitably committed from that point on to the categories there established. There may be truth in the statement. It may also be the fact that anyone who has immersed himself in Adolf Harnack, and particularly in his "search for the reality," cannot but be influenced in his own method to search for the *center*, the *key*, the "reality of Harnack."

Therein lies a danger, with several facets. On the one hand, we can quote Harnack's own statements as to what his problem was. In the choice of those statements there will therefore be a commitment for all that follows. On the other hand, Harnack was no different from other men in stating "his problem" in different ways at different times. And since, like all of us, he carried his cultural baggage with him, there are at least nuances in the different expressions which leave us with the bad feeling that all may not be as simple as it appears. The danger is that we will beset Harnack with too many categories, or with the wrong categories, and will end up with an "ideological" representation. It helps little to recall that this is what Troeltsch believed Harnack did in the writing of his own history,[3] and in turn, Löwith believes that Troeltsch did the same thing.[4]

Can there be any cutting of the Gordian knot? Can anyone completely divest himself of the *a priori*? Should we not rather run to the Goethean refuge: "Not all that is presented to us as history has really happened; and what has really happened did not really happen the way it is presented to us; moreover, what has really happened is only a small part of all that has happened. Everything in history remains uncertain, the largest as well as the smallest."[5] Or, in the words of a contemporary, shall we not admit that

[3] *Op. cit.*, p. 369.

[4] Karl Löwith, *Meaning in History* (Chicago: The University of Chicago Press, 1949), p. 225: "When Troeltsch and Dilthey endeavored to 'overcome' the dogmatic presuppositions of the theology and metaphysics of history, their actual standard of judgment was their dogmatic belief in the absolute value of history as such." Löwith takes radical exception to this denigration. For a more complete discussion of the "historicist" point of view and the extent of Harnack's adherence to it, see Part Five. For a brief discussion of "the problem of certainty" as this affected Lutheran thought, see Jaroslav Pelikan, *From Luther to Kierkegaard* (St. Louis: Concordia Publishing House, 1950), pp. 58–59. Bibliographical references on this problem are given by Pelikan on p. 142 of the same work.

[5] Quoted by Wilhelm Pauck in *The Heritage of the Reformation* (Glencoe: The Free Press of Glencoe, Inc., 1961) p. 342. Harnack has used the quotation in his lecture on "Die Religion Goethes in der Epoche seiner Vol-

More intelligent than the superior vision of philosophers and theologians is the common sense of the natural man and the uncommon sense of the Christian believer. Neither pretends to discern on the canvas of human history the purpose of God or of the historical process itself. They rather seek to set men free from the world's oppressive history by suggesting an attitude, either of skepticism or of faith, which is rooted in an experience certainly nurtured by history but detached from and surpassing it, and thus enabling man to endure it with mature resignation or with faithful expectation.[6]

That is a way out of the difficulty, but even if it were taken (we doubt its efficacy), it can be only at the end rather than at the beginning of a search. The vaunted "common sense of the natural man" or, indeed, "the uncommon sense of the Christian believer" is no less subject to the permeative influences of a "culture" than is the vision of the theologians. Our problem, therefore, is to recognize that we are shaped by culture, to recognize that anyone we study was also shaped by culture, to "sin bravely" with respect to the categories we employ, to be honest—this above everything else—in allowing these categories to arise out of the material at hand, and to remember, with Cromwell, that "we might be wrong." If these are the principles that guide us, we can in good conscience attempt to assess the "reality of Harnack," setting him in the historical background from which he came and orienting him to the intellectual world to which he contributed.

In the original preparation of this work, "the statement of the problem" took ten pages. I present this statement now, aware of the legitimacy of the charge that such a presentation represents tangential and profligate, rather than brave, sinning. But nothing in the past ten years has changed my mind on the basic *questions*. If the answers to those questions are given in a more muted cadence, with more panegyric and less criticism, it will only be because subsequent study has provided "richer points of view."

"How can I become his disciple?": this was the existential question. And the question must be answered, in order to be true to the limits within which man exists, solely by an appeal to the historical.

---

lendung," *Reden und Aufsätze*, Band IV, Neue Folge: *Erforschtes und Erlebtes* (Giessen: Töpelmann, 1923), p. 157. Hereafter items in this series will be designated *RA*, with the appropriate volume number, and NF in the case of the new series. The five volumes of the new series have titles; the two volumes of the original *Reden und Aufsätze* do not.

[6] Löwith, *op. cit.*, pp. vii–viii.

On the surface this appears to be a modest goal. But for Harnack, who early had been introduced to historical-critical methodology, who had accepted the Ritschlian viewpoint, historical investigation must be carried out without theological assumptions. The orthodox theology, he wrote to Ritschl during the Giessen years, "probes behind the historical facts. . . . You stand upon them."[7]

Fidelity to historical method as Harnack conceived it depends upon this abjuring of all dogmatic bias. We suggest that Harnack was faithful to this principle when the bias was of an orthodox or a speculative variety. The crucial question, however, is whether he was also willing or able to abjure the bias of the "new" theology (i.e., Ritschlianism). Harnack seems to have believed that precisely here lay the strength of Ritschl's formulation: that his historical-critical method had no theological axes to grind. In his *Christianity and History*[8] there is a passage that reminds one of the supreme confidence that characterized Hegel. Harnack's object was not speculative reasoning, to be sure, but history: "In the place of shallow talk about divine nature and profane history, about the 'eternal truths of reason' and casual records, we have arrived at the knowledge of *history*; of the history from which we have received what we possess, and to which we owe what we are."[9] In place of Hegel's Reason, we have Harnack's History; but in both cases there is a fundamental confidence that "we have arrived."[10] Perhaps this is one clue to Harnack's impatience with form-criticism, with Schweitzer and the eschatological school, with the *Religionsgeschichtliche Schule*, and with Barth and the dialectical theology: that they went beyond the "new" to something newer. For Harnack, with his confidence that "history has brought us to our destination,"[11] this could only be regarded as regression or betrayal. Like Hegel, who evidenced a proprietary jealousy with respect to his own system, and a colossal disdain of Schleiermacher's *Abhängigkeitsgefühl*,[12] Harnack bore the

[7] Agnes von Zahn-Harnack, *Adolf von Harnack* (Berlin: Hans Bott, 1936), p. 127. Hereafter all references to this work will be designated AZH.

[8] Adolf Harnack, *Christianity and History*, tr. Thomas Bailey Saunders (London: A. and C. Black, 1896). Hereafter, Harnack will signify, not surprisingly, *Adolf* Harnack!

[9] *Ibid.*, p. 24.

[10] *Ibid.*

[11] *Ibid.*

[12] Cf. H. R. Mackintosh's reference to this fact in *Types of Modern Theology: Schleiermacher to Barth* (London: Nisbet and Company, 1937), p. 102: "Hegel . . . declared that if the feeling of absolute dependence be the core of religion, then of all creatures the most religious is the dog, whose sense of dependence on his master is unqualified."

heavy burden of having to defend as final a particular methodological bias.

Where the presupposition that history has brought us to our destination operates, this history involving as it does for Harnack the dual emphasis on *development* and *personality*, a further complication is introduced. For the historian of such a *complexio oppositorum* as Christianity must seek to find *the* person who embodies the *Wesen* (the *Geist* is always expressed through great men), and trace the historical course of this reality. This set Harnack's two central concerns: Jesus and Christian dogma. It is with reference to these two prime concerns of his vocation as church historian that we may state the thesis of this work; indeed, we borrow Harnack's own argument and claim that this thesis arises from the material itself. We shall approach the thesis by stating a difficulty which is at the same time the most exasperating and the most demanding of a solution if one is to understand Harnack: How could the same person write a work as profound as the *Dogmengeschichte*, and another as simple as *Das Wesen des Christentums*? To be sure, there are similarities in these two works, especially in the identification of the reality of Christianity as the "kernel" which grew into a historically multiform institution with an elaborate cultus, organization, and system of doctrine. But in breath of conception, as well as treatment of subject matter, these two works stand on widely separated levels. The obvious answers attempting to explain this disparity are not adequate: that the former work was a sustained scholarly effort, and the latter a series of extemporaneous lectures; or that Harnack had different audiences in mind.

We believe that *the* problem can be identified by considering three concerns which Harnack juxtaposed in a letter written at the age of seventeen to Wilhelm Stintzing.[13] In this letter Harnack, in effect, declared it as his purpose "to understand Christianity historically and to set it in living relation to all historical event, to work beyond the dogmatic . . . to the inner form of Christian truth, and to confess and defend . . . the independently won position in all sincerity."[14] Harnack from the beginning was dominated by a passion to isolate an axiological essence and he was committed to doing this by means of a historical procedure. Hence we must demonstrate what the axiology was, how it was related to history, and what effect this "historical axiology" had on Harnack's theological work.

In carrying out our purpose in this work, we shall raise the follow-

[13] AZH, pp. 39 f.
[14] *Ibid.*, p. 40.

ing questions: (1) What is there in Harnack's background that helps to explain this "historical axiology"? (2) How does Harnack conceive of history, and what does he regard as a valid historical method? (3) How does the principle "to work beyond the dogmatic . . . to the inner form of Christian truth" operate in practice? (4) How does the principle "to confess and defend . . . the independently won position in all sincerity" operate in practice? Each of these first-order questions brings forth a variety of subsidiary questions, however, and in order to make explicit the thesis of this work, we shall detail these, with certain explanatory comments, in the paragraphs below.

As to background, we shall consider Barth's characterization of the "eighteenth-century man"[15] as "absolute," inquiring whether this is a fair analysis of the *Geist*, and whether Harnack is influenced by this passion for absoluteness. Was Harnack influenced by romanticism, combining it with a Ritschlian "ought"? Insofar as he is a Ritschlian, how far is the Kantian element in Ritschl determinative? Are there not covert strains of Hegelian influence still operative in Harnack, mediated, along with certain conceptions about historical knowledge, via Baur and the Tübingen school? What was the main contribution of the Dorpat-Erlangen school? What significance is to be attached to the fact that Harnack was *persona non grata* in the orthodox circles which controlled the ecclesiastical machinery? Is Ritschl indeed the one who provides for him a way between the Scylla of orthodoxy and the Charybdis of Tübingen? Was not Overbeck's "wounding criticism"[16] truly a wound that never healed, forcing Harnack to construct an axiology which would be useful to modern men, and thereby suggesting a dichotomy between historical and axiological norms? So far as his contemporary environment is concerned, is it not true that materialism provided *the* challenge that must be met? In Harnack's assertion that he must "confess and defend" the position won by scientific historical labor, is he deliberately answering this monistic interpretation of human existence, as well as his own past? Does this mean then that Jesus *must* be made contemporary to the late nineteenth-century situation, at least to the extent that he will be able to provide the power to overcome these polar positions? But is this to subordinate the historical by raising

15 Karl Barth, *Die protestantische Theologie im 19, Jahrhundert, Ihre Vorgeschichte und ihre Geschichte*, Zweite Auflage, verbesserte (Zürich: Zollikon, 1952), pp. 16–114.

16 AZH, p. 90. Overbeck had accused the "believing theologians" with "risking nothing." See Chap. V.

the question of contemporary efficacy to a dominant position? And, insofar as the axiological norm is concerned, is it derived by making "man and the world" the fundamental polar rubrics, rather than "God and the soul," as Harnack was wont to claim?[17]

Inasmuch as Christianity is to be understood historically, we must ask what is involved in Harnack's conception of history. Fortunately, he dealt with the problem of the certainties and the limits of historical understanding in explicit writings.[18] It must be noted carefully, however, that as necessary as this approach is for Harnack, it involves him in real perplexities as he applies this approach to Christianity. For though Christianity is to be understood historically, church history has a "special" character. It is in the delineation of this "special" character of church history that Harnack's axiological norm is particularly apparent. We shall argue further, when we come to a consideration of his historical method, that though it is a monumental synthesis, it contains traces of those elements which he derogated: partiality, absolute standpoint, and either/or interpretations. This is true, we believe, partly because no person can completely eviscerate such elements, and partly because Harnack held real commitments to the content he was concerned to explicate, viz., Christianity. In order to do justice to this content, he introduced Kantian, Hegelian, and romantic elements into the definition and the description of scientific knowledge. His "responsible action" ("to overcome history by history"), for example, presupposes an *Entwickelung* doctrine. Is not his view of "Mittleren"[19] only a scarcely concealed admission that one must indeed employ propositional formulations as well as value-judgments in order to act historically? Does he not, as many of his critics charged (the *Religionsgeschichtliche Schule* and the dialectical theology particularly), throw out dogmatic formulations at the beginning, but admit his own preferred brand under the name of "stages of scientific knowledge"[20] in his historical *modus operandi*? Finally, is it not feasible to evaluate Harnack as one whose dogmas were different from those held by orthodoxy or materialism, but nonetheless dogmas? To document this, do not the *Dogmengeschichte* and *Das Wesen des Christentums* indicate, respectively, Harnack's debt to his past and his superb

[17] See AZH, p. 516.

[18] Harnack, "Über die Sicherheit und die Grenzen geschichtlicher Erkenntnis," and "Was hat die Historie an fester Erkenntnis zur Deutung des Weltgeschehens zu bieten?," *RA*, IV, NF, pp. 3–23 and 171–195, respectively.

[19] AZH, p. 487.

[20] Harnack, "Stufen wissenschaftlicher Erkenntnis," *RA*, V, NF: *Aus der Werkstatt des Vollendeten* (Giessen: Töpelmann, 1930), pp. 202–205.

ability to analyze that past, and his powers as apologist when he is speaking to the "cultured despisers"? Was Troeltsch justified, then, in declaring that Harnack counterpoised his *Humanitätslehre* to his historicist method?[21] And is this not to say, in the final analysis, that if the "inner form" eludes the dogmatician, as Harnack claimed, so does it elude the historian? Harnack's "historical axiology," which had been drawn together from many sources, is a protean effort to grasp this "inner form."

In discussing Harnack as historian, our primary concern is to discover how the principle "to work beyond the dogmatic . . . to the inner form of Christian truth" operates in practice. This principle is to be implemented, as we have stated, by a historical method of procedure. In this section it will be argued that Harnack is true to this method in the *Dogmengeschichte*, that history does control. It is a wise caution, however, to recall that categories are never as neat with respect to history as they can be in other scientific disciplines. That is, we are not taking the either/or position that axiology is completely lacking in this work; but we are claiming that those stages of the historical method which are more scientific predominate here. Perhaps it was because there was less of cultural apologetic required in the situation out of which this work was written, and to which it was directed, in contrast to the prevailing situation at the time of the production of *Das Wesen des Christentums*, that Harnack could set forth his interpretation in a more dispassionate manner. Yet, as certain of Harnack's critics pointed out, there are numerous places within this work where the principle "to work beyond the dogmatic . . . to the inner form of Christian truth"[22] involved Harnack in real difficulties. It is therefore necessary that this work be evaluated with extreme care. Is the work dependent on the definition of the Gospel which Harnack here sets forth, and later defends in *Das Wesen des Christentums*? Does Harnack not hedge and qualify this definition in such a way that it becomes very difficult to say exactly what he means? And if this is true, does it not give an important clue as to the limits of historical knowledge? Is Harnack's definition of dogma adequate? Is his division and organization of the material defensible? We shall argue that in the final analysis it is *history*, as Harnack conceives it, which controls in the *Dogmengeschichte*, although Harnack's axiological norm is too intimately involved in the history to be considered absent.

In discussing Harnack's axiology, our primary concern is to dis-

[21] Troeltsch, *op. cit.*, p. 529.
[22] AZH, p. 40.

cover how the principle "to confess and defend . . . the independently won position in all sincerity" operates in practice. The position of which Harnack speaks is, of course, determined by the inner form of Christian truth which has been arrived at via history. Since this inner form of Christian truth is nothing else than the "kernel," or the "reality" of Christianity, the crucial work to be considered is *Das Wesen des Christentums.* This work provides a demonstration of Harnack's axiological norm, and the result is a "symbolic concatenation"[23] of liberalism. Though history is not abandoned, it is, in spite of Harnack's affirmation to the contrary, subordinated. For cultural apologetic is demanded, and this work gives evidence of this apologetic throughout.

The particular problems that emerge in connection with *Das Wesen des Christentums* are controlling for any balanced study of Harnack. We ask therefore whether his definition of the essence of Christianity is identifiable, and whether it is adequate. If this essence as defined has elements of Kantian moralism and Goethean romanticism within it, as we maintain, in what way is it transmuted by Harnack so as to provide that efficacy for contemporary Christianity which is demanded? But is it defensible to regard *this* work as the central clue to Harnack's achieved position with respect to axiology? Are we justified in claiming that the clue to his hermeneutics is to be found here? And again we must ask, particularly in this context, what the relation between Harnack's achieved axiological norm and his history really was.

Finally, we must ask what effect this "historical axiology" had on Harnack's biblical interpretation. How far is the Gospel defined by a sole dependence on *history*, as Harnack conceived it, and how far is it defined "apologetically," i.e., vis-à-vis the demand for cultural utility? If the latter predominates, does this not already determine what content *must* be placed in the traditional rubrics (e.g., authority and revelation)—rubrics which Harnack employs only as repristinated with proper meanings? Perhaps the most instructive treatment with respect to Harnack's hermeneutics is that which deals with the problem of the canonicity of the Old Testament. We shall see that when this problem is considered, it is dealt with almost entirely with reference to value. And the historical judgment which Harnack makes as to the way in which the Old Testament ought presently to be regarded[24] follows necessarily. For where contemporary utility con-

[23] Troeltsch, *op. cit.*, p. 42.

[24] *Marcion, das Evangelium vom fremden Gott* (Leipzig: J. C. Hinrichs, 1921), pp. 248–249.

trols as a presupposition, where the contemporary situation is regarded as unaddressable save from the standpoint of an ethical norm, and where the nisus to essence procedure is employed, then, if the essence is identified as the Gospel, the Law must go. In short, we raise this question: Was the Old Testament adjudged noncanonical by Harnack simply because he did not believe it contributed to the needs of his time? Does this not mean, then, that the central category of interpretation must always be "worthfulness"? But is this not to exhibit a fateful provincialism with respect to the richness of the forms—cultic and dogmatic, as well as ethical—in which the Christian Gospel has been carried in the course of history? And is it not to set oneself over against the Church, but also over against everyone with an alternative interpretation? Finally, is not this precisely the key problem: that Harnack, master craftsman as a historian, could therefore produce a *Dogmengeschichte*, and yet, operating as a spokesman to his culture, could repristinate the historical Jesus in such a way that Jesus could be effective in this culture? In the two key works themselves, is there not this problem: that Harnack's "work beyond the dogmatic . . . to the inner form of Christian truth" implies a far greater confidence in the ability of the Gospel to survive its multitudinous perversions than is credible? And therefore is Loisy not correct in his critique when he remarks that on the face of it, Harnack's formulation of a "husk and kernel" theory demands a far greater miracle than those alternative formulations of the Church which Harnack attacked?[25] Is there not an alternative interpretation which does justice to the historical dimension without doing violence to the multiform character of Christian faith?

By way of summary, our formulation would run as follows: in the *Dogmengeschichte* one sees Harnack's historical conception and method at its best. His understanding of history was derived in part from Dorpat (Engelhardt), in part from Tübingen (Baur), and in part from Ritschl. Here is Harnack as historian par excellence. Furthermore, he is here dealing with a subject which is of fundamental importance to the Church, within whose debt he stands, and the audience to which he is writing is comprised of theologians. In *Das Wesen des Christentums*, by contrast, the axiological norm is much more in evidence. The apparent influences are Kant (as interpreted by Ritschl), the romantics, and the Dorpat-Erlangen heritage. Here he is speaking to culture (confessing Christianity), trying to overcome materialism (defending Christianity), and doing it, perforce,

[25] Alfred Loisy, *The Gospel and the Church*, tr. Christopher Home (New York: Charles Scribner's Sons, 1909), pp. 1–22.

by abstracting an essence from Christianity which he believed he had discovered there in his historical investigation, but which was actually a "given."

To state the problem in this way is, admittedly, to run a great risk of oversimplification. The complexity of Harnack's thought demands cautious and qualified explication. Even to deal with his history and his theology in *separate* sections is to suggest a fissiparity which is questionably valid. The writer, to be candid, would have to admit that in the course of the following pages he has ridden the pendulum from the "history" to the "axiology" hundreds of times—and arrived at "historical axiology." The final decision, if indeed there must be one, lies "in the mean." What Harnack insisted on throughout his scholarly life—that the truth lies in the mean, not in the extremes—will find ample documentation in these pages, as we explicate this thesis:

Harnack's theology is based on a complex axiology which contains elements derived from Kant, from romanticism, from Dorpat-Erlangen, and from Ritschl. This axiology necessarily shaped Harnack's conception of history, and though he disavowed presuppositions, he meant thereby that kind of dogmatic prepossession which prescribed what history must discover. His own axiological norm, present throughout his writings, but most evident in Das Wesen des Christentums, *set the limits for his own endeavor. With respect to his hermeneutics, we hold the position (1) that Harnack's most important contribution lay in his insistence on historical interpretation, but (2) because his "historical axiology" was derived in part from contemporary cultural elements as well as from biblical faith itself, the categories of interpretation which he employed were reductive.*

A concluding word may be added with regard to the categories which Harnack employs in his biblical interpretation. The dialectic of history and value is never absent, but the categories which Harnack employs are either explicitly axiological, or the older categories—revelation, authority, continuity, particularity—are recast in such a way that they become axiological. If traditional questions cannot be dealt with by means of this procedure, as in the case of the unity of the Scripture, they must be denied validity. It is on this basis that one can account for Harnack's famous Marcion judgment.[26] The interpretation of Scripture which emerges by the use of these categories is utilitarian. This is to remove nothing of the significance

[26] *Marcion* , . . . , pp. 248–249.

from Harnack's "scavenger's labor,"[27] which remains as a noteworthy heritage along with his insistence on the historical character of Christianity.

Admitting, then, the positive contribution which Harnack made to historical study, one must go on to insist that his greatness did not lie at the point of his biblical interpretation. The process exemplified in his *Marcion, das Evangelium vom fremden Gott*, in which worth is judged by Harnack's particular norm, is evident in all of his interpretation of Scripture. The Gospel itself is cut to the measure of this norm, and the first-century Jew of Nazareth emerges with an efficacious message for nineteenth-century Germany's cultured despisers.

That was the statement of a decade ago. We are no longer restricting Harnack's work to his biblical interpretation—though, previously, it quickly became obvious that such a restriction was not viable in any case. For, as these pages upon pages of questions make clear, Harnack was in the fullest sense of the term a "contextual thinker." However pedantic or restrictive the questions may appear to be, Harnack was no pedant and he did not cripple his creative capacities with term-mongering. Prolific he was; and it is just this *range* which creates the problem for his interpreter. Two comments may be appropriate: that it will be a service if, doubting that *all* of these questions are germane to Harnack, and all these categories relevant, the reader is sent to the sources—to Harnack's own corpus of over sixteen hundred items. And the other comment: *mea culpa.*

We will deal, substantively, with two categories only: *history* and *theology*. Prefacing this consideration with a section that attempts to set Harnack in the historical background from which he came, we will follow it with a summation that also relates him to the theological currents which succeeded him.

[27] *The Sayings of Jesus,* tr. J. R. Wilkinson (New York: G. P. Putnam's Sons, 1908), p. xii.

II

Adolf von Harnack

HARNACK WAS born in 1851, in Dorpat, Esthonia. He was the son of Theodosius Harnack, a professor of practical theology and, later, of systematic theology at the University. In 1853 the father became a member of the faculty at the University of Erlangen, returning to Dorpat in 1866 to complete his professional career. It was in this little Esthonian island of culture that Adolf attended the *Gymnasium* and, electing theology in his final year, matriculated at the University. In October of 1872 he left Dorpat for Leipzig, where he took his doctoral examination in 1873 and habilitated in church history in 1874. His thesis on the latter occasion was on the "Monarchianism of Apelles the Gnostic."

Harnack began his teaching career at the University of Leipzig in the winter semester of 1874–75, and immediately began a career of publication that was to end only with his death. Already, in 1875, he became co-editor, along with von Gebhardt and Zahn, of the *Patrum apostolicorum opera.* In the following year, the *Theologische Literaturzeitung* was founded in collaboration with Emil Schürer, and in 1881 Harnack became its editor "for a year"—and kept it for twenty-nine!

In 1879 Harnack accepted a call to Giessen as *Professor Ordinarius*, and it was here that the first volume of his *Dogmengeschichte* was completed and published in 1885. Harnack had long since made it clear, through the number and the quality of his publications, that his would be a name to be taken seriously. In 1882 he had initiated the *Texte und Untersuchungen* series, fifteen volumes of which appeared up to the time that the series was taken over by the Commission on the Church Fathers of the Prussian Academy of Science. But it was the publication of the *Dogmengeschichte* that put his name on the lips of all German theologians, in approbation or in epithet. It was this work that marked a poignant break with his father and, therefore, though this was not yet clear, with his Dorpat-Erlangen heritage of Lutheran confessionalism. And it was this work which, though too recently published to create a significant deterrent to his appointment at Marburg (1886), became the center of controversy when his appointment to a chair at the University of Berlin was under consideration.

The battle over Harnack's appointment to Berlin went on for nine months, from December of 1887 till September of 1888, and was finally resolved by the Kaiser himself. Here it should simply be noted that this battle was one of the *eight* major controversies which raged around Harnack's head in the course of his life. For all the protestations which he himself made with respect to the effect of such controversies, it would be an egregious oversimplification to fail to note these effects. They are unmistakably clear, perhaps even fateful with respect to the later course of his life.

In 1888 Harnack took up his duties at the University of Berlin. In 1890 the Evangelical-Social Congress was formed, and within this movement Harnack took an increasingly active part: he was its president from 1903 to 1911. In 1890 he was elected to membership in the Prussian Academy of Science, and was chosen in 1896 to prepare a history of the Academy, this to be completed in time for the bicentennial celebration in 1900: and so it was. In 1891 the Academy had decided, on Harnack's urging, to bring out an edition of the Greek Church Fathers, and two years later the Commission on the Church Fathers was established by the Academy. Harnack headed this Commission to the end of his life.

These are the activities, directly related to Harnack's fundamental vocation, which were begun, pursued with an unfailing competence and dedication, and brought, in many cases, to fruition in the first half-century of his life. Although one can see diversity within this period, Harnack's daughter and biographer is correct when she describes the events of the first fifty years as "strung like pearls upon a single thread."[1] She is no less correct when she judges that at the turn of the century Harnack "was in the most significant climacteric-year" of his life, and that from this point on "many threads weave themselves together in a many-colored tapestry, criss-crossing, dividing and interlacing; and the eye must simultaneously encompass them all in order to become conscious of the wealth in form and colors which gives the weaver's masterpiece its significance."[2]

We shall have occasion later to return to Harnack's own assessment of his standpoint at this climacteric stage. It is essential to note, however, that from this time on, Harnack's activitics take on a scope and breadth practically coterminous with the cultural life of Germany. If there is a unity between the former and the later years; if there is not just an imposed but an actual integrity of purpose; and if the watershed (*Das Wesen des Christentums*) is the key to discovering this unity and the manifestation of this integrity of purpose—all of which we believe—these things above all must be demonstrated in the succeeding pages.

But to continue with "the life": in addition to his primary vocation, in relation to which he taught at the University of Berlin, served as Rector of the University, headed the Commission on the Church Fathers of the Prussian Academy of Science, edited the *Theologische Literaturzeitung*, and remained active in the Evangelical-Social Congress, Harnack took on new duties. In 1905, at the urging of Althoff, he became Director of the Royal Library, and held this position until 1921. In 1909 he prepared, on request, a memorandum recommending the establishment of a number of scientific research institutes, and there followed, at the one-hundredth anniversary celebration of the founding of the University of Berlin, the announcement by the Kaiser of the establishment of the Kaiser-Wilhelm Foundation. Harnack was chosen as the first President of the Senate of the Foundation, and for the rest of his life was active in the work of the various branches of the Foundation. His scientific interest found further expression in his election, in 1917, to the chairmanship of the executive committee of the German Museum in Munich. He held this position for six years.

There were other "activities" which demonstrate the scope and breadth of Harnack's cultural involvement. From 1900 until the time of the Kaiser's abdication, Harnack was *persona grata* in the royal court, serving as a privy counselor on a wide range of questions. He had received the Order of Merit in 1902, and from 1920 to the end

1 AZH, p. 294.
2 *Ibid.*, pp. 294–295.

of his life was Chancellor of the Order. His esteem in the eyes of the leaders of Germany is attested by his ennoblement in 1914.

Yet, in spite of all the honors heaped upon him, the twentieth-century years of his life were years of almost constant controversy. The "theological battles" had begun earlier, centering around the *Dogmengeschichte*, his appointment to the faculty of the University of Berlin, and the position he took regarding the Apostles' Creed—all of these in a seven-year period. With the publication of *Das Wesen des Christentums*, the controversies resumed. Of varying intensity, to be sure, the succeeding struggles (over "Babel-Bibel" in 1903, the "Jatho-affair" in 1909, the publication of the *Marcion* in 1921, and the emerging "dialectical theology" in 1923) declare, unmistakably, a resistance to that for which Harnack stood. The resistance was centered, of course, in the Church.[3] But just because it was Harnack's intention to serve the Church, the constant bombardment from synods, ecclesiastical newspapers, and theologians of a different ilk remained a continuing thorn. There is no reason to doubt the private agonies, expressed only in correspondence with his closest friends. At the same time the positions won in the workshop could not be left unstated. For Harnack knew, with that certainty of conscience attested by his hero at Worms, that ". . . only he is true to the spirit of this Church who wishes to be bound in nothing save the *sola fide*. . . ."[4]

[3] *Ibid.*, pp. 299 ff.
[4] *Ibid.*, p. 97.

PART TWO

THEOLOGY AS VOCATION

III

Theodosius Harnack

THE SOURCES for estimating the relationship between Adolf Harnack and his father Theodosius are scanty. That they are so is itself, in all probability, the most significant thing to note. With all due regard for the dangers of the *e silentio* argument, it can be said that what we have in the way of direct correspondence and indirect allusion is sufficient to justify certain conclusions about this relationship and its effect on Adolf Harnack. We have no competence or inclination to attempt here a psychological analysis of the father-son relationship. It may be, indeed, that the poetic sensitivity of the father accounts for the idealism of the son; that the death of Harnack's mother when he was six years old, with the consequent necessity that the father rear the children until, seven years later, a stepmother came into the home, marked Adolf indelibly; that the pietistic influences of Theodosius' paternal home carried into the strong Lutheran confessionalism of his adult life in sufficient measure to set ineluctable patterns of devotion in the children—indeed, we know that this is true of Adolf. We know, furthermore, that among those "elementary factors," he received from his parents unusual intellectual gifts and rigorous training in their use, a home environment where the *notae* of culture flourished, and the vigorous atmosphere of quest and creativity that characterized nineteenth century Dorpat.[1]

But the record, such as it is, will be allowed to speak for itself. It is a sufficiently ample record to make clear a poignancy of relationship, without thereby being ample enough to justify large theories.

> With negative jealousy I have always taken great care that no person who came under my tutelage should ever feel himself in the least degree bound or influenced by such a consideration, whether it be in ecclesiastical or theological respects. . . . For what that means I have myself experienced across the years in relation to my father.[2]

Thus did Harnack write to Karl Holl in 1915, twenty-six years after his father died. There are evidences of approval of the son's work by the father—Theodosius wrote warmly of the address which Adolf gave on the occasion of the celebration of the four-hundredth anniversary of Luther's birth: "Among the many addresses about Luther, I believe yours is the best, both in arrangement and, for the most part, in execution; and I do not believe that I give a partisan judgment."[3] Yet it is simply the fact that from the time Adolf left Dorpat for Leipzig, the gulf that already was developing continually widened. This is evidenced in the limited correspondence of that period, but, more precisely, in the elder Harnack's reaction to the publication of the first volume of the *Dogmengeschichte*, and in the younger Harnack's reaction to the anti-Ritschlian preface of the second volume of Theodosius' *Luthers Theologie mit besonderer Beziehung auf seine Versöhnungs- und Erlösungslehre*.

Theodosius Harnack (1817–1889) was a member of the "Erlangen School," and gladly accepted the designation which Ritschl gave to its members, that of "learned repristinators."[4] He had been educated at Dorpat and Erlangen, with brief stints at Bonn and Berlin. On returning to Dorpat as associate professor, he quickly made known his confessional commitments in his *Grundbekenntnisse der evangelisch-lutherischen Kirche* (1845). "Theology," so he declared in his *Die Kirche, ihr Amt, ihr Regiment* (1862), "is, above all else, called to hold to the unity and the purity of the confessions and Christian

[1] Agnes von Zahn-Harnack, in the biography, has provided a warm and human evaluation of the early years of Harnack's life at Dorpat and Erlangen. The section entitled "Kinder- und Jugendjahre" is on pp. 11–52.

[2] AZH, p. 238.

[3] *Ibid.*, p. 133.

[4] Theodosius Harnack, *Luthers Theologie mit besonderer Beziehung auf seine Versöhnungs- und Erlösungslehre*, Band 2, Neue Ausgabe (München: Kaiser Verlag, 1927), p. 3.

doctrine."[5] This position was consistently held throughout his adult life. He had served, in his twenties, as a tutor in the family of a Livonian nobleman, and had there strengthened a pietistic influence gained from his father; but his studies of Luther had led him to regard pietism, particularly as manifested at Herrnhut, as sectarian and incomplete. He therefore entered with great energy into the church life of Livonia, headed a committee of the synod of Livonia to improve the liturgy, and defended a pure Lutheranism in his influential book *Die lutherische Kirche Livlands und die herrnhutische Brüdergemeinde* (1860).

How did the father appear to the children? Adolf, at the time of his father's death, wrote a sensitive and impressive memorial to the man from whom so much of his theological training had been derived, but from whose positions he had now departed:

All that a father can be to his sons in their critical years, that he has been to us. First through him, and under his never wearying guidance, I gained my knowledge of all that constitutes experience, education, and discernment in the realms of personal life. When I think back to how much time we cost him, and how much time I devote to my children, there is simply no comparison. He labored much in his life, and up to the last corrected his proof sheets; but how much satisfying work he renounced to wear himself out with us! That becomes ever clearer to me in the later years. And if I think back to his strictness with us in our youthful days, it is quite clear to me that it was an outflow of the conscientiousness which first of all he exercised on himself. In my whole life I have never seen him in a bad humor or depressed. He never gave way to temper, and he never left us in doubt as to his judgment. We always knew how we stood with him. But perhaps the most impressive and noble thing about him was that he was never solicitous about things which did not lie in the province of human decision. He was solicitous only and exclusively that he and his family should remain in firm trust in God, without pretence or posturing, that they should do their duty and take care of their health. In truth, everything else was outside the range of his thought. He was glad if things went well, but he did not regard so-called misfortune as really misfortune; especially as this concerned matters of external success, livelihood, and the like, he always showed a sovereignty as if that did not concern him.[6]

Yet he was indeed a stern taskmaster, as Adolf's daughter records:

He led his son with the utmost precision. The first sermon which Adolf was to preach . . . had to be rewritten and learned anew between Saturday

[5] Theodosius Harnack, *Die Kirche, ihr Amt, ihr Regiment* (Gütersloh: C. Bertelsmann Verlag, 1862), p. 9.

[6] AZH, pp. 29–30.

and Sunday at his father's request, as it did not satisfy the requirements of this scholarly homiletician. The son learned from him the art of exact and strict arrangement, which makes impossible all lack of clarity of thought, all mere playing with words; he learned as well the tenacity which sticks to a problem until it is actually worked out.[7]

A letter written during Harnack's stay at Leipzig will indicate the father's characteristic concern for the intellectual development of his son, and his estimate of the dangers toward which he is tending:

Had I been more faithful, you would take a more positive position than you do. I beg of you, my dearest Adolf, for the sake of everything which is of worth and dear to you, neither to allow yourself to be imposed upon, nor to suffer your vanity to be charmed by the negative criticism of the modern theology, in which a leaf can be torn from the Bible, or the whole Bible can be thrown away. Do not follow the consciousness of the time, but rather that of the church, for our only choice is between these two.[8]

Ten years later, in 1885, the first volume of the *Dogmengeschichte* was published. In an exchange of correspondence with Loofs, Harnack dropped the mask of equability to which all who knew him publicly attest.

I thank my God and Lord that . . . I have had an opportunity in this book to say what I think about crucial questions, without anyone being able to cast in my teeth the charge that I have sought opportunity for expression. . . . It has been such a high joy that I have been privileged to say what I think, and not to appear to be other than I am, that in the strength of this joy all the tortures with which I have been wracked will vanish.[9]

Loofs reminded him that his book would hardly be received with joy by the older generation. Harnack responded, poignantly:

You have spoken of your father; I also have a father who thinks as yours does. I need not say to you what that means to me. As well as I could, I have sought, without at all compromising the truth in silence or in speech, to maintain my cause and yet to bear in mind his standpoint. But that has its limits, and these can be transgressed only by sullying the conscience. My father also knows that. . . . I know that to piety all force is dangerous, but each person must estimate for himself where the greater

[7] *Ibid.*, p. 47.
[8] *Ibid.*, pp. 106–107.
[9] *Ibid.*, pp. 138–139.

danger threatens his own individuality, and how he can maintain his position with a good conscience.[10]

There were immediate reactions from every point of the theological compass; but weeks passed, and Theodosius Harnack remained silent. Further, he made known to the Dorpat faculty his preference that they not speak to him about Adolf's work. Finally, two letters arrived from his home: one from the father, the other from the stepmother. Theodosius wrote:

Our difference is not simply a theological one, but one so profoundly and directly Christian that if I should pass over it lightly, I would be denying Christ; that no one can desire or expect of me, even if he stands as close to me, my son, as you do. To mention only the most decisive issue, whoever takes the position which you take on the Resurrection is in my eyes no longer a Christian theologian. I simply do not understand how anyone can appeal to history when he indulges in such historical machination, or I understand it only if one thereby degrades Christianity. Therefore: either/or. . . . For me Christianity stands and falls with the Resurrection.[11]

And the stepmother:

Papa's silence is not at all to be understood as basically indicating a lack of love or even an estrangement. But you have caused him deep grief. For as your positions now are made known, they can only give him a stab in the heart. Regarding this, you know the precise situation, and you know your father. I cannot judge to what degree it was necessary for you to write thus, and I must restrain myself from taking sides—my heart feels enough pain in what I see in you and in ourselves. I have not been able to understand the *manner* in which you love your father, nor the way you deal with him, my Adolf. You are the most tender and loyal son, and Papa is a father with whom few can be compared—and yet on both sides there is so much sorrow of heart![12]

A stab in the heart—what this meant to Adolf Harnack was never directly shared. But without an unseemly probing into what for Harnack remained a silent sorrow, it is clear that this judgment affected him deeply at the same time that it did not alter the direction of his effort. That direction lay increasingly along a path marked out by Ritschl. And if Ritschl, as was the case, represented the *bête noir* for Theodosius Harnack, this cross would simply have to be borne.

It is clear that Harnack believed that a way might be found between

[10] *Ibid.*, pp. 139–140.
[11] *Ibid.*, p. 143.
[12] *Ibid.*, pp. 143–144.

the position of the "learned repristinators" of orthodox Lutheranism and the historical-critical approach which he and Ritschl supported. Even after it became obvious to him, sometime in the Giessen years, that such a way did not exist, he tried to maintain a positive relationship to those of differing persuasions. But the judgment of his father was unequivocal:

> . . . in his central thought, that of justification, and especially in the separation rather than differentiation of faith and knowledge, he has worked radically and destructively. . . . He will not get by with it, no matter how much he gives the church to do. For as you know from church history better than I, it has been the fate of all middle parties that they have been crushed. That is the inevitable judgment of history. And because I value your work highly, I do not want this judgment to fall on it. . . . I know, to be sure, that there remains a good deal to unite us (you and me) but I also know what stands written in Matthew 13:12, and in that can rejoice only with trembling.[13]

Finally, in 1886, Theodosius Harnack's long-deferred second volume of *Luthers Theologie* appeared, containing in its preface a slashing attack on Ritschl. Adolf immediately wrote to Ritschl:

> The feeling with which I have read the preface is beyond description, and I cannot attempt to put it in words. You will understand it, and will be sympathetic toward me, since I can imagine the impression which this attack must make on you. But just on that account there is now a deep necessity for me to thank you for all which I have learned and received from you, and to assure you of my abiding gratitude. In the fixedness and strength of your evangelical knowledge, and in the consciousness that you have not been teaching in vain, you will have, as heretofore, a shield against all attacks. Kindly accept these lines! In heartfelt loyalty. Yours, A. Harnack.[14]

Ritschl's reply was gracious, ending with the assurance, "The kingdom must still remain to us."[15] And though the daughter tells us that in this assurance Adolf Harnack found renewed joy for his theological tasks, it is not to be doubted that in these tasks there remained a shadow of sadness that the theological *rapprochement* both he and his father had desired could not be effected. Yet in the desiring there was unity; and who can doubt that in this desiring, which was exemplified in his own commitment to "theology as vocation," a gifted father gave the determinative mark to a gifted son?

[13] *Ibid.*, pp. 129–130.
[14] *Ibid.*, pp. 130–131.
[15] *Ibid.*, p. 131.

IV

Dorpat and Erlangen

FROM THE father, a commitment to "theology as vocation." From Dorpat and Erlangen, with its Lutheran neo-confessionalism, its ecclesiological passion, its Christological concern, and its strong devotional emphasis (mediated by way of Schleiermacher and Herrnhut), a solid grounding in church history, particularly the history of Christian dogma, which was to be Harnack's corner of the theological vineyard. And church history at Dorpat meant one person: Moritz von Engelhardt.

Engelhardt was born in Livonia in 1828, and came under the Herrnhut influence through one of his early teachers. He studied under Phillipi at Dorpat from 1846–1849, under Hofmann at Erlangen in 1850, and subsequently, for a brief period, at Bonn. In 1858 he became professor of church history at the University of Dorpat, where he remained until his death in 1881.

This meager biographical note does no justice to the man who, as Harnack later emphasized, had a most determinative influence on the direction of his life. In 1916, forty-four years after he had left Dorpat for Leipzig, Harnack wrote a short piece entitled "Baltische Professoren." In a general discussion he takes particular note of the genius of Engelhardt:

In the approximately twenty-five years (d. 1881) of his work as a professor, he not only achieved a high position as a developing scholar, in complete control of his data; but as a teacher, he possessed a power of penetrating and convincing presentation of a kind that I have never experienced at any time with any other professor. What he understood historically he comprehended in its own right, and was able so to portray it to his hearers that they might internally appropriate it: only then would follow the critique. For this reason every great historical event was an experience of inner enrichment for the student.[1]

Harnack then reports that Engelhardt, in addition to his greatness as a teacher and scholar, acted as a pastor to anyone who came to him, in the strongest and deepest sense of that word. Thus, he concluded, "Anyone who had come into contact with this professor would never forget him, and to this day this Baltic country owes a great part of its ethical strength to the influence of a single man."[2]

It had been a passion with Theodosius Harnack that all of his sons should be thoroughly grounded in historical, philosophical, and literary subjects.[3] When Adolf elected theology and matriculated at the University of Dorpat, it was Engelhardt with his rigorous method who taught him the foundations of his art: textual criticism and the investigation of the sources.

"*Magister*, *patronus*, and *amicus*"—these were the words that Harnack used to describe his teacher.[4] On a significant day in his life, the day the thesis for the licentiate was delivered, he wrote to his once and future mentor:

On the threshold of a new and decisive stage for me, . . . naturally looking back, let me try to express to you what it is that moves me. And that means first of all, my deepest gratitude to you. I know very well that for all of the theological education I carry in my head and heart, and for all which I perceive of a Christian-historical view, I have you to thank for the most significant part; and that without the strong and secure edifice which you have built for me, it would have been infinitely harder for me in the past, and in the present, to preserve my Christian faith.[5]

Earlier, he had borne an eloquent testimony to the contribution

[1] *RA*, V, NF, p. 152. Cf. also here Reinhold Seeberg, *Die Kirche Deutschlands im neunzehnten Jahrhundert* (Leipzig: Deichert, 1903) for a laudatory estimate of von Engelhardt's work and influence "in the great days of the Dorpat faculty" (pp. 344–345). It is of interest that Seeberg finds the seed of the famous "Hellenization" thesis which Harnack employed in his history of dogma in Engelhardt's work on Justin.

[2] *Ibid.*

[3] AZH, p. 37.

[4] *Ibid.*, p. 54.

[5] *Ibid.*

Engelhardt had made to him, and did it by comparing him with the teachers at Leipzig:

If you could only stand for a week or two before these three hundred students, Uncle Moritz, and give here a few lectures to bring people to the right point of view! You know that this is no flattery; but the longer I am separated from you, and the more I look into the theological, ecclesiastical, and Christian life here, the more I note that in little Dorpat, on the border of Europe, and there alone is there clearly recognized and employed that conception which will and must break the path if Christianity is not to end with barbarism or with an unchristian humanity. This I know, that my work in the service of the kingdom of God, so far as I am able to achieve it, will be rooted in that which I have learned with you, for which I and all your students cannot now or ever thank you enough.[6]

The regard which Harnack held for Engelhardt, as master, patron, and friend, is undeniable. An exchange of letters at the time of the publication of Harnack's dissertation (*Zur Quellenkritik des Gnostizismus*) indicates, however, that beyond methodology Englehardt saw basic theological differences emerging. Harnack had expressed apprehension to Engelhardt lest this first scholarly effort be regarded as unworthy of his tutelage. Engelhardt's answer reveals his own fundamental scholarly commitments, as well as his joy in seeing these exemplified in his pupil:

It captivated me quite incredibly and inwardly pleased me deeply. I can say that today I am going about, as it were, in a holiday mood. You have succeeded splendidly. The presentation is in form so straightforward and simple, so transparent and clear, that it is not merely a joy to read the book, but even from the form the mastery of the material is to be recognized. On the other hand, a few stylistic and even grammatical infelicities scarcely come into consideration. The tone of the polemic is very appropriate, and a noble moderation prevails in the criticism. As concerns the research itself, everywhere there is to be recognized scrupulous care, laborious industry, a significant learned apparatus, and keen investigation of details. The result scarcely seems further in doubt.[7]

Engelhardt went on to another question, however, that of Adolf Harnack's commitment to orthodox, "believing" theology:

I thank God the Lord that he is awakening among the believing theologians men who have the passion and the strength to surpass the enemies

[6] *Ibid.*, pp. 54–55.
[7] *Ibid.*, pp. 65–66.

of his Kingdom in the driest and most laborious toil. Only in this way can we again set our battle in array, and win the respect of our opponents.

May the Spirit of God rest upon you young men! May he give to all of you, but especially to you, strength to continue in this way; and may he protect you from jumping at conclusions and from the lazy confidence in their positions of the great mass of the so-called believing theologians. It is possible that I put almost too much emphasis upon the advantages of the scholarly trend, to which I myself am scarcely in position further to contribute. But for my part I will at least have encouraged, and by my cooperation cheered, everyone who is in position to take the right path and direct others to it. In spirit I see a new day dawning in which a succession of young and strong men will direct the wars of the Lord better than we could—and here I disregard myself.[8]

At the same time that Engelhardt's approbation for Harnack's impressive achievement is expressed, therefore, there is a foreboding of things to come: speaking of Adolf's *general* view of his subject, Engelhardt writes, "It does not rightly correspond with your vibrant language and with the magnificent construction of historical relations as the excellent substructure of carefully hewn stones."[9] Harnack answers, profusely:

In the first place, the hopes which you have attached to my person have depressed me in view of what I am aware myself of being able to do and not to do. And you are not alone, for there are many others also. It is necessary to hew more stones where palaces are to be built. That is certain. But to know that one will never get any further, and yet will always in idea see a marvellously beautiful palace, here and there to be sure still veiled in mist, yet clear enough to be recognized as the right one; and yet to have neither word nor pen to fix permanently the picture, and to know that one will never quite succeed—and then to hear words of praise because one has carved a few chips correctly and is expert at curling shavings. . . . !

That the Lord wishes to use me all through my life in dressing stones which sometime, long, long after my time, shall perhaps be in place—and then it will be well: rather would I entreat him to open my lips and make my heart valiant and joyous, immediately to bear witness from his inmost sanctuaries, than that I should be obliged to tarry in the outer courts. However, there is joy in the small task even if the feelings during and after the work are so different. Which are the right ones? Should one even ask?[10]

[8] *Ibid.*, pp. 66–67.
[9] *Ibid.*, p. 67.
[10] *Ibid.*, pp. 67–68.

The immediately following years brought Engelhardt's foreboding to reality; for the influence of Ritschl was making itself increasingly felt at Leipzig, and it was this orientation which Harnack came to share. What this meant to Engelhardt we hope to make clear in the subsequent discussion dealing with the Leipzig period.

Theodosius Harnack and Moritz von Engelhardt—these are the two most important *personal* influences on Adolf Harnack, not only in the formative years, but in all of his life. In themselves, they represented a major part of those *elementary* factors, the evaluation of which Harnack regarded as basic to the work of the historian. Those who see Harnack as "simply a Ritschlian" fail to note that he *became* a Ritschlian. *Pace* his most famous historical judgment, Harnack was a work of the Ritschlian theology on the ground of Dorpat-Erlangen.

And what was this "elemental" ground?

Item: A letter to Wilhelm Stintzing, written when Harnack was seventeen years old, from Dorpat to Erlangen:

> As you will know, I shall study theology. I do not know whether you belong to those who regard everything which is called religion and theology either with contempt or indifference. But regard Christianity as you will; yes, even admit that it is an error; is it not still of the greatest interest to trace the history of this error, and to reach conviction as to what world-stirring events, what revolutions, this error has brought about, into what unaccustomed channels it has steered the spirit of the centuries, how it has permeated our entire present-day culture and civilization, and is inseparable from it? But even further—the longer I live (and how brief a time we as yet have behind us), the more I daily learn by experience how all problems and conflicts run back finally into the realm of religion and find their issue there, and how therefore a Christian viewpoint can never be gotten rid of. Therefore I am an enthusiastic theologue, for I hope to find in this science the way to the solution of the chief problems of our life. Not, to be sure, the entire solution; but nevertheless the right way to a solution; and I know well that one must begin this way anew daily. I do not want a profusion of ready-made creedal utterances, but I want to produce for myself and make my own every single tenet in the fabric. Perhaps you are reading over these lines hastily, or you may be wondering about these things in a similar way. But here among my school comrades I am often forced to bear witness to my opinion, and in that have had the experience that I am always best understood when I speak out most frankly what is in my heart.[11]

Item: A letter to Fanny von Anrep, written when Harnack was twenty-three years old, from Leipzig to Dorpat, referring to Jesus:

[11] *Ibid.*, pp. 39–40.

The correct way to begin is 1. to inquire what we and our entire world would be today without this person, and 2. to attempt to imitate him and suffer with him, to bear our cross, and to become joyfully certain of God as our Father. This experience with him, of which the Apostle speaks on every page of his letters, is the main point, and all statements concerning the worth of this person have value only insofar as they spring from and are enlightened by this life with him. The first question to be asked therefore is certainly not *this*, what was this Christ in and for himself, but the first and most important question is, "How can I become his disciple?"[12]

Item: A letter to von Engelhardt, also written when Harnack was twenty-three, from Leipzig to Dorpat:

I will never become weary of repeating to myself and to others that nothing may be achieved with respect to a blessed and joyful life from the strength of our thought, and that this redemption of which we must lay hold can be solely a *historical* one. There is no conviction which I hold with greater certainty than this, and it is the fundament of my total outlook on life. Therefore all philosophical speculation about our Savior and that which we possess through him is, in the ground of my soul, an offense, and I will be the prophet of no other faith, if God grant it to me, than this, that it is necessary . . . to lay hold of [Christ] himself.[13]

"I shall study theology": the influence of Theodosius; "I am always best understood when I speak out most frankly what is in my heart"; "to attempt to imitate him and suffer wth him, to bear our cross. . ."; "how can I become his disciple?": the influence of Lutheran devotionalism, possibly touched with pietistic Herrnhut; "this redemption on which we must lay hold can be solely a *historical* one": Engelhardt, *magister*, *patronus*, and *amicus*; "all philosophical speculation about our Savior and that which we possess through him is, in the ground of my soul, an offense": the yeast of Ritschlianism is working.

Theology as vocation, passion for the inner form, history as the instrument of release—these are the contributions of the Dorpat-Erlangeners to Harnack. They remained with him all his days.

[12] *Ibid.*, pp. 93–94.
[13] *Ibid.*, p. 95.

V

Leipzig and Giessen

THE THEOLOGICAL faculty at Leipzig, according to Harnack's own testimony, contributed little to what he had brought from Dorpat. A letter to Engelhardt makes this clear:

Entangled in a web of a thousand threads, from which, thank God! we in Livonia are free; in a web composed of the Christian and the worldly, of prejudices and narrownesses, of superficialities and rudeness, of lovelessness and passionate zeal for the kingdom of God—all so synthetically interwoven that the head quite as much as the heart appears bound and chained. Even if they were free, the hand would refuse to carry out orders; they are caught in a thousand concerns of church politics and are already engaged in so many undertakings and so continually occupied that they are no more suited to the faithful service of the refined heart and mind. Considerations here and considerations there, politics and the affairs of church politics taking precedence, the direction they take is determined by a whole range of factors, among which actual zeal for the house of God is only one. . . . According to Luthardt, a "mountain of ice" lies between the men of Erlangen and those of Leipzig!!! For myself, I have no desire to enter further into these melancholy relations, and am pained even to have to report them. If God does not look into them, showing people through shock what is black and what is white, I see no help.[1]

[1] AZH, pp. 59–60.

As Harnack entered on his teaching career at Leipzig, the theological situation he had described underwent a transformation, and certainly Harnack had a major part in it. Not only did he attract the ablest students in Germany to Leipzig—and then to Giessen, and then to Marburg, and then to Berlin[2]—but once having them he regarded their proper instruction as of the first importance. The testimonies to his skill are legion; but one from the Leipzig years will have to suffice to make the point:

His animated way of teaching worked upon his pupils in an electrifying way, for he combined a fine understanding of the nature and needs of youth, a friendly approach and unselfish encouragement, a strict scholarly passion for truth and religious ardor, earnest work and a free unruffled easiness of manner. The earnestness he exhibited provided a kind of pastoral unction, and at the same time he possessed humor, wit, and presence of mind of a magic kind. One also experienced in him that characteristic of the Baltic regions, the open and deep interchange of ideas, in distinction from the cut and dried ecclesiasticism in Germany. It is significant that the majority of his most intimate and enthusiastic students came from the orthodox-pietistic circles.[3]

Indeed it is significant; as is also the fact that a constant correspondence was continuing with the man who, without doubt, was more responsible than any other for the *way* material was presented as well as the *matter* of it. Early in 1873, the twenty-one-year-old had adumbrated, in a remarkable way, a concern which was to occupy his attention for the next decade and a half, and to result in his monumental study of the history of dogma:

The practical demand which I feel, if I may be permitted to speak of such a thing, amounts to this: to give to the system of dogmatics such form that it will deal first with that which is the original standard and

[2] To list the students of Harnack who later became renowned would be, practically, to compile a "Who's Who" of late nineteenth- and twentieth-century theologians. The *Festschrift* for Harnack's seventieth birthday (*Harnack-Ehrung*, Leipzig: Hinrichs, 1921) was presented on behalf of 215 theologians of all countries and specific vocations; of these 155 had actually studied with Harnack for longer or shorter periods. Among the names: Borneman, W. A. Brown, S. J. Case, Clemen, O. S. Davis, O. Dibelius, von Dobschütz, Goodspeed, Heussi, Klostermann, Krüger, Loofs, Lyman, McGiffert, Rade, O. Ritschl, J. H. Ropes, C. Schmidt and K. L. Schmidt, G. B. Smith, von Soden, Vischer, Windisch, and Wobbermin. The effect on the subsequent course of theology can hardly be demonstrated; but it takes little imagination to affirm it.

[3] The comment is by Wilhelm Bornemann, later a professor in Frankfurt. Quoted in AZH, pp. 74–75.

foundation, and to be certain that everything else will actually appear as derivative, and never again can be ascribed as having any other value. Through our usual arrangement presently, a fateful error is suggested, and undeniably it produces much harm. If one prefixes to the valid doctrines of justification and redemption all the sections concerning God's essence, the Trinity, and Christology, the misunderstanding that the latter conditions the former certainly arises, while the fact is precisely the reverse, that we attain to the latter only through the former. The fact that anyone—and there are many—can still doubt Christianity because they doubt the Trinity (better, perhaps, there are still many who put a justifying garment on their unbelief), is ground enough to build the edifice from the beginning up, not from the abstract to the concrete, but from earth to heaven.[4]

Later in the same year he presents a caustic criticism of the scholarship of the so-called "believing theologians":

With deep humiliation I admit that Overbeck is right when he scornfully estimates the total impotence of the believing theology as a meaningful sign that the so-called believing scholarship no longer ventures to believe. In no sphere within a decade has it accomplished anything worthy of mention on the burning questions. No life of Jesus, no critical investigation of the Johannine question, nothing about Paul, nothing about primitive Christianity.

Simply read what Overbeck says about today's young "believing" theologians, who no longer venture to undertake anything other than a petty patristic or a linguistic-Old Testament investigation, far away from the burning mountain which no one is willing to approach too near.[5]

A year later, another fundamental concept makes its first appearance:

To be sure I am of the opinion that we must learn to strip off from the forms of our Christian belief much which through habit and custom we believe to be united with its inmost being. I am convinced that we must learn to do this in order not to come into conflict with the truth, but I believe I sufficiently estimate how many hot battles one will have to fight, and how bitter and hard on the conscience such conflicts are.[6]

But in spite of the bitterness and the conflicts, Harnack plunged with an incredible versatility into the work of making visible the results of his historical study. We have already noted the main projects

[4] AZH, pp. 82–83.
[5] *Ibid.*, pp. 90–91.
[6] *Ibid.*, p. 80.

which he took on in the Leipzig and Giessen years; the Smend bibliography of Harnack's works lists over one hundred items up to the time that he left Leipzig, and 367 items by the end of 1886 (the year he left Giessen).[7] Admittedly, many are book reviews, or new editions of previously published material. But 367 items at age 35!

Of greater significance than his formal theological instruction at Leipzig were the friendships that Harnack formed with Kaftan, Schürer, Baudissin, and Gebhardt. Not only was Harnack thereby able to establish rich personal contacts with brilliant young scholars; in the common life which they shared, it became clear that the most important constitutive element was the work of Albrecht Ritschl. The five friends dubbed themselves, indeed, "Koryphäen der Ritschlschen Schule," and it is unmistakably clear that Harnack increasingly *belonged* in the chorus. Harnack had come to Leipzig in 1872, and began his teaching career in 1874; Ritschl's great monograph on *The Christian Doctrine of Justification and Reconciliation* began to appear in 1870, with the third and last volume following in 1874. Hence in the precise period when Harnack was receiving his theological education, Ritschl's most influential work was making its impact in the theological circles of Germany.[8]

Harnack's letters to his cousin and to Engelhardt make clear the intensity of the *personal* struggles through which he was passing. The Dorpat-Erlangen "existential question," how to become Jesus' disciple, remained, but the content of the answer increasingly took on a Ritschlian tone. Specifically, Harnack broke with his heritage on three points, and in the case of two others his view was altered. The first and perhaps crucial point had to do with the doctrine of the person of Christ. In 1873 he wrote to Engelhardt that he could no longer hold to the doctrine of the preexistence of Christ:

> I cannot, so far as I see—and I believe I overlook nothing essential—comprehend how one can hold the doctrine of preexistence. If I should hold it, I should have to assume that revelations of God which are to be esteemed very highly have taken place among heathen peoples; for from all which I can perceive, this doctrine comes out of heathen philosophy, which at about the turn of the ancient period mixed noticeably with Semitic ideas of angels and of preexistence.[9]

[7] Friedrich Smend, *Adolf von Harnack: Verzeichnis seiner Schriften* (Leipzig: Hinrichs, 1931). This bibliography contains 1611 items.

[8] Harnack had doubtless been introduced to Ritschl's work at Dorpat. Seeberg, *op. cit.*, pp. 344–345, points out that von Engelhardt had been one of the first to understand the significance of Ritschl's work and to give it intensive study.

[9] AZH, p. 93.

A year later, he writes to his cousin (the letter was quoted near the end of the last chapter), concluding with these words:

There can be no doubt among us that we should try, in sorrow and in joy, to live such a life of struggle as he lived; a life of struggle against ourselves and the world about us; the world which always tries to draw us down into the common stream of life, and by a thousand diversions—many a time very serious ones—calls us from our proper task of being men established in God. Out of this struggle alone it should dawn upon us that it was he who set the goal for us—and who can struggle without a goal?—and that it was he who gave and pointed out to us the resources for the struggle. As this man he stands among us in his spirit even today, and I see his power in those masterful Christians who have not yet died out; concerning whom even the world must acknowledge that they walk among us as transfigured. They do not appear as if they belonged to this world, and of them we still feel that they are just what we must be. I have come to know many men, great and good men, but only a few of whom I have involuntarily thought, "If we were all so, we should have heaven on earth." . . . These Christians were all such Christians as would know nothing of any Christianity without Christ as the eternal and living kernel and guiding star. They would have smiled and looked astonished if anyone had spoken to them of such a thing! They know assuredly that all they are they have through his spirit, and that he has given them power in the great battle which they are fighting. Is anyone to be able to take this from them?[10]

The second point on which Harnack broke with his heritage had to do with the valuation of the tradition. Harnack admitted that he was torn between two *Angelpunkte*; on the one hand

. . . every historical movement . . . has so worked (to express it crudely)—rationalizing, leveling, and deteriorating—that the *tradition* current with the great multitude is certainly on the whole far removed from true remembrance. But I cannot convince myself that God has guaranteed to his Church a special and differently constituted tradition, authenticated as pure. . . . These two opposing thoughts are for me cardinal points about which my theological thought moves. . . .[11]

The third point dealt with the sacraments, and Harnack took this position:

The sacraments are acts instituted by Christ for his community and, as does the Word itself, and not otherwise, should assure those who use them and receive them believingly of the grace of God and the forgiveness of their sins. The act itself and the elements are symbolical tokens; but

[10] *Ibid.*, pp. 94–95.
[11] *Ibid.*, p. 96.

we use them because Christ has ordered them, and we would gladly do as he has said. To be sure, regarding the defense of the baptism of children, at least as to its necessity and saving effect for the child who as yet cannot think or believe, I offer no theories.[12]

On the point of the confessional writings, he declares:

I cannot bind myself unreservedly to the creeds. When I bind myself to them, it is done in the sense that I promise with my heart and my head to stand in the line of continuity of development which was instituted by Luther, and which in the time of the Reformation could in no way have found a better and more wholesome expression than that which appears in the first symbols of the Reformation period. . . . [I mean that] while I hold to the symbols of the Reformation Church, I believe only he is true to the spirit of this Church who wishes to be bound in nothing save the *sola fide* and who does not understand the Scripture principle in the sense that it is in any way to be constituted as equal to the material principle. I am no longer able to ignore the fact that even the writings of the New Testament contain a variety of very different forms of teaching, which simply cannot all be harmonized.[13]

Finally, on the point of the forgiveness of sins, he admits an altered understanding.

If we really believe in our justification, it is proved to us simply by our placing our whole life, active and passive, into God's fatherly hand. I mean thereby that the assurance "thy sins are forgiven thee" is only a part and an excerpt, although at the same time it is the best part. Do you not also find in our Church the danger of referring the gift imparted in faith in a one-sided manner, to compensation for our unfitness? . . . I have experienced in myself, that led by the doctrinal tradition, I stand in danger of doing injury to my Christian faith in its determining power when I give greater import to getting rid of something rather than attaining something. Now with God's help I want to bring it to pass that the faith, God forgives thee thy sins, will be only a special case in a whole lifetime with him. I have become much happier since this has become inwardly clear to me, and I have by this thought scared away many evil spirits. It is not unknown to you that one can learn this particularly today from Ritschl. But I can affirm that I did not learn it from him—what I did learn from him is limited to the *formulation* which makes it possible for me . . . to say what I mean.[14]

[12] *Ibid.*, p. 97.
[13] *Ibid.*, pp. 97–98.
[14] *Ibid.*, p. 98. The italics are mine. Cf. here the reported statement of Harnack, in a 1920 conversation with Karl Barth and Eberhard Vischer. Pauck

All the while that these theological and historical matters were being transmuted, Harnack remained existentially involved by virtue of his heritage. He confesses that the problem of the person of Christ has weighed more heavily on his heart than on his head. His father, until his death in 1889, kept a steady pressure on him, warning him that he should not fall into the camp of the destructive critics, in which he placed Ritschl, but should remain true to the Bible and the confessions. Theodosius Harnack regarded any subjectivistic elements with horror, and by act and writing sought to uphold a high ecclesiological position. There was no turning back for Adolf, however, for in his choice of friends, in his historical investigation, and in his apologetic work,[15] he had set his course. He remained something of an enigma to his friends, as he pursued his "destructive" historical labors on the one hand, and maintained a deep personal piety on the other. When asked how these things could be, he remarked that in the *Vaterunser*, the *Bergpredigt*, and the hymns of Paul Gerhardt he found resources which, taken symbolically, could enable one to "follow Christ" in spite of conflicts.[16] In fact, he held tenaciously to the belief that the old and the new theology could be reconciled, as is evident from his correspondence during the early Giessen period with Ritschl and Engelhardt. But Harnack was wrong in believing the two might be brought together. The biographer records that "If Ritschl, half in vexation, half in jest, called Engelhardt a 'Knight of the Order of the Sword,' 'who does not cultivate agreements but wants to discover contradictions,' " Engelhardt writes to Harnack about Ritschl at the same time in an almost pathetic tone: "If I could only get behind the riddle of this man! This problem pesters me, and I seek means to discover the fundamental failure, and to separate the great and powerful and true which is contained in his teaching from the heretical, and so to master him."[17]

By the beginning of the Giessen years Harnack's position was firmly set. Henceforward there were changes only in the sense of nuances. The works that poured in a rising tide from Harnack's pen,

---

quotes it (*op. cit.*, p. 358) from a letter Barth wrote to Thurneysen: ". . . the sum of what they said amounted to this, that the forgiveness of sins is something very simple and a part of the love of the neighbor, and Harnack said that he practiced it constantly."

[15] This was exercised, among other ways, by the founding, with Emil Schürer, of the *Theologische Literaturzeitung*.

[16] AZH, p. 108.

[17] *Ibid.*, pp. 128–129.

and especially the *Dogmengeschichte*, only buttressed the achieved position. And that position was—"Ritschlian."

Though it is not possible or desirable to attempt any full explication of the work of Ritschl, the "elemental factors" entering into the career of Adolf Harnack cannot be accurately represented without some attention to him, and particularly his relation to Baur.[18]

Baur's significance lay in the fact that he was the first historian to apply seriously the methods of critical empirical investigation to the history of the Church, and in the fact that he insisted that one must always be seeking for interpretative principles by which the flux of historical event can be given meaning. The interpretative principles which Baur employed were Hegelian. The philosophy of religion which subsumed the Hegelian attempt at a dogmatic, as essayed by Baur and his school, was deduced from a definite concept of the divine nature and of the logical principles of its evolution. Hegel's view of history, in which the Absolute Idea is seen as slowly coming to its fulfillment through the rational working of the process of thesis, antithesis, and synthesis, enamored Baur. In this view, Christianity was regarded as "the self-realization of the divine spirit in a historical movement which redeems finite spirits to itself."[19] Seen as a logically necessary result of the history of religion completing the self-evolution of the divine spirit, Christianity represents the perfect religious idea actually come to expression. Dogmatics is therefore nothing else than the exposition of the content of the God-Idea, absolute and final both for philosophy and religion. Such a dogmatic should make clear that the content of the God-Idea is the real inner meaning of the traditional ecclesiastical formulas, and should be practically expounded as such.

The significance of Baur was by no means restricted to his Hegelian interpretative scheme, however, as contemporary theological scholarship is recognizing. Indeed, the Hegelian interpretation rapidly passed out of favor. Idealistic monism had attempted to bring nature, man, and God within its rationalistic orbit, but it was overcome, at least temporarily, by the multiple blows of an intellectually creative century. Whatever Hegel might have thought of this crowning achievement of all thought, there were options which, when actualized, pronounced the Hegelian achievement relative like all other intellectual syntheses.[20]

18 See the other works in this series on Baur and Ritschl.

19 Troeltsch, "The Dogmatics of the *Religionsgeschichtliche Schule*," *American Journal of Theology*, XVII (Jan. 1913), p. 7.

20 Cf. Barth, p. 487, for an assessment of Feuerbach's influence in this respect.

Marx and Kierkegaard contributed to the dissolution, each transforming the absolute philosophy of spirit in his own way: Marx by his analysis of the external conditions of the life of the masses, challenging the bourgeois capitalist world, and Kierkegaard by his analysis of the internal existence of the individual, challenging the bourgeois Christian world and Christian secularism.[21]

Baur had criticized the rationalists of his time for their "mere" empiricism, and the orthodox historians like Neander for their lack of an interpretative principle that emerged out of the material itself.[22] He believed that he had discovered in the Hegelian philosophy the means by which the errors of his contemporaries could be corrected. When he adopted Hegelian philosophical categories, however, he in turn was criticized by Hase and later by Ritschl for depersonalizing man and failing to take history in its full concreteness.

Ritschl eviscerated from his thought not only Hegelian speculation, but all forms of speculation. What he did not reject, however, when he turned away from Tübingen, was Baur's *historical-critical method*—that which distinguished him as *Bahnbrecher*. Dilthey in 1865 made a judgment concerning Baur which has been repeated many times since: that Baur, because of his insistence on understanding Christianity as a historical phenomenon, ranks with Schleiermacher as an equal genius given to German evangelical theology in the nineteenth century.[23] But because this was a period in which an old norm was passing and a new was being born, and because this was probably not recognized even by those participating in the process, much of Baur's significance was ignored. Further, when his Hegelianism was rejected, many of his particular interpretations of early church history were rejected also. What remained as his enduring contribution, however, was his understanding that *Christianity must be viewed as a historical phenomenon*, and *investigated by a historical-critical method.*

[21] Karl Löwith's "L'achèvement de la philosophie classique par Hegel et sa dissolution chez Marx et Kierkegaard," *Recherches Philosophiques*, IV (1934–1935), pp. 232–267, is a suggestive essay which points out that Hegel departed from his own early declared principle, "Fini absolu contre infini absolu," in his achieved system. Kierkegaard held that Hegel's "existence" was, therefore, always abstract and ideal rather than real.

[22] Barth, *op. cit.*, p. 453, declares that such a history of dogma as that of Harnack, basing everything on the Gospel of Jesus, would have been regarded by Baur as hopeless; for it rested essentially on a pragmatism by means of which the riches of history could never be possessed.

[23] Emanuel Hirsch, *Geschichte der neuern evangelischen Theologie in Zusammenhang mit den allgemeinen Bewegungen des europaischen Denkens*, Fünf Bände (Gütersloh: C. Bertelsmann, 1950), V, p. 625.

In this respect Harnack was his heir, in spite of the fact that he rejected many of Baur's specific formulations.

Harnack assessed the significance of Baur and the Tübingen school, and the advances made in the generation following, in a lecture given at Giessen in 1885, entitled "The Present State of Research in Early Church History."[24] He begins by admitting that in 1855 Baur dominated the field, and anyone who dared to question his Hegelian interpretation of the development of the early Church was written off as an apologist. For Baur, this development "was an immanent process, which, beginning with the appearance and preaching of Jesus Christ, branched into two opposite tendencies, the Petrine and the Pauline, and advanced through a cycle of antitheses and syntheses till it culminated in the Catholic Church."[25] "Jewish Christianity" and "Gentile Christianity" were interpreted in terms of the philosophical concepts of "Consciousness," "Image," "Idea," and "Reality." As dubious as this practice was, the historical importance of the Tübingen school cannot be gainsaid, Harnack declares, for it rightly defined the main problem as the rise of Catholicism, it adopted a methodologically sound procedure in beginning with Paul and Paulinism, and it sketched a picture of the early development on the basis of these understandings.[26]

But this picture was not just, and historical-critical science had to revise the picture as it became "richer in historical points of view."[27] With this revision, in large part a result of Ritschl's work, the following six viewpoints were altered: Tübingen saw the Judaism contemporary to the rise of Christianity as a homogeneous structure, whereas now it is seen as a richly multiform phenomenon; Tübingen identified the standpoint of the original Apostles with that of the legalistic and exclusive Jewish-Christians, whereas the picture at present sets forth three strands: the Pauline, the Pharisaic Judaeo-Christian, and that of the "Pillar-Apostles"; Tübingen identified Paulinism with Gentile Christianity, but we now know that it was really a Jewish-Christian doctrine, distinct from first- and second-century Gentile Christianity; Tübingen resolved all second-century antagonisms into one great antithesis between Jewish and Gentile Christianity, whereas at present we recognize that in the second century Jewish Christianity was no longer a factor; Tübingen concentrated on images, conceptions,

[24] *RA*, II (Giessen: Töpelmann, 1904), pp. 217–235.
[25] *Ibid.*, p. 219.
[26] *Ibid.*, pp. 219–220.
[27] *Ibid.*, p. 220.

and dogmatic statements, but today we have learned that the Christian religion was, above everything else, a new life and a new form of human society; and Tübingen, in criticizing the New Testament writings, always asked as its first question whether they were genuine or counterfeit, but today, by a more developed method, we push behind this question to ask whether the books have been transmitted to us purely and without additions.[28] The result of these "richer historical points of view" has been a greater caution, and withal, a more traditional view of the authenticity of many of the writings.

But what are the causes which have made this advance possible? Harnack suggests three: The science of history has been emancipated from its slavery to philosophical systems. After the death of rationalism, romanticism provided a wholesome reaction, but it was no more than that. It, too, had to be overcome, by means of a genuinely historical temper. Ecclesiastical history has come to be seen as a part of general history, occupying no sheltered status. And there have been a vast number of wide-ranging new discoveries.[29]

A close examination of the six listed contrasts evokes two comments. In the first place, with the exception of the fifth point there is no necessary contradiction between Baur and the positions Harnack sets forth. We say "necessary"—for obviously there are differences. But Harnack in making these points is dependent on the historical-critical method to which Baur had contributed so seminally; and "the richer historical points of view" means simply the further development of that which was implicit in Baur's *method*, sans his Hegelian presuppositions. Secondly, there is a real point of difference in *conception* expressed in the fifth difference. It is hardly fair to point out that if Harnack stated the options correctly, then Baur is much nearer modern biblical conceptions than is Harnack. But it is fair to emphasize that as of 1885 Harnack had already decided what the Christian religion was, viz., "a new life and a new form of human society,"[30] and that (*pace* Harnack's "presuppositionless" history), the Ritschlian influence was already thereby clearly marked.

Of the causes assigned by Harnack for the advance, the first is the only one that requires comment. And here we dissent from Harnack's judgment if he means what he appears to mean. For that romanticism was not overcome, at least in Harnack, but it was repressed in favor of "richer historical points of view." Joining with his Ritschlian

[28] *Ibid.*, pp. 221–223.
[29] *Ibid.*, pp. 223–227.
[30] *Ibid.*, p. 222.

axiology, it emerged increasingly in his later years as an *Humanitätslehre*, counterpoised to his historicist tendencies.

Ritschl himself, as every theologian knows, had announced his break with the Tübingen School in the second edition of his *Die Entstehung der altkatholischen Kirche*, published in 1857:

When I prepared *Die Entstehung der altkatholischen Kirche* in its first form, I was in a position to raise a number of differences with certain representations of the Tübingen school; but at that time I still had not arrived at the point of opposition to this school which would have made the opposition principal and thoroughgoing.[31]

With this second edition, Ritschl did take a diverse position to that of Tübingen, and throughout the rest of his life he sought to make good and to document this divergent position. Ritschl's "revolution" touched on almost all aspects of the theological enterprise of his time.[32] This was due to the fact that he was concerned with historical, exegetical, and systematic problems, and did significant work in each.[33]

Ritschl helped to clear away many difficulties by limiting theology to the point of view of faith in the God of Jesus Christ, and by his recognition that affirmations about God, sin, Christ, *et al.*, are meaningful only in a Christian context. He put his finger on the weakness of solely intellectual approaches, he helped "to clear up the discrepancies between religious and non-religious views of the same event," he "gave impetus to the historical examination of Christian faith," and of the life and faith of the historical Jesus, and he strengthened the emerging social gospel.[34] Yet, after insisting on the centrality of the Church, and declaring invalid the traditional theological method which worked from natural theology to revelation, he

[31] Bonn: Marcus, 1857, p. v.

[32] In spite of this fact, Barth declares (*op. cit.*, pp. 598–599) that the estimates of Ritschl which see him as marking an "epoch" in the history of theology are overdrawn. He comments: "In the development alluded to the Ritschlian School played the assuredly important role of a reaction. As such, but not as the beginning of a new epoch, it distinguishes itself from the flood of events and personalities."

[33] Consider the judgment of Philip Hefner, "The Role of Church History in the Theology of Albrecht Ritschl," *Church History*, XXXIII (Sept. 1964), pp. 338–355, where he develops the view that "that career took the shape it did because Ritschl understood church history as he did, because he was committed to this understanding, and because he accepted the responsibility for the theological activity which commitment to such an understanding of church history entailed."

[34] H. Richard Niebuhr, *The Meaning of Revelation* (New York: The Macmillan Company, 1941), pp. 26–27.

too proceeded "to analyze God's nature simply from the point of view of a member of the human community confronting nature."[35] That his point of view was that of a scientific, historical-positivist, nineteenth-century enlightened man may have justified it to him as standing outside the relativities that impinge on and generally corrupt all systems; it did not justify the point of view to a later deluded generation, nor to the orthodox confessionalists and hard-headed Lutherans of Dorpat-Erlangen. His "new mediating theology,"[36] based on a positivist-historical rather than a speculative-pietist ground, was rejected by the orthodox confessionalists, in spite of its foundation in biblical revelation.

During the Leipzig years Harnack clung to the hope that some *rapprochement* could be effected between the rival camps.[37] Ritschl had scorned the idea, and by the time Harnack had lived through the strife over his appointment to the University of Berlin and the *Apostolikumsstreit* that followed, he was ready to agree with Ritschl. This agreement is intimated in a significant review article of a book on Ritschl and his school; the book, written by Gustave Ecke, was reviewed by Harnack in *Christliche Welt* in 1897. In introducing the review, Harnack declares that in order to understand Ritschl, three things must be set forth: (1) the fact that Ritschl was concerned to develop a unified theology; (2) the fact that Ritschl was interested in the historical, rather than in natural theology; and (3) the fact that Ritschl was always seeking to defend and strengthen the Protestant position:

> What a noble purpose, and what an idealism! The mighty faith in the possibility of achieving a strong, unified knowledge of God and the world! The renunciation of philosophy in favor of history! The conviction that the Reformation of the sixteenth century had won a positive, impregnable possession to enrich religion and thought, which only needed to be purely developed in order to drive back Catholicism and forever adjudge it wrong! Ritschl lived within these structures of thought, they were his objective, and every noble or acid word is to be understood from this point of view. Where among us is there still existent the complete certainty which this great theologian possessed?[38]

Harnack describes Ritschl's "unified theology" as achieving the following: it made possible the scientific treatment of *Glaubenslehre*, it

[35] *Ibid.*, p. 29.
[36] Hirsch, *Geschichte der neuern . . .*, V. p. 558.
[37] *Supra*, p. 41.
[38] "Ritschl und seine Schule," *RA*, II, p. 355.

successfully overcame speculative rationalism, and it presented valid criticisms to an unsound piety. This achievement was effected by centering upon the greatness of Jesus Christ, the forgiveness of sins, and the necessity of using the Christian community as *Ausgangspunkt*.

Admitting that Ecke is correct when he says that such "Ritschlians" as Häring, Kattenbusch, Loofs, Herrmann, and Kaftan are returning to a positive biblical-Reformation confessional position, Harnack inquires why there must continue to be a conflict between the Ritschlians and the orthodox.[39] For one reason, Harnack suggests:

> They all esteem the Bible, as did Ritschl, "only" in its historical originality as a source for Christian faith, and will not give it the authority of revelation. "But for the Christian community," he [Ecke] declares, "this witness to Christ has the value of revelation as the enlightening paraclete."[40]

In short, the orthodox held firmly to the dogma of the inspiration of the Scriptures, as interpreted in the old way, and rejected the viewpoint and the findings of historical criticism. Harnack is quite clear as to what influence historical criticism has had on such matters: "The dogma of the New Testament, as it has, not without basis, been called, can no longer live in the scientific theology in the sense of an exclusive inspiration doctrine; indeed, it will in the future most certainly be overcome through the historical representation."[41] This does not mean that the essential content, which Ritschl sought to discover in the New Testament forms, has been overcome, but just the opposite. Through a historical understanding it will be possible to discover the real strength and power of the biblical writings.

What then, we ask, is Ritschl's "theology of moral values"?[42] When Ritschl rejected Baur, in part because Baur underestimated the historical importance of Jesus in Christianity's beginnings, he turned to a strictly historical method, with all speculative patterns abjured. By this method he saw Christianity as a historical religion centering in the revelation of God through Jesus, and in the experience of faith and salvation produced by this revelation. This revelation was ethical, and determined that Christianity would be a teleological religion. That is, the faith and salvation is dynamic, its impulsion being that final "kingdom of ends" which serve as hope and therefore as motivating source in religious living. It is in the historical Jesus that one sees

[39] *Ibid.*, p. 366.
[40] *Ibid.*, p. 367.
[41] *Ibid.*
[42] This is the term used by Mackintosh, *op. cit.*, pp. 138–180, to describe Ritschl's position.

this process actually operating; he is the one datum in history who brings all the experience of man into perspective. The fateful consequence of this insistence is two-pronged: on the one hand, Jesus is interpreted as the *one* revelation, and the problem of *praeparatio evangelica* and its consequent, the "unity of the Scriptures," is denied validity; on the other hand, by his insistence that this revelation is strictly a *historical* revelation, Ritschl implies that the "scandal of particularity" is meaningless, and, as Tillich has pointed out, adopts the view that Jesus is the "extraordinarily regular" medium of revelation.[43] Thus it is admitted that the Logos is divinely disclosed, but the relation of this Logos to the realm of divine mystery is bypassed. "Where I find mystery," Ritschl had declared, "I say nothing about it."[44]

But how could Ritschl affirm the finality of the revelation in Jesus, and still insist that theological speculation as to Jesus' relation to God was pointless? Or, asked in a different way, what is the norm from which such a position could be set forth? The clue is to be found in his fundamental anthropocentrism, and this not in the sense that all formulations are man-made, and therefore relative, but in the sense that the norm is made to be *the value for man*. This norm is to be arrived at not by the employment of fundamentally biblical categories, in which man is always seen to be under God, but by the employing of idealist speculation (*sic*) concerning man's relation to nature. Thus: "What is sought . . . is a solution of the contradiction in which man finds himself as both a part of nature and a spiritual personality claiming to dominate nature."[45] Or, again: "A religious value-judgment can be made only as one has experienced the way in which the particular religion makes available the power of God to secure man's dominion over the world of nature."[46] God is thus made instrumental to the achievement of man's end, which is the actualization of his dominance over nature. To ask the question "What is God worth for man?" is an infinite methodological distance from asking "What is man worth under God?"

From this viewpoint, however, Ritschl proceeded to explicate his views; and all of the characteristic features of the Ritschlian theology

[43] Paul Tillich, *Systematic Theology* (Chicago: The University of Chicago Press, 1951), I, p. 119.

[44] Quoted with no source given in Mackintosh, *op. cit.*, p. 160.

[45] *Ibid.*, p. 150.

[46] Robert Koenig, "The Use of the Bible in Albrecht Ritschl's Theology and the Significance of His Method for Today" (unpublished Ph.D. dissertation, The Divinity School, The University of Chicago, 1953), p. 30.

are outgrowths of his insistence that apart from Christ we cannot know or grasp God as a redeeming Father,[47] that "every claim to teach something concerning God in Himself apart from some real revelation on his part, felt and perceived on ours, is baseless,"[48] and that this essentially ethical revelation of historical Christianity is, indeed, the Word of God which is to be found in the Scripture. Ritschl's Christocentric method, his emphasis on Christian experience as against confessionalism, on the historical nature of Christianity as against speculative thought, and on the ethical and social in Christianity as against mysticism, all root in this fundamentally anthropocentric method.

Karl Barth has accused Ritschl of going behind romanticism and idealism to the fundamental tenets of the Enlightenment.[49] This charge is an oft-repeated one, and is used by Schweitzer in his description of the weakness of certain nineteenth-century historical investigation, laboring as it did under the colossal presupposition of a "presuppositionless Kulturprotestantismus":

> It is, indeed, not the least service of the eschatological school that it compels modern theology, which is so much preoccupied with history, to reveal what is its own as its own. Eschatology makes it impossible to attribute modern ideas to Jesus, and then by way of "New Testament Theology" take them back from him as a loan, as even Ritschl not so long ago did with such naïveté. Johannes Weiss, in cutting himself loose, as a historian, from Ritschl, and recognizing that "the real roots of Ritschl's ideas are to be found in Kant and the illuminist theology," introduced the last decisive phase of the process of separation between historical and "modern" theology.[50]

This criticism requires evaluation, for if, as we hold, it is true that the clue to understanding Harnack lies in his axiology, and if he got this axiology primarily (not exclusively) from Ritschl, it must be asked whether it is indeed the Kantianism in Ritschl which prescribes the norm.

How far is it true to declare that "the real roots of Ritschl's ideas are to be found in Kant and the illuminist theology"? Ritschl, it is true, accepted the Kantian limitation of pure reason. With this limitation, "the belief that has controlled theology, that the Christian con-

[47] Mackintosh, *op. cit.*, p. 145.
[48] *Ibid.*
[49] *Ibid.*, p. 141.
[50] *Quest of the Historical Jesus: A Critical Study of Its Progress from Reimarus to Wrede*, tr. W. Montgomery (London: A. and C. Black, 1911), p. 141.

ception of God and Christ must be demonstrated as a universal truth of reason, has been shaken to the foundation."[51] Thus far, Ritschl and Kant agree; but Ritschl welcomed this limitation, believing that it opened the possibility that Christian experience might be regarded as an independent source of truth. "Religion and theoretical knowledge are different functions of the spirit, which, when they deal with the same objects, are not even partially coincident, but are divergent throughout."[52] But this is to depart from the positive view of religion which Kant explicated, for, as Kattenbusch remarks, religion for Kant is practically "an annex to morals."[53] The practical reason which produces value-judgments deals *only* with moral judgments. Ritschl's religion, it is true, was also concerned with the ethical, but he surpassed the religion of Kant by his insistence that religion must be given an independent basis. For Ritschl, the *historical* was the starting point, and he was the one who broke the pattern of imposing philosophical schemes on church history.[54] Individuals, not ideas or institutions alone, were to be centered upon; and he then went on to make his correlation between the historical (Jesus) and the ethical (love), in attempting to solve the dilemma of man in nature.

The basis value-judgment of all of Ritschl's thought is simply this: that man, though a part of the order of nature, has intrinsic worth over against nature by reason of his constitution as spirit. It is because Christianity solves this problem that it is to be regarded as the absolute religion. The problem itself, as has been suggested, was bequeathed to Ritschl and later to Harnack by the flourishing materialism of the time. How does Christianity solve this? "The revelation of God in Jesus, when responded to in active faith, gives man actual freedom and mastery over nature. It redeems him from sinfulness through the divine forgiveness, and implants in him that motive of love which aims at the moral organization of mankind."[55] This reconciliation with God takes place only within the Church. Because we possess this reconciliation, access to the kingdom of God, and a program for the mastery of life, we can say that we have God in Jesus Christ.

[51] Eugene W. Lyman, "Ritschl's Theory of Value-Judgments," *Journal of Religion*, V (Oct. 1925), p. 505.

[52] *Ibid.*

[53] Ferdinand Kattenbusch, *Die deutsche evangelische Theologie seit Schleiermacher: ihre Leistungen und ihre Schäden*, Vierte Auflage, umgearbeitete (Geissen: Töpelmann, 1924), p. 51.

[54] *Ibid.*

[55] Lyman, "Ritschl's Theory . . . ," p. 508.

Ritschl has been accused of anthropocentrism, of rationalism, and of a culture-oriented Christianity. Too often, doubtless, he has been sold out by using the straw-man technique and interpreting him in terms of later denatured varieties of Ritschlianism. It is true that for Ritschl moral faith is regulative. This norm was evolved, at least in part, as a reaction to Baur's Hegelianism, as Ritschl discovered the vast resources for theological work resident in the new "presuppositionless" historical method. But as he rejected the notion that "the idea works itself out in history," he sought, unsuccessfully, to take a stance which would bear no presuppositions with regard to historical data; and, as in the case of his most famous disciple, the axiological presuppositions intruded. For Ritschl failed to take account of the fact that he too was an heir of German idealism, and in one of the fundamental categories of his thought (man over nature), he depended on the great idealists for the setting of the problem.[56] Nature, man, and God, and the relations between these entities, were very much his fundamental concern. But further, he failed to take account of his own historical situation in his implied acceptance of the positivistic dictum that "the latest in time is the best in fact." Couéism is scarcely concealed in his optimistic appraisal of man, in his impatience with any mystical position which sought, at least, to point to an ultimate mystery that could not be plumbed, and, in patent form, in his confidence that the essence of the Gospel could be discovered by a historical method and applied by sensible men.

How was Ritschl's theological labor received by orthodox Lutheran confessionalism, and how did it diverge from the older view? In a striking letter to Ritschl written in 1882, Harnack specifies four points of contrast between Ritschl and the orthodox. On theory of knowledge, they probe behind the historical facts; Ritschl stands upon historical events. As to method, they want *loci*; Ritschl desires a system. In dogmatics, the Augustinian concept of sin and the Anselmian reconciliation doctrine are decisive for the older theology; this is not true for Ritschl. Practically, they seek to master all knowledge, defining everything through an ecclesiastical, *loci*-dogmatic; Ritschl abjures this and places the problem of the Christian on the ground of religious virtue.[57] The orthodox, therefore, seek to write history with transhistorical objects intruding; the new theology remains conscious of the limits of history, though it holds a high view with respect to the efficacy of historical knowledge. The orthodox speak of Jesus and

56 Although, of course, he rejected this solution.
57 AZH, pp. 127–128.

of the events concerning his life from the standpoint of a dogmatic position which emphasizes his relation to God; the new theology remains silent when it confronts mystery, and above all does not bring a dogmatic prepossession to this historical person. The orthodox confess that Jesus is the Christ, *a priori*; the new theology takes the position that "he has the value of God for us," which position is based on a historical examination. So Harnack believed.

Yet, in spite of the fact that Harnack viewed Ritschlian theology as providing a way of mediation between the old and the new theology, the differences proved to be unbridgeable, as we have noted. Harnack's naïveté was somewhat dissipated when pamphlets began to appear roundly condemning his own work as "destructive Ritschlianism," and Ritschl's own books were burned by the zealots. Ritschl entertained no sanguine hopes about the possibility of a *rapprochement*, and passed on to his disciples the advice to "Trust in God, keep your powder dry, and write textbooks!"[58] And indeed, this was just the cathartic that Harnack employed to make clear to himself and to others where he stood. In 1885 he published the first volume of his *Dogmengeschichte* and sent the first copy to Ritschl. Affirming his great debt to Ritschl, continuous since 1868 when he first read the *Entstehung der altkatholischen Kirche,* he declares that "without the foundation which you laid, the *Dogmengeschichte* probably would never have been written."[59] The critiques, praises, and bombasts which greeted this work made it clear that Harnack had staked out a position from which he would henceforth be judged. From this point on, Harnack was *persona non grata*, theologically speaking, in orthodox circles; all possibility of mediation was gone, and he became the storm center of the liberalism of the time.

[58] *Ibid.*, p. 129.
[59] *Ibid.*, p. 135.

VI

Berlin

It is neither possible nor necessary to follow Harnack's career after his appointment to the theological faculty at the University of Berlin with the same attention to detail we have thus far attempted. Not possible because, to mention only one aspect of his multiform activity, there were over a thousand publications that issued from his study to the time of his death. Not necessary, because the pattern of his activity and the manner of his thought had been set by the time he moved to Berlin, and what follows is an explication of a point of view already described.

Therefore we will deal with this period by focusing on several paradigmatic episodes which illumine all of his activity. We will be particularly concerned to examine the fate of his attempted mediation *within the Church*, the reinterpretation which Harnack gave to his vocation at about the turn of the century, and the direction of the attempted mediation between *the Church and the culture*.

Harnack's career, almost from the beginning, had been such as to require taking into account the live theological options of his day. The Dorpat-Erlangen confessional Lutheranism had been challenged by the Tübingen interpretation. He had found a way between this Scylla and Charybdis in the ship of Ritschlianism. This way of thinking had become the *bête noir* of the rigid confessionalists, making necessary, because of personal loyalties, an attempt on Harnack's part to find tangents of commonality. But these he did not find, and increasingly as Harnack's name became *the* symbol of historical study from a Ritschlian viewpoint, he became aware that this was true.

A letter to Loofs, written shortly after the appearance of the first volume of the *Dogmengeschichte*, makes clear, perhaps, why Harnack failed to achieve the "mediation" he desired:

I do not believe we will advance further without an iconoclastic element. Since we may not employ such an element directly, because neither the pulpit nor the instruction of the Church is the place for it, it ought not, in my opinion, to be wanting in our books. If we wish to free Protestantism from its pettinesses and be ready for the crisis which must come, and if our cultured Christian people are to have their confidence renewed in the whole of evangelical Christianity, not simply in this or that fragment, this must be done. I do not want to keep any student of theology from a decisive crisis. The three ways of escape which they can take are apostasy from theology, confirmation in authority, or understanding. Any of the three is more to be desired than the spongelike attitude of mind and thought which they conserve, through indifference, in the university, only then to be wet down by what is termed "experience in office," which in the majority of cases is simply routine. Thus, as our conditions presently exist, *that person* seems to me to be the best teacher who knows how to combine the *fortiter scandalizare* with the living witness to the plain Gospel, to whom the one is as much an inner necessity as the other.[1]

This was written in 1886. Harnack had "guessed," in writing to Loofs, that the publication of the *Dogmengeschichte* would free him from the confessional war; but if he meant more than a personal emancipation, he could hardly have been more wrong.[2] For it was his method of handling church dogma that cost him a chair at Leipzig,[3] and set the defenders of ecclesiastical orthodoxy on his trail in a way hitherto unknown to him. In fact, the years between the publication of the *Dogmengeschichte* and *Das Wesen des Christentums* are Harnack's *Sturm und Drang* period so far as the Church is concerned; and finally, we believe he saw that he had failed, and

[1] AZH, p. 141.

[2] It was the *Dogmengeschichte* that marked his coming of age as an established and recognized scholar in his own right, and with the recognition, he became the target of those of different persuasion. See AZH, pp. 141 ff. for a summary of some of the results.

[3] *Ibid.*, p. 146. Eighty-five of eighty-six votes from the Leipzig faculty were cast for Harnack; but the appointment was blocked by the high consistory.

this recognition brought on what his biographer calls "Harnack's inner change."[4]

After a short tenure at Marburg, the Berlin appointment was broached and a prolonged controversy broke out. The Berlin faculty, on December 10, 1887, unanimously proposed Harnack for the chair in church history vacated by Semisch.[5] In the old Prussian provinces, the Evangelical *Oberkirchenrat* had the right to express itself regarding the doctrinal and confessional position of anyone called to a university chair. The council was split, but Brückner, one of those who took a neutral position, wrote to Harnack, asking for a statement of his views on the Resurrection and on baptism as a sacrament. Harnack answered, referring him to his published writings. The ecclesiastical press of Prussia entered the fray against him, with Stöcker's *Deutsche Evangelische Kirchenzeitung* leading the pack. When the judgment of the council went to the Ministry, Harnack was voted against on three counts: that he had shattered the New Testament canon, that he left open the question of miracle, and that he denied that the Trinitarian formula for baptism had been instituted by Jesus. The Ministry of Worship now had a chance to reply, and Harnack's defenders were Althoff and Weiss. At this crucial juncture, Wilhelm I died and the young emperor inherited the problem. Through the active support of Bismarck in the Ministry of State, Wilhelm II, previously under Stöcker's influence, made a favorable decision, with a characteristic flourish: "Ich will keine Mucker!"[6] The decision came on September 17, 1888, over nine months after the recommendation of the faculty.

Harnack's expressed hope that he would be allowed to go about his work unimpeded proved again to be illusory. In 1892 the most bitter of all the controversies surrounding him, the *Apostolikumsstreit*, broke out. Though the problem was older than this, dating from the eighties, and including, as was customary, political factors, Harnack's involvement was precipitated when he was specifically asked for his judgment on the "Schrempf case." Schrempf, a young ecclesiastic, had performed a baptism without using the Apostles' Creed. Harnack answered the request with nine points, which he published in *Christliche Welt*. Among them, he held that the Church should prepare a shorter confession which would be grounded in the Reformation position, and also take account of later understand-

[4] *Ibid.*, p. 294.
[5] *Ibid.*, p. 156.
[6] *Ibid.*, p. 171.

ings of the Gospel. This confession should be required of everyone. Further, either the Apostles' Creed should be removed from liturgical worship, or its use should be left to the discretion of congregations. On specifics, he declared that certain elements of the Creed cannot be interpreted in their original sense, but must be seen in the light of evangelical belief—e.g., "the communion of saints"—and that the phrase of the Creed "conceived by the Holy Ghost, born of the Virgin Mary" cannot any longer be received by many believing Christians as fact. His generalization was that there should now be required of all future ecclesiastics the study of the history of dogma and of symbolics.[7] Harnack appended a statement in which he specified what he regarded as the essentials of any evangelical creed:

> The essential content of the Apostles' Creed consists in the confession that in the Christian religion the goods "holy Church," "forgiveness of sins," and "eternal life" are given, that the possession of these goods is promised to those believing in God, the Almighty Creator, in his Son Jesus Christ, and in the Holy Spirit, and that these are won through Jesus Christ our Lord. This content is evangelical.[8]

With this statement the controversy flared into violence. Cremer of Greifswald, an opponent whom Harnack honored, argued, in *Christliche Welt*, against his position; but Stöcker requisitioned the columns of *Deutsche Evangelische Kirchenzeitung* to pour out his journalistic vitriol, accusing Harnack and his ilk of "no respect for history, no honor for the confessions, no regard for the Church and community. Hypotheses, quite often giddy hypotheses . . . are given greater reality than the foundation beliefs of the Church."[9] Stöcker concluded with the declaration that "confession, biblical authority, and finally the historicity and the personality of Christ himself are thrown into the witches'-kettle of frothy criticism."[10] At Kassel a consistorial paper printed a sonnet ending with the lines:

> If Harnack is for you the light of the world,
> Then he must also now your Savior be.[11]

The Catholic press also joined the controversy, and an unbelievable number of letters appeared in the papers, most of them opposing Harnack's position. There were supporters, however: Rade, through

[7] *Ibid.*, pp. 196–201.
[8] *Ibid.*, p. 201.
[9] *Ibid.*, p. 202.
[10] *Ibid.*
[11] *Ibid.*, p. 203.

his influential *Christliche Welt*, and the *Akademie der Wissenschaften*. And Harvard University took occasion to offer Harnack for the second time, a full professorship.[12]

Harnack was supported by the Ministry, and was not reproved.[13] It is significant that in spite of the many requests that poured in, including one from his brother Otto, asking Harnack to make explicit what he would put in the place of the Apostles' Creed, he refused. On the one hand, he confessed a great fear of agitators, for he held that in any agitation the truth suffers; on the other hand, he affirmed that he was not willing to destroy the faith that meant so much to so many people. Thus, though he was accused of a failure to follow through on his position, he took as his motto "Ich bin kein Reformator," and refused to say anything further.[14]

The *Apostolikumsstreit* can stand as paradigm for Harnack's relation to the ecclesiastical authorities of his day, but there were many subsequent occasions when he came into conflict with them. After the publication of *Das Wesen des Christentums*, he was challenged from many sides for his statement that "the Father alone, and not the Son, belongs in the Gospel as Jesus preached it."[15] Two years previous to this he had declared to Rade his intention to continue in his vocation of serving the Church and serving science at the same time;[16] this in spite of the fact that the Church would not even let Harnack act as examiner for his own students. A year after the publication of *Das Wesen des Christentums*, Harnack had desired to be appointed as the faculty representative to the meeting of the Brandenburg Synod, but when he contacted his friends to inquire whether this would be possible, they retorted that it would be an affront to the Synod if Harnack were appointed.[17] Even the liberal party among the churchmen did not find Harnack acceptable, for

[12] *Ibid.*, p. 210.

[13] However, as a concession to orthodoxy, Adolf Schlatter, a conservative, was appointed to the Berlin faculty. *Ibid.*, pp. 208–209.

[14] *Ibid.*, p. 212.

[15] (Leipzig: Hinrichs, 1900). Tr. by Thomas Bailey Saunders as *What is Christianity?* 4th ed. rev. (New York: G. P. Putnam's Sons, 1923). The notation suggesting "revision" is misleading, and amounts only to such trivialities as italicizing. In the German edition, which I have used in several instances ("zum 45. bis 50. Tausend," issued in 1903), Harnack remarked that he deliberately left the text unchanged because he wanted it to remain as it had been delivered and transcribed. See p. iv. The Saunders translation is a good one, and I have used it. Hereafter the work is designated *WC*.

[16] AZH, pp. 295 f.

[17] *Ibid.*, p. 300.

Harnack held that the Church was too much dominated by the ecclesiastics, and in his appeal for more lay participation he found few clerical supporters.

The sole place where his interest in action could be exercised was in extra-Church movements and organizations, and this doubtless accounts, in considerable measure, for his acceptance of the directorship of the Royal Library. When the call to this position came, in 1905, he wrote about it to Rade, and in the course of one of his letters made a significant statement with respect to his relation to the Church:

> You learn to know the world only insofar as you influence it. My new position will not make me so much a "librarian" as an organizer. I hope that my friends will find that theology does not thereby lose anything, but that science, and theology also, will win. I have *done* so little in my life, and I would like to supplement my lectures and writings in a modest way by an *action* from which the entire community profits. The Church has not offered me an opportunity in this regard, and such work would now come too late for me.[18]

This is certainly seriously understated. Though Harnack had, in his writings, declared his concern to be the defense of Protestantism—to be sure, as understood under its Ritschlian form—though he had been actively interested since his Leipzig years in the "social question" in the Church, though he had supported foreign missions in numerous writings, though he had been president of the *Evangelisch-Soziale Kongress* for three years at the time of the writing of this letter, and was to continue for five more, though he was active in the Inner Mission, though he was co-founder and president of the Evangelical Union, he remained *persona non grata* to the institutional church and its leaders.

If the desired mediation *within* the Church could not be effected, perhaps a grander mediation, between culture and the Church, could: perhaps he could "confess and defend the independently-won position." And here we arrive at one of those *idées fixes* with which most of the interpretations of Harnack have begun as presupposition. *Kulturprotestantismus!* and all the pieces of the puzzle fall into position like the turning of a kaleidoscope! This is the essence of oversimplification.

For the biography makes it crystal clear that Harnack (always according to his own light of understanding—and of whom can it

[18] *Ibid.*, p. 325.

be any other way?) was aware of what he was doing as he entered, from the turn of the century on, into wider cultural duties. Further, it is clear that he always regarded theology as his fundamental vocation, and his work in the Royal Library and the Kaiser Wilhelm Foundation as *Nebenrufen*. And finally, it would be grossly unfair to fail to take account of the cultural situation itself as a crucial element in his decision thus to participate in wider scientific and cultural affairs.

The *Wesen* had been declared. All of the strands that had fed into this "symbolic concatenation of liberalism" were as visible to the perceptive eye as they would ever be. In a real sense, that position which Harnack espoused *had* developed as far it could, and in 1900 he stood, not only at the height of his own powers, but at the end of a quest to understand Christianity historically and penetrate beyond the dogmatic to the inner form of Christian truth. That *his* understanding and *his* penetration by *his* method were to be "overcome" by new ways of thinking need not deter us here. The fact is that those things which his way of investigating could begin *had* been begun. It was a time of harvest. And Harnack saw it as essential for himself that he move into new fields.

Action: this is the final responsibility of the historian. We are not in the world simply to contemplate it, but we are in it to prepare for the future in a responsible way. This was an elemental article of faith for Harnack. And it is because he believed this, and because he believed that any belief must be expressed in what one does, that he expanded the range of his activity in the last three decades of his life.

Positively, this is the motivant. Were there negative reasons? If it is true, as we have declared, that at the time of *Das Wesen* a watershed had been reached, and from this point on, as it were, Harnack moved on a vast plateau that touched all facets of Wilhelmian and Weimar Germanic culture, was this not because the newer directions of theological science had turned to "system-building" and away from Harnack's "scavenger-labor" of historical investigation? And also because those who continued in his ways were simply mopping up? And still further, because the established Church, governed as always by ecclesiastical politicians, went on its way as if there had never been a Baur, a Ritschl, or a Harnack? It is vastly instructive, in order to understand which, if not all, of these reasons really controlled, to examine Harnack's own assessment of his "inner change" at the beginning of the twentieth century.

This change is described in a series of letters to Martin Rade, written in a two months period in late 1899. On the direction of theological scholarship, he writes:

They want today to get at things which in my opinion should remain a secret to general discussion as well as to science; for they are the secret of personality and its inner life. Whoever refuses to participate in this immodest and indelicate exposure is counted a pallid scholastic who has no feeling for "life." On the other hand, that work which makes real the ordering, the development, and the understanding of what is knowable, is little prized, as is the cultivation of the common resources of knowledge.

Further, I cannot share in the whim of ignoring all that we have learned from history about religion and Christianity (although it may be that I myself, in my own personal development, have very imperfectly appropriated it), in order to introduce some sort of elementary, antediluvian frame of mind, as though we were Titans. If anyone feels that way—and I do not doubt that some who represent Neo-Rousseauism do thus honestly feel—then I have neither the vocation nor the capacity to influence him. Perhaps history is preparing something actually new in and through these spirits. I am willing to believe it and, therefore I will not malign them. But personally I cannot go along with them.

Finally, as to the structure which I have learned from Paul, Luther, and Ritschl—and I think they learned it from someone Greater—faith in Christ, trust in God, peace in God, humility, patience and industry in one's calling and status, I pledge myself with all the strength which God has given me, and dare not let it be plucked to pieces, or regarded as belonging to a religion of secondary rank. In contrast to this, all high revelations, spirits, and ecstasies are to me as nothing; they are merely individual protuberances.[19]

Against all attempts to interpret Christianity psychologically, or mystically, to interpret it according to its variations rather than its central principles, Harnack entered the strongest objection. *He never altered his position*, whether the opponent was the eschatological school, the *Religionsgeschichtliche* school (with whom he felt some affinity), the dialectical theology, the newer forms of mysticism, "neo-Buddhism," or the reviving pietistic influence within the Church.[20]

[19] *Ibid.*, pp. 295–296.

[20] See H. Weinel, "Religious Life and Thought in Germany Today," *Hibbert Journal*, VII (July 1909) especially pp. 732–728, for a fascinating analysis of the role of Schopenhauer, Wagner, and von Hartmann in this "movement."

Indeed, so committed was Harnack to his particular way of "understanding Christianity historically," that he courted the disfavor of his liberal colleagues in his rectoral address at the University of Berlin. The address bore the title "The Problem of the Theological Faculties and the General History of Religion," and in the address Harnack opposed that movement which "drew upon the popular traditions of the non-Christian religions for the interpretation of Christianity, . . . hoping to find in the mythology of the heathen religions a primitive religious property, from which Christianity would be seen as one derivative alongside others."[21] Harnack's position was stated sharply: "Christianity is not *one* but *the* religion."[22]

Yet Harnack could not, on principle, oppose "new" directions:

It is out of my line to be *laudator temporis acti*, and I believe I have a feeling for the progressive and the productive; but I look very cautiously into the future. I do not want nor do I have the ability to drive violently into it. Therefore I will remain absorbed in my work, and leave to the broader stream the course of its own development. . . . Perhaps something of importance may yet come out of the venture. Sometimes it all seems inhuman.[23]

He repeats to Rade—no, he protests—that his desire is to *serve* the Church:

I will at no point quench the spirit, nor will I let scholarship be cheapened; I want to serve the Church, our much afflicted Reformation Church. I want to do it because I feel the obligation to do so, and I cannot renounce that obligation so long as I stand in a semi-ecclesiastical position; further, I recognize no incompatibility between the two tasks. It would be much easier for me to let the Church go its way, and who could blame me for doing it? The churches would rejoice; for they have never had anything for which to thank me. But my historical conscience and consideration for my students, which have been laid on my soul, forbid me to do that.[24]

[21] AZH, p. 297.

[22] Harnack, "Die Aufgabe der theologischen Fakultäten und die allgemeine Religionsgeschichte," *RA*, II, p. 172.

[23] In a letter to Rade, AZH, p. 298.

[24] *Ibid.*, p. 299. As Harnack said of Luther, it could be said of him, "Never did he think to fight against the Church, but always *for the Church* against a false and soul-dangerous practice; never did he dream that the Gospel had been really lost—no, but it was to be freed from a captivity into which . . . the theologians had led it." Quoted from Lyman Abbott *et al.*, *The Prophets of the Christian Faith* (New York: The Macmillan Company, 1896), p. 115. Harnack's essay in this volume is entitled "Martin Luther, the Prophet of the Reformation."

Yet this is the question: how can he most effectively serve the Church? Harnack is very certain that the Church as he meets it in his own *Sitz im Leben*, even among the liberals, is not a viable place for him to work. It "is completely encumbered with the mortgage of town hall free thought. Individually some of the men are excellent; as a group they are under the influence of the Communists. Perhaps I should make the attempt to change all this, but I have no inclination and no time for it."[25]

And so, his daughter records:

> He felt himself called to the task of administration; the heritage from his grandfather Ewers, re-organizer of the University of Dorpat and of the spiritual life of Livonia, was in his blood, and it drove him in this direction. He would not be untrue to himself, and he would not withdraw from the path marked out for him; rather, he followed the same law by which he had always walked when, at the height of his manhood, he undertook new tasks often far removed from theological science.[26]

One might choose from a number of minor or major alternatives as illustrative of Harnack's *practical* attempt to mediate between the Church and the culture. But just because it represents most dramatically the divergence from theological historical work, we will use Harnack's work with the Kaiser-Wilhelm Foundation as example.

As early as 1898 Harnack had presented a suggestion to the Ministry of Public Worship and Education regarding the naming of associates and assistants in the Royal Academy, the purpose being to support fundamental research that could not be carried out by those with professional duties. A year later he had expanded this suggestion to include the natural sciences. In the succeeding decade, many conversations with Althoff and succeeding ministers confirmed the judgment that the state should sponsor such fundamental research. Therefore, when the Kaiser, in 1909, sent to the ministerial director, Schmidt-Ott, a query "as to what could be done by him in the interest of science on the occasion of the jubilee of the University," Schmidt-Ott asked Harnack to prepare a memorandum "regarding the founding of institutes of research."[27] The memorandum was prepared, containing a strong rationale for the founding of such institutes, but also setting forth what was to become the organizational structure of the Kaiser-Wilhelm Foundation. Harnack had the help of a number

[25] AZH, pp. 300–301.
[26] *Ibid.*, p. 302.
[27] *Ibid.*, p. 425.

of scholars, of course; but Schmidt-Ott later affirmed that "it bore the stamp of Harnack's genius"[28] in its structure.

In 1911, the Kaiser announced, at a convocation of world leaders in education, the founding of the Kaiser-Wilhelm Gesellschaft zur Förderung der Wissenschaften. Deissmann, who was present on that occasion, remarked that "The Kaiser spoke, but another had thought out and shaped the work."[29]

Harnack served as the first president of the Foundation, and presided, for the succeeding years, over the establishment of a whole series of institutes. (In the first year alone, institutes of Chemistry, Coal Research [Krupp von Bohlen was vice-president!!!], Experimental Therapy, and Industrial Psychology were opened, and in addition, support was extended in the areas of biological research, air traffic, and Islamic archaeology.) Well might Harnack's friends ask, as they did ask, what justification there could be for one whose vocation was theology that he take on this "third" call. And that is, of course, the crucial question.

Harnack was not unaware of the question, and his answer to it is instructive. In 1929, at the dedication of the Harnack-Haus of the Foundation, he interpreted his eighteen-year presidency in this way:

> It has been a deep concern of mine that wherever I see clefts, I should encourage the romance that will bring about a marriage. I have certainly made this my life's task. But I am not merely concerned that things should be joined together. They do not join themselves if men do not act, and I have had the splendid experience of seeing, in many areas, that not only industry but the industrialists, not only agriculture but the agriculturists, not only banks but the bankers, not only mining companies but the workers, not only cities but the burgomasters, have come into a hearty and occasionally inner relationship. . . . I have never observed such a mutuality developing where I have not also gained something for the life of the soul.[30]

That he sought to relate this work to his fundamental vocation is attested further in a letter to Rade written in 1929:

> The Kaiser-Wilhelm Foundation has laid on me great sacrifices, and does still. Yet I have not made a capricious choice, but have taken on me a destiny, and have then acted according to the principle: "Exactly or not

[28] *Ibid.*
[29] *Ibid.*, p. 427.
[30] *Ibid.*, p. 431.

at all." It has not been entirely without fruit for the evangelical Church and Christianity, even if my professional colleagues do not discover it. For myself, I am still theologian as before, and my spare hours belong as from youth to our theological science.[31]

"I have not made a capricious choice, but have taken on me a destiny"—is this indeed the case? The writer of those lines was seventy-eight years old. The destiny had been "taken on" at least a quarter of a century earlier. Why?

"The culture," so he believed, demanded it. New and unforeseen powers had brought their armies to the field, and these must be met, yes, even by a Christian theologian. Above all, these powers were represented in the variant forms of materialism which had grown apace in the last years of the nineteenth century. "Materialism": that representation of human life which rests on nontheistic assumptions. This view had been espoused in varying ways by Feuerbach, Schopenhauer, Vogt, Moleschott, Darwin (and his German interpreter, Haeckel), Marx and his interpreters, and a veritable host of lesser personages. From the beginning of Harnack's scholarly activity he had been aware of their influence in the cultural background, and of their challenge to any "religious" interpretation of human existence; thus they must be answered from the Christian point of view. Harnack explicitly admitted, in his essay on "The Double Gospel in the New Testament,"[32] that the formulation of the position he there sets forth has been determined by the contemporary situation: materialism has denied any validity to Christianity. Two points need to be noted here. First, Harnack claims that this denial rests on a *false* historical view with respect to what Christianity *really* is.[33] He then proceeds to specify what it *really* is—in overtly Kantian terms. Secondly, this is, for better or worse, a utilitarian argument. Christianity *must* be defended against materialism; to do this, one must demonstrate on a scientific historical basis, against these thinkers (but also *for* these thinkers?), what the Gospel really is. Harnack claims to do this on the basis of historical truth. But what he is actually using as the basis of his argument is the contemporary *value* of the Gospel. The "second" Gospel cannot suffice to meet the contemporary challenge; the "first" Gospel, interpreted in terms

[31] *Ibid.*, p. 432, note 2.

[32] Harnack, "Das doppelte Evangelium im Neuen Testament," *RA*, II, NF: *Aus Wissenschaft und Leben*, Band II (Giessen: Töpelmann, 1911), pp. 211–224.

[33] *Ibid.*, pp. 222–223.

of Kantian ethics, can. Therefore, the Gospel must be interpreted under this latter form.

It is to be noted further that the mode of development of his argument buttresses this conclusion. Scientific investigation is implicitly lauded as the only way to truth in the affirmation that any statement that does not begin, proceed, and end with Jesus' historical existence must be abjured.[34] Revelation is here cut to the necessary measure; it "can only take place in the uniqueness of personal life, and only the result that issues in history can tell us whether God has so acted through individuals."[35] These are "results" that can be studied "scientifically." Finally, then, even in his valiant and necessary attempt to save the uniqueness of Jesus, the apologetic situation with respect to the culture is apparent, perhaps to the detriment of the question of truth: Jesus is unique because history has found in him a way to a "personal higher life" which "overcomes the world."

We believe it is clear that Harnack is trying to "confess and defend" Christianity, but that he is caught in the necessities of a situation which subordinated even his fundamental question of truth to the question of contemporary efficacy and value in such a way that a certain content must be given in the answer.

It is obvious in this connection that what Harnack cannot say argues as decisively as that which he says. For though he had declared in numerous writings that there are two fundamental foci which are the objects of man's concern, "God and the soul,"[36] in actual practice these are not the true foci. Rather than God, the *world* is the "given" that confronts the liberal, and the relation of the soul to this world becomes his overarching problem. For of these two things one can speak in an age when autonomous reason reigns with some assurance that one will be heard. To speak of God is immediately to insert the concept of mystery into religion, at least from Harnack's point of view. The only option then is to speak of revelation in such a way that it can be drawn within the orbit of man's experience, and therefore can be known by him. It is Jesus, in the full range of his humanity, as one who provides the power to overcome the world, to whom Harnack looks for the answer. And if the Church should agree, but claim that there is a mystery in the relation of Jesus as Christ and God as Father, Harnack could only say, with

[34] *Ibid.*, p. 223.
[35] *Ibid.*
[36] AZH, p. 516.

Ritschl, "Where I find mystery, I say nothing about it."[37] Harnack then proceeds to examine Jesus' teaching in the light of the necessities of the situation, and what stands forth as the "first Gospel" is Kantian ethics with a nimbus.

Harnack's situation, then, with respect to the contemporary cultural challenge, was essentially ambivalent. He had to speak to culture, but he had to defend Christianity. The solution of this problem has been perennially vexing to Christian thinkers, and Harnack was no exception. But the fact that it was *this* problem that motivated much of his work is what we wish to emphasize here. He did not solve the problem, if indeed it is capable of "a" solution. But to understand him, one must be aware of the threat which he felt from the materialistic interpretation of life. This much is certain: Harnack did not evade, and he did not escape, involvement in the intellectual warfare that raged during his lifetime. Nowhere is this fidelity to "becoming involved" more patent than in his challenging of the materialistic interpretations of human existence which have dominated intellectual circles since 1850. But it may be argued that his own solution to the problem of Christianity and culture has proved to be as questionably valid as those against which he contended.[38]

[37] Quoted in Mackintosh, *op. cit.*, p. 160.

[38] Cf. the critique of liberalism by H. Richard Niebuhr, *Christ and Culture* (New York: Harper & Row, 1951), pp. 15–19.

VII

The Setting and the Norm

HOWEVER NECESSARY it may be, it is a dangerous practice to try to place the man of genius in a particular temporal and cultural setting. No one knew this better than Harnack himself. In his theory of history, he writes of the necessity to evaluate elementary, cultural, and individual factors. The elementary factors are, mainly, the natural givens within which a man lives his life. The cultural factors include the institutions which carry tradition, and the customs, the art, and the science of an epoch. The individual factor has to do with the talent, the genius, the personality of men—that is, with their "individuality."

The danger is at least twofold. One part is sheerly methodological. For when one tries to do justice to the range of influences bearing in upon a nineteenth-century German church historian, the *volume* of material with which one is confronted is staggering. Barth recognizes this, as we shall see, and deals with it as well as anyone might. But just so: "as well as anyone might." For the other danger is that ideology will inevitably rear its head, that for the sake of not omitting, one will oversimplify, that the besetting sin of theologians, propositional categorization, will in truth beset.

There is no help for it. To say nothing is inexcusable. To say a little is dangerous. And to say too much is diversionary. The effort must still be made.

Who is the guide in the attempt? Will it be Pauck, who, in response to a paper on "Nineteenth Century Theological and Cultural Influences on Adolf Harnack,"[1] commented that *Paul* and *Luther* were the two dominant influences on Harnack? Will it be Emanuel Hirsch, who in his monumental work, completed in 1954, *deliberately* wrote a *Geschichte der neuern evangelischen Theologie in Zusammenhang mit den allgemeinen Bewegungen des europäischen Denkens*?[2] Will it be Barth, who in his *Die protestantische Theologie im neunzehnten Jahrhundert*[3] has no chapter on Harnack, and a very scant, if provocative, chapter on Ritschl? Or should it be, among other possibilities, Seeberg,[4] Stephan,[5] Elert,[6] Hermelink,[7] Drummond,[8] Troeltsch,[9] Kattenbusch,[10] Mackintosh,[11] McGiffert,[12] Kissling,[13] Perriraz,[14] Moore,[15] Walter,[16] or Zahn?[17] Not to speak of the *sources* themselves!

The point of this not so forceful *tour de force* is one that any historian of nineteenth-century German theology neglects at his peril.

1 Given at the 83rd meeting of the American Society of Church History, New York, Dec. 27, 1957.

2 *Op. cit.*

3 *Op. cit.*

4 *Die Kirche Deutschlands im neunzehnten Jahrhundert.*

5 Horst Stephan, *Geschichte der evangelischen Theologie seit dem Deutschen Idealismus* (Berlin: Töpelmann, 1938).

6 Werner Elert, *Der Kampf um das Christentum* (München: Beck, 1921).

7 Heinrich Hermelink, *Das Christentum in der Menschheitsgeschichte von der französischen Revolution bis zur Gegenwart* (Stuttgart: Metzler, and Tübingen: Wunderlich, 1951–52), 3 Bänden.

8 A. L. Drummond, *German Protestantism Since Luther* (London: Epworth Press, 1951).

9 *Gesammelte Schriften*, especially Band III, *Der Historismus und seine Probleme.*

10 *Op. cit.*

11 *Op. cit.*

12 A. C. McGiffert, *The Rise of Modern Religious Ideas* (New York: Macmillan, 1915), and *Protestant Thought Before Kant* (New York: C. Scribner's Sons, 1915).

13 J. B. Kissling, *Der deutsche Protestantismus, 1817–1917* (Münster in Westf.: Aschendorff, 1917–1918), 2 Bänden.

14 L. Perriraz, *Histoire de la théologie protestante au XIXme siècle surtout en Allemagne* (Neuchâtel: H. Messeiller, 1949–56), 3 vol.

15 Edward Caldwell Moore, *An Outline of the History of Christian Thought Since Kant* (New York: Charles Scribner's Sons, 1912).

16 Johannes Walter, *Die Geschichte des Christentums* (Gütersloh: C. Bertelsmann Verlag, 1938).

17 Adolf Zahn, *Sketch of a History of the Evangelical Church on the European Continent in the Nineteenth Century* (Stuttgart: J. B. Metzler, 1888).

It is not possible to read the totality of "the heritage,"[18] and dangerous to entertain the delusion that, having read what one can, he can understand and delineate this complex tapestry "wie es eigentlich gewesen ist."

Yet, in spite of this *apologia*, the effort must be made. The goal in mind for this total work is, to be sure, a *monograph*. The method must be the close study of the sources—*Harnack's* own writings. We have sought in the preceding pages to identify those contemporary influences which, on Harnack's own testimony, were the most determinative in shaping his positions. Before moving on to an examination of his work—his theory and practice of history on the one hand, and his theological positions on the other, we will present a summary of the eighteenth-century intellectual forces which set the problems, in many ways, for the nineteenth century; and we will seek to identify, all dangers incident thereto notwithstanding, the "theological norm" which we have denoted Harnack's "axiology," or *Lebensideal*. Hopefully, having seen in the preceding pages the living human being, this summarization, since it is Harnack's background, may itself take on some semblance of life.

A final defensive note is in order. To the possible charge "Have you not claimed all things for Harnack, finding Kantian, Hegelian, and romantic influences, in addition to more specific ones?" there should be a double rejoinder. First, there is a *most* significant influence, and it is Ritschl, and we have said so. But Ritschl was no *sui generis*, historically fatherless creature either—Kant and Baur *were* there, shaping problems and setting the limits for alternatives. Second, *mea culpa*! But the question is not whether the claim has been made, but whether it can be, itself, historically demonstrated from the sources. The question is not even whether *Harnack* judged that thus and so were the determinative influences, but whether a broader historical perspective judges them, again on the basis of

[18] But consider here the judgment of a major thinker in American Protestantism: "I believe that it is still possible to attain a responsible scholarly grasp of those sources in a lifetime. . . ." Pelikan goes on to make his own apologetic point: "I believe, moreover, that such scholarship, if carried out with modesty and boldness, also has something to say as an apologetic, demonstrating to the cultured among the despisers of religion that scholars who could have devoted their talents to Isocrates or Sebastian Brandt have chosen instead to study the development of the Christian tradition." J. Pelikan, "Tradition, Reformation and Development," *The Christian Century*, Jan. 6, 1965, pp. 8–10. The point made in the text above is clear, however; and Pelikan is aware of it in recommending "modesty and boldness."

evidence, to have been so. For example, Troeltsch found Hegelian influences in Harnack where Harnack did not. And, as we shall see, the romanticism of Herder and Schleiermacher, mediated by way of the historical-critical movement and by way of certain of the Erlangeners, was far more influential than Harnack would have judged.

Kant and romanticism, Theodosius Harnack, Moritz von Engelhardt, Dorpat-Erlangen confessional Lutheranism, Baur and Ritschl —these, therefore, are the most "immediate" influences. And the greatest of these is, without doubt, Ritschl.

But not unequivocally. And in those three words, the secret of "the reality of Harnack" must be sought. For though it would be a mistake to take away from Harnack the adjective "Ritschlian," it is an oversimplification, almost universally the fashion among historians who have discussed Harnack, to limit him to that adjective. We need to look more deeply into the century that preceded Harnack.

Karl Barth has characterized the eighteenth-century man as "the man who no longer has an emperor."[19] Historians and theologians have affirmed and documented the bifurcation which, though it originated earlier, finds a renewed vitality in the Reformers: on the one hand, the "Protestant principle" which successively challenged, in the name of God, all those heteronomous structures which became idolatrous by claiming God's *imprimatur* for particular formulations; on the other hand, an increasing anthropocentrism and preoccupation with man's possibilities in shaping his culture.[20] In this "absolutist" genus of the eighteenth century, the theological species appeared also. In the discussion of Church-state relations, issuing in the territorial and collegial theories; in the "ennoblement" of Christianity into a natural and a reasonable religion; in pietistic subjectivism, challenging "dead" orthodoxy not only with its moralism, but, much more significantly, with the internalization of all authority, one discerns a single intoxicating spirit: "Er handelt gut."[21]

Barth's characterization of the eighteenth-century man can be fruitfully employed for understanding certain features of the nineteenth-century milieu within which Harnack developed. Indeed, there are those who are willing to say of Harnack that he represents in

[19] *Op. cit.*, p. 24.

[20] Cf. here the suggestive essay by H. Richard Niebuhr, "Religious Realism and the Twentieth Century," *Religious Realism*, D. C. Macintosh, ed. (New York: The Macmillan Company, 1931), pp. 413–428.

[21] Barth, *op. cit.*, p. 55.

paradigm that autonomous reason which has come to characterize more and more the "modern man."[22] If the designation of the eighteenth century as the "Age of Enlightenment"[23] is to communicate any meaning, one must ask what constituted the nature of this "enlightenment." Barth's answer to this question, clearly, would be *man's* reason, *man's* discoveries, *man's* faith, *man's* educability, *man's* confidence, *man's* power. For the eighteenth-century "enlightened" man, the anthropic referent dominates every activity, to whatever object it may have been directed. To be sure, a great deal of energy was expended in discussing God, but the presupposition of most of this declamation was that of Leibnitz' "pre-established harmony."[24]

Barth has described this eighteenth-century man as follows: he is "aware" of himself; he has a basic confidence in the goodness of the world; he walks and talks with his "buddy," God; he, like God, is spiritual, powerful, wise, and good; he can solve on his own initiative the problem of theodicy; and he has the sublime confidence that God speaks to his *Vernunft* through nature.[25] Barth argues that the eighteenth century was a re-eruption of Renaissance humanism following its submersion by the Reformation. One might similarly argue that Harnack's variety of theological liberalism was a part of this re-eruption, with this difference: the nineteenth century's "certain knowledge of history" had been substituted for the eighteenth century's "natural truths of reason," and "inevitable" progress had to be given up because this history demonstrated with what struggle and effort progress is made. It is instructive that Harnack would state that Leibnitz, who "represented the eighteenth century in microcosm,"[26] was the only philosopher to whom he would gladly listen.[27]

If one were to attempt a diagram of the theological and philosophical development of the eighteenth and early nineteenth century, the most striking pattern that would emerge would be the relative purity which the orthodox-confessional defenders maintained. Embattled though this position was, it did on occasion assimilate to itself the insights of its more liberal brethren, at the same time that it provided a steady tradition with which liberalism must perforce contend. Particularly, the orthodox never forgot, and frequently reminded the

[22] This was the formulation used by Paul Tillich in a personal conversation.

[23] Cf. Isaiah Berlin, *The Age of Enlightenment* (New York: The New American Library of World Literature, 1956), for a critique of this term.

[24] Hirsch, *op. cit.*, II, p. 33.

[25] *Op. cit.*, pp. 54–55.

[26] *Ibid.*, p. 57.

[27] AZH, p. 546.

liberals, that it was churchly theology which should provide the point of departure. This was an integral part of Dorpat-Erlangen's view, and was burned deep into Harnack's consciousness. Basing its position on the Reformation assertion of theonomy as against the heteronomy of the medieval synthesis, orthodoxy was accused of unduly exalting the Bible and the confessions. It was against this hard orthodoxy that Pietism had affirmed, in the name of Luther, the primacy of the "faith of the heart," thereby playing into the hands of the emerging "autonomous man" of the eighteenth century. But within orthodoxy there remained the power to synthesize the validities of the Pietist position at the same time that the dangers were challenged. The received orthodoxy of the early nineteenth century was, then, at worst colored; it was not corrupted.

When one turns to the philosophical-theological-historical development stemming from Leibnitz, the pattern is no longer simple and linear. Leibnitz took truth as his province, truth seen as the reconciliation of all the concerns of life and thought, including the harmonization of faith and reason, and thus he became "the decisive turning-point in the history of German evangelical theology."[28] Can Christian faith and *Lebensgefühl* be harmonized? Can all contradictions touching faith and reason be resolved by reason? Leibnitz answered affirmatively, and by his introduction of the concept of a "pre-established harmony" laid the foundation for the theories of *Entwickelung* and *Humanitätsideal* which were to obsess the minds of the succeeding generations.

As briefly as possible, the process may be thus described: Wolff systematized Leibnitz, making it evident that philosophy's apprenticeship to theology had been completed, and that now theology must come to terms with its erstwhile servant; Wolff's challenge was taken up by the neologists, especially by Semler, as all provinces of knowledge became matters of concern. Increasingly, from Semler's time, the necessity for a thorough investigation by biblical scholars of all linguistic, cultural, and historical questions is apparent; and though fought at every step, and seen in paradigm in the *Fragmentenstreit* over the Wolffenbüttel discoveries, a complete historical-critical attempt was in the offing.

Lessing, in many ways a stranger to his time, was significant for theological development as he attempted, by insisting on the primacy of reason, to replace positive Christian affirmations with his *Humanitätsideal*. Herder also was preoccupied with this grand concept

[28] Hirsch, *op. cit.*, II, p. 17.

and, as a leader in the emerging romanticism, opened many questions for future consideration. The future, in fact, belonged to those movements which stemmed out of romanticism, on the one hand, and out of the profound Leibnitzian-Pietistic revolution effected by Kant, on the other.

Romanticism, that turbulent and complicated stream of the *Zeitgeist*, included Herder, Schleiermacher, Hegel, and Harnack's favorite poet, Goethe, in its amorphous ranks. The romantic, above all impressed by the richness and variety of the experiences which the individual discovers in the world, is obsessed, at the same time, with the necessity to bring into a unified synthesis all that is knowable in the realms of nature, history, and art. Completeness is his passion, and therefore he announces himself an enemy of such restrictive systems as that of the Enlightenment. Above all else, history becomes the means by which man's fullest appreciation of himself and his world is to be actualized. But this is no narrow concept of history; history as the romantic conceived it meant *Geist*. And this "spirit that prevails in history"[29] must be revered as one studies the personalities and the development which history manifests. It was further characteristic of romanticism that it tended to separate religion and metaphysics.[30] Such a separation tends to obscure the close relation of faith and truth,[31] and it has been convincingly argued that there are evidences of such a fissiparity in Harnack.[32]

It is particularly in his *Humanitätslehre*, with which his axiological norm is so intimately involved, that Harnack shows the marked influence of romanticism. This doctrine of humanity shows many striking parallels to the doctrine held by the early leader of the group, Herder. Herder's "humanity" was a complex fusion of many elements, including feeling, individuality, and religion, which is the highest humanity. History, when it is properly seen in all its concrete reality, reveals to us the developing city of God on earth. This passionate concern for the concrete reality of history made possible a new approach to the problems of theology.[33] For Herder, God is to be found in the common experience of history, and revelation is nothing else

[29] Harnack, *Christianity and History*, p. 25.

[30] Hirsch, *op. cit.*, IV, p. 446.

[31] *Ibid.*

[32] Troeltsch, *Der Historismus . . .*, p. 529.

[33] "Herder's significance for subsequent theology is seldom estimated highly enough. Without Herder no Schleiermacher and no de Wette. Without Herder the specific pathos of the theological history of the nineteenth century would be impossible. Without Herder no Erlangen School and no *Religionsgeschichtliche* School. Without Herder no Troeltsch also." Barth, *op. cit.*, p. 282.

than the meeting of spirit with spirit in living men. It is through great men that God speaks in his self-mediation, and through such great men culture is shaped and transmitted. Evil in such a view can mean nothing more than incompleteness, and Christ is the enlightener who speaks to our humanity through his own, meeting this incompleteness. Any Christology which goes beyond this must be renounced. The Bible therefore is to be read in order that the spirit of the living man who stands at its center—Jesus—may speak to our spirit. It is through his pure human understanding of God as Father and men as brothers that he is validated to our understanding as preeminent—and in no other way. Herder was particularly incensed at those productions which questioned the concrete historical particularity of Jesus.

Harnack would have been able to assert every one of these propositions! History had refined its method in the succeeding century, to be sure, and here or there a minor change in emphasis might therefore have been necessitated. But at that point which is crucial for understanding Harnack, the axiological norm embodied in the *Humanitätslehre*, the influence of Herder is decisive.

Then, there is Goethe, by all odds the most quoted author in the writings of Harnack. Nor can one explain this simply by recalling the German preference for Goethe. Actually, as is clear from his laudatory essay on Goethe's religion "at the time of his maturity,"[34] Harnack shares many of Goethe's views. There is the same aspiration after perfection in science, the same reverence for all that is above, beside, and beneath us, and the same awareness that perfection forever eludes man's grasp. There is the same emphasis on the richness and variety of life experience as containing within itself revelatory significance, though Harnack is certainly more concerned than Goethe to relate this to the Gospel as he conceives it. An important question with respect to the Goethean influence lies at the point of the interpretation of love. For Goethe, the Eros quality was so emphasized that there could be no real appreciation for or understanding of the Christian doctrine of reconciliation. For Harnack, vague though he may be at certain points, it cannot be doubted that there was too much influence from Lutheran orthodoxy operating upon him, plus Kantian ethics by way of Ritschl, to allow him to capitulate completely to Goethean Eros. The danger, however, is never absent, and it is an open question whether in the final analysis Harnack's "essence" is not as much determined by this Goethean concept as by Johannine Agape.[35]

[34] "Die Religion Goethes . . ." *RA*, IV, NF, pp. 141–170.
[35] Cf. *infra*, Chap. XII, B, on the meaning of Christ's redemption.

Harnack would *not*, of course, agree with the estimate of the influence of romanticism on his own thought which we here claim. In the middle of the controversy centering around the dismissal of Traub, *his* estimate of the influence of romanticism is incidentally set forth:

From many years of study of the history of dogma and the confessions, I have reached the conclusion that complete sincerity has never prevailed in the Church from about the fourth or fifth century. . . . Always, much more extended expressions of faith were promulgated than could be defended. Always men expressed themselves in their dogmatic formulas more eccentrically than they actually believed and were determined to carry out in life. And always, in defence of liturgical formulas, they went further than they should.[36]

Continuing, he affirmed that the Reformation had

. . . produced a strong impulse toward improvement, but this was lost again in the ensuing dogmatic struggles. The Enlightenment revived the impulse toward veracity, but it was sloughed off by romanticism, in its will vital and powerful, but "showing a complete deficit so far as actuality and the feeling for truth" were concerned. The Church as it has come down to us today has fortified itself with romanticism. It takes its stand without regard to the fact that modern natural science, the theory of knowledge resting upon Kant, and the recently founded science of history "have produced among us a new, inexorable, joyous, and trustworthy sense of actuality and truth in all questions of knowledge. The church must reckon with this new condition. *It must come to the place that it can say openly, These definite assertions and teachings in the confessions are not correct, and no one is compelled in the worship of God to confess things he does not need to confess.*"[37]

That is Harnack's testimony. *E pur si muove!*

The bedeviled eighteenth-century theologian might well have taken Jesus' didactic demoniac[38] as his patron saint; there was Leibnitz, then Wolff, Lessing, Goethe and the *Sturm* and *Drang*, full-flowered rationalism, and many varieties of each type. Higher criticism was emerging, and Semler and Herder were laying the groundwork for the historical effort which was to come into its own in the following century. Well might theology look to the awakened giant of Königsberg as the deliverer from confusion, failing to see that if he had shattered the epistemological premises of rationalism, no less had he

[36] AZH, p. 404.
[37] *Ibid.*, pp. 404–405. The italics are Harnack's.
[38] Matt. 12:43–45.

challenged the competence of the reason of orthodox theologians. The options that remained open for theology in the succeeding century after the epistemological reduction effected by Kant were three: it could be argued that Kant was correct in challenging the adequacy of pure reason, and in substituting the moral maxims of a practical reason; it could be argued that though he had effected a partial liberation, his formal ethic did not take account of the element of feeling which is plainly a part of being human; and it could be argued that there was "a perfect identity of being and thought, real and ideal, in one great dialectical evolution."[39]

The first of the options suggested was taken up by Ritschl, and his formulation was most determinative for Harnack.[40] The third option was followed by Schelling and Hegel, and found theological expression in Baur and the Tübingen school. The second option was chosen by Schleiermacher, whose influence has permeated all subsequent theological development.[41] Schleiermacher brought together strands of idealism and of romanticism, with a Kantian solvent; but he stood, squarely and self-consciously, within the Church as a servant of the Church. What he attempted to do was to work out a normative Christian dogmatics; in this attempt, the supreme stage of religious development, monotheism, was resolved into ethical theism. This alone, Schleiermacher held, could stand as the final perfection of the religious idea, and such a theism actually exists historically in Christianity. Therefore dogmatics sets forth the essential ideas of Christianity concerning God, the world, and man, as they radiate from the central redemptive personality of Jesus. Further, such a dogmatic, for practical purposes, must relate itself with sympathy, but with freedom, to the ideas of the Protestant ecclesiastical tradition. "The central redemptive personality of Jesus," related to "the ideas of the Protestant ecclesiastical tradition"[42]—these were the concerns that occupied nineteenth-century theologians, and Harnack is no exception. He, also, was the heir of Schleiermacher.

Doubtless one may discern traces of the avoidance of metaphysical thought with respect to religion prior to Kant; but Kant's profound treatment of the epistemological problem was carried out in such a

[39] Friedrich Schelling, *The Ages of the World*, tr. Frederick deWolfe Bolman, Jr. (New York: Columbia University Press, 1942), p. 4.

[40] See Chap. V.

[41] These categories are, of course, too neat, for there was a great deal of overlapping. However, their usage can be justified as types to represent the direction of development.

[42] Troeltsch, "The Dogmatics . . . , p. 7.

way that all nineteenth-century thinkers had to come to terms with him. By his denial that the "thing-in-itself" can be known, and his limiting of knowledge to the realm of practical reason, he seemed to threaten some of the dearest tenets of orthodoxy.[43] Harnack as historian would have held different positions from those of Kant, particularly with respect to the estimate of the worth of historical study, but at the point of metaphysical skepticism he agreed completely. Kant had also sought to save faith by identifying it with the practical reason, investing the postulates thereof with the full deist meaning. His contribution to Harnack lies in this positive identification of religion as the highest ethical striving. Harnack's identification of the "first" Gospel, "as Jesus taught it"[44] is, in effect, nothing else than the three postulates of the practical reason. "The ethical, life with God"[45] is declared to be of almost equal power as the laws of nature. The new which came into history in Jesus Christ is the ethical ideal of the Kingdom of God, a kingdom of ethical ends which lays its demands upon us.[46] It is "the ordinary canons of morality" which Jesus invoked, and from which "he expected everything."[47] Kant's ethics is determinative, therefore, of the content which Harnack places in the highest form of religion, and, as we shall see, Troeltsch was correct in judging that for Harnack Christianity was essentially "the preaching of Jesus concerning the Kingdom of God interpreted in terms of Kantian ethics."[48]

In the letter to Stintzing,[49] Harnack made plain his awareness and understanding of the live options for the Christian theologian in the late nineteenth century. To recapitulate, he saw himself as required to do three things: "to understand Christianity historically and to set it in living relation to all historical event, to work beyond the dogmatic . . . to the inner form of Christian truth, and to confess and defend . . . the independently won position in all sincerity." We contend that these statements constitute a valid summary of Harnack's life-long purpose and position. We believe further that an assessment of his background and environment makes obvious the sources from which

43 Harnack, "Immanuel Kant," *RA*, V, NF, p. 176.
44 Cf. *infra*, p. 238.
45 Cf. *infra*, p. 190.
46 Cf. *infra*, p. 191.
47 Cf. *infra*, p. 271.
48 Troeltsch, "The Dogmatics . . . ," p. 12.
49 AZH, pp. 39–40.

this position was derived, and the setting with respect to which it was employed. Finally, we believe that "*historical axiology*" is the best descriptive term to which these principles can be reduced. It is desirable that these contentions be dealt with in a summary statement.

We have seen that nineteenth-century Germany, rich though it was in system, exacted a high mortality on these systems. At the beginning of the century, Kant had made possible several new approaches to theological concern, but his own interpretation of religion was meager. Romanticism, a spirit more than a movement, brooded over the century like a benign presence, occasionally striking a solitary soul with its pagan fire. Schleiermacher's effort, never completely overcome, was rendered less effectual within the Church by neoconfessional and neosupernatural revivals. Hegel's school collapsed with the dissolution of his metaphysic, and the displacement of the notion of an absolute rational religion by the recognition of the concrete historical character of Christianity. Baur at Tübingen exerted a powerful influence through the historical-critical approach, but joined it with Hegelian philosophical presuppositions; with the collapse of Hegelian idealism, Baur went into eclipse.[50] Eighteenth-century supernaturalism, torn by inner conflict, rendered ineffectual by rationalism, by-passed by the multiform historical-critical evolutionary thought, could still revive sufficiently, as at Dorpat and Erlangen, to reclaim temporarily some of its lost domain. Ritschl accepted Kant's reduction, but rejected his interpretation of religion as mere morality, seeking an independent basis for religion in moral faith.[51] Materialism was challenging any religious interpretation of human life, and seducing thousands from the churches. And pietistic-biblical supernaturalism was in control in these churches, flavored on occasion with cultural influences, but in the main avoiding scientific questions, or leaving them to ethnologists, philologists, and philosophers. This was the situation within which Adolf Harnack did his work.

The significance of this situation for an understanding of Harnack is clear when we remember four things: that Harnack was a son of Dorpat-Erlangen orthodoxy; that he had been strongly influenced by Tübingen historical criticism; that he was thoroughly conversant with all of the cultural components just set forth; and that the position he came to adopt had as its self-conscious purpose an attempted mediation. This attempt at a mediation between the old and the new theology within the Church was transmuted, in the course of Harnack's

[50] Cf. Troeltsch, *Der Historismus . . .*, p. 53.
[51] Cf. Hefner, "The Role of Church History . . . ."

development, into an attempt to mediate between the Church and culture. It attempted to utilize the historical-critical approach, and was rigorously faithful to the "scientific" canons thereof. Though Ritschl, in certain distinctive ways Harnack's "enlightener," had restricted his vocation to historical theology (in its fullest sense), Harnack moved on a larger stage. To summarize the sequence of development by which this ultimate result came about, we must go back to the crucial Leipzig period. Harnack confessed that he was glad to leave Dorpat, for the theology here was of a single variety, and any expression of doubt brought the charge of insincerity. Harnack had many doubts, as his voluminous correspondence shows, and he was unable to repress them lest he become hypocritical. *Sicherheit* and *Einheit*, key clues to his entire life, are frequent words in his early letters.

Having completed his doctoral work at Leipzig, he prepared a *Habilitationsschrift* defending this proposition: "There is no other method for the exegesis of Holy Scripture than the grammatical-historical."[52] Until 1879, when he accepted a call to Giessen, he was implementing this text. There were four main problems for which he sought answers in the Leipzig period, and these can almost be taken as paradigmatic for his entire life. First, he was concerned with the problem of historical method, which for him was answered by the word *science*. He was always concerned with the discovery of new manuscripts, with improved editions, textual purity, and chronological accuracy. Secondly, he sought to deal with the problem of understanding church history properly and representing it fairly; this could be done if church history was viewed as a part of the total spiritual history of mankind, to be assessed by historical means and methods, and if it were at the same time recognized that God's hidden but present revelation to man was contained therein. Thirdly, the problem of the representation of the rise and development of Christian dogma provided the particular special focus of interest. Finally, the problem of organizing the developing new science so as to make it yield its full potential demanded a practical solution. The latter question was in part answered by the founding, with Schürer, of the *Theologische Literaturzeitung*, which became the organ of the Ritschlian school.[53]

The three questions have been stated in a slightly different way here, but the essential direction is the same, and answers are clearly set

[52] AZH, p. 69.
[53] *Ibid.*, pp. 81–85.

forth. "To understand Christianity historically" meant for Harnack scientific method; "to set it in living relation to all historical event" would be achieved by this method, and by the organization of church history so as to make it yield its full potential; "to work beyond the dogmatic . . . to the inner form" meant to *know* the history of dogma, and to recognize that within the husks of this "spiritual history" was hidden God's revelation to man; "to confess and defend the independently won position" required that an apologetic stance be taken with respect to culture, leading to *action* within the broader cultural world.

It is clear that in this statement *history* and *value* are both emphasized. The former is so obvious as to need no underlining; the latter is to be seen in such respected phrases as "total spiritual history," "this is God's revelation to man," and "full potential." We would argue that these phrases show, respectively, the influence of (1) romanticism and Hegelianism, (2) Dorpat-Erlangen and Ritschl, and (3) romanticism and materialism. We refuse to admit that this is a strained exegesis of Harnack's phrases. Indeed, Harnack's universal concern, making necessary as it does a full evaluation of the many currents already discussed in this chapter, is precisely the controlling emphasis of the interpretation we are setting forth. We submit that it is those interpreters who fall prey to the "fallacy of simple location" who do the real violence to Harnack. Few men in the history of theology have borne within themselves the multiform heritage which Harnack enjoyed; and few have been as concerned to do justice to all facets of a heritage. Harnack's daughter has communicated this concern for completeness on her father's part in a significant comment about him during the Leipzig years. It was customary, of course, for young theologues to take some position which would be identified and then defended. But Harnack took no such position: "His critics were not certain in which camp he belonged—for that anyone could belong to *no* camp was unheard of."[54]

Harnack's "universality," characterizing the post-Leipzig period, was achieved only after he had encountered severe criticism of his early work. When his Leipzig publications began to appear, and the reviews of the many theological faculties of nineteenth-century Germany followed, one in particular disturbed Harnack. This was the critique of his work by Overbeck, to which we have already referred.[55] Overbeck had charged the "believing theologians," with "risking

[54] *Ibid.*, p. 87.
[55] *Ibid.*, p. 90.

nothing," and Harnack had admitted that Overbeck was right.[56] He had been a son of Dorpat-Erlangen; he had been influenced by Tübingen; and he had believed that the orthodox theology could be reconciled with the newer historical criticism. On the basis of Overbeck's criticism, he squarely faced this question, and passionately declared to Engelhardt that he could find no way between the "mummified dogmatic" of the "believing theologians" and the *Tendenzkritik* of Baur and his school.[57] Admitting the attraction of the latter, which had had a glorious dawn but no following sunrise, dissatisfied with the heritage which would not come to terms with the burning questions posed by Baur, he resolved the conflict, sometime during the Leipzig years, in favor of neither. It was Ritschl who opened a way of mediation; in Ritschl, Harnack declared, "lies the future direction of Protestantism."[58]

How does one summarize Ritschl's contribution to Harnack, and are there significant points of deviation? It was Ritschl who raised real questions in Harnack's mind as to the legitimacy of the Tübingen interpretation. Harnack followed Ritschl in renouncing metaphysical speculation; Ritschl, as we have seen, "emancipated" Harnack from his uneasy tension between Dorpat-Erlangen and Tübingen; Ritschl communicated his passionate concern for the historical to Harnack; Ritschl stood as an ardent defender of Protestantism; Ritschl tried to defend Christianity against the growing threat of materialism; Ritschl centered on the problem of value, and interpreted Christianity in terms of moral faith—his *Lebensführung*. In his essay on "The Present Position of Protestantism," Harnack uses terms nearly identical to those of Ritschl in defining "religion": "Religion is only a steadfast temper of the soul, rooted in childlike trust in God."[59] This trust "is inescapably bound up with the plain, simple rule that the moral life, in all its solemnity and earnestness, is the correlative of Religion, and that without it Religion becomes idolatry."[60] Harnack then ascribes the achievement and reaffirmation of this Reformation understanding of Christianity to Ritschl. This is, indeed, according to Harnack, modern Protestantism's debt to Ritschl, that "he grasped the fundamental ideas of the Gospel and of the Reformation with insight and

[56] *Ibid.*

[57] *Ibid.*, p. 91.

[58] *Ibid.*

[59] *Thoughts on the Present Position of Protestantism*, tr. Thomas Bailey Saunders (London: A. and C. Black, 1899), p. 54.

[60] *Ibid.*, pp. 54–55.

vigour,"[61] and separated them from those extraneous entanglements and fetters with which they had been bound up. Thus far, Harnack was indebted to Ritschl, and so deeply were these influences inculcated that it cannot be doubted that Ritschl is the *main* contributor to him.

However, in the last phase of Harnack's life—from *Das Wesen des Christentums* on—there are signs of deviation. Though there is the continued emphasis on historical-critical endeavor, as signified by the publication of Harnack's great work on Marcion in 1921, and though the full-blown axiological norm to which Ritschl had contributed significantly is still apparent, Hegelian strains are more pronounced. The final "stages" of scientific knowledge—those stressing the individual and spiritual aspects—are colored with Hegelianism, as seen in the essay "Uber die Sicherheit und die Grenzen geschichtlicher Erkenntnis."[62] Yet the truth is still in the mean here, for in the development, in this essay, of the "stages" of knowledge, it is the Ritschlian category of worth that dominates. In his fundamental assertion that the historian must assess that which is of moral worth in the work of a man, he is clearly depending on Ritschl. It is this latter tenet of the position held by Ritschl and Harnack that made them vulnerable to the charge of *apriorism*; for to determine "moral worth," a stance must be assumed, and it is clear (*pace* Harnack) that such a stance was present. This stance was apologetic: he would, he *must*, speak to culture. He would, as a mediator, redeem for the Church those masses who could no longer accept the Gospel as the churches preached it. One cannot but confess sympathy with Harnack at this point when the effusions of certain of the highbrow fundamentalists of his time are recalled. His heritage made it imperative that atheistic materialism be rejected. But his passion was to try to make his contemporaries see that these two—atheism or fundamentalism—were not the only options. There could and must be a *via media*. This middle way must on the one hand be intellectually and scientifically respectable, to speak to the cultured; it must also take full account of the uniqueness of Jesus, to speak to the Church. Harnack believed he had found such a middle way in Ritschlian liberalism. History, which had come into its own as a science, had made possible for men the recovery of the historical power of the essential in Jesus, his Gospel; but this history as Harnack conceived it thereby incorporated within itself a full-bodied doctrine of humanity. History could tell us about Jesus and his power, his purpose, and his in-

61 *Ibid.*, p. 56.

62 Harnack, "Uber die Sicherheit . . . ," *RA*, IV, NF, *passim.*

fluence in history. Thus could man overcome his past and lay the foundations of the future.

Where is the "tragic flaw" in this fundamental stance? It lies, we believe, in the real decision to regard the world and the overcoming of that which one finds in the world as the primary referent. What difference would it have made if, instead of attempting to answer via history the question "How can one grasp the inner form of Christianity, and defend it?" Harnack had asked the question "How can I be faithful to God, whether I see the immediate relevance of this fidelity or not?" The former question suggests the extent to which Harnack remained under the influence of the romanticism in his background, with its passion to "know all," to "experience all"; and it also has as its clear objective to "defend Christianity" to the culture. Our judgment is that Harnack was preeminently influenced by this latter objective, so that it is true that his fundamental referent was the culture, and his purpose to find meaning for the embattled soul within this culture.[63]

How does one summarize the background and environmental influences on Harnack? Materialism and "mummified orthodoxy" provided the challenge. Romanticism dictated the nisus to essence procedure. The Dorpat-Erlangen, Tübingen, Ritschlian background prescribed the historical method of procedure, which in the last phase reasserted certain Hegelian themes. But the *content* of the essence, once identified, was *Ritschlian axiology* with a nimbus.

[63] Rade, in his essay in *Harnack-Ehrung*, "Der Begriff der Kirche bei den Kirchenhistorikern," p. 457, wrote, "In the ceaseless turning of the Church of God to the world, and vice-versa, the history of the Church is fulfilled." It is certainly a Harnackian theme.

PART THREE

HISTORY

The appropriate organization of this section is difficult, because Harnack presupposed every part of his history and his theology in every other part. What follows in the next two sections of this work therefore amounts to a *theologoumenon*: the separate treatment of "history" and "theology." Further, *within* each part the same principle obtains. For example, a possible organization of the section on "History" might be:

I. Harnack's Conception of the Nature of History
II. The Historical Method of Harnack
III. Harnack's Historiography
  Contributions to church historical knowledge
IV. Harnack's Conception of Christianity as a Historical Phenomenon, His Approach to It as a Living Faith, His Interpretation of It by the Historical Method, and His Judgment of Its Validity[1]

This is *not* the organization that will be used. Simply, we contend that the subject, Harnack, and the subject-matter—his works—yield to a better understanding if a division, however artificial, is employed. It is possible to make a fairly discrete separation of "Harnack's Conception of the Nature of History" and "The Historical Method of Harnack," and to treat these two subjects separately, without doing violence to either. It is *not* possible to avoid some artificiality if "Harnack's Historiography" and "Harnack's Conception of Christianity . . ." are separated. But because of the substance of the material itself, there would be a much greater artificiality if they were joined, and if both were treated under history. Therefore the first three categories only will be examined in this section and, as is more appropriate, the last category will be considered under "Theology." Insofar as there is an overlapping, it must be ascribed to the dominance, even within the history, of the axiological component.

[1] The categories are derived from Pauck's essay on "Adolf von Harnack's Interpretation of Church History," in *The Heritage of the Reformation*, pp. 337–351.

VIII

Harnack's Conception of History

WILHELM PAUCK, in his Inaugural Lecture at the Union Theological Seminary in New York, took as his theme "Harnack's conception and interpretation of Christianity as a historical phenomenon."[2] He set aside, as not of primary interest, on that occasion, "Harnack's contribution to church historical knowledge," pointing out that "the results of his research on the history of the ancient church may today be unduly neglected, but they cannot but come into their own wherever and whenever scholarship turns to the fields which he chiefly explored."[3] He continued:

> It is his approach to Christianity as a living historical faith which needs to be freshly understood and re-evaluated, because the major trend of contemporary theological thought is marked by a blindness to those ways of thinking which Harnack practiced not only in his historiography but also in his judgment of the validity of the Christian faith. We therefore direct our attention to his insistence that Christianity must be understood as a historical movement and that it must be interpreted by the historical method.[4]

Pauck, under a different and more felicitous phrasing, is dealing here with that which we have denominated the "axiological" com-

[2] *Ibid.*, p. 338.
[3] *Ibid.*
[4] *Ibid.*

ponent of "historical axiology." Pauck's interest differs from that of Pelikan, who wrote in the Torchbook introduction to Harnack's *Mission and Expansion*:

We need to learn from him once more that without sound historical study Christian theology inevitably falls victim to the pressures of denominational (or interdenominational) bureaucracy, to the changing fads of the most recent theological masters and dogmatic system-builders, or to the murky subjectivities of a religious solipsism that cannot see beyond the borders of its own century and therefore regards itself and its own time as utterly unique.[5]

Harnack faced in his time all of the vicissitudes which Pelikan here mentions. His response was to continue with that historical research which alone, he thought, could redeem the time. To be sure, he was not loath to point out that in spite of all the efforts of the theologians and historians, this victimization would probably continue, just because few were willing to "earn their heritage in order that they might possess it."[6] Thus, in the Babel/Bibel controversy, after remarking that Delitzsch's views regarding the dependence of certain Old Testament myths on Babylonian sources were not new to "science," he went on to observe: "But this knowledge had not become common property. No blame for this, however, attaches to the theologians. They had indeed done their duty in books, pamphlets and lectures. . . . But Church and School in league together have suppressed this knowledge, banishing it from their respective domains."[7]

Harnack continued to "do his duty." For him, the great problem with which the Christian who is also a historian of Christianity must wrestle until, in his Peniel, it yields, is just this:

The whole substance and meaning of religion—life in God, the forgiveness of sins, consolation in suffering—she [the Church] couples with Christ's person; and in so doing she associates everything that gives life its meaning and its permanence, nay the Eternal itself, with an historical fact; maintaining the indissoluble unity of both.[8]

[5] *The Mission and Expansion of Christianity in the First Three Centuries*, tr. and ed. by James Moffatt (New York: Harper & Row, Torchbook ed. 1962), Introduction by Jaroslav Pelikan, p. vi.

[6] Pelikan cites an aphorism from Goethe as applicable, for contemporary church historians and theologians, to Harnack's work:

Was du ererbt von deinen Vätern hast,
Erwirb es um es zu besitzen.

[7] Harnack, "Der Brief Sr. Majestät des Kaisers an den Admiral von Hollmann," *RA*, II, NF, pp. 65–66.

[8] *Christianity and History*, pp. 17–18.

Over against the deified nature and the hypostatized reason which the eighteenth century had enshrined, there had been a mighty reaction. Led by Herder and the romantics, abetted by "Hegel and his great scholar Ranke," and due, "not least of all, to the powerful reaction of Christian faith," the reaction had issued in a "knowledge of *history*; of the history from which we have received what we possess, and to which we owe what we are."[9]

Assuredly, this is the key word for Adolf Harnack: historian. The adjectives that precede or the prepositional phrases which follow in qualification ought never to deter one from this insight. And for Harnack, *history* is one species of that genus *science*.

There are few words which occur with more frequency in Harnack's works than the word *Wissenschaft*, and there are none used with more unequivocal approval. From 1883, when he first used the word in a lecture title,[10] through his years of membership in the Prussian Academy of Science, he is reflecting on the meaning of the concept and setting down his reflections. In 1895 he published anonymously in *Christliche Welt* a number of reflections, "*Über Wissenschaft und Religion.*"[11] Increasingly from this time one finds the word recurring. Harnack himself declared in his late autobiographical reflections that *Wissenschaft* was a dominant concern of his life from the beginning.[12]

Wissenschaft must be taken in its most heavily freighted meaning, connoting "science," "learning," and "knowledge." Narrowness is the cardinal sin for Harnack, and this is illustrated by his antipathy toward the practice of restricting "science" to *Naturwissenschaft*. Harnack's daughter remarks that Söderblom showed how well he understood Harnack when "he referred to the spiritual emancipation and clarification which he owed to Harnack: science must be 'a higher form of life, not only a way to "results."' One could point to this sentence as the key to Harnack's personality."[13]

What is this "science" which is lauded, sought after, and followed as beacon? One does not need to speculate here, for Harnack dealt overtly with the subject. Two of his statements in particular require

[9] *Ibid.*, pp. 23–24.

[10] So far as I can determine, the first use is in his lecture, fittingly, on "Martin Luther, in seiner Bedeutung fur die Geschichte der Wissenschaft und der Bildung." The lecture was published in various editions, and is in the initial *Reden und Aufsätze* volume (Giessen: Töpelmann, 1904), pp. 141–169.

[11] "Über Wissenschaft und Religion. Angeeignetes und Erlebtes," *RA*, II, pp. 369–379.

[12] *RA*, V, NF, Part I, pp. 3–48, *passim*.

[13] AZH, p. 438.

analysis. In 1907 he contributed an essay to the first issue of the *International Wochenschrift für Wissenschaft, Kunst und Technik* entitled "Gedanken über Wissenschaft und Leben."[14] Six years later he gave a lecture entitled Über Wissenschaftliche Erkenntnis" at the first annual Fortbildungskursus der Baltischen Literarischen Gesellschaft.[15] The 1907 essay took its title from a statement of Humboldt, which also served as the text for explication: "Science often renders its most beneficent blessing to life when it appears to forget itself."[16] This paradoxical statement must be taken to mean that all that is transitory should be forgotten; "but all the more sharply should his observation be directed to the living interplay of real powers and the true content of life."[17] This last phrase, "the true content of life," specifies for Harnack the task of that branch of science which comprises philosophy and history, *Geisteswissenschaft.* "Its object is life, the life of humanity, insofar as this is distinguished from and elevated above the stage of nature. This life can be grasped only through a study that includes the present as well as the past."[18] From this it follows that the life of the historian who would be true to his calling must be rich, many-sided, and deep, in order that he may interpret that which he investigates from the substance of an inner conviction. The historian who does not possess this inner conviction and that deep knowledge of life which comes from responsible participation in the institutions of men will be at best a hack, passing on someone else's wares. This lack of conviction was castigated by Harnack with a categorical statement: "He who has no conviction always lies, no matter what he says."[19]

In the 1913 lecture, though Harnack in no way qualifies the demand which this position requires, he systematizes his meaning of "scientific knowledge." That this position remained constant for the rest of his life is proven by two other statements: one, written in 1930, the year of his death, was entitled "Stufen wissenschaftlicher Erkenntnis,"[20] in which Harnack abstracted a portion of this lecture with very little editing; the other is his "Fünfzehn Fragen an die Verächter

[14] *RA,* NF: *Aus Wissenschaft und Leben,* Band I (Giessen: Töpelmann, 1911), pp. 1–9.

[15] *RA,* III, NF: *Aus der Friedens- und Kriegsarbeit* (Giessen: Töpelmann, 1916), pp. 173–201.

[16] "Gedanken über Wissenschaft . . . ," *RA,* I, NF, p. 3.

[17] *Ibid.*, p. 4.

[18] *Ibid.*

[19] "Über Wissenschaft und Religion . . . ," *RA,* II, p. 379.

[20] "Stufen wissenschaftlicher Erkenntnis," *RA,* V, NF, pp. 202–205.

der wissenschaftlichen Theologie unter den Theologen,"[21] written as an open challenge to the dialectical theology of Barth and his confrères.[22]

"Science is the knowledge of the Real turned to purposive behavior."[23] This is not the totality of life; for when we become aware of ourselves three psychological compulsions bear upon us: the desire to know, to appreciate, and to honor. These correspond to the intellective, the aesthetic, and the religious aspects of man, whose objects are, respectively, science, art, and religion. In this essay, it is "knowledge [*Erkenntnis*], i.e. science [*Wissenschaft*] with which alone we have to deal."[24]

The following are the stages of *Wissenschaft*:

(1) The first and most basic stage consists in *identification*, *analysis*, and *organization*. All knowledge begins with these operations.[25]

(2) The second stage is to be designated as *the knowledge of the causal relations between things*. . . . In a word, it concerns itself with the knowledge of the powers of the world, insofar as they can be represented quantitatively and mechanically.[26]

(3) To investigate life is the third stage of knowledge. A structure, analysis, and order is necessary here, as in the first stage, but in a higher manifestation; new questions are thereby raised; questions concerning the fleeting and the fit, the idea and the direction and the purpose. Here we have to deal with the living world *in its concrete reality*.[27]

(4) The fourth stage of knowledge is closely related to this third stage, and one might be disposed to connect them, for originally it uses the same means and methods, epistemologically, as the third stage; and its object in any case is included in the concept of "life." But the knowledge of men . . . is lifted above the knowledge of "life" because we encounter something at this point which other living things do not manifest: conscious spirit.[28]

Specifically, what is encountered when we study men are the categories of "norms" and "worth." It is only in this fourth stage that

[21] *RA*, V, NF, pp. 51–54.

[22] For a translation of this short article and an analysis of its contents, see Chap. XIII, B, *infra*.

[23] Harnack, "Über wissenschaftliche Erkenntnis," *RA*, III, NF, p. 178.

[24] *Ibid.*

[25] *Ibid.*, p. 179.

[26] *Ibid.*, pp. 179–180.

[27] *Ibid.*, pp. 187–188.

[28] *Ibid.*, p. 191.

we really can speak of history; for history is involved only when the spirit of an event is grasped. The creative leader among historians is the one who sets forth such "norms" and "worth," which means to exercise that law of the spirit which gives freedom. "Through this law he creates above and in this life a second life, above and in nature another nature, a second world above nature—the human. It must express itself first in ideas, which appear to be as abstract as the ideology of mechanistic power-systems."[29] But as these ideas are grasped, they bring about a conquest of nature, and thereby prove themselves to be of worth in the creation of "supermen"—for all those who live in this law of spiritual freedom are supermen. But does this provide a final measure of worth? There is only one answer, and it is absolutely crucial: "The measure and the directive for all higher motives in the life of men is the conviction that we are not mere fragments of nature, but bear within ourselves an eternal life as the citizens and creators of a spiritual kingdom."[30] This is the measure, the standard of worth, the norm to which all activity is held accountable. Everything which contributes to the emergence of this new, "überempirisch" man, this true humanity, is worthful; everything that hinders it is evil. "And all history in its essence is nothing else than the leading forth of humanity from the gloomy depths of nature to the pinnacle of this knowledge."[31] Thus spoke Harnack in 1913; "da brach der Weltkrieg aus."[32]

Certainly this is an interpretation on the grand scale of the possibilities of human knowledge. There is nothing here—literally *nothing* —that suggests narrowness in the conception of *Wissenschaft*; this is "learning" and "knowledge" and "science" all together, conquering the merely temporal and finite limits of creatureliness through the freedom of the human spirit. Harnack had not always been so Olympian in his estimate of man and of "gloomy nature"; in his lecture entitled "The Pursuit of Education," delivered before the Evangelical-Social Congress in 1902, he had sounded the theme, but with a qualifying variation:

> If . . . we consider man in his relations to that Nature of which he is a part, education will be seen to have a two-fold function to perform. On the one hand, it will be a weapon of defense against Nature, a protection against her threat of overwhelming force; so far as possible it will master Nature, gaining possession of her secrets by cunning and skill, in order

[29] *Ibid.*, p. 194.
[30] *Ibid.*
[31] *Ibid.*, p. 195.
[32] *Ibid.*, p. 174.

to subjugate her and make her a willing servant. On the other hand, it is the office of education to lead, by the knowledge of Nature, to reconciliation with her; to disclose the intimate connection between all things that have life; and to knit yet closer every healthy bond by which they are already connected. From this standpoint, again, the highest aim in view is power and liberty.[33]

More important here than the fact that he speaks for a protean effort to overcome and in part to be reconciled to Nature is the fact that his problem is set within *this* context of "man in nature." For whether the judgment is qualified or unrestrainedly confident, with the giddiness of a 1913 German optimism, the breadth of the claim here made is breath-taking.

Identification, analysis, and organization; the knowledge of the causal relations between things; the investigation of life; the knowledge of men, in whom we meet axiological norms, and through whom the *Geist* of an epoch is communicated to us, raising us above nature: this is *Wissenschaft* as Harnack conceived it. More precisely, this is *Geisteswissenschaft*, whose proper end is achieved by a joining of the knowledge of the past and the wisdom of the present. And ultimately, we note, it is this latter present wisdom which is determinative. Lacking inner conviction, the historian lies, no matter what he says. But this inner conviction, this wisdom of the present—what is it? It is Harnack's *Humanitätsideal*, as derived from Herder, Goethe, and Ritschl; but, involving a "rich and many-sided wisdom of life," as it does, other strands are also present.

It is noteworthy to recall that, although the faculty of the University of Berlin had voted unanimously for Harnack's appointment, the evaluation of his work was not unambiguously favorable. The faculty had adverted to the fact that Harnack's work was based on "independent investigation of the primary sources," and that it had "contributed to the dispersal of opinions and prejudices drawn from the past," "had set old problems in a new light," and "had for the most part yielded fruitful and positive results."[34] However, the faculty statement went on to note:

Of course we cannot conceal these judgments: that the objectivity necessary for a historian is still frequently lacking in him; that conclusions, often too hastily drawn out of his otherwise well-founded premises, are

[33] Harnack and Wilhelm Herrmann, *Essays on the Social Gospel*, tr. G. M. Craik, ed. Maurice A. Canney (New York: G. P. Putnam's Sons, 1907), pp. 106–107.

[34] AZH, p. 157.

also (at least in the opinion of some of us) too strongly influenced by his dogmatic standpoint; and that, especially in his History of Dogma, his conception of the formation of ecclesiastical dogma is too crude and one-sided. Hence the wisdom befitting a Christian theologian in handling ecclesiastical matters is to some extent still lacking. On the other hand, we would say that this kind of extravagant judgment does not rest on any eccentricity of character, or on any want of regard for Christianity and the Church; rather, he seems to be carried away by his zeal to bring into effect the new historical viewpoints which he champions, and it is to be hoped that with increasing experience and in vital contact with circles differently disposed, he will learn to find the correct measure.[35]

Certainly the comments regarding "objectivity" and "dogmatic standpoint" must have been cutting, for these were, according to Harnack, elemental considerations. A little over a year after he moved to Berlin, a lecture on "Legends as Historical Sources" provided an occasion for an impassioned defense: "The historian above all else has to deal with the establishing of the facts. It is his sacred duty to ascertain the truth of the facts. Pity the historian who takes this problem lightly, or who falsifies it! There is in his case no excuse: he is a traitor to his sacred call."[36]

The full-blown statement of his conception of history was set forth somewhat later in a remarkable lecture, and then published. He gave the lecture the title "Über die Sicherheit und die Grenzen geschichtlicher Erkenntnis." His earlier position regarding the requirement of objectivity is reaffirmed: "In the writing of history the investigation of facts, which is severely exact, is placed first; after this a measure of the wisdom of life, which estimates the inner relationships, is required. All progress in historical knowledge is conditioned by the degree to which the interpreter brings to his material . . . a rich, deep, and many-sided personal wisdom and experience."[37] These statements suggest the fundamental problem which any historian must face: the relation of "facts" and "interpretation." It is from his "objective" commitment that Harnack challenges those "dogmatic" or "metaphysical" or "theological" preconceptions which, when deliberately inserted into historical work, ruin its value. Harnack, of course, did not believe that one could constitute himself *tabula rasa*. He knew that he had a position, but the question was whether the position one took was based on a valid method and whether the judgment

[35] *Ibid.*
[36] "Legenden als Geschichtsquellen," *RA*, I, p. 23.
[37] *RA*, IV, NF, p. 19.

emerged from the study of the material, or whether the presuppositions were brought to the material and impressed forcibly upon it. Of those who announced a position of partiality, he was unqualified in his critique. In his *Date of the Acts and of the Synoptic Gospels*, he remarked of a colleague's conclusions: "This is a way out of the difficulty which can be acquiesced in only by one who has not studied in detail the actual coincidences and is content to quiet his intellectual conscience with preconceived opinions."[38] In his *Acts of the Apostles*, he makes clear the distinction between "apologetic" study and "openness":

In any age wherein critical hypotheses, once upon a time not unfruitful, have hardened themselves into dogmas, and when if an attempt is made to defend a book against prejudice, misunderstanding, and misrepresentation, scornful remarks are made about "special pleading," it is not superfluous to declare that the method which is here employed is influenced by no prepossession of any kind.[39]

In critical study, then, there is no place for "prepossessions" of a "dogmatic" or a "metaphysical" kind to operate, but this is not to say that the historian comes to his sources as though he had no interest in the matter at all. Though "in a historical work, there is no room" for asking about the standpoint of the author, "the question here is whether the author is in sympathy with the subject about which he writes, whether he can distinguish original elements from those that are derived, whether he has a thorough acquaintance with his material, whether he is conscious of the limits of historical knowledge, and whether he is truthful."[40] Of the interpretation of the first two chapters of Matthew, Harnack declares: "Critics may call this narrative late, but in saying this they only express the fact that they find themselves out of sympathy with it; and to be in sympathy with a narrative of this kind is especially difficult for us westerners of the nineteenth and twentieth centuries."[41]

It is not, therefore, simply the knowledge of the facts, but the way in which one deals with the facts and the tradition which constitute faithful historical labor. For Harnack, these two facets of the his-

[38] Tr. J. R. Wilkinson (New York: G. P. Putnam's Sons, 1911), p. 3.

[39] Tr. J. R. Wilkinson (New York: G. P. Putnam's Sons, 1909), pp. xlii–xliii.

[40] Harnack, *History of Dogma*, tr. Neil Buchanan (Boston: Little, Brown & Company, 1899), I, vi–vii. This is in the "Author's Preface to the English Edition," and is not in the German. On Buchanan's translation of the *Dogmengeschichte*, more later.

[41] *The Date of the Acts . . .*, p. 142.

torian's task represent the Scylla and Charybdis which, one or the other, wreck many efforts. In his *Sayings of Jesus* he indicates the internal tensions represented in each of these tasks, and suggests in an indictment the ways in which an incomplete attention to the stringent internal demands of competent historiography brings grief:

One can scarcely hope that there will be an end of wild hypotheses in regard to . . . history. The temptation to confine one's gaze to isolated details, and to view these as reflected in the distorting mirror of prepossession and prejudice, without deep and reverent study of tradition, is too great for us to expect that these strivings will ever cease.[42]

Further,

The situation here [with regard to the investigation of Q] is the same as in the case of a dozen other important problems of the criticism of the gospels: men soar away into sublime discussions concerning the meaning of "the Kingdom of God," the "Son of Man," "Messiahship," etc., and occupy themselves with investigations into the "history of religion," and with problems of genuineness, in the light of "higher" criticism (as if the critic were inspired with absolute knowledge of historical matters from some secret source); while the "lower" problems, whose treatment involves real scavenger's labor in which one is almost choked with dust, are passed by on the other side. . . . Hence the wretched plight in which the criticism of the gospels finds itself in these days, and indeed has always found itself with the exception of the work of a few critics.[43]

Harnack then unloads his ire on those "compelled to take their knowledge of the criticism of the New Testament at second hand"; unable to stand on their own exegesis, they are "like reeds swaying with the blasts of mutually exclusive hypotheses."[44] Jesus is now a Tolstoyian monk, now a Buddhist world-denier, now an eponymous hero. Being abreast of the latest hypothesis "is more important by far than the knowledge of the facts themselves, which indeed do not so much concern us, seeing that in this twentieth century we must of course wean ourselves from a contemptible dependence upon history in matters of religion."[45]

There are other questions, however, of first-order importance, and it is characteristic of Harnack that he does not dodge them. One such question has to do with the purpose of historical study, and Harnack's

[42] Tr. J. R. Wilkinson (New York: G. P. Putnam's Sons, 1908), p. xii.
[43] *Ibid.*, pp. xii–xiii.
[44] *Ibid.*, p. xiii.
[45] *Ibid.*

answer is developed as follows: He describes history as the bond between all the sciences; without historical knowledge, routine reigns, and purposeful work is not possible. Only through history can one come to a positive view of the world and of life; neither the knowledge of nature nor pure reason can provide this. One must know his tradition in order to serve the present and prepare the way for the future; only within the framework of historical knowledge, therefore, can significant work be done. History is not, as Ranke had said, simply the representation "wie es gewesen ist"; and Ranke did not believe this in a positivist sense, for he did not write history in this way. The inevitable question that arises when one says he wants to know "how it was" is "Why would you know it?" The answer cannot be curiosity, or entertainment, or the mere possession of knowledge: "What we strive for in historical knowledge is not the knowledge of an abundance of important or unimportant details, but we would learn to know the material and spiritual structure of past life, and we would understand it as the progressive concretion of the spirit, and, therefore as the progressive mastery of the material circumstances of life."[46]

Harnack rejects Goethe's statement that "the best thing about history is the enthusiasm which it engenders,"[47] not because it is untrue, but because it is incomplete. Similarly, the suggestion that history is to be studied in order to "have great experiences" is insufficient; meeting great personalities can evoke a deep response, but biography is not the same thing as history. Why then should men study history? Harnack's answer is clear:

> *Only one* satisfactory answer can be given: if it is true that no work is fitting for men which does not qualify them for *deeds* and *action* . . . then historical knowledge must prove and justify its right to existence *here*. And it can do this! *We study history in order to intervene in the course of history*, and we have a right and duty to do so; for without historical knowledge we remain either passive objects of development, or we mislead people irresponsibly.
>
> . . . .
>
> To intervene in history means that we must reject the *past* when it reaches into the *present* as a hindrance; it means further that we must do the right thing in the *present*; and it means finally that we must prepare prudently for the *future*. There is no doubt that, with respect to the past, history assumes a judging, or even a regal function; for in order to decide

[46] Harnack, "Über die Sicherheit. . . ," *RA*, IV, NF, p. 5.

[47] *Ibid.*, pp. 6–7.

what of the past shall continue to be efficacious and what must be done away with or transformed, the historian must judge like a king. But everything in historical knowledge must finally be utilized for the preparation of the future; *for only that knowledge has a right to exist, which prepares for that which is to come*; otherwise it is a superfluous and pernicious dilettantism which deprives necessary work of its required strength. Man is in the world for action, not for contemplation![48]

Does this not amount to a doctrine of progress, with Hegelian overtones? The Hegelianism is certainly implicit, as Troeltsch remarked.[49] But Harnack, unlike some of his followers, was quite clear that any "inevitable progress" doctrine was indefensible. In this instance, he employs a biological analogy to make the point. Living nature has two great secrets: the secret of the species, which is in transition at the same time that it is an end in itself, and the secret of individuality, which suddenly appears in a higher development. Mommsen perfectly expressed the mystery when he declared: "It is an ineffable secret of nature that it can blend *normality* and *individuality* in their most perfect manifestation."[50] To affirm only the first characteristic, as is often done, is to write shallow, misrepresentative history. Is it really true, Harnack asks, that a later people is more advanced than an earlier? Is the thought and art of a later time necessarily higher than that of an earlier time? On the contrary, what poet has surpassed Homer or Dante, what philosopher has equaled Plato, and who of more recent vintage has outdone Moses or Phidias or Bach? These giants exceed any maximal normality, and for that reason they are regarded by us as high points.

Indeed, Harnack overtly denied any such inevitable progress theory. In his 1922 edition of Augustine's *Maximen und Reflexionen*, he refers to those virtues which Augustine espoused—the sense of the real, the deep search after truth, the love of the neighbor, the sharp-

[48] *Ibid.*, pp. 7–8.

[49] Troeltsch, "Adolf v. Harnack und Ferd. Christian v. Baur," *Festgabe zu Harnacks 70. Geburtstag*, pp. 272–291. I was unable to secure this work except on microfilm from the Deutsche Staatsbibliothek, Berlin. No publication data were given on the microfilm. Remarking on the fact that "the camp-followers" of the Tübingen School saw only the contrasts between Baur and Harnack (and did not see these at the right place), and that Harnack himself "at the beginning probably judged similarly," Troeltsch goes on to say that from the time of the publication of *Aus Wissenschaft und Leben* (1911) "one senses a strong emphasis on the Idea of a general development of the spirit, almost exactly in the sense of the dialectic of Hegel; the development of Christian institutions and the Christian spirit is imbedded in this general development."

[50] Harnack, "Über die Sicherheit . . . ," *RA*, IV, NF, p. 5.

ening of conscience—and then declared: "In all of these we have made no progress; we have won a useful knowledge of nature, and we have achieved better techniques!"[51] Harnack's daughter is just in her evaluation of Harnack's position:

With these words Harnack declared himself free from any easy culture- and civilization-optimism, with which his critics had so often charged him. He knew very well out of what depths mankind cries to God, but at the same time the saving power of Christianity had revealed itself to him, not only in the personal life of the individual, but also in the history of humanity.[52]

It is this latter *Sicherheit* which permitted Harnack, even in the dire situation of 1920, to distinguish between "progress" and "inevitable progress." In his criticism of Spengler's pessimistic work, he had pointed out that the denial of progress of *any* sort is inconsistent with the plain fact that modern science has learned many of the secrets of nature, and therefore can control it. But is there a continuous progress in history? Certainly not. Regress is also present, even though, as in Hegel, such regress may be only apparent as antithesis, and may make possible a broader progress. The further question as to whether progress might cease entirely and mankind relapse into barbarism is regarded by Harnack as "unanswerable from the standpoint of history."[53]

Harnack was not unmindful of that fundamental criticism which questioned any attempt to understand human life historically. In his essay on Goethe, he quoted the uncomplimentary remarks which the great man had made concerning the possibility of getting at past events: "Not everything that is represented to us as history has really happened, and what really happened did not happen as it has been represented, and furthermore what has happened is only a small segment of all that has happened. Everything in history remains uncertain, the greatest as well as the smallest."[54] Harnack was by no means as pessimistic as Goethe in this regard, but his optimism, bearing within it a recognition of the limits involved in historical knowledge, was nurtured by ethical rather than historical convictions. A further limit for Harnack, self-consciously accepted, was that suggested by the categories of nature and super-nature. Writing to Loofs in 1901, he declared: "For me the supernatural is not, on the

[51] AZH, p. 517.
[52] *Ibid.*, p. 518.
[53] "Was hat die Historie . . . ," *RA*, IV, NF, p. 194.
[54] "Die Religion Goethes . . . ," *ibid.*, p. 157.

whole, a concept: I am continually learning more about the greatness and the extensiveness of God-given *natura*. God and all that he gives of himself to our hearts are absolute; we and all of our knowledge are relative."[55] But, this being so, what is the proper activity of man? It is to study that which can give the maximum human certainty, history. This can be known because there is a bond between our minds and the minds that have shaped and created institutions. But it must always be remembered that "we and all of our knowledge are relative."

Within this position one can discern the emphasis on the salutary quality of "mediation," an emphasis characteristic of Harnack's work. He was the despair of his friends, for he was always surprising them by supporting something which they felt alien to his "position."[56] His daughter comments that in the post-World War political crisis he would join no particular party, but was sympathetic to the center group. He contemplated writing a *Psychologie der Mittleren*, in order to "honor this species," whose great contribution lay in the fact that they did not see "positions" but points on a line: "Therefore they have no precise standpoint, but only a *direction*; they are as true to this direction as the extremists are to their positions, but these latter can never understand them."[57] Harnack, many-sided as he was in interest and attainment, believed that narrow partisanship always obscured elements of truth. We can observe these antinomies in his own "direction": while one must master isolated details, these must be treated with wisdom and sympathy, avoiding prepossession and prejudice; while the historical understanding of the past is indispensable, this does not mean that the historian possesses absolute knowledge from above, for all knowledge is relative; while deep and reverent study of the tradition is required, one must overcome history by history, rejecting that part of the past which reaches into the present in a debilitating way; and while dogmatic prepossession may not be forced upon historical material, historical study issues in and contributes to experience and judgment and wisdom.

One can argue that the stone of stumbling in Harnack's theory of history is far-set in antiquity: in the conflict, indeed, between Jewish prophetic understanding and Greek intellectualism. Löwith has stated this as the dilemma of the modern historian, at least insofar as this

55 AZH, p. 248.
56 Cf. here the account of the "Jatho affair," given in AZH, pp. 395–401.
57 AZH, p. 487.

historian holds to the view that Harnack espoused: that we must "overcome history by history in order thus to build a platform for new productive action."[58] He quotes Hermann Cohen:

The concept of history is a concept of prophetism. . . . What Greek intellectualism could not produce, prophetism has achieved. In Greek consciousness, *historein* is equivalent to inquiry, narration, and knowledge. To the Greeks history remains something we can know because it is a matter of "fact" [*factum*], that is, of the past. The prophet, however, is a seer, not a scholar; his prophetic vision has created our concept of history as being essentially of the future. Time becomes primarily future, and future the primary content of our historical thought. For this new future "the creator of heaven and earth" is not sufficient. He has to create "a new heaven and a new earth." In this transformation the idea of progress is implied. Instead of a golden age in the mythological past, the true historical existence on earth is constituted by an eschatological future.[59]

That some such problem is the one with which Harnack wrestled is attested by his "the Eternal itself" on the one hand and "historical fact" on the other, when these are conjoined with his (and Troeltsch's) "overcoming history by history." This is the most obvious dichotomy that one sees in Harnack's work. The historian of dogma, on the one hand; the seeker after the "reality" of Christianity on the other.

To summarize and evaluate Harnack's conception of history, we refer to the basic contention of the initial chapter: "Harnack from the beginning was dominated by a passion to isolate an axiological essence and he was committed to doing this by means of a historical procedure."[60] The fundamental question then becomes: If Harnack's history was influenced by his axiology, what are the ways in which the latter shaped the former?

Harnack held that the final purpose for the study of history is *action*. One studies the past, and determines the ways in which the past has come to shape the present; then one applies in this present all the wisdom of which he is capable in order to act responsibly. Lacking this wisdom, the past will lie like a dead hand on all his efforts. Harnack here saw himself as a fighter on two fronts: against the materialism of his day, which was all for "overcoming history," but not "by history," he asserted the necessity of understanding one's heritage; against ecclesiastical orthodoxy, which he saw as living "by history" but not "overcoming history," he asserted the necessity

[58] Quoted in Pauck, "Adolf von Harnack's Interpretation . . . ," p. 341. The quote is from Troeltsch; but Harnack *espoused* it.
[59] In Löwith, *Meaning in History*, pp. 17–18.
[60] *Supra*, p. 8.

of responsible deeds. But he was emphatic in his assertion that the history by which one overcomes history must be understood in terms of a scientifically oriented method, where, as nearly as man can, prepossessions are excluded. At the same time, one must possess a "rich and many-sided wisdom of life." Put into a formula, History (Tradition) is overcome by History (Responsible Acts), when Tradition and Responsibility are understood by a method which combines scientific fidelity and *Lebensweisheit*. The judgment of fact and the judgment of value thus merge to bring forth, in given historical situations, creative activity.

But it is just at this point that the basic problem becomes evident. Whether the conflict be expressed by the use of the categories of "scientific knowledge" and "life," or "judgment of fact" and "judgment of value," or "fact" and "interpretation," or "history" and "axiology," the problem is constant, as Troeltsch understood when he characterized Harnack's history as an "ideological-dogmatic" representation. To be sure, Harnack seems to have believed that he had overcome the tensions and achieved the *Sicherheit* and *Einheit* which he so ardently sought. Yet, conceding the brilliance of his understanding and the protean character of his achievement, our judgment is that this *a priori* axiological norm is integral to his concept of history; that his attempt to understand Christianity historically is dominated throughout by his concern to isolate its axiological essence; that the commitment to historical procedure, issuing in a *Dogmengeschichte* or a *Marcion*, was under the suzerainty of this *a priori*; that the presence of this fundamental tension explains—or makes necessary—a doctrine of "Mittleren," and may help to explain the announced but never completely achieved "impartiality"; and that the methodological principle, "the same mind is at work in history and in us" is interpreted in such a way that the mind "in us," i.e., the nineteenth-century culturally conditioned mind, is made determinative in a too simple way.[61] As we shall have occasion to note, Troeltsch disagreed with aspects of Harnack's thought, charging him with bringing to his historical labor a given which was not itself historically derived; and Harnack disagreed almost entirely with Barth, expressing an inability to understand or to appreciate the dialectical theology. This, we believe, was due to the fact that Barth categorically rejected Harnack's nisus to essence procedure and the content which was discovered by means of this procedure.

[61] The full development of this interpretation is in Chap. XV.

Harnack, almost "from the beginning," had emphasized the necessity to distinguish man in his freedom from that stark nature which is about him, and of which he is a part. This determined in large measure his concentration on *history* rather than natural science or philosophy. Only history, seen in the full richness of the above description, could give that certainty and unity which man requires. Harnack in his youth had studied Kant; he had felt himself required to know what Schopenhauer and Hartmann and Nietzsche were thinking; he had made it a point to master natural-science monism.[62] But in all the range of philosophical and scientific thought which he encountered, he admitted that he could find only one person "to whom I would gladly listen"—this is the universal man, Leibnitz.[63] In a letter to Rade written in 1888, he traced his pilgrimage from philosophy to history: "Through the study of Marcion and the Gnostics, I was strengthened in the distinction between positive religion and theology. The . . . study of Kant and the English philosophers confirmed my conviction of the impossibility of metaphysics. For a year, I was a 'strict positivist.' "[64] But then the light broke: "Gradually it became more certain to me that history is sovereign, . . . that it is worth nothing to speculate, but that we need to make friends with the great personalities of history in order to enrich ourselves thereby. But all of them since Christ appeared to me to be his servants."[65] It was in this historical understanding of "knowledge" that Harnack believed true knowledge inhered; and yet, in historical understanding, one is dealing constantly with "life." Knowledge and life, science and behavior, seen as interpenetrating each other, provide the essential rubrics.

This was expressed by one of Harnack's students, Heinrich Scholz, who evaluated his contribution in a letter of 1916. Scholz first stated his conviction that Harnack had, in the historical field, done more than all of his students; and at the same time, "you stand in relation to this investigation as Goethe stood in relation to his poetry; one understands him quite inadequately, if one sees him only as a poet."[66] Unlike his students, who for the most part oscillated between knowledge and life without any inner consistency, Scholz saw Harnack as practicing a "terminal osmosis" which demanded the synthesizing

[62] AZH, pp. 545–546.
[63] *Ibid.*, p. 546.
[64] *Ibid.*
[65] *Ibid.*
[66] *Ibid.*, p. 547.

of knowledge and life; this, he declared, is "the key to your existence."[67]

The conception of history is magnificent; the achievement sporadic. In the *Dogmengeschichte* he comes closest to the ideal; this is most nearly *Geisteswissenschaft* as he conceived it. In the *Wesen* and many of the occasional writings, the history has been swallowed up by the axiological prepossession. The unhappy fissiparity between the knowledge of the past and the present inner conviction is apparent, and the latter prevails. Troeltsch is correct: Harnack counterpoised a doctrine of humanity to his historicism.[68] Perhaps this was because of the necessity which he felt to speak to his time; in any case he brought to his interpretation a standard which did not arise from the material itself. "Wissenschaftlich" theory became, in practice, a schizoid historicist axiology.

[67] *Ibid.*
[68] *Der Historismus . . .*, p. 529.

IX

The Method of the Historian

HARNACK WAS not disposed to speculate about method. His daughter reports that "he was not a slave to method in the scholastic sense, and he disposed of all questions as to 'how it has to be done properly' with the answer: 'Method is mother-wit.' "[1] To be sure, Harnack wrote and spoke often on the broader problems of historiography. In these comments it is quite clear that he was aware of the contributions made to the "science of church historiography" by his eighteenth- and nineteenth-century forebears, and that he was abreast of the contemporary theories of the church historians, the "secular historians," and the philosophers of history. The *Reden und Aufsätzen* series makes this all very clear: the names of Mommsen, Möhler, Döllinger, Troeltsch, and Dilthey—to pick only a few—adorn the pages.

But when he spoke of "method as mother-wit" he was bearing witness to the fact that he was simply not interested in that kind of "practical" introspection which is much the fashion with twentieth-century church historians. Rather, he would have supported the view that there is an objective givenness about the material to be studied, that one should learn his method by sitting down before the material, and that any conclusions about the appropriate way to proceed should *follow* rather than precede the doing. It is therefore not sur-

[1] AZH, p. 72.

prising that when he finally does put in writing some of his reflections on the nature of the historiographical task, these reflections should be allusive and evocative rather than precisely descriptive.

What follows therefore is a construct, using as sources those addresses and lectures to which we have already given attention. And though the various elements of this construct must, of necessity, be dealt with *seriatim*, it is a wise caution to recall that, just because history is concerned ultimately with the *human*, a rigidly consecutive pattern would be completely artificial.

Harnack insisted that source-work was basic to any sound historical method. We have seen with what passion he proclaimed the historian's responsibility to "the facts." From the beginning to the end of his work, critical, grammatical, philological competence is held to be *sine qua non* for the historian. The most striking evidence of his conviction in this regard is the critical edition of early church documents which he edited in cooperation with a large company of scholars, and to which he contributed.[2] He was actively engaged in searching for new manuscripts himself, and his writings constantly refer to newly discovered materials. If Harnack had written no *Dogmengeschichte* and no *Das Wesen des Christentums*, if he had practiced no historiography, but had attended only to the critical editing of source material, his contribution to historical scholarship would still be very great. He had nothing but professional contempt for those who had to take their material second hand, and in his *Luke, the Physician* he inveighs against a kind of scholarship which did not begin, he judged, with source-study: "The method which I have followed in this book is little in accord with the impressionism which is the style in biblical criticism today. . . . The problem before us . . . can be really mastered by a method which comprises close and detailed examination and discussion of vocabulary and style."[3]

The historian, having mastered the sources, is in a position to distinguish and assess the various factors that enter into and shape historical events. Harnack believed that there were three kinds of factors which must be assessed if the historian is to provide the necessary order to the fabric of his history. In the first place, there are "elementary" factors: the setting, the climate, the natural conditions, and those physical and mental givens which are as they are. These constitute an important element in history; and in fact they are

[2] We refer here to the *Texte und Untersuchungen zur Geschichte der altchristlichen Literatur* series (Leipzig: Hinrichs).

[3] Tr. J. R. Wilkinson (New York: G. P. Putnam's Sons, 1907), pp. vii–viii.

so powerful that the attempt is constantly recurring, as witness the materialistic historians, to attend *only* to these factors.

In the second place, there are the "cultural" factors. All that has been previously experienced by a people or an outstanding individual, and found worthy of preservation, is included here. Tradition, customs, ethical and religious power, art and science, as these are carried in the institutions of culture—the state, the Church, the schools, the societies—these constitute this factor. It is because these institutions of "culture" have caught and carried the activities and the experiences of human beings, structuring these, with all their interrelationships and contradictions, in constitutions and memorials, that they make up so powerful a factor in history. Indeed, "they work almost as a second nature to a people and to individuals,"[4] and it is for this reason that it is possible to portray a great part of the development of a people by attending to them.

But there is a third important factor which one must distinguish and assess if he is to fulfill the highest calling of the historian. This is the "individual" factor. "Individuality, personality, talent, and above all, genius, the *great men*, are here to be represented."[5] Indeed, "the great ideas and institutions . . . are, as a rule, the lengthened shadows of great men, and our spiritual, mental, and technical possessions are the capital which they have won, and which represents their continuing life."[6] It is not enough to say that "times produce men": "In history the rule obtains that a development is really *fulfilled* and a *new situation created* only through great personalities, who do not come when they *must* come—ach! how often are they obliged to come!—but they come when they come!"[7]

It is in connection with this third factor that Harnack raises another concern, one which might be denominated "the problem of continuity." Harnack's total historical conception and method hinges upon his view at this point. The problem may be stated in this way: What assurance does the historian have that he can "get at" the life of the past and understand it? The answer lies in the fact that the key to the past is the institutions—here seen in the broadest sense—which have been bequeathed to us. But *all institutions stem from ideas.* There is no such thing as a cultural institution which did not have an idea behind it.

[4] Harnack, "Über die Sicherheit . . . ," *RA*, IV, NF, p. 10.
[5] *Ibid.*
[6] *Ibid.*, p. 11.
[7] *Ibid.*

To be sure, all history is institution-history; but behind these rest the idea and idea-history. Therefore: just as it is certain that what is mere ideology and has not been embodied in institutions can never be called history, it is equally certain that institution-history without the driving force of ideas would never penetrate; but the ideas *are mind*.[8]

It is because institutions are produced by ideas, and "all history is the history of the mind"[9] that one can claim a continuity with the life of the past and can understand it. "How much or how little we may possess from it, it is always one and the same mind which works in all the products of history *and in us*. . . . A deep unity is discovered between all events and the essence of our own highest life."[10] There follows a quotation which may very well be the key to Harnack's position with regard to the understanding of history: "*Homo sum, nil historicum a me alienum puto.*"[11] Or perhaps even stronger, "You yourself are all that has preceded and precedes you in history, and it only depends upon your grasping it with your consciousness."[12]

Only when these three factors are considered with respect to the material is a true picture possible; and even then, one has not discharged one's total responsibility as a historian. For the historian is also a man, and as a man, he will have reasons for what he does. Harnack was not coy in expressing his judgment as to what these motives ought to be. And though such an expression may not appear to be a part of historical methodology proper, Harnack was not bound by little consistencies. His basic position on this question, integral both to his conception of history and his method, has already been quoted:

We study history in order to intervene in the course of history, and we have a right and duty to do so; for without historical knowledge we remain either passive objects of development, or we mislead people irresponsibly. . . . Only that knowledge which serves the present has a right to demand that it become the subject of knowledge *for us*.[13]

The historian has an obligation, therefore, as Epictetus implied, to represent the facts in such a way as will arouse men, not simply to know the facts. Harnack understood the dangers of taking such a position; he recalls that Goethe had criticized history as resting on

[8] Harnack, "Was hat die Historie . . . ," *RA*, IV, NF, pp. 186–187.
[9] *Ibid.*, p. 187.
[10] *Ibid.*
[11] *Ibid.*
[12] *Ibid.*
[13] Über die Sicherheit . . . ," *RA*, IV, NF, pp. 7–8. See note 48, Chap. VIII.

tradition, and all tradition is either false or partisan, or both, constructed out of blind hate or blinder love. Furthermore, the historian is always too late: the returns are already in! Harnack regards the situation as not so hopeless; though it is true that "quo accuratius, eo falsius," if one goes on to ask the threefold question, "what *powers* were effective in a given epoch, in what *direction* did they proceed, and what was the *production* of the epoch,"[14] the decisive question of history can be raised, and the Goethean criticism met. What are the sources which provide the material for answering this question? "*The epoch-making events, the understanding of memorials, and the investigation of institutions constitute the backbone of history.*"[15]

And, now, returning to the *fons et origo*, one further quality must be stressed as an essential—indeed *the* essential—mark of the exemplary historian. In order to represent the facts properly, a historian must possess the practical wisdom which can grasp the inner relationships between facts, and a "rich, deep, and many-sided wisdom and experience of his own which he brings to the interpretation of the material."[16] A reflexive relationship is here involved: the wisdom and experience of the historian clarifies and arranges the historical material, and, in turn, the material strengthens his wisdom. He then can determine that which may still be useful from the past, declare what is to be done in the present, and how one may prepare responsibly for the future. These are the minimal conditions for gaining certainty in history.

Yet these "minimal conditions," viewed as a totality, may impress the less universal man as being impossible to fulfill. Especially when one considers the valency of "rich, deep, and many-sided wisdom and experience," the conditions seem appalling. Harnack was not unaware that his model historian must be a paragon of wisdom and virtue. In fact, as he became more involved in "culture" himself, his own pyramidal career manifested an increasing catholicity of interest; so much was this the case that Troeltsch rightly saw him as turning more and more toward idealistic philosophical tenets. Harnack's 1913 lecture, *Über Wissenschaftliche Erkenntnis*, bears directly on this point:

Just as Goethe, in his investigation of nature, remained certain of his main points (in spite of the mistakes that he made) because he knew

[14] *Ibid.*, p. 14.
[15] *Ibid.*, p. 15.
[16] *Ibid.*, p. 19.

the direction and the road; just as he avoided pessimism, internal schism, and uncertainty with regard to his knowledge—at the same time that he avoided arrogant certainty, fanaticism, and impudence—so Ranke also could always be positive in his investigation of history because he was guided by the conjectural and directional evidence which he had divined from his view of history. To be sure, the problems of historical knowledge are complicated not only because we are dealing with elemental questions and with freedom, but because we must deal with entirely new problems regarding norms and values. . . . There are some color-blind monists who perceive nothing in history except a canon of force and declare all ethics to be out of date; but even in this "monist century" Hildebrand recently opposed the editor Ostwald and spoke out for the obligatory demand of the old duties and virtues even if this demands the sacrifice of life. Indeed, those who oppose the great guiding ideas of goodness, love, and self-sacrifice resemble a swarm of gnats flying against a window. Nor is one able to tear out of one's heart the ideas of sin and guilt, atonement and forgiveness, punishment and vicariousness, regardless of the difference of conception and evaluation and regardless of their point of origin; for they are the greatest advances of the spirit which structures his highest life. . . .

Is there a still higher level? Assuredly. There still remains the task of investigating the whole in its totality, of understanding mechanism, life, ethics, history and, indeed, the spiritual instruments of investigation themselves which lead to this knowledge. This is the task of philosophy. To be sure in the last two generations numerous philosophers have abstracted from this task one piece after another, and nothing more remains for this kind of investigation than that kind of psychology which we share with the apes, a thin theory of knowledge, and logic. But as soon as a real philosopher arises, a Plato, Aristotle, Spinoza, Kant, Schopenhauer, Hegel, or Hartmann, he sweeps all the insufficient and paltry fabrications into a corner. A true philosophy begins where all other disciplines have finished their work, where we set out to unite and to find a higher unity of mechanism and life, external and internal life, object and subject.

It has been said that it is impossible to solve such a task, because the greatest minds have tried and failed. Failed? To be sure, they have not found the formula by which mechanism, life and spirit can be explained in its unity. But does that mean they have labored in vain? Let us look at the ascending history of our race and at the history of culture! That which has raised us to higher levels, aside from the message of the great founders of religions, was the intellectual labor of men who looked at the whole under the dominion of the inner life, the spirit, and its norms. Mankind has not found its way upward by the brilliant torches of quantitatively testable individual cognitions, but under the guidance of men who posited a central sun and had the courage to press on from physics to metaphysics, from history to metahistory, from ethics to meta-ethics. They also had the courage to subordinate the whole to the norms and values which they had recognized in their intellectual life and thus to recognize in mechanism and unconscious life the means and foundation of a given and yet growing realm of freedom and goodness. Their every observation led them to something eternal and infinite, to problems which lie behind the world accessible to our powers of imagination, to the necessity for modes of thought which go beyond transparent concepts. But as bold sailors they set their sails and dared the trip on the endless ocean; for in contrast of those of faint heart they felt that at least they had found *their* way. All the coasts that they saw turned out to be deceptive, but the *direction* in which they traveled was still the right one; for as often as they returned to their fellow-man they brought back to them an enhancement of life.[17]

The complexity of Harnack's conception and method is apparent. An attempt at summary would issue in something like the following: Historical knowledge is knowledge of the material and spiritual structure of past life, to be seen as the progressive concretion of the spirit and its mastery of material circumstances. Such progression is undoubtedly present, but it is not inevitable. The historian should proceed to his task with a frank admission of the limits of historical knowledge, and should seek insofar as possible to root out all preconceptions and prejudices; he would further be well advised to seek the truth in the "mean" rather than the extreme. History is to be studied in order to intervene in the course of history and prepare for the future in a responsible way. The extent to which one becomes effectively engaged in that responsible action which is the purpose of historical study will be determined by: his possession of a "practical wisdom" which can grasp the inner relationships between facts, and of a "rich, deep, and many-sided wisdom of life" which contributes to and is continually strengthened by historical investigation; his philological and critical competence in the use of the sources; his attention to and ability to assess the elementary, cultural, and individual factors as embodied in the memorials, events, and institutions of history; his ability to identify the *Geist* of an epoch as seen in the powers operative in it and the direction and result of it, all this being possible because "the same mind is at work in history and in us"; and his fidelity and power in representing the facts.

[17] *RA*, III, NF, pp. 197–200.

X

Marcion, das Evangelium vom fremden Gott

To WHAT extent was Harnack successful, in his own historiography, in practicing what he preached? The evidence for answering this question might be sought generally, in his total corpus. It lies at hand, however, in a most paradigmatic way, in the monograph to which he gave sustained attention throughout his life: the *Marcion*. The six "steps" involved in his conception of history and his method will be assayed, therefore, against this model.

We have already remarked that Harnack's "affair with Marcion" had begun in his student years at Dorpat. Here, in 1870, he had won a prize in a competition whose problem was "Marcion's Doctrine as Represented and Explicated in Tertullian's *Adversus Marcion*." So impressed were the faculty by this effort that they not only gave Harnack the gold medal in the competition; they also suggested that he revise and publish the essay. Harnack did: fifty years later! As he put it, "I kept the subject in mind and broadened it."[1] When the "broadened" work was published, in 1920, it contained 623 pages.

[1] *Marcion, . . .*, p. iii.

One can say without fear of contradiction that it contained every shred of evidence then extant regarding the man from Pontus.

"The possession of a 'practical wisdom' which can grasp the inner relationships between facts, and of a 'rich, deep, and many-sided wisdom of life' which contributes to and is continually strengthened by historical investigation."

Whether or not Harnack possessed these qualities is, in the final analysis, a matter of judgment on the part of the interpreter. On the basis of the evidence, not simply the *Marcion*, but a life of "theological vocation" and "scientific" work, it is unreasonable to doubt that he possessed what he lauded. One can advert to Friedrich Smend's *Adolf von Harnack, Verzeichnis seiner Schriften*,[2] with its more than sixteen hundred entries, to substantiate the point; one can, of course, also refer to the cultural and scientific organizations of which Harnack was an active member. *This* quality, in any case, does not lend itself to demonstration of an explicit sort. Let him who has a bibliography of 1611 entries deny it to Harnack!

"Philological and critical competence in the use of the sources."

The reader is advised to leaf the pages of the *Marcion* in order to encounter at first hand what may here appear to be only a cataloguing of data. The ten appendices, taking up 358 pages, include the following: On Marcion's life: eleven "certain" and three "uncertain" witnesses; on Cerdo: eight witnesses; on the development of Marcion's doctrine, and on the Marcionite Church: in the first two centuries, twenty witnesses; in the third century, sixteen "certain" and four "uncertain" witnesses; from the fourth century, thirty-four eastern witnesses and nineteen western witnesses. *Und so weiter!* In addition, one of the appendices reconstructs Marcion's *Apostolikon*, and another reconstructs Marcion's *Evangelium*—these reconstructions carried out, of course, on the basis of the evidence provided by the "witnesses" Harnack cited. There is also, in the main body of the work itself, a reconstruction of the *Antitheses*, of which Harnack remarks that "it is certain that no other work besides the *Antitheses*, written by Marcion himself, is known."[3]

It is in connection with this reconstruction of the *Antitheses* that we can indicate the nature of Harnack's "source-work," and identify thereby a problem which later scholars have not failed to notice. In

[2] Axel von Harnack, one of Adolf's sons, indicates that it is not at all certain but that Smend missed some items. But the point is gratuitous.

[3] *Marcion*, . . . , p. 68.

Harnack's reconstruction, he remarks that the work "probably" contained a dedication, and cites Tertullian as his source.[4] It also contained, he believed, a prologue, the famous "O Wunder über Wunder, Verzückung, Macht und Staunen ist. . . ," for which Harnack cites as his source an early Syrian anti-Marcionite source.[5] There then follows in Harnack's reconstruction three pages of references on the relation of Paul to the early apostles (Marcion judged that Paul regarded them as "false brethren"), for which Harnack cites Irenaeus eight times and Tertullian eighteen times.[6] Later, to use one more example, Harnack's documentation of the antithesis between Christ's "knowing the thoughts of men" while the Old Testament God asks Adam, "Where are you?" includes one certain and one probable reference from Origen, one from Jerome, and thirteen from Tertullian.[7]

The source-work has been done: that is certain. But has it been, if possible, too well done? Is Grant not correct when he says "Had Harnack not collected every possible witness to Marcion's teaching, including some which are highly improbable, we should not have so many opinions about Marcion, but we might have more knowledge."[8] Specifically (and this is a most ambiguous kind of question to raise), did Harnack depend far too much on Tertullian in constructing his basic thesis about Marcion, as in reconstructing the *Antitheses*, the *Apostolikon*, and the *Evangelium*? Particularly when one discovers, as Burkitt made clear, that Tertullian plagiarized his own third book *Against Marcion* when he wrote his treatise *Against the Jews*,[9] and adds the evidence of Quispel[10] that this third book was already a plagiarization of Justin's *Dialogue with Trypho*, the question which Grant has asked becomes troubling. The locus of the malaise, however, is not at the point of "source-study." No one in his right mind would fault a scholar for completeness. The question is whether something in the way of a prior "wisdom of life" was operating, a judgment with respect to the validity of Marcion's religion, to which the collection of the data was *not* foundation, but embellishment. Cer-

[4] *Ibid.*, p. 81.

[5] *Ibid.*

[6] *Ibid.*, pp. 81–84.

[7] *Ibid.*, pp. 93–94.

[8] Robert Grant, book review of E. C. Blackman, *Marcion and His Influence* (London: S. P. C. K., 1948), in the *Review of Religion* (Jan. 1950), p. 176.

[9] F. C. Burkitt, *The Gospel History and Its Transmission* (Edinburgh: T. & T. Clark, 1906), pp. 306–307.

[10] Gilles Quispel, *De Bronnen van Tertullianus' Adversus Marcionem* (Leiden: Burgersdijk & Niermans-Templum Salomonis, 1943).

tainly Harnack would have been horrified at such a suggestion; and after much chiding at this point by the critics, he issued a revised edition and, through the *Texte und Untersuchungen* series, wrote a *Neue Studien zu Marcion.*[11]

"Attention to and ability to assess the elementary, cultural, and individual factors as embodied in the memorials, events, and institutions of history."

Harnack's "sources" for the study of Marcion were, of course, mainly literary. The qualifying adjective is necessary only if one accepts Harnack's own final judgment that Marcion's influence, albeit a negative one in his time, had carried over into the institutions of the great Church, manifesting itself in canon, creed, and organization. Positively, the Marcionite church had disappeared, and its organization and constitution could not, therefore, be studied. The factors which one must attend to and assess, therefore, must be discovered in the literary heritage.

Harnack's attention to these factors is clearly marked in the organization of the work itself. Setting, climate, natural conditions, and physical and mental givens are dealt with in his chapters on "The Religious and Historical Presuppositions of Marcion's Christian Preaching, and the Internal Situation of Christianity at the Beginning of His Work"[12] and on "Marcion's Life and Work."[13] There is little in the work having to do with art and science, and only allusions to customs, but, in the chapters "The Holy Church of the Redeemed and Its Regimen (Cultus, Organization and Ethic)"[14] and "The History of the Marcionite Church,"[15] Harnack deals with that institution within which tradition, religion, and ethics were embodied. It is certainly the last factor, the "individual" one, which is given primary attention in the work. Harnack here considers, successively, "Marcion's Starting-Point: Law and Gospel; Salvation from the World, the Law, and the Creator";[16] "The Critic and Restorer. Marcion's Bible";[17] "Marcion's *Antitheses*";[18] and "Marcion's Christianity and His Preaching."[19]

It is Harnack's judgment, of course, that he is dealing with one of

[11] (Leipzig: Hinrichs, 1923).
[12] *Marcion*, . . . , pp. 1–20.
[13] *Ibid.*, pp. 20–27.
[14] *Ibid.*, pp. 181–190.
[15] *Ibid.*, pp. 191–230.
[16] *Ibid.*, pp. 27–32.
[17] *Ibid.*, pp. 32–68.
[18] *Ibid.*, pp. 68–135.
[19] *Ibid.*, pp. 135–181.

the great men of Christian history, "who comes when he comes." It is difficult to assent to this judgment, particularly in the light of later scholarship on Marcion,[20] but also when one considers the troubling question as to whether Harnack did not indeed "put his own flesh and blood" into this second-century form. Yet it remains patently true that for Harnack, Marcion was one of the geniuses of Christian history: whether one cites his comparison of Marcion with Paul and Augustine,[21] or with Luther,[22] or with Schleiermacher,[23] the fact that this is the "league" in which Harnack places Marcion makes clear his judgment.

"Ability to identify the Geist of an epoch as seen in the powers operative in it and the direction and result of it, all this being possible because 'the same mind is at work in history and in us.'"

There were powers at work in Marcion's great Idea, and the direction which his work took produced results which became embodied in institutions. It is the task of the historian to unravel this tapestry, to work back through the institutions to the Idea which brought them into being. As we have remarked, what has come down to us is the Christian literature, and the continuing influence, whatever its nature, on the great Church. It is in the literature that one finds Marcion's Idea, the redeeming Idea—"Gospel." That this was true Harnack demonstrates by citing many explicit references; in addition, he calls attention to the fact that what Marcion allowed to remain in Luke after he had practiced his "exegesis by excision" makes quite obvious what he regarded as the central part of the Gospel. One explicit reference which Harnack cites is the opening line of the Prologue to the *Antitheses*: "O wonder beyond wonder! what ecstasy, power, and astonishment lies here, that one is able to say nothing of the Gospel, nor even to think of it, nor to compare it to anything whatsoever."[24] In fact, the whole of the *Antitheses*, and the very fact that he wrote

[20] In addition to Blackman, *op. cit.*, and Quispel, *op. cit.*, the following works may be cited: R. S. Wilson, *Marcion: A Study of a Second Century Heretic* (London: James Clarke and Company, 1932); John Knox, *Marcion and the New Testament* (Chicago: University of Chicago Press, 1942); Robert Grant, *Second Century Christianity* (London: S. P. C. K., 1946); and numerous articles by Rendel Harris, A. Loisy, R. B. Tollinton, etc. Hans von Soden wrote a negative review of Harnack's *Marcion* in the *Deutsche Literaturzeitung* (1921, pp. 44–61), in which, with some sarcasm, he accuses Harnack of placing Marcion in the succession of the prophets, Jesus and Paul.

[21] *Marcion, . . . ,* p. v.

[22] *Ibid.*, p. 25.

[23] *Ibid.*, p. 220.

[24] *Ibid.*, p. 81.

them and gave them this title, is an indication of Marcion's belief in the radical disparity between the Law and the Gospel. Tertullian is called as a witness to Marcion's "Paulinism"—at least in his emphasis on the Gospel—where, in a scornful denunciation of Marcion's denial of the wrath of God, Tertullian asks why Marcion does not then indulge his lusts. Yet even this unfriendly witness testifies that Marcion declared "Absit!" to all such antinomian suggestions.[25] A person who experiences grace does not act this way.

Harnack had summed up in another place the result of his search for the dominating Idea which Marcion preached, and in terms of which he must be understood:

To Marcion belongs the credit of having extracted the opposition between Gospel and Law from Paul's Epistles, and of having formulated it for all time. In Paul it is only implicit. . . . Only Marcion discovered it. According to Tertullian and Irenaeus, there can be no doubt that it was just in the contrast between Law and Gospel that he expressed the distinction between the old and the new religion. It is also clear that he used the word not only for the written Gospel, which he had put together for himself from Luke and which he entitled simply 'Ευαγγέλιον, but also for the whole content of the new religion as distinguished from all that was legal. In Marcion as in Paul "gospel" and "salvation" must have stood in the closest relation to one another; echoes of this are still heard in Apelles. The fundamental distinction discovered by Paul between the religion founded on faith, and the religion of the Old Testament, was now imparted into the expression "Gospel and Law."[26]

The point we are here concerned to make is clear enough: that the way in which Harnack wrote history was to seize, on the basis of critical study, that basic Idea which a particular person (or movement, or epoch) manifested, and then to identify its power, chart its direction, and describe its result.

"Fidelity and power in representing the facts."

It is this step which, if it is not effectively carried out, will seriously limit the value of a particular historian's work. And it is a difficult step, for only one who possesses practical wisdom and "rich, deep, *Lebensweisheit*" can represent the facts properly.

An example of Harnack's attempt to achieve the desired result, combining factual knowledge with a double wisdom, is to be found

[25] Harnack, *Neue Studien . . .*, p. 8.

[26] *The Constitution and Law of the Church in the First Two Centuries*, tr. F. L. Pogson; H. D. A. Major, ed. (New York: G. P. Putnam's Sons, 1910), pp. 331–332.

in his account of the famous meeting between the Roman presbyters which led to Marcion's expulsion from the Church.[27] Harnack concludes his account of this incident with these words: "It will remain noteworthy forever that at the first Roman Synod of which we know, a man stood before the presbyters and set forth to them the distinction between Law and Gospel, and pronounced their Christianity to be Judaistic. Who could help but think of Luther at this point!"[28] Harnack is not content here simply to report the fact that Marcion raised a good question, probably an embarrassing one, as to the meaning of the pericopes dealing with the wine-skins and the garments; that the presbyters responded with an answer which, according to Epiphanius, interpreted the Pharisees' hearts as the old skins, and Judas as the old garment who caused a rent in the circle of the Twelve; and that Marcion, rejecting this interpretation in favor of one emphasizing the radical disparity and absolute discontinuity of the Old and the New, declared, "I will rend your Church, and put a rent in her forever."[29] Rather, Harnack calls up for comparison an event which would be more freighted with overtones of value for his readers than any other possible event. And this would be true not only positively of Marcion as compared by Harnack to Luther, but negatively of the presbyters as compared with the antagonistic Diet of Worms, representing the legalism of the medieval Catholic Church. Yet, without denying that Harnack recognized what an effect such a comparison would have in evoking favor for Marcion, there is no reason to doubt that he believed that it was historically justifiable so to represent Marcion. The question that must be put to Harnack at this point would be whether he had brought to his study more of a presupposition than he would have admitted with respect to this "Gospel" which Marcion was preaching. We believe that this is actually the case; and that the Idea which he finds in Marcion and which he makes the basis for his "representation of the facts," is so warmly lauded just because it fits Harnack's own conception.

As to the other aspect of the desideratum, fidelity, one is permitted therefore to say only that Harnack was faithful to *his own conception* of history and its method. What we see in *Marcion* in this respect is no isolated phenomenon: this was the method which he

[27] In the full meaning of this step, one could cite the whole of this work. However, an example will better illustrate it.

[28] *Marcion*, . . . , pp. 24–25.

[29] Harold Smith, *Ante-Nicene Exegesis of the Gospels* (London: S. P. C. K., 1925), I, pp. 13–14.

practiced in all of his historiography. Challenging his "fidelity" therefore would be tantamount to challenging his whole way of looking at life and history. This has been done, as we shall see immediately.

"Action."

The final step, one which many would question as properly belonging to the specific vocation of the church historian, is to use all the previous steps "in order to overcome history." The historian is not a dilettante; he is not studying history "for the sake of history"; he is not simple enough to believe that the task of the historian is to represent "wie es gewesen ist"; he is not interested simply in knowing facts. *Why* would he study the past, then? "We would learn to know the material and spiritual structure of past life, and we would understand it as the progressive concretion of the spirit and therefore as the progressive mastery of the material circumstances of life."[30] Men study history in order to overcome history, which means "to accept one's fate, to love it, and to turn it into something better."[31] The final step is to act with cultural responsibility in terms of the situation within which one finds oneself, utilizing all of that knowledge which the previous steps have supplied.

The most famous judgment in the *Marcion* provides an excellent example of what Harnack means. In a discussion of antinomianism and the value of the Old Testament for contemporary men, he makes this assertion:

> The rejection of the Old Testament in the second century was a mistake which the great Church rightly refused to make; the retention of it in the sixteenth century was due to a fatal legacy which the Reformation was not yet able to overcome; but for Protestantism since the nineteenth century to continue to treasure it as a canonical document is the result of a religious and ecclesiastical paralysis.[32]

In the same chapter, in a discussion of the "gospel of the strange God," other judgments illustrative of this same point are made: (1) "*The concept of faith which Luther held is really very close to that of the Marcionites*";[33] (2) "He preached . . . the new God. In Christ, and only there, he had experienced the new God; *therefore he elevated the historical reality of the Christian experience to the zenith*";[34] and, drawing these judgments together with a final recommendation,

[30] Harnack, "Über die Sicherheit . . . ," *RA*, IV, NF, p. 5.
[31] Harnack, "Ernst Troeltsch," *ibid.*, p. 365.
[32] *Marcion*, . . . , pp. 248–249.
[33] *Ibid.*, p. 256.
[34] *Ibid.*, p. 259.

"One could only wish that one could find some Marcionites in the multitude of God-seekers yet today."[35] The last affirmation confirmed in some minds the suspicion "that something resembling the Marcionite Church would satisfy the ideal which a great many now hold of the Church of the future. Dr. Harnack has described a form of Christianity essentially subjective, more dependent upon individual experience than upon any historic faith."[36]

In a valuable background description, Harnack's daughter has related something of Harnack's purpose in publishing the *Marcion* when he did, and here also one may see the emphasis on the "responsible action" which constitutes this final duty of the historian. Posing the questions, "Why was this book completed just at this time, in the revolutionary crises and the post-war need, and why did it evoke such a deep response, particularly in lay-circles which stood at this time in no close relation to scientific theology?"[37] she then suggests three answers: Marcion had preached the "strange God," the God who had nothing in common with this sorrowful, ill-conceived creation, or with the general history which takes place within this creation, and this was natively attractive to those who had lived through the war and the revolution; Marcion had also preached the coming of the Redeemer who is love and nothing but love, who would save man from the bondage of the Law and from the evil and the travail in the created world; and Marcion had thrown out the Old Testament with its Law in favor of the Gospel alone, while the contemporary Church, as a result of a "religious and ecclesiastical paralysis" was trying to hold on to it.[38] The responsible action which *should* have been taken, but was not, is then described, with the consequences of inaction indicated:

> Religious and ecclesiastical paralysis—this was what countless earnest Christians felt in these years. . . . It is tragic that the Church at this time, as it undertook the process of rebuilding, could not find the power to free itself from dogmatism, and to place the entire Old Testament under the same valuation which Luther had given to the Apocrypha, as "good and profitable to read," but not to regard it as Holy Scripture; how much difficult contemporary strife it would have spared itself through such a decisive and honest deed.[39]

[35] *Ibid.*, p. 265.

[36] F. J. Foakes-Jackson, *Christian Difficulties in the Second and Twentieth Centuries* (Cambridge: W. Heffer and Sons, 1903), pp. 138–139.

[37] AZH, p. 511.

[38] *Ibid.*, pp. 511–513.

[39] *Ibid.*, p. 513.

One of the reasons why "such a decisive and honest deed" was not effected lay in the response to Harnack's recommendation by his own liberal colleagues, as well as the orthodox. Though there was enthusiasm for the way in which he had treated the sources, for his careful and complete evaluation of all the references, and for the genius of his historiography, his liberal critics saw also "that he had given his own blood to this spirit from a nether world, and called it again into life. It appeared to them as if Harnack had himself become a Marcionite."[40] Particularly, Harnack's estimate of the place which the Old Testament should henceforth hold was challenged. Loofs, reminding Harnack of Harnack's own knowledge of the shaping power of tradition, finds it inconceivable that Harnack had really meant what he said.[41] Holl, also, admitting the difficulties of "reading the Old Testament to the children in evening worship," held that the situation was not much different than it was in the second century: "We must keep the Old Testament in order to use it, and the New Testament, in freedom."[42] Interestingly enough, the most laudatory statements came from the laity. Harnack's daughter chose one from the "many witnesses," a Heidelberg interne by the name of von Krehl, to speak for all:

This man's passion for God has touched me at the deepest level of my being; it strengthens us and gives us new courage. . . . There is a unity in the knowledge which your Excellency preaches, and it is this: that we, both in our practical activity and in our science, must proclaim the hidden God.[43]

[40] *Ibid.*
[41] *Ibid.*, pp. 513–514.
[42] *Ibid.*, p. 514.
[43] *Ibid.*

XI

The Dogmengeschichte

"I AM far from disparaging the historical importance which belongs to the Tübingen school. . . . the main problem, the rise of Catholicism, was first rightly defined by this school as problem . . ."[1]

These words were spoken by Harnack a year before the appearance of the first volume of his *Dogmengeschichte*. What had been adumbrated in all of his study thus far, and what was clearly expressed in his lecture on "The Present State of Research in Early Church History," comes, in a sense, to fulfillment in the History of Dogma. It is interesting to note in passing that the judgment of a contemporary Lutheran scholar reinforces Harnack's (and therefore Baur's) definition of the problem. Pelikan cites "the issue of the relation between Judaism and primitive Christianity," "the analogies between early Christianity and its Gentile environment," and "the origins of Christian polity and . . . the Roman claims to primacy," as well as "the nature of the apostolic ministry and the legitimacy of Catholic Christianity"[2] as examples of Harnack's correct *questions*.

Harnack was thoroughly aware of the difficulty of treating such a subject as the history of dogma. This awareness was deepened as a result of the critiques of the early editions of the *Dogmengeschichte*,

[1] Harnack, "The Present State of Research . . . ," *RA*, II, p. 220.
[2] Introduction to Harnack, *The Mission and Expansion* . . . , p. v.

as is evident from the attention he gives to these critiques in later editions; in the third edition, a number of significant prefaces and expansions of the text itself directly refer to and attempt to answer his critics. The second edition of the first volume, issued only two years after the first, had already taken account of one of these criticisms, in which an unnamed critic had opined that the chapter on "Presuppositions" was inappropriate. In answer, Harnack *expanded* this section, asking his readers "not to forget how difficult, both intrinsically and because of the nature of the sources, the questions there considered are, and how the historian who attempts to state his position on them exposes himself to criticism."[3] The questions he had dealt with in the chapter on "Presuppositions" were not methodological or introspective in nature; they were questions substantive to his basic thesis itself, according to which there is no dogma, strictly speaking, in the earliest period of the history of Christianity. To these intrinsically difficult questions we shall return presently.

There is no better way to study Harnack's *Dogmengeschichte* than the way Harnack adopted in studying dogma. That requires a study of the source itself, the identification of the predominating Idea, and the representation of the facts.

Before he embarks on the actual subject itself, Harnack deals with a number of fundamental questions in a chapter on "Prolegomena." He defines the term "dogma" and describes the task of the historian of it, he presents a brief history of dogma, and he discusses the division and the principles of organization of the work.

"Dogmas are the doctrines of Christian faith (the knowledge of God, the world, and the activity of God in behalf of man's salvation) as these have been logically formulated and expressed for scientific and apologetic purposes."[4] The Christian Church looks upon these dogmas as revealed truths from Holy Scriptures, but actually, they

[3] *Lehrbuch der Dogmengeschichte,* Drei Bände, Dritte Auflage, verbesserte und vermehrte (Leipzig: Mohr, 1894 and 1897), I, p. viii. Hereafter all references to this work will be designated *DG,* with the appropriate volume numbers following. We have already referred (Chap. VIII, note 40) to the Neil Buchanan translation of this work. It is not a usable translation, and all subsequent translations from the *Dogmengeschichte* will be my own. This is an appropriate place to indicate the "history" of the editions of the DG: Vol. I, 1st ed., 1886, 2nd ed., 1888, 3rd ed., 1894, 4th ed., 1909; Vol. II, 1st ed., 1887, 2nd ed., 1888, 3rd ed., 1894, 4th ed., 1909; Vol. III, 1st and 2nd ed., 1890, 3rd ed., 1897, 4th ed., 1910 and 1920.

[4] *Ibid.*, p. 3.

were not possessed from the beginning. This inevitably raises two questions: what is the origin of these dogmas, and how can the development of these dogmas be adequately described?

In this definition of Christian dogma, several elements are taken into account: the fact that "dogma is always based on an authority" and the resulting recognition "that a social element is introduced into the concept of dogma: those who confess the same dogma form a community."[5] But even the inclusion of these two elements does not give a complete picture of the real nature of Christian dogma:

> What Protestants and Catholics call dogmas are not only ecclesiastical doctrines, but they are also (1) *conceptually expressed theses which, taken together, form a unity; these theses establish the contents of the Christian religion as a knowledge of God, of the world, and of sacred history as demonstrated truths; but further,* (2) *these theses have emerged at a definite stage in the history of the Christian religion; in the way in which they are conceived, and in many details, they show the influence of this stage, viz., the Greek period, and they have preserved this character in all later epochs in spite of qualifications and additions.*[6]

Seen in this way, the Christian religion seems to parallel the ancient philosophical schools. But the difference lies in the fact that Christianity has, by its inclusion within its system of an authoritative principle, "eliminated the process of thought which led to the dogma, represented the total dogma as a revelation, and . . . has not taken account of the powers of the human understanding"[7] which led to the promulgation of the dogma.

The conclusion at which Harnack arrives is unequivocally clear:

> Dogmatic Christianity is therefore a definite step in the historical development of Christianity; it corresponds to the ancient mode of thought, and continues in large measure into subsequent epochs, though undergoing some variations. Between that Christianity which one sees in the Gospel, based on personal experience and having to do with motives and deeds, and that Christianity which one sees as a religion of cultus, sacraments, ceremony, and obedience—in short, superstition—stands dogmatic Christianity, which can unite with either of the others.[8]

Since dogmatic Christianity is in essence intellectual Christianity, it always stands in danger of substituting knowledge for religious faith,

[5] *Ibid.*, p. 15.
[6] *Ibid.*, pp. 15–16.
[7] *Ibid.*, p. 16.
[8] *Ibid.*

confusing faith and doctrine, and failing to base faith on God and living experience.

It was the Reformation, particularly Luther, which in principle overcame this, and it did so by insisting on the primacy of faith. The purpose of the historian of dogma is to complete that which began with the Reformation, to discern what the Christian religion originally was, and to compare the history of dogma to this original Gospel. How is one to study this subject in order to achieve this purpose?

The answer, of course, is that dogma must be studied historically. Until the eighteenth century, no attempt had been made to carry out such a study, nor, indeed, was it practically possible. In the early and medieval Church, and in modern Roman Catholicism, dogma was regarded as unchangeable. Though the Protestant Reformation *theoretically* made possible a critical treatment of the history of dogma, the subservience of historical investigation to confessional standards in the Protestant churches of the sixteenth and seventeenth centuries prevented the attempt. The sources, however, were collected and edited during these centuries, and when the Pietistic challenge to confessional requirements emerged, the time was ripe for a critical investigation. Mosheim, "the Erasmus of the eighteenth century,"[9] pioneered in this work. In his impartial and methodical work, he raised church history to the rank of a science; but to avoid controversy, he devoted himself to church history proper rather than to the history of dogma. Walch, in the sixth decade of the eighteenth century, focused attention on the history of dogma as a special discipline, but his standpoint was still under the domination of ecclesiastical dogma. Harnack interprets the rationalism which dominated the mid-eighteenth century as a necessary though triflng reaction against the past. It was necessary because the central dogmas "on which Protestant system as well as that of the Catholic rests" could be challenged only on the basis of "the absolute certainty which rationalism had found in the religious philosophy of this era."[10] It was trifling because the rationalists lacked in large measure the requisites of sound historical work: knowledge of the subject, candid criticism, and the power of understanding alien ideas. By challenging the dogmas of canon, inspiration, the Trinity, and Christology, however, the rationalists made necessary a historical-critical examination of the received dogma. Semler adumbrated this in his important

[9] *Ibid.*, p. 26.
[10] *Ibid.*, p. 29.

work, but it was S. G. Lange who first sought to treat this subject as a separate and special discipline. He did not complete his work, and Münscher became the first to produce a complete history of dogma. Unfortunately, he employed a *loci* method, which could not help obscuring the subject, and he failed to evaluate sufficiently the relation between the developing dogma and the historical situation.

With the opening of the nineteenth century, a spiritual revolution occurred, of such proportions that all phases of church historical scholarship were affected. Rationalism broke down under the triple impact of Schleiermacher, the Hegelians, and the confessional revival. What these tendencies had in common was

> the attempt really to understand history, and to learn from it, i.e., to permit the idea of development to come to its rightful place, and to grasp the fact of the individual's power and possibility; in this, in the deepened conception of the essence and the meaning of positive religion lay the great advance beyond rationalism.[11]

Yet here also there was a fateful debility; for the obsession to understand history fathered a carelessness with respect to facts. Speculation transcended factualness, "the immanent unfolding of the spirit" precluded scientific history, and led to the erroneous identification of religion with theology rather than faith. Such a speculative procedure was almost worse than rationalism; the latter threw out the baby with the bath, but to neglect the faith and keep the theology is to throw out the baby and keep the bath. Even Baur, for whom Harnack employs his most laudatory adjectives, was misleading at this point; but he did "give a unified general interpretation of the history of dogma, and attempted to enter into the whole process in his own experience, without thereby giving up the critical achievements of the eighteenth century."[12] His abstract view of history was remedied by Neander, but in regressing to a *loci* method, Neander failed to take account of the historical character of dogma and its developmental progress. Kliefoth, the representative of the confessional theology, attempted to interpret dogma in such a way as to legitimize a return to the theology of the Fathers. Thomasius of Erlangen paid insufficient attention to the history of the era in which dogma arose, in many ways depending on the Hegelian notion of the unfolding of that which is immanent within the dogma itself. Nitzsch represented a real advance by his faithful attention to the monographs

[11] *Ibid.*, p. 32.
[12] *Ibid.*, p. 33.

that have been prepared in this area, but more importantly, by the arrangement of his work. For "in the main divisions: 'The Establishment of the Old Catholic Church Doctrine' and 'The Development of the Old Catholic Church Doctrine,' the most important problem with which the history of dogma is concerned is finally given its just rights."[13] Nitzsch was free of that speculative obsession which reads ideas into the history of dogma, thereby concentrating on philosophical and theological points and neglecting the more important aspect, the expression of religious faith.

The direction for the future in this discipline, Harnack believed, must be that of concentration on the history of the dogma itself, deliberately extruding present prejudices, but at the same time paying the closest attention to the history of the Church. Progress will depend upon "an accurate understanding of what the Christian religion originally was; for only this understanding permits us to distinguish that which was born out of the original strength of Christianity from that which was assimilated to it in the course of its history."[14] For the purpose of criticizing the history of dogma, two standards are possible: "Either (one) compares the history of dogma—insofar as this is possible—to the Gospel, or he judges it according to the historical circumstances of the time and the result."[15] It is Harnack's judgment that Protestantism must recognize the first standard.

The Gospel, therefore must be identified; for it is "on the ground of the Gospel" that dogma was conceived and developed. Once the Gospel has been identified, one can go on to study dogma in the same way that the canon has been studied: first to ask how it originated, and then to consider its development. Harnack admits that to divide the history in this way implies a precision which can be misleading, for the two rather "merge into one another."[16] However, a final point of division can be set, and it is that point at which some particular article of faith was declared by the Church to be obligatory on all believers. This happened at about the end of the third or the beginning of the fourth century.

Harnack divided his description of the *origin* of dogma into two parts: the preparation (roughly from 50–150 A.D.), and the laying of the foundations (roughly from 150–260). His description of the *development* of dogma is divided into three parts. First, dogma is

[13] *Ibid.*, p. 36.
[14] *Ibid.*, p. 39.
[15] *Ibid.*
[16] *Ibid.*, p. 3.

represented as theology and Christology and this development takes place in the period of the great Councils. The Eastern Church has never gone beyond this stage. Secondly, dogma, as interpreted by Augustine, is given a "churchly" basis, and is expanded and remodeled by introducing sin, grace, and the means of grace as the fundamental concepts. Augustine's purpose of joining old and new was of the highest significance, since he did this within the context of the Church *qua* institution. As this institution developed and shaped itself into a legal, political entity, the operative power really resided in it rather than in the dogmas. Thus one has the strange anomaly of an accepted *dogma* without practical efficacious power, and an undeclared "dogma" of an authoritative papacy and Church which did exert this power. The third stage of the development of dogma began with the Reformation. Two tasks are incumbent on the historian of dogma with respect to this third stage: "To present the Roman dogma as the product of the medieval-ecclesiastical development under the influence of the rival Reformation faith," and "to portray the conservative new form which original Protestantism shows to us, and to define its relation to dogma."[17] For, with the setting forth by the Reformers of a repristinated Paulinism and Augustinianism, the whole ecclesiastical tradition, including dogma, underwent a revision. This revision issued from the fact that the Reformers insisted on grounding the dogmas they retained in the Scriptures—in this, indeed, they did not differ from the Roman Catholics—but the principle of authority which they found within these scriptures devalued or entirely rejected the tradition. Furthermore, they questioned the Roman conception of the place of the empirical Church with relation to dogma, and "they tried to put forward a formulation of the Christian religion which went back to a pure understanding of the Word of God."[18] The result was that they effected a threefold "issue": Roman Catholicism, which retained dogma, albeit developed, *as* dogma; Anti-Trinitarianism and Socinianism, which rejected dogma completely; and Protestantism, which in principle rejected dogma, but lacked the historical understanding so to assess it.

With respect to the principles on the basis of which his History of Dogma will be written, Harnack declares that it is impossible to state *in abstracto* what these principles are; "for general rules to keep the ignorant from overlooking that which is important or fastening

[17] *Ibid.*, p. 7.

[18] Harnack, *Dogmengeschichte*, Vierte Auflage, verbesserte (Tübingen: Mohr, 1905), p. 3.

on the unimportant cannot be set forth."[19] Yet the way in which the material is arranged is crucial, and any true understanding of the history of dogma will depend upon finding the rules according to which the material ought to be grouped. Harnack warns, initially, against any attempt to interpret the history of dogma which does not take into account all of those diverse factors which were operating in the process of origin and development. In addition to the attempt to define doctrine according to the salvation which it gives, these following factors present in the process of the formation of Christian dogma must be considered:

(1) The concepts and sayings contained in the canonical Scriptures; (2) the doctrinal tradition produced in an earlier period of the Church, but no longer understood; (3) the requirements of cultus and polity; (4) the effort to interpret religious teaching in terms of the prevailing knowledge; (5) political and social conditions; (6) changing moral ideals; (7) the interpretation of one dogma according to the scheme of another in terms of abstract analogical thought; (8) the attempt to interpret different directions and contradictions within the Church; (9) the purpose of stating definitively why a doctrine regarded as erroneous should be rejected; (10) the hallowing power of blindly accepted tradition.[20]

Second, Harnack points out that there are certain characteristics of the dogma itself which make necessary a particular kind of organization. Because the Church has recognized her faith in her dogmas, it is important for the historian to demonstrate the unity of the dogmas in a given period, the relation between the various dogmas, and the main ideas that are expressed. Actually, such a unity can be seen only in the Greek Church; both Augustine and Luther (for Harnack, these three "styles of construction"—Origen's, Augustine's, and the Reformers'—exhaust the possibilities in Christian dogma) expressed a new view concerning the nature of Christianity, and grafted the old dogmas onto it. Therefore, when the history of dogma is written in a unilinear fashion, these new conceptions may be ignored. Harnack holds that the historian of dogma must include in his method, as a principle of organizing his material, the unities, the new conceptions that are introduced, and the interrelationships between these two.

Third, the historian must remember, in organizing his material, that dogmas arise, develop, and are utilized through theology, not

[19] *DG,* I, p. 13.
[20] *Ibid.*

the obverse. They are the product of theology, which in turn is dependent on many factors operating at the time the "theological thinking" is done. First Origen, then Nicaea; first the Scholastics, then Trent; and both Origen and the Scholastics are dependent in their theological thinking on given historical situations and challenges which make necessary the presentation of the faith. However, once Nicaea and Trent have spoken, Origen and the Scholastics and their theological concerns are forgotten, the dogmas are declared to be *θεοῦ δόγματα* and the whole process is flipped over on its head, dogma being declared the source of theology. Indeed, so perverse can this relationship become that the Origen or the Schleiermacher many be condemned by the dogma which his theology made possible. Ecclesiasticism tries to squirm out of this indictment, Harnack charges, by distinguishing the work of theology, as expressing only the form, from that of the Church, which presupposes the substance; but such *hysteron-proteron* reasoning should be left to the Catholic Church, which can "overcome history by dogma," and, indeed, cannot get along without such reasoning. The Protestant historian of dogma, on the other hand, must judge the development with reference to "Gospel Christianity," insofar as this is possible. And yet he is able to show, as he views the tenacity of dogma (in its "Greek spirit on the ground of the Gospel"[21] character) and the changes that it has undergone, that in Augustine and Luther there was a real recovery of this Christian character, though this actually proved to be a fissiparous influence on the dogma itself.

Finally, Harnack reaffirms a familiar methodological principle which also has relevance to the way in which the material will be organized: "The method of explaining everything, wherever it is possible, from the principle that 'Dogma tends to explicate itself' must be given up as unscientific; in fact, all such empty abstractions are to be avoided as scholastic and mythological."[22] For "dogma has had its history in the individual living man and nowhere else."[23] When this is recognized, the actual situations in which intelligent and believing men have lived will be investigated, and that medieval realism which can pull anything out of its magician's hat will be given up. There is "one simple, fundamental principle" which "has never been given its rights in the historiography of the history of dogma": the principle that "only that is Christian which can be

[21] *Ibid.*, p. 18.
[22] *Ibid.*, p. 13.
[23] *Ibid.*, pp. 13–14.

authenticated in the Gospel."[24] Harnack does not presume to believe that a first attempt to implement this principle can succeed fully; but this is his declared purpose.

On the basis of his definition of dogma, and proceeding according to his announced division and principles of organization, Harnack produced a work of more than two thousand pages. What follows is an attempt at summary, divided into "Origin" and "Development."

A. ORIGIN

The Gospel was first expressed in the thought-forms of Palestinian Judaism, which stamped upon it a certain form. In a short time, this Gospel—"which was Jesus Christ"[25]—broke the bonds of Judaism and became a world religion; this was done by the appropriation of the Old Testament, the setting forth of the claim that the Christians were truly the people of God, and the initiation of a world mission. The bridge by which the Gospel was transformed into a world faith was non-Palestinian Judaism, as represented preeminently in Paul. The Gentile churches which Paul founded did not understand his problem, however. For Paul, though he could become "a Greek to the Greeks," appropriating this heritage in the service of the Gospel, always subordinated this knowledge to his central confession—"Christ crucified"—and his view of the Spirit and of justification had nothing in common with the moralism and idealism of Hellenism. His churches, on the other hand, saw in the Gospel "the certain message of the blessings and the obligations which they had already sought in Hellenistic Judaism."[26] Because of this misunderstanding, that part of Paul's message which linked it with the Gospel was obscured: a fact of fateful consequence for the process of dogmatic formulation which was to follow.

An excellent example of Harnack's basic thesis is provided in his discussion of the influence of Philonic exegesis. This influence had penetrated widely into non-Palestinian Judaism because it provided a way of dealing with difficulties in interpreting a sacred text. Because it had been proved efficacious, and because the Christians were under the necessity of proving that the Old Testament was in reality their possession, it was taken up by certain of the Christian apologists. Thus a Hellenic "device" was used in order to meet what was regarded

[24] *Ibid.*, p. 14.
[25] *Ibid.*, p. 43.
[26] *Ibid.*, p. 56.

at this time as a real Christian difficulty; but this was "on the ground of the Gospel" inasmuch as the referent was Jesus Christ. The point is summarized by Harnack:

To find the spiritual sense of the sacred text, in part beside and in part excluding the literal sense—this became the purpose of "scientific" Christian theology. Indeed, such a theology was possible only on this basis, as it tried to join into a unity the extensive and disparate material of the Old Testament with the Gospel, and both with the religious and scientific culture of the Greeks.[27]

Harnack dates the period of *preparation* for church dogma from c. 50 to c. 150. In this period, Jewish Christianity declined, and certain syncretistic tendencies arose. The attempt to fuse the Gospel with the religious interests of the time led to a correlate: the necessity to separate the Gospel from those of its own presuppositions which could only provide difficulty in a Hellenic life situation, and to provide it with foreign presuppositions. "*To this latter tendency belongs, above all, the Hellenic view that knowledge is not a (charismatic) adjunct to the faith, or one exposition of the faith beside others, but that it is identical with the essence of the faith itself.*"[28]

Harnack admitted that the problem which gave him the greatest difficulty in the entire project was "The Common Faith and the Beginnings of Self-Recognition in The Gentile Christianity Which Was to Develop into Catholicism."[29] This difficulty is emphasized in a footnote:

The statements made in this chapter require a particular forbearance, for we cannot stop to justify our selection from the rich and varied material, . . . our emphasis upon certain elements, and our placing in the background of other elements. It is not possible, . . . to give expression to the elasticity and the variations of idea and thought which were characteristic of the Christians in this earliest period. There certainly was . . . a complex of tradition which was in many ways established, but this complex still remained under the domination of enthusiastic phantasy, so that what appeared to be fixed at one moment had already disappeared in the next. Finally, we must take note of the fact that when we speak of the beginnings of knowledge, we no longer refer to the members of the Christian community in its totality, but only to those individuals who were the

[27] *Ibid.*, p. 111.
[28] *Ibid.*, p. 135.
[29] This is Chap. III of Book I of Part I.

leaders of the community. If we had no other writings from the time of the Apostolic Fathers than the first Epistle of Clement and the Epistle of Polycarp, it would be relatively easy to set forth a clear history of the development which connects Paulinism with the old-Catholic theology (Irenaeus), and to justify thereby the traditional picture. But in addition to these two letters, which are the classic memorials of the mediating tradition, there are a great number of documents which show us how manifold and complicated the development really was. They also show us how careful we should be in the interpretation of the post-Apostolic documents which stand closest to the Pauline Epistles, and we must pay particular attention to those sections which deviate from Paulinism.[30]

In the period in which this preparation was taking place, organized communities existed, outwardly free with respect to each other, but inwardly bound to their particular interpretations of the Gospel. The Old Testament was accepted as divine revelation, to be interpreted as belonging to the new people of God. Jesus was increasingly elevated, and speculation concerning his person went on apace, with docetic, adoptionist, and Logos Christological positions emerging. An incipient institutionalization of worship is to be noted, and rudimentary forms of sacramental "mysteries" can be discerned. In short, the elements for the formation of a system of doctrine were in existence before the great Gnostic controversy broke out.

When this movement did become an overt threat to the Church, it attempted to assimilate Christianity as a peculiarly elevated form of γνῶσις to its *corpus permixtum* drawn from many sources. As such, it was rejected by the great Church, which accepted only those speculative thinkers of the period from c. 60 to c. 160 who sought to save the Old Testament by a spiritualizing of its contents. Harnack holds that historical inquiry cannot agree with the great Church here:

Rather, it sees in Gnosticism a range of undertakings which in certain ways is analogous to the Catholic expression of Christianity in doctrine, ethics, and cultus. But the great distinction here is essentially that the Gnostic systems represent the acute secularization, or the Hellenization of Christianity (rejecting the Old Testament), while the Catholic system is to be seen as a gradual process (with the conservation of the Old Testament.)[31]

This insight, which has been consistently overlooked in the history of dogma, means that the Gnostics

[30] *DG*, I, pp. 140–141.
[31] *Ibid.*, p. 215.

were, in short, the theologians of the first century. They were the first to transform Christianity into a system of dogma; they were the first to work up the tradition systematically; they were the first to attempt the explication of Christianity as the absolute religion . . . but absolute religion to them was identical with . . . philosophy of religion.[32]

This attempt of Gnosticism to master Christianity by the Greek spirit was rejected; but in the end it prevailed in its gradual rather than its acute form. The result was that speculative-philosophical, cultic-mystical, and dualistic-ascetic ideas became a part of the synthesis as it eventually worked itself out.

Book II of the section of the work dealing with origin covers the period from 150 to c. 260, and is entitled "The Laying of the Foundation." In this period, the following characteristics are to be noted: "the victorious struggle with Gnosticism and with the Marcionite Church, the gradual development of an ecclesiastical doctrine, and the suppression of the early Christian enthusiasm."[33] This took place "through the establishment of a great ecclesiastical society formed as a coterminous political community, school, and society for worship, and based on the strong foundation of an 'apostolic' law of faith, an 'apostolic' collection of writings, and . . . an 'apostolic' organization—in short, *the Catholic Church.*"[34]

There are two dominant problems for the historian of dogma in this period: to describe the origin of Catholicism as a Church (with canon, creed, and office), to be regarded as the apostolic, true, and holy Church, and to describe the rise of the system of dogma. Harnack's treatment of the first problem may be summarized as follows: in the conflict with Gnosticism and Marcion, the main articles of Christianity were raised to the status of "apostolic ordinances and laws"; the fact that they challenged the sense of freedom characteristic of the early Christians was not noted until the Montanist outbreak and its suppression in the name of this "apostolic tradition"; doctrinal law was thus substituted for the fellowship of faith; on the one hand, this incipient Catholicism destroyed "acute secularization" by its preservation of an important part of the early Christian tradition; on the other hand, it bound Christianity to rules (protecting against "acute secularization") which, because they were seen as "right doctrine" rather than "new life" actually lowered the standards of Christianity (making possible a "gradual seculariza-

32 *Ibid.*, p. 215.
33 *Ibid.*, p. 303.
34 *Ibid.*

tion"); all of which is to say that the Church "was no longer a community of faith, hope, and discipline, but a political community in which the Gospel took its place alongside many other things."[35] Yet this is only one side of the matter. For after her victory over Gnosticism, achieved with the weapon of "apostolicity," the Church went on the offensive. She put to work the "cultured Greeks" who had come into the Church, eager as they were to justify the faith "to themselves and to the world, and to present it as the desired and certain answer to all those pressing questions which moved the men of this time."[36] This process, initiated by the early Apologists, came to its fruition in the theology of Origen.

When one turns to the Apologists and their successors, those who interpreted Christianity as "the true philosophy," the second problem, the rise of the system of dogma within the Church, has been engaged. "What is here represented as Christianity is in reality the idealistic philosophy of religion of this epoch, certified by divine revelation, made available to all through the Incarnation of the Logos."[37] It is important to note that what is "Hellenized" here is not the Gospel, but ecclesiastical Christianity; and this process became necessary the moment the converted Greek turned to look at the religion he had accepted. From Justin on, this "looking process" is in operation, with those differences which the continuing fusion made necessary. The early Apologists, for example, had no New Testament canon to which they could appeal; their problem was to deal with the Old Testament and the teachings of Christ. But when one comes to Origen, the problem is vastly more complicated. It grew out of the claim which had been made that the Church possessed in her tradition everything philosophy taught, and this in its true form; but inasmuch as the Christian charters by this time comprised the Old Testament, the New Testament, and the rule of faith, the task of setting forth "the true philosophy" was immense. Not only must these three elements be included in the synthesis, but all that knowledge which the philosophical systems of Philo and Valentinus had sought to explicate must be set within the system, but in its true perspective. Clement tried this, "but the task was too much for him."[38] "Under even more difficult circumstances Origen

[35] *Ibid.*, p. 306. The summary included in this paragraph was derived from pp. 303–306.

[36] *Ibid.*, p. 308.

[37] *Ibid.*

[38] *Ibid.*, p. 313.

took up the problem, and in a certain sense brought it to a conclusion. He, the rival of the Neoplatonic philosophers, the Christian Philo, wrote the first Christian dogmatic, which rivaled the philosophical systems of the time."[39]

The influence of Origen on the rise of dogma cannot be overestimated; the range of his concerns was extremely wide, but it was in his speculation on the Logos that he exerted the widest influence. And wherever the Logos was considered, Christian Hellenism was present. This concept, indeed, became the catalytic agent for the process of development of an official scientific theology. The Catholicism which was eventually to result was "a mixing of Christianity with the ideas of antiquity," and Catholic dogma, "as it developed after the second or third century on the ground of the Logos-doctrine, is Christianity conceived and formulated from the standpoint of the Greek philosophy of religion."[40] It was this Christianity which conquered the ancient world and became the basis for the development in the Middle Ages. Harnack concludes this first part of the *Dogmengeschichte* with a historical judgment:

> The union of the Christian religion with one definite historical phase of human knowledge and culture is lamentable both in the interests of the Christian religion, which was thereby secularized, and in the interest of cultural development, which was thereby retarded(?). Yet to lament here would be presumptuous; for everything that we possess and value we owe to this union which was formed between Christianity and antiquity, in which neither was able to overcome the other. It is upon the tensions which were here brought into existence that our inner and spiritual life rests even today, not in any significant measure on the empirical knowledge which we have achieved.[41]

B. DEVELOPMENT

The first book of the three comprising the second part of the total work considers the first *Baustil* of ecclesiastical dogmatics, that of Origen. The central concept for this kind of dogmatic formulation was Christology, and particularly the Logos Christology. We have already pointed out that all theologians had to relate themselves in some way to Origen's thought on this subject. Harnack specifies three other contributions which Origen made, and the development which resulted from them: Origen distinguished "between Pistis and Gnosis

[39] *Ibid.*, p. 313.
[40] *Ibid.*, p. 315.
[41] *Ibid.*, pp. 315–316.

—he kept these separate, unified only by his common aim."[42] This distinction between the faith of the Church and the science of faith was rejected by the Church. Further, Origen revealed himself to be at bottom a philosopher "in the rich variety of his speculations . . . and the balance which he maintained between the various factors in his system, relating all to his one central purpose."[43] Athanasius, though in many ways a disciple of Origen, challenged this philosophical approach. Motivated throughout by a determination to center on that which was of practical efficacy in the life of the Christian and the Church, "he defined the Christian faith exclusively as redemption through the God-man whose essential nature was identical with God's, and thereby he restored to the faith fixed limits and a specific content."[44] Finally, Origen presented a great problem to the Church "in the biblical stamp which he gave to his theology by a strict dependence on the text of Holy Scripture."[45] Eventually, he was rejected; but the results of this rejection were by no means an unmixed blessing. Though Athanasian theology had prevailed to check the Hellenization and secularization, theological science after Chalcedon almost came to a standstill. There was a cultic mysticism, dependent on a combination of Neoplatonism and superstition, and there was a scholasticism which presupposed the dogma as declared. For "through the condemnation of Origen and the Antiochenes man stood defenseless against the massive biblicism and the superstitious realism, and this was something which had not been originally desired."[46]

The second book of Part II is, in the main, a monument to Augustine, who represents the second *Baustil* in the history of dogma. Of the four basic elements which enter into the history of dogma in the West in the thousand years preceding the Reformation—the heritage of Tertullian and Cyprian, the theology of the fourth-century eastern theologians, Augustinianism, and the needs of the western nations—the third is by far the most determinative. Indeed, "the history of piety and dogma in the west from the fifth century to the time of the Reformation was so thoroughly under the domination of Augustine that one must consider this entire period as a single unit."[47]

Harnack's interpretation of Augustine's essential contribution is

[42] *DG*, II, p. 14.
[43] *Ibid.*
[44] *Ibid.*, p. 25.
[45] *Ibid.*, p. 14.
[46] Harnack, *Dogmengeschichte*, p. 259.
[47] *DG*, III, p. 3.

highly instructive: "This is his secret and his greatness . . . : *he recognized his heart as the lowest, and the living God as the highest good; he lived in the love of God, and he possessed a thrilling ability to set forth his innermost observations.*"[48] Though he separated nature and grace, he bound together religion and morality; though he destroyed the old intellectualism of antiquity, he revived it in the insistence that man, who finds his true being in the love of God, can thereby bring his intellect into the service of God. He placed religion where it belonged, in the heart, and released it from its cultic accretion. "Love, unfeigned humility, and the power to overcome the world—these are the elements of religion, and its blessedness; they arise from the possession of the living God."[49] As against the received conception of *sins*, Augustine located *sin* in the disposition to independence; against the received emphasis on baptism as an *Einmaligkeit* for the forgiveness of sins, he spoke of grace as the repose of the soul in God. Yet there was also a strong element of Catholicism in the piety of Augustine: he "*transformed the authority of the Church into a religious power*," "*exchanged the personal relation to God for a sacramental communication of grace*," joined a conception of the necessity of merits to his view of the sovereignty of faith, and generally accepted the Catholic quietistic view of piety as against the working in faith and love which his thought seemed to make necessary.[50]

We shall not enter into the intricacies of the Augustinian theology; it must be remembered, however, that there were several levels in this theology, and that Augustine bound these together into a unity. It was above all in his polemical struggles, against the Donatists and Pelagius, that he worked out the meaning of his basic categories of sin, grace, and the means of grace; and all of this took place under the aegis of his Catholic concern. It was this multi-hued theology which was accepted into the Church, worked and reworked by Gregory, Alcuin, Erigena, Gottschalk, and Bernard, and combined with the papal conception of the Church and Aristotelianism in Thomas. In this process, Augustinianism was dissolved almost totally into dogmatics; but "*this dissolving of Augustinianism was not due essentially to external pressures; it was in great part the working out of an inner development.*"[51] For Augustine had allowed three

[48] *Ibid.*, p. 57.
[49] Harnack, *Dogmengeschichte*, p. 270.
[50] *DG*, III, pp. 68 ff.
[51] *Ibid.*, p. 525.

elements, "*merit, gratia infusa, and the hierarchical-priestly element,*" to stand alongside his doctrine of grace; and these "continued to work until they had completely transformed the Augustinian way of thinking."[52]

The concluding book of the total work is entitled "The Three-Fold Issue of the History of Dogma." The first of the four chapters is a historical survey, and the next three deal, respectively, with the issuing of dogma in Roman Catholicism, in Anti-Trinitarianism and Socinianism, and in Protestantism.

(1) *Roman Catholicism:* The old Church became even more decidedly the papal church. It fixed the Augustinian-medieval doctrines as dogmas at the Council of Trent, finding their particular type of Augustinianism a useful weapon against the Reformation positions. But their position was thereby rendered ambivalent: on the one hand, Trent placed itself *above* dogma by using it as a regulative device in the interests of the Church, on the other, the need to meet the spiritual force of the Reformation with spiritual force introduced compromises which curialism would have preferred not to make. It took another three centuries and a huge assist from the French Revolution and Napoleon to overcome the ambivalence in favor of an absolute papacy. The promulgation of the dogma of the Immaculate Conception marks the victory, and from this point on the idea of dogma "*as the faith* that animates every Christian heart, and makes the Christian a Christian" is completely obscured, and in its place is put "the intention to believe what the Church believes."[53]

(2) *Anti-Trinitarian and Socinian Christianity:* This type of Christianity broke with the old dogma and discarded it. Harnack admits that the inclusion of this type may appear to be out of place in a history of dogma, but justifies it with three considerations:

> the certainty that Anti-Trinitarianism and Socinianism can be connected with the medieval development (Nominalism), the fact that the Protestant dogmatic of the seventeenth century wrestled with it as with its worst enemy, and finally, the fact that the criticism applied to dogma in the eighteenth and nineteenth centuries by evangelical theologians is very close to this Socinian criticism.[54]

Harnack feels very strongly that this movement has been given far too little attention:

[52] *Ibid.*
[53] *Ibid.*, p. 581.
[54] *Ibid.*

Any movement which collects the greater part of that which had been existing in diffuse form for many centuries alongside the Church, but above all a movement in which the critical thought of the ecclesiastical theology of the fourteenth and fifteenth centuries had come to a free explication, and at the same time had taken up into itself the impulses of the new age (the Renaissance) must not be judged of secondary importance. That which is characteristic of the Anti-Trinitarian and Socinian movements of the sixteenth century is this: it represents that destruction of Catholicism which could be brought about on the ground of Scholasticism and the Renaissance, without thereby deepening religion.[55]

(3) *Protestantism:* This third "issue" of dogma is in many respects the most complicated. For on the one hand it represented

a new point of departure for the characterization of the Christian faith, won from the Word of God, and it discarded all infallibilities which could provide an external certainty to the faith, the infallible organization of the Church, the infallible doctrinal tradition of the Church, and the infallible codex of Scripture.[56]

This meant the setting aside of that view of Christianity from which dogma had arisen. But, on the other hand, the view of Christian faith that was set forth ("the absolute certainty of having received from God, as the Father of Jesus Christ, the forgiveness of sins, and of living under him in his kingdom")[57] had all dogmatic support removed from it. Even so, the Reformers did not explicitly reject the old dogma, assuming without a close examination that it actually did correspond to the contents of Scripture. True, it was not as dogma that it continued authoritative for them, but as a confession of the faith which they transferred, uncritically, from the immediacy of its effect upon them into the dogmas. The more the Reformation insisted on faith, therefore, the more disastrous did the issue become, "for this faith, and that knowledge of faith and law of faith were, unknown to them, forced together."[58] With Augsburg, under the manifold pressures of antinomian Anabaptism, the process of "pouring new wine into old bottles" (without, indeed, denying the evangelical principle) was begun.

In summary, then,

Did the Reformation (in the sixteenth century) put an end to dogma? It is more valid to answer this question with a No than with a Yes. But if one understands that it uprooted the basis of dogma, . . . that

[55] *Ibid.*, p. 655.
[56] *Ibid.*, p. 582.
[57] *Ibid.*, pp. 582–583.
[58] *Ibid.*, p. 583.

it is a powerful principle and not a new system of dogma, and that its history through the eras of orthodoxy, Pietism, and Rationalism to the present is not an apostasy, but a necessary development, then one must also grant that the quite conservative position which the Reformation took toward the old dogma belongs not to the principle but to the history.[59]

It would be unfair to Harnack to conclude this summary without some representation of his treatment of Luther. Indeed, Protestantism is dealt with almost exclusively in terms of Luther's contribution: while Calvin is mentioned, *passim*, on fourteen pages, Luther gets the entire last seventy-four pages. It is instructive of Harnack's own convictions that no part of the total work is so interlarded with German interstices as these last pages. We note the following emphatic points: (1) "*The Reformation, as represented in the Christianity of Luther . . . is an old Catholic or even a medieval phenomenon, but if judged with respect to its kernel is not such a phenomenon, being rather a restoration of Pauline Christianity in the spirit of a new time.*"[60] (2) "*He was great only in the fact that he rediscovered again in the Gospel the knowledge of God.*"[61] (3) "The same man who had released the Gospel of Jesus Christ from ecclesiasticism and moralism *had at the same time strengthened its value in the forms of the old Catholic theology, and was the first to bestow sense and meaning again into these forms which had been quiescent for many centuries.*"[62] It follows that (4) "*Luther was the restorer of the old dogma.*"[63] But (5) he accomplished this restoration only in the sense that "*the old dogma itself encountered the new conception of the Gospel which he preached.*"[64] Though Luther lacked the historical understanding to develop fully his insights, he was eminently right in his understanding that (6) "this old dogma was really the expression of *the religion* of ancient times: *that which those times bound together with dogma, thereby limiting it, had not been taken up into the dogma itself.*"[65] Luther's own Christianity can be summed up in his grasping of the "Wesen": (7) "*the revelation of the gracious God in the Gospel, i.e. in Christ.*"[66] This was Luther's reductionism, and (8) "*this reduction meant nothing else than the restoration of*

59 *Ibid.*, pp. 583–584.
60 *Ibid.*, p. 691.
61 *Ibid.*, p. 693.
62 *Ibid.*, p. 695.
63 *Ibid.*
64 *Ibid.*, p. 697.
65 *Ibid.*, p. 699.
66 *Ibid.*, p. 702.

religion."[67] For him, the source of this religion was the Holy Scripture, especially the New Testament. The basis of the Church is indeed something "given," but this is not priesthood or statutes or papacy; it is (9) "*the Word of God as purely understood.*"[68] In insisting on this unprejudiced understanding of the language of Scripture, Luther laid the foundation for the scientific investigation which was to follow in its time.

Luther's view on predestination and the bondage of the will yields what Harnack considers one of his most important contributions to theology:

> Here, in contrast to the medieval view, his basic thought is that God . . . *gives faith and creates penitence.* The medieval theology . . . had relaxed this thought . . . in its essentially religious aspect . . . . But for Luther this religious central point was decisive, namely, that it is God who creates faith, who plants and nourishes the good tree. Just this, which appears from the outside to be subjectivism, and therefore is regarded by the reason as an achievement of man, appeared to Luther (who always held in view that real experience through which he had passed) to be a really objective thing, created within him from outside. This is perhaps Luther's greatest significance with respect to theology . . . . *This significance lies in the fact that he completely broke with the idea that religious experience is made up of historical and sacramental acts, which God performs and holds in readiness, joined with subjective acts which are in some way man's affair.* To describe this experience in this way meant to deprive it of its power and to turn it over to reason; for reason may then register, describe, and evaluate, in an objective way, the "activities of God," and it may also fix and prescribe the possibilities for men. That this was the falsely famous art of the Scholastics, the doctrine of reason and of the devil, was recognized by Luther; therein stands his greatness as a theologian. He did away with the proud pseudo-theology of "objective" reckoning, and that basically godless morality which claimed to be religion. He overcame, in the experience of faith, that severing of the objective and subjective, of divine and human factors. *Thereby he produced a complete confusion in religion for anyone who approached it from the outside, because religion cannot be thought about if this separation of the activities of God and the possibilities of man is denied; but thereby he made religion clear for those who believe, and restored to it that representation which truly describes what the believing Christian has experienced and continues to experience.*[69]

In this declaration, Harnack affirmed, Luther took his stand squarely on the fact of Christian experience; and though he did not yet per-

[67] *Ibid.*
[68] *Ibid.*, p. 705.
[69] *Ibid.*, p. 714.

ceive that by so doing the experience of faith is identified with revelation (lacking this perception, he, too, speculated in scholastic fashion on certain matters), he

> gave religion back to religion, affirmed the independence of the knowledge given through faith, and declared that the experience of the revelation of God in the heart, i.e., the begetting of faith, constituted a *noli me tangere*, a stumbling-block to the Jews, and foolishness to the Greeks. But who understood him![70]

This understanding was not achieved in the sixteenth century. For in the discussions which followed, even Melanchthon reverted to the old understanding.

c. THE CRITICS

The predominant Idea of the *History of Dogma* is "the Gospel." It is the dominant idea of Harnack's life. It was very clearly *not* in the first instance an intellectual concept. Those who have interpreted Adolf Harnack and his career by fastening on the "Wesen" or "essence" of Christianity, interpreting this as fundamentally intellectual, have missed the point. "Reality" is a better word, just because it suggests a going-behind the purest cognitive structure. It may be that Harnack was not able, as Aquinas was not, to communicate in words—just because words are taken as intellectual intercourse only—the "reality" which lies in the very *Urgrund* of human existence. It may be, further, that his own intellectual baggage and "elementary, cultural, and individual" factors got in his way:

item: "Where I find mystery, I say nothing about it"[71]—Ritschl, but also Harnack;

and: "He himself therefore is Christianity. . . . We cannot state the 'doctrine' of Jesus; for it appears as a supramundane life which must be felt in the person of Jesus, and its truth is guaranteed by the fact that such a life can be lived."[72]

yet: "In taking up a theological book we are in the habit of inquiring first of all as to the 'stand-point' of the author. In a historical work, there is no room for such an inquiry";[73]

and, "Progress will finally depend upon an accurate understand-

[70] *Ibid.*, p. 715.
[71] Quoted in Mackintosh, *op. cit.*, p. 160.
[72] *DG*, I, p. 69.
[73] Harnack, *History of Dogma*, "Author's Preface to the English Edition," not in the German, I, p. vii.

ing of what the Christian religion originally was"[74]—certainly a "stand-point."

To juxtapose these elements is to recognize the difficulty which Harnack—and every other historian—faces. His critics centered on this difficulty also; and they raised questions, in the first instance, as to what this "now you see it, now you don't" evanescent "Gospel" is.

Harnack had defined the Gospel, in the original edition of the *Dogmengeschichte*, as follows:

> The Gospel is the glad message of the government of the world and of every individual soul by the almighty and holy God, the Father and Judge. . . .
>
> the Gospel . . . is inseparably connected with Jesus Christ . . . He is the Son who knows the Father.
>
> Jesus Christ by no definite statement thrust the connection of his Gospel with his Person into the foreground. . . . The religion of the Gospel is based on this belief in Jesus Christ, which signifies that by looking to him, this historical person, the believer becomes certain that God rules heaven and earth, and that God the Judge is also Father and Redeemer.[75]

In the preface to the third edition of the third volume of the *Dogmengeschichte*, issued in 1897, Harnack takes account of this continuing criticism, and of three others, all of which we shall note in due course. "It has been said that in this account the development of dogma is judged by the Gospel, but that we do not learn clearly what the Gospel is."[76] Harnack's answer to this charge must be quoted in full:

> As to the first objection, I believe that I have given a fuller account of my conception of the Gospel than has yet been done in any textbook of the History of Dogma. But I gladly give here a brief summary of my views. The preaching of Jesus contains three great main sections. First, the message of the approaching Kingdom of God or of the future salvation; second, the proclamation of the actual state of things, such as are given in Matthew 6:25–34; 7:7–11; 9:2; 10:28–33. . . ; third, the new righteousness (the new law). The middle section connected with Matthew 11:25–30, and therefore also combined with the primitive Christian testimony regarding Jesus as Lord and Savior, I hold, from strictly historical and objective grounds, to be the true main section, the gospel in the gospel, and to it I subordinate the other portions. That Christ himself

[74] *DG*, I, pp. 38–39.
[75] *Ibid.*, pp. 57–59, *passim.*
[76] *Ibid.*, III, p. ix.

expressed it under the form of eschatology I know as well as the antiquarians who have so keen an eye for the everlasting yesterday.[77]

Harnack had declared, in the text itself:

The history of the Gospel contains two great transitions. . .; from Christ to the first generations of believers, including Paul, and from the first, the Jewish-Christian, generation of these believers to the Gentile Christians; in other words: from Christ to the brotherhood of believers in Christ, and from this to the incipient Catholic Church. . . . As to the first, the question has frequently been asked, Is the Gospel of Christ or the Gospel concerning Christ to be the authority? But the dilemma is false. The Gospel certainly is the Gospel of Christ. For in Jesus' sense it has only fulfilled its mission when the Father has been declared to men as he was known by the Son, and where life is dominated by the realities and principles which ruled the life of Jesus Christ. It is, to be sure, in accordance with the mind of Jesus, and at the same time a fact of history, that this Gospel can only be appropriated and adhered to in connection with a believing surrender to the person of Jesus Christ. Yet every dogmatic formula is suspicious, because it effects a wound on the spirit of religion; it should not in any case be put before the living experience in order to evoke it. . . . The essence of the matter is a personal life which awakens life around it, as the fire of one torch lights another. As early as a weakness of faith can be discerned in the Church of Christ, it is no earlier than the practice of making, as the foundation of faith, a formulated and ostensibly demonstrable confession—on the basis of which a demand for subjection to this confession is made. Faith surely is propagated by the testimony of faith, but dogma is not itself that testimony.

The peculiar character of the Christian religion is conditioned by the fact that every reference to God is at the same time a reference to Jesus Christ and vice-versa.[78]

Finally, note must be made of the *further* encystation of this Gospel as it moves from the first to the second transition:

. . . it brought with it the most important changes which became obvious, however, only after several generations had passed. These appear, first, in the belief in holy consecrations, having their own efficacy, and administered by chosen persons; further, in the conviction that the relation of the individual to God in Christ is conditioned, above all else, on the acceptance of a definite and divinely attested law of faith and the canon;

[77] *Ibid.*
[78] *Ibid.*, I, pp. 69–70.

further, in the view that God has established certain structures for the Church, the observance of which are necessary and meritorious, and that this Church as the people of a new covenant is a visible earthly community. These assumptions, which constitute, formally, the essence of Catholicism as a religion, have no support in the teaching of Jesus; indeed, they are an offense to that teaching.[79]

Agreement with Harnack's identification of the Gospel—the great Idea, the *Geist* that animates his effort—was by no means achieved in his time, or subsequently. But one point is not open to debate—that "the Gospel" was "the inner form" of Christian truth for him. To the question, Is the Gospel a dynamic principle or an historically specifiable content, he would answer, "In its reality, the former." Is it living faith, or defined doctrine? The same answer.

It may be objected that when one considers the more than sixteen hundred writings in the Harnackian corpus, it is a patent *reductio ad absurdum* to reduce the Idea that animated Harnack to this single crux. The obvious rejoinder must be that if it is indeed a "reductionism," we shall have to make the most of it; for the position Harnack sets forth is clear. Further, if it is a reduction to *this* Gospel, this Gospel then becomes the torch from which other lights are lit, the burning center which is what it is but which throws off, centrifugally, new light in myriad hues. Some such figure must be used to connote Harnack's position. For, in his own formula, this "reality," the Gospel, worked in history with its *Kräfte* (powers) and with its *Richtung* (direction, aim), to bring forth a certain *Leistung* (result, accomplishment).

In summary, then, Harnack identifies the Gospel as "Jesus Christ." But he also makes it quite apparent that he implies no dogma of the Person of Christ in this statement. In *Das Wesen des Christentums*, where this question is specifically central, it is the *message* of Jesus which is emphasized. This message is described in the threefold identification, "the kingdom of God and its coming," "God the Father and the infinite value of the human soul," and "the higher righteousness and the commandment of love."[80] Here, in the *Dogmengeschichte*, the identification of the Gospel with this "message" of Jesus is already present, and Harnack views it in terms of a dynamic experiential relationship. Thus, Augustine's greatness is seen to lie in the fact that he "recognized his heart as the lowest, and the living God as the highest good"; that he "placed religion where it belonged, in

[79] *Ibid.*, pp. 70–71.
[80] *WC*, pp. 45–67.

the heart, and released it from its cultic accretion."[81] In the laudatory sections on Luther, Harnack makes plain his own judgment that the greatness of this man rested on his grasping of the Gospel, although at the same time he held on to certain parts of the old dogma. Thus "the Christianity of Luther . . . judged with respect to its kernel is . . . a restoration of Pauline Christianity"; "he . . . rediscovered again in the Gospel the knowledge of God," he "released the Gospel of Jesus Christ from ecclesiasticism," he preached a "new conception of the Gospel"; and he grasped "the revelation of the gracious God in the Gospel, i.e., in Christ."[82]

What we mean when we say that for Harnack the principle is dominant over the content may be indicated by saying that the *experience* of the soul in communion with the merciful God defies all verbalization. Though historical forms must always be present to transmit this Gospel, and though man must try to state what it means, it is fatal to confuse these statements with the experience itself. Man can never fully succeed in making clear, through language or the full range of symbolism, what the essential nature of this experience means; and he runs a great risk if he attempts to break this barrier by proclaiming as revealed dogma the speculations of men who have in turn taken prior speculations of men when they "affirmed the independence of the knowledge given through faith, and declared that the experience of the revelation of God in the heart, i.e. the begetting of faith, constituted a *noli me tangere*."[83] This "experience" is the inviolate principle, dynamic and gerundial in character, and it simply cannot be captured in propositional formulas. This view, which is in effect Harnack's doctrine of revelation, is set forth in his final characterization of Luther's influence.[84] Though he is, presumably, explicating Luther's influence, the value-words that are used, the overtly indicated emphases, and the *Geist* that is communicated in these passages make it clear that Harnack regards Luther's understanding of the Gospel as the true understanding. "It is God who creates faith": "this religious central point was decisive"; and in his understanding of this, Luther "*made religion clear for those who believe, and restored to it that representation which truly describes what the believing Christian has experienced and continues to experience.*"[85]

[81] *Supra*, p. 138.
[82] *Supra*, p. 141.
[83] *Supra*, p. 143.
[84] *Supra*, p. 142.
[85] *Supra*, p. 142.

It is in this sense that he interpreted the "material" principle of the Reformation, and sought to bring it to its modern fulfillment; and it is in this context that his rejection of dogma as in any sense θεοῦ δόγματα must be viewed.

Two other criticisms of Harnack's work had to do with definitions, one with his definition of "dogma" itself, the other with his definition or characterization of "the Greek spirit." Both are implicit to some degree in the three remaining criticisms to which he paid particular attention in the Preface to the third edition of the third volume; but we will consider these two criticisms directly before returning to this Preface.

In his "Present State of Research in Early Church History," Harnack had stated his essential thesis; "Christianity has throughout sucked the marrow of the ancient world, and assimilated it; even dogma is nothing but the Christian faith nourished on ancient philosophy, and the whole of Catholicism is nothing else than the Christianity which has devoured the possessions of the Graeco-Roman world."[86] In the *Dogmengeschichte* he sought to make it quite clear what he did and did not mean. He held that the term "dogma" has been used in three distinct senses: it can mean "(1) the historical doctrines of the Church, . . . (2) the historical facts upon which the Christian religion is professedly or actually based, and (3) every definite explication of the contents of Christianity."[87] This multiform usage of the term, he believed, "gives rise to all sorts of misunderstandings and errors."[88] He then goes on to say that he is using the term "dogma" only in the first sense, and adds that when he speaks of the disintegration of dogma, he is not denying "the historical facts" or calling into question the necessity of the Church to have a creed. "My criticism does not apply to the general genus 'dogma,' but to the species, namely to that definite dogma which was formed on the soil of the ancient world, and, though modified, is still powerful."[89]

Loofs, in his *Leitfaden zum Studium der Dogmengeschichte*, took issue with the limitation which Harnack gave to dogma in this definition of the term. "As compared with previous usage," he writes, "Harnack's narrowing of the concept 'dogma' appears to be only individually justified."[90] He then describes Harnack's work as "a

[86] *RA*, II, p. 233.
[87] *DG*, I, p. 22.
[88] *Ibid.*
[89] *Ibid.*, pp. 22–23.
[90] Friedrich Loofs, *Leitfaden zum Studium . . .*, Dritte Auflage (Halle: Max Niemeyer, 1893), p. 6.

monograph on the rise and development of the dogma of the fourth century."[91] What is the significance of this criticism? It lies in the claim that Harnack, by limiting the term "dogma" to "the historical doctrines of the Church" has chosen to give to this term a meaning to suit his purpose. Minimally, Loofs is suggesting, this amounts to a rejection of the common meaning of the term. But there is a much deeper significance to this "narrowing of the concept." For it is clear that unless the concept is so limited, Harnack's conception, division, principles of organization, and therefore the interpretation itself are rendered dubious. Harnack's total conception of history and his method require just such a definition.[92] The criticism implies, therefore, that even in his historical work Harnack was operating with a presuppositional bent. The charge is not that of inconsistency: given the conception of history and the definition of dogma, Harnack's *Dogmengeschichte* holds together as a convincing demonstration. But to concede this to Harnack is to concede all. It is here that one must raise the basic question of the validity of the *Dogmengeschichte*, and Loofs recognized this fact in his criticism.

We may note here that Harnack's "limitation" is made necessary by his presupposition that there is an inner form, that there is an explication of this inner form, and that both of these are distinct from "dogma." *This* is the conviction which Harnack brings to his studies of Christianity, the *Dogmengeschichte* included. The question may be asked why, if this was so patently obvious to Harnack (that there was an inner form, an explication, and "dogma"), it escaped every other interpreter of the subject until the nineteenth century. The answer lies in the fact that though Harnack truly allowed "history as he understood it" to control in the *Dogmengeschichte*, "history as he understood it" is seen from the perspective of a nineteenth-century *Entwickelung* doctrine.

One of Harnack's American critics, writing a third of a century after the *Dogmengeschichte* had been completed, charged that Harnack nowhere defined the Greek spirit, which plays so important a part in his interpretation, and nowhere indicated at what point this spirit began to operate.[93] It would appear that this charge is half true, and perhaps reflects more upon the understanding of the one who made it than upon Harnack. It is true that Harnack does not develop in

[91] *Ibid.*

[92] See Chap. VIII and IX.

[93] See the vitriolic attack on Harnack's position by Finley DuBois Jenkins, "Is Harnack's *History of Dogma* a History of Harnack's Dogma?" *Princeton Theological Review*, XXI (July and Oct. 1923), pp. 424–425.

great detail a definition of this term, since he is not primarily concerned to write a history of Greek thought. It is not true, however, that Harnack failed to make clear what he meant by the term. He speaks of the Christian message as "clothed in a knowledge of the world and of the world-ground,"[94] and declares that he means that "ancient mode of thought" which is characterized by a definite philosophy of nature and of history, a certain view of man, and a particular metaphysic.[95] As to the second part of the charge, Harnack explicitly admitted the difficulty of finding the historical locus for the beginning of the Greek influence. It is true that this was not enough for his critic; but it shows, at least, a salutary hesitancy about claims to a complete understanding of second-century thought and development. One suspects that what the critic is really reacting against is Harnack's recognition of the limits of historical knowledge; and this charge is probably to be understood in the light of the earlier diatribe against Harnack's "chronic . . . affectation, of knowing that you do not know"[96] and his (Harnack's) insistence on distinguishing "dogma *quoad nos* as opposed to dogma *quoad se*."[97]

A more telling criticism by far is that of Tillich, who centers upon Harnack's *interpretation* of the Greek spirit. In the first volume of his *Systematic Theology*, Tillich challenges Harnack's judgment that dogma represents an intellectualization of the Gospel. In order to set the problem in context, we quote the relevant passage in full:

> The doctrine of revelation has been developed traditionally as a doctrine of the "Word of God." This is possible if Word is interpreted as the *logos* element in the ground of being, which is the interpretation which the classical Logos doctrine gave it. But the Word of God often is understood—half-literally, half-symbolically—as a spoken word, and a "theology of the Word" is presented which is a theology of the spoken word. This intellectualization of revelation runs counter to the sense of the Logos Christology. The Logos Christology was not overintellectualistic; actually it was a weapon against this danger. If Jesus as the Christ is called the Logos, Logos points to a revelatory reality, not to revelatory words. Taken seriously, the doctrine of the Logos prevents the elaboration of a theology of the spoken or the written word, which is *the* Protestant pitfall.[98]

94 *DG*, I, p. 17.
95 *Ibid.*, pp. 121–122.
96 Jenkins, *op. cit.*, p. 389.
97 *Ibid.*, p. 418.
98 Tillich, *op. cit.*, I, p. 157.

There then follows a footnote in which Tillich relates this charge to the Ritschlians, and particularly to Harnack:

This statement is a complete reversal of the doctrine of the Ritschlian school that the reception of Christianity by the Greek mind meant an intellectualization of Christianity. The Greek mind can be called "intellectualistic" only in its limited and distorted manifestations, but not as such. From the beginning to the end, knowledge means "union with the unchangeable," with the "really real." Metaphysical knowledge is existential; even in an empiricist and logician like Aristotle it has a mystical element. The reduction of knowledge to detached observation for the sake of control is not Greek but modern. This understanding of Greek philosophy demands a reorientation of that type of interpretation of the history of dogma of which Harnack was the classical representative.[99]

The point of Tillich's charge is twofold: he is asserting that the "Greek mind" was not understood by Harnack, and that Harnack, and the Ritschlians, actually forced into modern categories that which did not belong there at all. To the first part of this charge, it may be pointed out that Harnack's misunderstanding rested on his methodological principle that "the same mind is at work in history and in us," but, more importantly, his *a priori* commitment to a particular historical-critical way of understanding this mind which is at work in history. Or, in other words, it may be said that this principle lends itself to a *hysteron-proteron* kind of reasoning, particularly if it is joined with a renunciation of "philosophical-metaphysical" reasoning. By this "kenosis" of metaphysics, it becomes well-nigh inevitable that the second part of Tillich's charge should be actualized. To fail to understand the Greek mind on its own terms—"existential," if Tillich is correct—is to understand it in alien terms. If Logos points to a revelatory reality, that is, and if one's method makes it impossible for one to deal with any such metaphysical concept, the only way that is open for the explication of "historical" material is by means of a (covert) "theology of the spoken or written word."

Since Harnack regarded his task as a critique of "that definite dogma which was formed on the soil of the ancient world," i.e., a work of the Greek spirit, the explication of "Greek spirit" (or mind) is crucial. However, Tillich holds, Harnack's own presuppositions about knowledge, antimetaphysical (and therefore, antiexistential) as they were, made it impossible for him to understand this Greek spirit. He interpreted it as an "intellectualization" because, on the

[99] *Ibid.*

grounds of his Kantian assumptions about knowledge, the traditional sense of revelation "as a doctrine of the 'Word of God' " had lost all valency. But if it is true that for the Greek mind knowledge in its logos-character points to a revelatory reality which cannot be controlled, circumscribed, or limited by intellectual formulas, and if Harnack's antimetaphysical bias removed from possibility any consideration of this logos-character of knowledge, it follows that Harnack did not really understand the Greek mind. How debilitating this must be, if true, is readily apparent by considering the frequent points in the *Dogmengeschichte* where this "Greek spirit" argument is absolutely controlling.

In effect, what we have said is that the same tendency which Harnack evidences with respect to the Gospel is operative in his estimate of the "Greek spirit"—he interprets both from his nineteenth-century, antimetaphysical, historical standpoint. This fact in itself need not completely destroy the value of the representation set forth; but to the degree that modern value-norms intrude, and are not recognized as such, and are allowed to determine the categories of interpretation, to that degree the representation will be qualified. Tillich believed that Harnack fell into these errors, and therefore a reorientation in the interpretation of dogma, doing justice to the Greek spirit, is demanded.

Another common criticism, the fourth that we shall note, and the second that Harnack took account of in his third edition Preface, is "that the history of dogma is depicted as a pathological process."[100] That Harnack was most sensitive to this criticism, and regarded those who made it as not understanding what he was intending to say, is evident from the frequent repetition of his disclaimer: "As I have been misrepresented by some as one who knew not how to appreciate the uniqueness of the Gospel history . . . others have conversely reproached me with making the history of dogma proceed from an 'apostasy' from the Gospel to Hellenism."[101] Again, "I have given quite as little ground for the accusation that I look upon the whole development of the history of dogma as a pathological process within the history of the Gospel. I do not even look upon the origin of the Papacy as such a process, not to speak of the history of dogma."[102]

The criticism was as continuing as it was puzzling. The 1887 second-edition Preface to Volume I mentions it; the 1893 rewrite of the

[100] *DG*, III, p. ix.
[101] *Ibid.*, I, p. vii.
[102] *Ibid.*, p. 22.

third-edition "Prolegomena" expands it; but it is not until the 1897 third-edition Preface to the third volume that Harnack meets it directly. And though he admits that on this objection, "I am at a loss," one finds it hard to believe that he could not understand why his critics made the charge, and, as a more troubling question, that he could not sense the degree to which his own categories were hypostatized by him. For this is his answer:

After the new religion had entered the Roman Empire, and had combined with it in the form of the universal Catholic Church, the History of Dogma shows an advance and a rise in all its main features down to the Reformation. I have described it in this sense from Origen to Athanasius, Augustine, Bernard, and Francis, to mystic Scholasticism and to Luther. It is to me a mystery how far the history should nevertheless have been depicted as a "process of disease." Of course *superstitions accumulated*, as in every history of religion, but within this encrustation the *individual ever became stronger*, the sense for the Gospel more active, and the *feeling for what was holy and moral more refined and pure.* But as regards the development from the beginnings of the evangelical message in the Empire down to the rise of the Catholic Church, *I have not permitted myself to speculate* how splendid it would have been if everything had happened differently than it did. On the other hand, I grant that *I have not been able to join in praising the formation of that tradition and theology which has lowered immediate religion to one that is mediated, and has burdened faith with complicated theological and philosophical formulas.* Just as little could it occur to me to extol the rise of that ecclesiastical rule which, when it speaks of faith, means, pre-eminently, obedience. But in this there is no "pathology"; the formations that arose overcame Gnosticism.[103]

What Harnack has done, it seems very clear from the italicized passages, is to state with unmistakable clarity his axiological presuppositions, his *Lebensideal*, at the same time he declares he has not permitted himself to speculate. Here is, once again, a paradigm of "the problem of Harnack." One can understand Loofs's judgment, "only individually justified," in this context also. Would an answer to this conundrum not require that one demonstrate, from the sources, what was "true" and what was not, from *no* standpoint? Assuredly. But if "no standpoint" is impossible, *pace* Harnack, then one should state his conception as clearly as he can. *Mirabile dictu*, Harnack did this without thereby admitting to a "standpoint." That he should defend "the historical investigation" of Christianity, as against those

[103] *Ibid.*, III, pp. ix–x; the italics are mine.

who would "overcome history by dogma," we can understand and appreciate; that he should at the same time intrude an axiology into his historical investigation marks him as "one of us men"; but that he should insist on "Abwesenheit des Gesichtspunkt" and still make such a statement as "I have not permitted myself to speculate how splendid it would have been if everything had happened differently than it did" provides an unsolvable riddle.

The fifth common objection, of which there were several varieties, centered around Harnack's principle of organization of the material and the way the use of this principle predisposed an answer. There had been an objection that since Christianity has been a faith from the beginning, the question of "origin" is invalid. Harnack answers that there was, of course, a Gospel "which had as its contents a definite belief in God and in his ambassador Jesus Christ."[104] But *this* faith and later dogma are not to be seen as theme and explication; in the dogma a new element entered:

> Its message is clothed in a knowledge of the world and the world-ground which was obtained without any reference to religion. Religion itself becomes a doctrine which, to be sure, finds its certainty in the Gospel, but contains only a part of its contents, and which can be measurably obtained by those who are neither poor in spirit, nor weary and heavy-laden.[105]

This does not mean that *no* philosophic view of Christianity is possible, for Paul had already begun to speculate in this direction. But Paul's knowledge is "foolishness"; the knowledge claimed by dogma is "wisdom," and even declared to be revelation itself. Actually, "*dogma in its conception and in its development is a work of the Greek spirit on the ground of the Gospel.*"[106] "The Gospel itself is not dogma; for in the Gospel, faith makes room for knowledge only insofar as knowledge comprehends disposition and action, i.e., a definite way of life."[107] Harnack admits that the spiritual character of the Christian religion will always make necessary a scientific apologetic; but what he is here considering is not *Unbestimmtes, Allgemeines*, but *das bestimmte Dogma.*

Another criticism of Harnack's principle of organization held that dogma as Harnack conceived it has validity only for a certain epoch in the history of the Church, and is therefore too limited to be applied

104 *Ibid.*, I, p. 17.
105 *Ibid.*
106 *Ibid.*, p. 18.
107 *Ibid.*

to its total history. Harnack replies that this objection would have point only if one carried the history of the development of dogma through the entire history of the Church. But this he does not propose to do, for the historical facts do not present this possibility. "The Greek Church after the time of the seven great Councils did not have a history of dogma"[108]—those who list all of the theologoumena of the various bishops notwithstanding. "That which concerns Roman Catholicism . . . is today essentially what it was fifteen hundred years ago, viz., Christianity as understood by the ancient world."[109] Finally, as to Protestantism, . . . dogma, as dogma, has had, strictly speaking, no development."[110] To be sure, a way was opened up in the Reformation by which the Gospel might be recovered from its dogmatic integument; but this was not worked out at the time, and many retrograde movements have since set in and qualified the discovery. Harnack declares his own purpose and rationale in the context of this discussion of the unfinished task of the Reformation:

> Historical knowledge can in no way be served by regarding as unimportant the unique character of the Christian faith as dogma, and allowing the history of dogma to be treated only in a general history of the various views of Christianity. Such a "liberal" view would agree neither with the insights of history nor with the real situation of the Protestant Church at the present time; for it is decisively important to recognize that what dogma describes is one unique stage in the development of the human spirit. . . . This stage . . . has in no way been overcome by us, though science has lifted itself above it. But the Christian religion, as it was not born of the culture of the ancient world, is not to be chained to it forever. . . . The Gospel since the Reformation, in spite of never-ending regressive movements, is emancipating itself from the forms which it once had to take up, and a pure knowledge of its history may help to hasten this process of emancipation.[111]

Clearly, it was this "emancipation" by history which Harnack sought to effect as he "worked beyond the dogmatic to the inner form of Christian truth." And equally clearly, this was not, in the mind of one of his most able critics, an emancipation. It was not even "history":

> It follows that, while it is not justifiable, with Thomasius, to make the Lutheran confession the goal, it must be a thorough perversion of historic

[108] *Ibid.*, p. 19.
[109] *Ibid.*
[110] *Ibid.*, p. 20.
[111] *Ibid.*, pp. 21–22.

verity to represent the History of Doctrines as closed before the Reformation . . . or to close it with a portrayal of Romanism, Socinianism, and a general characterization of the Christianity of Luther—the last method being based on the ground "that the entirely conservative attitude of the Reformation toward the ancient Dogma belongs not to the Foundation but to History!"[112]

Seeberg then continues, in a footnote, with a quotation from the last volume of Harnack's *Dogmengeschichte*:

To present in detail a narration of historical events until the time of the Formula of Concord and the Decrees of Dort and then suddenly to drop the subject, I consider a serious error, inasmuch as countenance is thereby given to the prejudiced opinion that the dogmatic structures framed by the churches of the Reformation in the sixteenth century constituted the classical completion of the movement, whereas they can only be regarded as points of transition. Seeberg's comment: "Such an argument in a historical work must fill the unprejudiced reader with amazement."[113]

It was no answer which Harnack gave as he commented, "Even Seeberg and Loofs break off with the Book of Concord and the Synod of Dort. In the case of the former, the adoption of this terminus is certainly intelligible. . .";[114] but the amount of attention which he gives to this question of "dogma and Protestantism" in the last volume of his work indicates his understanding of how integral it was to his total interpretation of Christianity.[115] It is particularly instructive that in discussing this question he depends heavily on the interpretations of his colleague at the University of Berlin, Dilthey, from whom, indeed, it could be argued, he gets his theory of the "threefold issue" in the first place;[116] and that he ends this excursus with ecstatic praise of the work of Philip Schaff and his American confreres in attempting the revision of the Westminster Confession.[117]

Harnack's last word, in the *Dogmengeschichte*, on this matter of the principles of organization, indicates that he stands by his original position:

[112] Reinhold Seeberg, *Text-book of the History of Doctrines*, tr. Charles E. Hay (Grand Rapids: Baker Book House, 1961), p. 23. This is a translation of *Lehrbuch der Dogmengeschichte*, first published in 1895 (Band I) and 1898 (Band II).

[113] *Ibid.*

[114] *DG*, III, p. 614.

[115] *Ibid.*, pp. 607–617.

[116] *Ibid.*, p. 607.

[117] *Ibid.*, pp. 616–617.

My critics have not convinced me that the conception followed by me in reference to the final offshoots of the history of dogma is unhistorical. But I readily admit that the history of dogma can also be treated as the history of ecclesiastical theology, and that in this way the account can bring it down to the present time. Little is to be gained by disputing about such questions in an either-or fashion. If we regard Protestantism as a new principle which has superseded the *absolute* authority of dogmas, then, in dealing with the history of dogma, we must disregard Protestant forms of doctrine, however closely they may approximate to ancient dogma. But if we look upon it as a particular reform of Western Catholicism, we shall have to admit its doctrinal formations into that history. Only, even in that case, we must not forget that the Evangelical Churches, tried by the notion of a church which prevailed for 1300 years, are no churches. From this the rest follows of itself.[118]

We come then to the final criticism to be considered here, and in many ways it is as important as the question of the identification of the Gospel. For it has to do with "the essence of Harnack the mediator," dealing as it does with the church, "science," and the liberal theology. Harnack states the criticism in this way: ". . . it has been declared that, although the account marks a scientific advance, it yet bears too subjective or churchly a stamp, and does not correspond to the strictest claims of historical objectivity."[119]

When we recall that these lines were written in 1897, just after the Apostles' Creed controversy, and just before the watershed of *Das Wesen des Christentums*, we may be certain that Harnack's answer is an existential one. Here are excerpts:

. . . I may apply . . . a verdict recently passed by a younger fellow-worker:—"The history of dogma of today is, when considered as science, a half-thing." Certainly it is in its beginnings and it falls far short of perfection. It must become still more circumspect and reserved; but I should fear, lest it be so purified in the crucible of this youngest adept . . . that nothing of consequence would remain, or only that hollow gospel, "religion is history." . . . We are all alike sensible of the labors and controversies which he would evade; but it is one of the surprises that are rare even in theology, that one of our number should be trying in all seriousness to divide the child between the contending mothers, and that by a method which would necessarily once more perpetuate the dispute that preceded the division. The ecclesiastics among Protestants, although they arrogate to themselves the monopoly of "Christian" theology on the title pages of their books, will never give up the claim to history and

[118] *Ibid.*, p. x.
[119] *Ibid.*, p. ix.

science; they will, therefore, always feel it their duty to come to terms with the "other" theology. Nor will scientific theology ever forget that it is the conscience of the Evangelical Church, and as such has to impose demands on the Church which it serves in freedom.[120]

This sensitive and fascinating statement makes it clear that Harnack was aware that he stood *in medias res*: challenged from one point of the compass—they thought it was the "fixed" point—by the orthodox Protestants, claiming Christianity, using history and science to make their claim, and, indeed, attempting a mediation of their own; from another point goaded by the young "fellow-worker"—was he, perhaps, a member of the *Religionsgeschichtliche Schule*, which would, contrary to Harnack's judgment, write no history of dogma, and leave those investigations, on the basis of which the imperfections might be wrought through, to turn in directions Harnack believed "mystical" and unhistorical—and, in the middle, "scientific theology," "the conscience of the Evangelical Church," not willing to settle for a "hollow gospel," not willing to concede history, science, *or* Christianity to the orthodox, but serving the Church *in freedom*.

This freedom—this "liberalism," as it came to be called—certainly was not as presuppositionless as it claimed to be. Whether it deserves all the invective poured upon it is another matter: certainly it is encouraging to see the grandchildren calling into question some of the grosser bases of rejection employed by the children. But so far as responsible and careful evaluation is concerned, few critiques of the liberal theology in general, and of Harnack in particular, have been as measured as that of Gustav Aulén of the Lundensian school. Aulén, in his *Christus Victor*, has a broader purpose than a critique of Harnack, but he has suggested an important criticism in his analysis of the position of liberalism with respect to the Bible and early Christian thought. Aulén holds that liberalism misunderstood the fundamental stance of the New Testament and the early Church, in large part because of its own "doctrinaire methods of interpretation."[121] *Religionsgeschichte*, indeed, represented an advance over liberalism, for "in place of the modernizing exegesis of liberalism, the 'primitive' features of Apostolic Christianity have been emphasized with great vigour, the features *which stand in such sharp contrast with the outlook of the modern man*."[122] Again,

120 *Ibid.*, p. x–xi.

121 *Christus Victor: An Historical Study of the Three Main Types of the Idea of the Atonement*, tr. A. G. Hebert (London: S.P.C.K., 1931), p. 80.

122 *Ibid.*, italics mine.

in actual fact, our eyes have been opened to perceive certain important features of primitive Christianity, which were equally hidden from the conservatism and from the liberalism of the nineteenth century; such, for instance, as the decisive importance of the eschatological outlook in the New Testament. But at the same time new light is being thrown on the ideas of salvation and atonement in the Apostolic Age.[123]

As against the orthodox, liberalism's historical criticism unearthed and interpreted a great deal of material, on the basis of which their criticism of orthodoxy was valid. Their historical criticism must be accepted. But their prepossessions made it impossible for them to go further to the real task of interpretation: to probe behind the understanding of the history and the psychology of the Bible to its religious dimension, and this *in terms of the Bible's own point of view.* To give content to this generalization, one would say that the *historical* method of the liberals, strictly regarded, was a valid tool for understanding the *historical* character of the Bible; but the theological presuppositions of liberalism prevented them from completing their task of attempting to understand the *religious* character of the Bible, and more particularly its presuppositional position.

That this makes a difference in the resultant interpretation is obvious. To illustrate this point, and to understand also how it relates to the intepretation of dogma, we may cite two examples of this type of procedure: one with respect to dualism, the other with respect to Christology.

Liberal Protestantism rejected dualism; "but the classic idea of the Atonement is dualistic."[124] Aulén summarizes the implications:

> The leading theology from the time of the Enlightenment to the nineteenth century lay under the influence of an idealistic metaphysic, and was definitely monistic and evolutionary. It had no place for the dualistic element in Christianity; and this theological attitude reacted on its studies in the history of dogma in the New Testament and the patristic period.[125]

Historical studies could not deny the fact that there was this dualistic element in early Christianity; but they could not accept it, and therefore (since "Jesus" had to be saved from his grotesque worldview) interpreted it solely as contemporary integument. But what does it mean when one proceeds in this way? "The historical study of origins was linked up with the question of the place and the

[123] *Ibid.*
[124] *Ibid.*, p. 27.
[125] *Ibid.*

meaning and value of the dualistic idea in Christianity; and the underlying assumption was that the dualistic outlook was to be set on one side as irrelevant."[126] But this meant, in turn, that "two questions were being brought together, which ought always to be kept strictly separate: the questions of origin and of value."[127] The result was that these theological presuppositions of liberalism, inextricably joined in spite of themselves with the liberals' method, dictated that that which was really essential for an understanding of early Christianity was regarded as nonessential. Aulén sums up the point: "But in reality it is an integral and necessary element in primitive Christianity, and in the early Church too. It is impossible to eliminate it without representing early Christianity as something quite other than it actually was."[128]

The second example, that respecting Christology, is discussed by Aulén in the same vein:

> If I am not altogether mistaken, it will become evident that the interpretation of the Christology of the period as a "work of the Hellenistic spirit," intellectualistic and metaphysical in character, and of its doctrine of salvation as "naturalistic" rests rather on the presuppositions of nineteenth century theology than on an objective and unprejudiced analysis of the actual work of the Fathers.[129]

There are two serious challenges here. The one is to Harnack's proclaimed "lack of prejudice and presupposition."[130] One must simply disagree with Harnack at this point. The other challenge has to do with the basic premise of the *Dogmengeschichte* that Christology as it was worked out in the early Church was really a work of the Greek spirit, an encysting and secularizing of the "simple Gospel." If it is true that Harnack really misunderstood the character of the patristic Christology (because his theological presuppositions prevented him from genuinely engaging the religious affirmation there contained) the total interpretation is to some degree qualified. Or, as Aulén has put it,

> if the patristic view of the Atonement has really the character which we have attributed to it, it will become impossible to maintain the common view of its Christology as merely metaphysical and its doctrine of

126 *Ibid.*, p. 28.
127 *Ibid.*
128 *Ibid.*
129 *Ibid.*, pp. 29–30.
130 Cf. *supra*, pp. 157–159.

salvation as naturalistic . . . there is in reality a close relation between the Fathers and the New Testament, and an essential difference between them and the Latin type of thought which gradually grew to its full development in the medieval scholastics.[131]

Aulén's critique here points essentially to that presuppositional bias which he regarded liberalism as holding. Their exegesis was "modernizing," and therefore they ignored, or regarded as unimportant, certain crucial features of early Christianity. We believe that Aulén is correct in his claim that nineteenth-century liberal histories of dogma—particularly Harnack's—lay under the influence of monistic, evolutionary thought. As one reads Harnack's works, the increasing problem that presents itself is that this man who saw so much could not see that he saw it from a particular point of view. There can be no reasonable doubt that Harnack was utterly convinced that he had repudiated all presuppositions. But if nature abhors a vacuum, so also does the mind of a historian; and perhaps all the more because he abjured such, his covert commitments operated.

D. EVALUATION

It is too simple, no matter how tempting, to "divide" Harnack's theological vocation—the fundamental category—into "history" and "axiology," and then to superimpose this ideology on his work, finding the former exemplified in the *Dogmengeschichte* and the latter in *Das Wesen des Christentums*. That there is something resembling this dichotomy of history and axiology at work in Harnack is clear, however, and the degree of the dominance of either is probably to be explained in the light of his immediate apologetic purpose. It is possible on these grounds to argue that history controls in the *Dogmengeschichte*; but this is always "history as Harnack conceived it," which, if obvious, is still very complicated. One can also state the problem at issue in terms of "analysis" and "synthesis." Harnack disclaimed in large measure the latter task, since it would have involved him in setting forth a systematic theology; he regarded his primary vocation as that of historian. Though it was "the inner form of Christian truth" that he would "confess and defend," this inner form must be discovered by a historical method. We believe he assumed, somewhat too simply, that all that was necessary was to employ the "objective" historical method, and after the "dogmatic"

131 *Christus Victor* . . . , p. 30.

accretion had been removed, the Gospel would remain, recognizable to any clear eye.

In this evaluation of the *Dogmengeschichte* we shall consider the significance of Harnack's presuppositional structure, relating this to his definition of dogma, his division and organization of the material, and his *explication* of the history of dogma.

Harnack rejected that explicit setting forth of a point of view which was the habit of the orthodox theologians on the one hand and the Hegelians on the other. In order to understand this avoiding of a standpoint, it is necessary to see what he regarded these rival theologians as doing. This is made clear in his discussion of the history of dogma. Catholics could speak of no such thing as a history of dogma, for dogma overrides history and dictates to it. Walch was under ecclesiastical authority; rationalism was incompetent methodologically; Münscher obscured the historical development with a *loci* arrangement; the Hegelians speculated and brought their logical necessities to bear in a way that forced history to the necessary truths of reason; Neander regressed to a *loci* arrangement; Kliefoth interpreted dogma out of a confessionalist motive; Thomasius paid scant attention to the history and employed Hegelian theories; Nitzsch alone worked through to a viable historiography, combining historical fidelity and a proper sense of arrangement. In summary, there are two canons to which the historian of dogma must be equally faithful; he must examine, evaluate, and interpret the material on the basis of a sound historical method (in their separate ways Catholicism, rationalism, Münscher, the Hegelians, Neander, Kliefoth, and Thomasius fail here); and he must, as a historian of *Christian* dogma, make the essential criterion that which *is* Christian, i.e., the Gospel, i.e., the essence of the Gospel. They all fail here, possibly excepting Nitzsch. And why does Nitzsch not fail? Because he was free of rationalistic or speculative obsessions, and tended to let the most important aspect, "the expression of religious faith," assert its own rights. One must assess highly the importance of Harnack's affirmation that "only that is Christian which can be authenticated in the Gospel"[132] if one is to understand what he means by the abjuring of standpoint.

But, of course, to rival interpretations this was only to state the problem. For they too held that one must be primarily responsible to the adjective "Christian," but they believed that *their* interpreta-

[132] *DG*, I, p. 14.

tion of what was Christian (including the dogma) *was* Christian.[133] And probably that is the final reduction which one can make of this problem. If Harnack is correct in his interpretation of the essence of Christianity, this which is the crux of his total work, the rest follows. If he is jaundiced by his "situation," or by his Ritschlianism, then the most that one could say is that the *Dogmengeschichte* is a magnificent monument to historical positivism, celebrating an evanescent "essence" which has no real existence. But even if the latter should be affirmed, it cannot be denied that his service to the history of dogma was estimable in two respects: in his comprehensive assessment of dogma and its milieu of development, and in his insistence that dogma must be held responsible to the Gospel.

Harnack had a standpoint, a presuppositional structure, and it operated crucially in his *Dogmengeschichte*. In his basic thesis concerning dogma—that it was "a work of the Greek spirit on the ground of the Gospel"—historical axiology is magnificently illustrated. Here Harnack takes an obvious fact—that Christian dogma in its conception and development was a compound of many elements, certainly including what he calls the Greek spirit (whether he defines it adequately or not), as well as the Gospel (whether he defines it adequately or not), as well as the background of Old Testament belief—and he elevates one particular aspect of this development, the Greek spirit. Why? Obviously, he would answer, because his historical investigation had demonstrated conclusively that this was the dominant factor. But this, we hold, is only to raise the fundamental question, that of method. For history, to Harnack, means (at least) "to permit the idea of development to come to its rightful place," "to grasp the fact of the individual's power and possibility," and to penetrate to the "deepened conception of the essence."[134] *Development, personality, essence:* these are nineteenth-century shibboleths. Hegel, Kant, Ritschl, and romanticism, however muted, are in the prompter's pit. (And, as the summary of the *Dogmengeschichte* makes clear, these are the themes which emerge over and over again. The passionate search for the original—this is the emphasis on essence; the architectonic pattern of the total work—this bespeaks development; and the emphasis on *men*—Origen, Augustine, and Luther—proves the centrality of personality.)

But the greatest of these—for Harnack—is Ritschl, for here is the source of that decisive norm of "moral faith," *Lebensideal,*

[133] Jenkins, *op. cit.*, e.g.
[134] *Supra*, p. 126.

Humanitätslehre. And just because Harnack included the "regal judging function"—on the basis of this norm—in his historical method, he can claim that his history has revealed what his norm has prescribed. On the basis of this presupposition, to which was added a rejection of metaphysics, and an affirmation of the centrality of the religious "self-consciousness," Harnack came to the study of dogma. The ancient mode of thought was *ex hypothesi* dead: *Entwickelung* decreed it. Dogma as θεοῦ δόγματα was dead: Kant had killed it, and Schleiermacher had set theology on a new way. Though the form of the old dogma lingered on, in its Greek "ancient mode," history had moved beyond it to a consideration of the essence. "Origin" and "development" are required as rubrics in this view of history, and these are dutifully brought to the history. "To work *beyond* the dogmatic to the inner form" Harnack had declared to be a binding duty: from the development of dogma to the origin of dogma, and beyond that to the essential Christian content. What precedes what? Nineteenth-century *Entwickelung* dogmas infest the method; therefore one works "beyond" the dogmatic. Nineteenth-century threats must be met; therefore one emphasizes that moral faith which affirms man's value against materialism. And nineteenth-century faith must be confessed; therefore one defines the problems in such a way that nineteenth-century answers will be efficacious.

Perhaps Harnack did not see this. No judgment of praise or blame is necessarily involved if one points out that Aulén and Tillich in another theological climate have seen it. For Aulén, Harnack's weakness with regard to the *Dogmengeschichte* lies in the way he evaluates the Church Fathers; for Tillich, this weakness lies in the way he evaluates the "Greek spirit." But both men go further. They believe —from different points of view—that Harnack's presuppositions made it impossible that he would properly estimate the character of revelation. This shows itself in Harnack's calculated limiting of the meaning of "dogma" to "the historical doctrines of the Church," categorically excluding the possibility of going "through"—not "beyond"—the spoken or written word to the "revelatory reality" (Tillich): and it shows itself in Harnack's rejection of dualistic categories, rendering extremely dubious the possibility of properly assessing the classical view of the Atonement (and all related dogmas), resting as they do on this "ancient mode of thought."

This presuppositional structure was at work from the moment the question was phrased "to work beyond the dogmatic to the *inner form*"; axiology is perforce in the picture from that point on. On the basis of his own historical canons, the question "*Is* there an inner form" should have been given priority; instead, it is nowhere asked, but an affirmative answer is always assumed. As he entered into his historical investigations, he found in the object (Christian dogma) that same principle of "husk and kernel" which he had already confessed to in the subject (Harnack). He arrived at the conclusion that the center of unity could not be found in the *total* Scripture. One must go further toward the center to discover, *within the New Testament*, and not even there, but *within the Gospels*, and not even there, but within the *teaching of Jesus*, and not even there, but within the *essence of that teaching* the inner form of Christian truth. Here, "at the silent center of the turning world,"[135] or perhaps more aptly, "at the eye of the hurricane," there is *certainty* and *unity*. Here is the simple Gospel, the essence, the peace of God that passes all understanding, openness, "the treasure which the soul possesses in the eternal and merciful God."[136] Is this then an Eckhartian mysticism, "God and the soul" in spiritual communion? It is saved from this because on the basis of this "total experience" of the God who is love, man, who by his given nature is an ethical being, is commanded and required to make manifest his possession of the treasure of eternal life by acting, here and now in the midst of time, in relation to this eternal referent. Just as the Kingdom comes by *coming*, so is man's citizenship in this Kingdom made real by *realizing* it. Thus, from the peace and unity of this intimate communion of the soul with God, men have moved out to explicate their experience in manifold ways: in the forming of creeds and dogmas, in worship and organization, in service and self-denial, i.e., in all the differing activities which church history reveals to us. In this process, man being what he is, there was a great deal of extraneous theological accretion—as well as cultic and "organizational" accretion. Thus Harnack could say, in *Das Wesen des Christentums*, speaking of Jesus' message, "Now . . . the spring burst forth afresh, and broke a new way for itself through the rubbish—through the rubbish which priests and theologians had heaped up so as to smother the true element in religion; for how often does it happen in history that theology is only the instrument for getting rid of religion!"[137] Men

[135] Paraphrasing T. S. Eliot, *Four Quartets* (New York: Harcourt, Brace and Company, 1943), p. 7.

[136] *WC.*, p. 67.

[137] *Ibid.*, p. 42.

forgot the essence, or so bound it in formulas which were declared to be θεοῦ δόγματα and therefore absolutely authoritative (to which was added the absolutely authoritative Church and an absolutely authoritative canon), that the simple essence was lost behind layer upon layer of turbulent metaphysical *blaue Dunst*. Into this hurricane flies the historical-critical *Wetterwarte*, with a full complement of instruments aboard, charting every breeze and gale. The *Meteorolog* responsible for theological currents was Harnack; and what we have in the *Dogmengeschichte* are his charts. It is just because his whole orientation is directed to the purpose of setting forth the interrelationships between the husk and the kernel, the "eye and the winds" (doing this, of course, on the basis of a historical method which he regarded as presuppositionless and impartial) as these have interacted in the centuries since the initial setting forth of the essence, that these charts become a prime document for understanding him.

What his charting procedure made clear to him was this: that dogma did not exist at the outset of the Christian enterprise: that it had some historical point of origin, before which it was not "dogma" and after which it was; that after it became "dogma" its historical origin as "*a work of the Greek spirit on the ground of the Gospel*" was denied or suppressed, and it became authority, θεοῦ δόγματα, to be regarded as revealed truth; that this "dogmatic Christianity" was but one stage in the historical development of Christianity, preceded by "Gospel Christianity" and followed by "superstitious Christianity," although both types have continued to the present with variations; that "dogmatic Christianity" was really an intellectualization of the Gospel brought about by the employment of the psychology, metaphysic, philosophy of nature, and philosophy of history of the received Hellenistic culture; and that there has been no significant development of dogma in the Greek Church since the seventh century (for all practical purpose, since the fourth), very little development within Roman Catholicism, and a great deal of complexity within Protestantism. Furthermore, in its discovery of the central importance of justification by faith, Protestantism made possible a challenge to the whole structure of dogmatic Christianity, and expurgated superstitious Christianity. It was not able to overcome dogmatic Christianity completely because it lacked *historical* insight. Dogmatic Christianity must be overcome, and this must be effected by breaking the identification of such Christianity with the Gospel. In doing so, one recognizes that "the way of dogma" was one possible way to explicate the Gospel (and therefore *not* pathological), and that it was, indeed, necessary in the givens of the early centuries; but just because it was the work of one historical epoch, it cannot be regarded as absolute. It is only the Gospel which reveals the essence of the human situation before God, and because it reveals this, it is not conditioned by particular historical formulations, but can be carried in diverse forms. Harnack did not deny—at least in theory—the necessity of such forms; but he did deny that *das bestimmte Dogma* must be accepted as the only valid form.

How does this structure of assumptions relate to his definition of dogma? In order to answer that question, several levels in his definition must be distinguished. There is, first, the matter of authority, there is what he calls the "social element," and finally there is the specific description of Christian dogma as the "work of the Greek spirit on the ground of the Gospel."

For Harnack, as for liberals of any hue, the first two problems are to be answered in the light of the recognition that all conceptualization is nothing more than man's reasoning about his experience. No matter if this experience is "the experience of the revelation of God in the heart"; when reduced to verbal formulas, it is the limited man who provides the categories. To say that dogmas are the revealed truths of God is impossible. God does not declare himself in authoritative propositions; therefore any authority which man claims in terms of propositions is man-derived. But there is that within men which requires that they explicate what it is that they have experienced in their religious self-consciousness. In his *Grundriss der Dogmengeschichte*, Harnack describes this constraint:

> The inclination to formulate the content of religion in articles of faith is as essential to Christianity as the effort to prove these articles true with reference to science and history. Therefore the universal and supernatural character of the Christian religion requires of its believers that it find some expression of it which will not be impaired by the weakness of our knowledge of nature and history. . . . The problem which thus arises cannot be completely solved, for all knowledge is relative; nonetheless religion attempts to bring its absolute to expression in the realm of knowledge.[138]

It follows from this that if there are dogmas, they have been formed by men who shared a common confession. But this does not mean, for Harnack, that the Church confessing the faith in words is equivalent to "dogma." "Dogma" is rather "the Church reasoning about

[138] *Dogmengeschichte*, pp. 1–2.

her faith and binding the propositional results of that reasoning on its members by means of ecclesiastical law." It is this definition of Christian dogma—from Harnack's point of view the only valid one —which he has in mind when he says that it is "a work of the Greek spirit on the ground of the Gospel."

And what is implied in this description? Harnack declares in his *Das Wesen des Christentums* that either the Gospel is something that came with its time and departed with its time, or it is something that is valid behind and beneath all the historical forms in which it has been cast. The latter position is the correct one, according to Harnack, for one finds a multiplicity of forms into which the Gospel has been cast in the course of its historical development. It is necessary that the Gospel be carried in *some* historical form, and Harnack on this basis rejects the criticism which was so often raised against him that he regarded the development of dogma as pathological. But the historical tragedy, he believed, lay in the fact that the separation of husk and kernel was so seldom recognized as a necessary corrective to the too-sure pronouncements of men. One must distinguish that which was born from the original strength of Christianity from that which was assimilated to it. He explicitly rejects the view that original Christianity and "dogma" stand in relation to each other as seed and tree; a more appropriate analogy would be that of the Johannine "spirit and flesh." Though the spirit can never be experienced unless there be a flesh to carry it, the flesh which then describes the experience can never capture and contain its essence in propositional formulas. The tragedy is that the propositions were formulated by a particular mind, the "Greek mind" and then were declared to be of equal revelatory authority with the experience itself. Actually, this propositional formulation (dogma) "had its history in the individual living man and nowhere else."[139]

Because this is always true—whether it refers to dogma, to cultus, to polity, or to *practica*, and whether it takes place in the milieu of Origen, of Augustine, or of Luther—no historical form can be declared absolute. Conversely, the essential Gospel cannot be transmitted except via historical forms. Harnack's thesis is that this essence provided the ground for the initial casting of "dogma"; that this casting was carried out by the ripened Hellenic mind; that this particular historical formulation was declared to be of equal revelatory value to the Scriptures, and to the Gospel therein; and that, in

[139] *DG*, I, pp. 13–14.

spite of later qualifications and additions, this form remained determinative within the Christian Church. But this form, as he defines it, and as he explicates it, this form which he describes as an intellectualization of the Gospel, always has as its referent *das bestimmte Dogma.*[140]

It is not difficult to understand why Harnack regarded the question of the division of the material as "the most important problem with which the history of dogma is concerned."[141] For where *the problem* of the history of dogma is stated in terms of origin and development, *all that Harnack believed about the Gospel, and all of that historical conception and method which he espoused, can* be justified and applied toward a solution of the problem. We do not intend this to be anything more than a neutral statement of fact. It should be noted here, however, how integrally this statement of the problem is related to Harnack's fundamental concerns. He was certain that there was an "essence" or an "inner form" to Christian truth—he had inherited the certainty that there was such an "essence" and the passion to discover it from romanticism. He early declared it as a part of his vocation "to work beyond the dogmatic" to this inner form via historical procedure—he had inherited this from Tübingen, to some extent from Erlangen, and from Ritschl. To state one's position in this way means, of course, that the dogmatic is not central —to be relevant to the challenge of ecclesiastical orthodoxy, on the one hand, and to speak to the culture, on the other, one must affirm this. Yet the dogma in some way encysts this "essence"—Harnack's historical understanding made it clear to him that institutions are necessary to carry and preserve even the pure Gospel. Harnack believed that if one could strip off the layers of dogmatic accretion, he would find first "theology," then "religious faith," and then the basis of faith. This final basis, "God and the soul," is the original reality; it could meet the challenge of Harnack's contemporary situation, overcoming both materialism and "ecclesiastical paralysis." Basic, therefore, to the total conception, is the necessity that this "original reality" be rediscovered. On this interpretation, one can understand Harnack's suspicion of all methods which interpreted dogma in any other way than as an explication of the religious self-consciousness.

We believe the division and organization which he sets forth is valid only if there is a reality to Christianity; if Harnack correctly

[140] *Supra*, p. 148.
[141] *DG*, I, p. 36.

identifies it; if the "Greek spirit" is what he says it is; if the content of revelation can never be set forth propositionally; if historical conditionedness always enters into conceptual activity; and if one can assume that the same mind is at work in history and in us. To all of these Harnack would agree. Yet his critics did not accept many of these propositions. Some said there was no such reality as Harnack discovered; some challenged his identification of the "Greek spirit"; some held that he overplayed the "cultural milieu" theme, to the detriment of the "Gospel" influence on the shaping of dogma; and some regarded Harnack as being insufficiently aware of his own "historical conditionedness" with respect to his historical presuppositions.

As the division and organization depend on the definition, so does the actual explication. The essential rubrics have been set: "the Gospel" and "the Greek spirit." When the reality is viewed as Harnack viewed it, and when "the Greek spirit" is defined as he has defined it, the main task becomes that of setting forth the interpenetrations of the one with the other as they first become "dogma" and then develop as "dogma." This task is carried through by Harnack with a consummate skill which at times becomes near evangelical in it passion, as in the sections on Augustine and Luther. He includes in his purview not only the creativity of the "individual living men," but that plethora of factors which obtained at various times in the process of dogmatic formulation and development. But the pattern has been set by the way in which he defines his basic terms. For when the Gospel is defined in the reductionistic way which Harnack adopts, it becomes almost impossible to get the complex system of Christian dogma unless there is a vast supplement supplied by some other force. This, for Harnack, was "the Greek spirit." He does not say that even on his definition of the "Gospel" the Gospel's contribution to this development was minor: he avows the opposite. And he does not suppress material which would be embarrassing to his thesis, though it may be held that he argues with all the subtlety of a scholastic in order to fit this material to his central thesis. But —to state the issue squarely—for Harnack it is not the Gospel (as he conceived it) but the Greek spirit (as he conceived it) which determines the shape of dogma (as he conceived it).

This is perhaps the crucial question in evaluating the total work: how valid are his definitions? Did Harnack's antiorthodox position penetrate his historical-critical work? Was he too aware of the necessities of his time which, he thought, demanded an undogmatic Christianity? Was he afraid of any taint of biblicism? Did his antimetaphysical, antispeculative bias make it impossible for him to carry on a conversation with Paul, and others? Did he, living in a complex century, employ *hysteron-proteron* reasoning as he looked at the "crucial period" between 50 and 150 A.D., as he was accused of doing also with respect to Jesus? Having found "certainty and unity" in a Gospel of "the merciful God seeking the soul," did he read this back into the first century as the "reality of Christianity"? These are all more or less familiar charges made against Harnack.

When applied to this work, the following development would be required: that there must be "something" within the Gospel of Jesus which raised it above the apocalyptic form in which it was cast; that whatever this "something" was remained active in spite of the cast that was given to it in this "paleontological epoch"; that this passed to the Hellenic world via Paul, who was, however, not understood; that because he was not understood, the "something" was simply interpreted in Hellenic forms as that which the Hellenes had been seeking all the time; that this Hellenic mind, which had penetrated widely into non-Palestinian Judaism, went to work with all its assiduity to join together the Old Testament and the "something" under the aegis of the scientific and religious culture which they had maintained as a residuum; that the "something" retained sufficient power for a century after Paul to throw back such threats as Gnosticism and Marcionism, even before a fixed authority was established; that once the Hellenic mind had taken over and misunderstood Paulinism, the presuppositions which had informed the latter had to be eviscerated in order to supply the former with presuppositions more amenable to it; that while the "something" was still present, Gnosticism had to be rejected because of its "acute secularization" of this "something," but after the Church had arrived at authoritative status, this Hellenism actually prevailed to bring about a "gradual secularization"; and this "gradual secularization" shows itself in the great Catholic Church which was formed, and in the dogma which it pronounced as authoritative.

It must be admitted that this is a scintillating thesis, and that Harnack has worked it out in scintillating fashion. Yet we maintain that even here "historical axiology" abounds; and in order to make the point we introduce here, as a theologoumenon, an alternative definition.

"Dogma is the work of the Church, in its several environments, effected on the ground of the Gospel." Even if one agrees with

Harnack that the Gospel was a powerful force, and that it was on this ground that dogma developed, and that dogma must be held responsible to the Gospel, it does not follow that Harnack has rightly identified it. In fact, we believe that Harnack's identification is dubious because his nisus to essence procedure led him astray. Whatever his motivation for the employment of such a procedure—and we have attempted to demonstrate that it was multiform—it is certainly a fact that he did employ it. We believe that he indeed "reduced" Christianity; that he did this in terms of his Ritschlian presuppositions, elevating that moral faith which he believed the situation of his time required; and that such a "reduction" made it possible for him to excise from Christianity everything—authoritative dogma, authoritative episcopate, and a part of the authoritative canon (or all of it—as "authoritative"?)—which he regarded as debilitating to modern Christianity. But we believe that he thereby misrepresented the Gospel. It is not so much a matter of "simple" versus "complex": it is a question of "moral faith" (axiology) versus the full New Testament kerygma. We believe, in short, that the "Gospel" cannot be reduced to three, or thirty, or three hundred "propositions," simply because it is concerned with the *Einmaligkeit* of God's self-disclosure, on the one hand, and with the totality of man's life, involving the ethical dimension, to be sure, but encompassing everything else that makes man the thing that he is, on the other hand.

Furthermore, our definition would emphasize the primacy of the fact that it is the community of faith and worship which reasons about its faith in the formulation of dogma; that this "community of faith and worship" was related to, and knew itself to be related to, the God of the Old Testament; that, of course, it was influenced by the "Greek spirit"—though not more than by the "Hebraic spirit"—and by every other cultural *Geist* in which it lived and reasoned; that this influence is inevitable for any "historical" faith; and that "dogma" therefore, so conceived, can never be regarded as Tridentine Catholicism has come to regard it. It is here that we see Harnack as employing a *tour de force* to make his point. For he can maintain his "Greek spirit" claim only if dogma is "individually justified," i.e., restricted in the way he has restricted it. Loofs, therefore, is correct in his statement that the *Dogmengeschichte* is a monograph on Christian dogma at the beginning of the fourth century, conceived, to be sure, with genius, and related to the subsequent history with massive learning.

What would Harnack's criticism of this formulation be? Of course, he would say that it was not true to historical fact, because the early Church contained no such unanimity of position as is here required. Yet it is clear from his own later New Testament Studies[142] that it behooves anyone to proceed quite cautiously at this point. The fact that the Church from the beginning laid claim to the Old Testament, interpreting it, to be sure, in most unusual ways, is of crucial importance here. For whatever the mode of interpretation, it was still to this content that it was applied. And the indisputable fact that the New Testament, when written by the Church, placed itself within the framework of Jewish thought ("the God of Abraham, Isaac, and Jacob," "God spoke of old to our fathers by the prophets,") is certainly presumptive evidence that the situation from which the dogma developed was by no means as "Hellenic" as Harnack assumes. Certainly he is correct in designating the crucial period as the century from 50 to 150 A.D. It is instructive that it is here, in the chapter entitled "The Common Faith and the Beginnings of Self-Recognition in Gentile Christianity which Was to Develop into Catholicism" that he admits the greatest difficulty of explication, declaring that "the statements made in this chapter require a particular forbearance, for we cannot stop to justify our selection from the rich and varied material, . . . our emphasis upon certain elements, and our placing in the background of other elements."[143] For this is precisely what must be done, if it can be done, in order to validate the total thesis. We would very much like to know what the basis of selection and emphasis was. On what basis, for example, can Harnack say that "when we speak of the beginnings of knowledge, we no longer refer to the members of the Christian community in its totality, but only to those individuals who were the leaders of the community," and

142 The series of studies which immediately comes to mind is the *Beiträge zur Einleitung in das Neue Testament*, although there were multitudes of other individual studies. The seven works published in this series are: Vol. I, *Lukas der Arzt* (1906); Vol. II, *Sprüche und Reden Jesu* (1907); Vol. III, *Die Apostelgeschichte* (1908); Vol. IV, *Neue Untersuchungen zur Apostelgeschichte und zur Abfassungszeit der synoptischen Evangelien* (1911); Vol. V, *Über den privaten Gebrauch der heiligen Schriften in der alten Kirche* (1912); Vol. VI, *Die Enstehung des Neuen Testaments und die wichtigsten Folgen der neuen Schöpfung* (1914); Vol. VII, *Zur Revision der Prinzipien der neutestamentlichen Textkritik* (1916). All were published at Leipzig by Hinrichs. The first six studies have been translated, excellently, and quotations are from the translations. In these studies it is notable that Harnack was quite cautious of bizarre theses; his results are generally "conservative."

143 *DG*, I, p. 140.

then proceed to tone down the value of Clement and Polycarp in order to exalt the "enthusiastic phantasies which show us how manifold and complicated the development really was."[144]

Harnack would also challenge this definition of dogma as omitting that element which he declared throughout to be characteristic of it: authority. Yet indeed this would appear to be the most obvious sort of "individual justification" of dogmatic origin and development. Certainly if one accepts this given which he has laid down, "that there is always an authority at the basis of dogma,"[145] it follows that one cannot speak of "dogma" until such an authority can actually be demonstrated to have been in existence. But, in this regard, is it not true that Baur's conception of the rise of Catholicism and the consequent formulation of dogma may be more true than that of Harnack? Or, at least, is this not an option which can be employed on the basis of the historical information available which holds as much initial credibility as Harnack's method? Remove the Hegelian "working out of the idea" from Baur's conception, and what remains would come closer to fitting the definition that we have given than that which Harnack gave. And even if Harnack's dictum were to be accepted, it does not follow that "authority" must be constituted in the way in which he implies. Indeed, in his very admission that for all of its "enthusiastic phantasies" the early Church was "inwardly bound to . . . particular interpretations of the Gospel,"[146] and therefore possessed the elements for the formation of a system of doctrine which could operate to throw off the Gnostic threat, has he not conceded that there was a standard of "the Christian Gospel" in existence very early (from the beginning)? And does this not run head-on into the "something" theory, thereby making necessary (from his point of view) a postponing of the formation of such an authority, and making necessary (from his reader's point of view) "a particular forbearance" for this sort of "individually justified" representation of dogma?

In summary, then, it appears clear that this great work is built upon Harnack's absolutely basic category of "the Gospel"—the reality of Christianity. To fail to understand this fact, or to fail to see what content Harnack places in this category, can only result in a failure to understand his definition of dogma, his division and principles of organization of the material, and his explication of the

[144] *Ibid.*, pp. 140–141.
[145] *Supra*, p. 124.
[146] *DG*, I, pp. 140–141.

origin and development. However, though the validity of the work rests essentially upon this definition, it cannot be held that the value of the work is destroyed if this definition is rejected. For it is in either case true that Harnack's encyclopedic knowledge of the sources makes of this work a monumental contribution to the literature of the history of dogma.

But clearly, in respect to Harnack's own purpose, this concession would be a mess of pottage to Esau. He believed passionately that he was restoring to the Church a correct picture of the origin and development of dogma, and thereby making possible a hastening of that process of emancipation which the Reformation had initiated. It is not unfair to say that he thought he had discovered the genuine Gospel of Jesus in its dynamic principle. Though this had been encysted in the dogmatic husks of ancient and medieval Catholicism, it had, nonetheless, emerged from time to time even in the period of dogmatic domination: with Athanasius, with Augustine, and even to some degree with Origen. Yet for Harnack it was Luther, above all others, upon whom the Light dawned; Luther who saw that "God gives faith and creates penitence," though he did not see that precisely *this* experience *is* revelation; Luther who deprived "Whore Reason" of her cavalier treatment of the Gospel, by his shattering of the old subject/object epistemology as it was applied to religion. Thus he "gave religion back to religion, affirmed the independence of the knowledge given through faith,"[147] and made of the Augustinian "God and the soul" *one thing*. So Harnack thought.

But *there* is the fundamental difficulty. What was the *one thing*? What was the Christian religion "originally"? Was it so simple a thing that any nineteenth-century historically trained "clear eye" could immediately identify it? Is it possible to reduce the multiform doctrinal, cultic, and institutional phenomenon which is Christianity to *a* reality? Harnack answered yes. And his final evaluation of Luther (he "restored the doctrine" that the Gospel is a "joyous message and the power of God"; that this is "the only principle of theology"; that "the power of God cannot be construed by thought, but must be experienced"; that "faith in God . . . cannot be evoked by reason or authority"; and that "all that is not born of faith is alien to the Christian religion"[148]) proves it. Yet of all these principles it may be said that they are seen by the "clear eye" of the nineteenth-century historian, and perhaps thereby transmuted.

[147] *Ibid.*, III, p. 715.
[148] *Ibid.*, pp. 759–764.

Harnack clearly conceived it as the binding duty of his vocation to carry to fulfillment these insights which Luther had bequeathed to the Church. For Luther had not dissociated the Gospel from his contemporary integument as thoroughly as it should have been done, limited as he was in historical understanding. And the epigons had confounded the problem by their misunderstanding of what Luther had done, forcing Christianity into the scholastic theology of the Lutheran symbols. But the yeast continued to work, even through the epigons, even through Pietism and Rationalism, importantly in Zinzendorf and Wesley, powerfully in Schleiermacher and Ritschl. It is in this succession that Harnack proudly stands.

PART FOUR

THEOLOGY

Some explanation for the division and organization of the material of this work may be appropriate at this point. The hypostatizing of "history" and "axiology"—the latter category to be seen as the animating norm for the more structured "theology" —has, quite probably, already been objected to by the critical reader. There is no virtue in belaboring the obvious, but there may be virtue in trying to make clear what is intended by this apparently artificial division, and there certainly is a command to be fair that requires the explanation.

There is artificiality, of course. The individual in history is just that—but an individual is also a totality of all that has entered into the person and made him what he is. As one seeks for the standard to interpret such an "individual totality," categories emerge. These categories are in the interpreter. The important question for the historian-interpreter is, finally—this one can learn from Harnack—whether they are in the material, whether they are responsibly derived from the sources, and whether they are faithfully represented, to the limit of the interpreter's ability.

Harnack's *Dogmengeschichte* is a paradigm for imitation here. In the Prolegomena to that work he took great pains to make clear what his principles of division and organization were. He was convincing to some, unconvincing to others. For the latter, Harnack was intruding his own theological positions at the same time that he protested his "historical objectivity." He may, indeed, have done so; but it is no less true that those who made the charge also intruded their theological positions, protesting their objectivity while they did it.

The lesson here is that it is not given to men to be historically unconditioned, purely objective beings. The interpreter is himself an "individual totality," bearing his categories with him. He must be as faithful to "the given" as he can be, at the same time confessing that he sees what he sees from his point of view. There is no claim made here, therefore, to "wie es gewesen ist"; the confession is that the interpreter sees Harnack in his individual totality as *not* first a theologian and second a historian, *nor* the reverse, but *always* as a historian *and* a theologian. The division therefore is didactic, and that only. To interpret Harnack in any other way would be, we believe, to fall victim to "the fallacy of simple location." And, as a final presuppositional confession, we believe that this is, indeed, a fallacy.

The three chapters that follow will underline Harnack's theological position by directing attention to central questions which he considered. As our purpose in Part III centered on "the historical interpretation of theology," here the coin will be reversed: we shall consider "the theological interpretation of history." Because the coin is single, one might choose from a substantial number of rubrics. The three we have chosen, "Jesus Christ and Christianity," "The Bible," and "The Reality (*Wesen*) of Christianity" are not random selections, of course. These were dominant questions for Harnack throughout his life. They possess an intrinsic unity of their own, so that the problem of writing about them discretely inevitably arises. But in addition to *their* intrinsic unity, the fact that they were fed through Harnack's rich, expansive, historically oriented consciousness (which at the same time was antisystematic in the sense of *loci* arrangement) deepens the problem. Themes emerge at unexpected places, and the method has been to deal with them where they emerge. For whatever redundancy this may create, a *mea culpa*; but this has been judged more appropriate than an index without context.

XII

Jesus Christ and Christianity

A. THE HISTORICAL JESUS

HARNACK'S PERSONAL struggles, as indicated in the Leipzig correspondence, centered in the question "How can I become his disciple?" One can discern in Harnack's own development that which he practiced in his historiography—the "stripping off" of the dogmatic forms to try to locate the inner form of Christian truth. Thus he relinquished belief in the doctrine of the preexistence of Christ, and the classical formulations of the doctrine of the Trinity and of the Logos. The "kernel" at which he arrived was the teaching of the historical Jesus: but this process was, as we shall see, by no means simple.

First consideration should be given to the source-problem. Harnack's critical work in this regard was, on the whole, conservative. He objected to the practice of many of his contemporaries whereby "everything which can possibly be a *hysteron-proteron* is at once pronounced to be such with absolute certainty. This seems to me to be a form of critical conscientiousness which leads to critical narrow-mindedness."[1] He believed that the eschatological school and, later, the *Formgeschichte* school had gone off on tangents in their means of investigation. He was convinced that one can depend upon the

[1] *Sayings of Jesus*, p. 204.

essential credibility of the Synoptics in giving a historically recoverable picture of Jesus. In *The Sayings of Jesus* he analyzes, in particular, the relation between the Gospel of Mark and the "Q" document. Q is older than Mark, and differs from it in that it shows no evidence of the influence of the "Paulinism" of that Gospel. "*The main theme of St. Mark—that Jesus, His death and resurrection, form the content of His own Gospel—is not to be found in Q.*"[2] He contrasts the two sources, finding Mark inconsistent, apologetic, lacking in discrimination, sometimes incredible, and yet providing us with our only concrete information about the life of Jesus; while Q is exact, profound, many-sided and free from bias in setting forth the teaching of Jesus, and yet gives us no history. To the question as to which has more value, Harnack answers: "Eighteen centuries of Christianity have answered this question, and their answer is true. The portrait of Jesus as given in the sayings of Q has remained in the foreground."[3]

A further evidence of Harnack's essentially conservative position regarding the sources is to be found in his article "Hat Jesus gelebt?" written in 1909 in connection with the Jatho controversy.[4] The fact that such a question could arise at all indicates the degree to which the historical investigations of the nineteenth century *had* gone unnoticed. Nor is this in itself the sum of the "shameful indictment." For the claim that Jesus was not a historical person and that the Gospels were essentially fabrications was being based on "scientific historical investigation." Harnack remarks that no reputable scholar would agree with this claim, and describes the three persons with whom this view is associated in Germany, Kalthoff, Drews, and Jensen, as dilettantes. In part the fact that the claim has been entertained at all resides in the sensationalist appeal which the debunking of great men always makes upon certain kinds of minds; in part the record itself, where encomium is piled on encomium to the point that the figure which emerges seems to be too good to be human, is responsible; and in part it is the stance of the critics themselves which accounts for the raising of the question. Specifically, it is their conviction that a man must be understood in the context of his environment and his heritage—which is true—and solely within this context—which is false—that caused them to question Jesus' historical existence. For Jesus could not be reduced to their categories.

The further question as to why these negative treatments of Jesus

[2] *Ibid.*, p. 248.
[3] *Ibid.*, p. 250.
[4] *RA*, II, NF, pp. 165–175.

should meet with the favor of so many people has a double answer. In the first place, there is a widespread lack of knowledge as to what *is* comprised in scientific theology, and consequently a distrust of everything that it suggests. Even so eminent a man as Haeckel judges theology solely on the basis of that limited and unscientific brand with which he has come in contact. There is guilt attached to the "scientific theology" here, for its proponents have not taken seriously the apologetic task and described in publications its purposes and limits. But there is another more powerful explanation for the fact that so many are enchanted with this negative position: it is argued that one can expect nothing but a partisan answer from anyone who holds that religion is something essential and valuable, for this person will always read history through partisan eyes. Thus, when a dilettante comes forward who claims to be absolutely neutral with respect to the whole question of the validity of religion, it is assumed that he can conduct an impartial historical investigation, and he gets a hearing.[5]

Harnack then summarizes the questions which cannot be answered unless the historicity of Jesus is accepted. Generally, these questions point out the absurdity of believing that the "fable-makers"—the Evangelists—would have deliberately included insoluble difficulties in their narratives—as in Jesus' instructions to his disciples not to go to the Samaritans and Gentiles, which they did shortly thereafter, or in the quoting of the statement from the cross, "My God, my God, why have you forsaken me?" Harnack remarks with some asperity that of course one can answer these questions through some kind of contrived knowledge; "but no satisfactory answer can be given if Jesus did not live."[6] Yet the certainty of the historical existence of Jesus does not rest on such individual questions or observations:

> Anyone who considers the first three Gospels, even taking into consideration what is said by the sharpest historical criticism, and does not feel that a powerful, compelling, uncontrivable personality is here at work, thereby declares his incapacity to extract historical and personal life from these records or to distinguish this life from fable.[7]

The argument may be less circumspect than Harnack is accustomed to use. But it makes unmistakably clear his position that Jesus was a historical person and that the primary sources for our knowledge about him are credible and valid.

[5] *Ibid.*, pp. 168 f.
[6] *Ibid.*, p. 174.
[7] *Ibid.*, p. 175.

On the basis of these sources what can be said about this historical Jesus? It is of more than passing interest that Harnack, with all of his writing, did not write a "Life of Jesus"; but even more instructively, his attention is concentrated almost entirely on the teaching of Jesus and its effect. We may note this characteristic of Harnack's representation in several connections.

First, he took issue with Loofs, in 1916, for having made the statement that "the life of Jesus was not solely human." Harnack wrote that the thesis should run as follows:

> The life of Jesus contains tensions for which we do not possess historical analogies. A scientific person can and should not use any other formulation. It was a solely human life, and yet the faith learned from him divine power and divine wisdom. That is the only possible formulation. One falls helplessly into Docetism or into the two-nature doctrine if one formulates the question in any other way. If Jesus had the consciousness, as no other (and no other after him was able to or could have it), that he was the Son of God, then he had this within a completely human consciousness.[8]

Here that which "the faith learned from him" is emphasized.

In another earlier encounter, centering in the strife over the Apostles' Creed, Cremer of Griefswald had challenged certain of Harnack's claims, and Harnack answered him by setting forth the relevance of historical study and its limits.[9] Cremer had argued that there were no new results of historical investigation that had relevance to the controversy. Harnack answered that questions such as "Does the Ascension of Jesus belong to the earliest Christian proclamation" and "What is the basis of the tradition that Jesus was not Joseph's son" *are* historical questions and can only be resolved historically, not dogmatically. Cremer's second argument had been that the question concerning the person of Christ can never be decided by means of historical investigation. Harnack admits that the statement is half true, but dangerous. Stated in Cremer's way, it means that the fanatics (*Schwärmgeist*) who create everything from their own inner revelation, the Roman Catholics who trust the authority of the Church to guarantee the picture of Christ they project, and the speculative rationalists who are satisfied with the idea of the Incarnation cannot be answered. By contrast, Harnack affirms, "The evangelical Christian uses history: for we want no other Christ, and no other Christ can

[8] AZH, p. 247.

[9] "Antwort auf die Streitschrift D. Cremers: zum Kampf um das Apostolikum," *RA*, I, pp. 265–298.

help us, than the real historical Christ whose words we still understand and whose tensions we can accept in our hearts."[10] True, historical understanding can never convince anyone that Christ is his Lord. "Here I am at one with my opponent when he says 'It is not historical investigation which speaks the last word about Christ.' "[11] But the Holy Spirit does work through the preaching of the Word. And for that majority who are not of the "Christian aristocracy" (i.e., the theologians), there is no way to build a bridge from the world to Christianity except by history. History can do this, but it is not therefore "religion." Religion in the final analysis has to do with nothing else than the soul's finding and holding onto God. Therefore the sentence of Cremer should be stated: "The question as to who and what Jesus is . . . can be strengthened by means of historical investigation; but the conviction that this historical Jesus is Savior and Lord does not emerge from historical knowledge, but from the knowledge of God and of sin as Jesus preached it."[12]

Harnack had declared, in *The Sayings of Jesus*, that the picture of Jesus given us in Q had remained in the foreground for eighteen centuries. Certainly this is an exaggeration. Equally certain, his belief that it *would* remain in the foreground was partial, at least, if not inaccurate. For those directions of investigation which he viewed with alarm were emerging into the foreground, in spite of his (perhaps apologetic?) judgment:

> Above all, the tendency to exaggerate the apocalyptic and eschatological element in our Lord's message, and to subordinate to this the purely religious and ethical elements, will ever find its refutation in Q. This source is the authority for that which formed the central theme of the message of our Lord—that is, the revelation of the knowledge of God, and the moral call to repent and believe, to renounce the world and to gain heaven—this and nothing else.[13]

Finally, in considering Harnack's interpretation of "the historical Jesus," it would be an omission to fail to note that fascinating section of the *Dogmengeschichte* in which Harnack identifies, in the strongest possible language, *the* essence of the teaching: "The . . . section connected with Matthew 11:25–30 . . . I hold, from strictly historical and objective grounds, to the true main section, the gospel in the

[10] *Ibid.*, p. 290.
[11] *Ibid.*, pp. 390–391.
[12] *Ibid.*, p. 293.
[13] Pp. 250–251.

gospel."[14] On the next to last page of the *Dogmengeschichte*, Harnack asserts that "Matthew 11:27 is the basis of faith and of theology."[15] From this verse, "All things have been delivered to me by my Father; and no one knows the Son except the Father, and no one knows the Father except the Son and anyone to whom the Son chooses to reveal him," the historical Jesus must be interpreted. For this verse, Harnack says elsewhere, "belongs to the best authority which we possess concerning our Lord, nor can any valid objections be alleged against its content . . . the whole emphasis is laid upon the knowledge of God and its revelation . . . the primary condition of the knowledge of God is simplicity . . . Jesus is represented as the revealer of the knowledge of God."[16] Those things which had been delivered to the Son, and revealed by the Son, are "God's sovereignty, the higher righteousness (the commandment of love), and the forgiveness of sin."[17] This Gospel is inseparably connected with him, for in preaching it he calls men to himself. Yet: "Jesus Christ has by no explicit statement placed the connection of his Gospel with his person in the foreground."[18] To be sure, he knows that he is the Messiah: "the speaker is a teacher, a prophet, one who is more than a prophet—*the final decisive Messenger of God*; but so surely as he demands unconditional *obedience* to His commands, in which the will of God is expressed, and calls upon men *to follow him*, so little does He do this with the expressed self-witness: 'I am the Messiah.' "[19]

The reason Harnack adduces here for Jesus' reticence to declare himself as the Messiah is that the words would not have proved the fact if there had not been a life, "the overpowering impression of his person. By living, acting and speaking from the riches of that life which he lived with his Father, he became for others the revelation of the God about whom they had previously heard, but had not

[14] *DG*, III, p. ix. The section to which Harnack refers reads (RSV): "At that time Jesus declared, 'I thank thee, Father, Lord of heaven and earth, that thou hast hidden these things from the wise and understanding and revealed them to babes; yea, Father, for such was thy gracious will. All things have been delivered to me by my Father; and no one knows the Son except the Father, and no one knows the Father except the Son and any one to whom the Son chooses to reveal him. Come to me, all who labor and are heavy-laden, and I will give you rest. Take my yoke upon you, and learn from me; for I am gentle and lowly in heart, and you will find rest for your souls. For my yoke is easy, and my burden is light.' "

[15] *DG*, III, p. 813.

[16] *Sayings of Jesus*, pp. 300–310, *passim.*

[17] *DG*, I, p. 58.

[18] *Ibid.*

[19] Harnack, *Sayings of Jesus*, p. 244.

known."[20] Therefore one may question whether it is, finally, the *teaching* which constitutes the Gospel; "the personal life which awakens life around it as the fire of one torch kindles another":[21] this *effect* appears to be the essence of the matter.

For Harnack, then, Jesus can be known as well as any historical person can be known. Such a statement presupposes Harnack's total methodological structure, formed within the context of nineteenth-century Germany. But because the faith that informed the erection of this structure was directed to the service of, and perhaps derived from the "situation" of this time, not derived from the biblical conception of faith (this was held impossible because of historical relativity), or from the biblical declaration of the action of God which evokes faith (this was held unknowable), what was actually explicated was one's own "inner certainty" as to what must have been true. That is, because of the limits that Harnack had already declared to be binding upon man (relating to his possibility of knowing), if Jesus was to be placed at the center (he had to be), then this Jesus had to be cut to the measure of man's highest apprehension of personality. For Harnack had said that the *Geist* that was at work in history and in us is the same *Geist*. Jesus was perfectly human, we are human. Only if we can receive by that antenna (Harnack's "clear eye") which feels and experiences that which has been sent by that "powerful, compelling, uncontrivable personality" can Jesus have any efficacy or worth for us. And this is the quintessential norm for Harnack: worthfulness, as against the impersonal mechanism of his time. When Barth asserted in 1920 that faith is not some pure and unsullied capacity, but sheerly gift, Harnack could only confess that he did not understand one syllable of what Barth was talking about. One need not doubt his testimony here. For certainly it is not inaccurate to say that when one makes worth for men the norm with relation to which all statements and systems must be judged, any theology which begins by emphasizing the infinite distance between God and man must appear to be irresponsible and incomprehensible.

B. CHRIST

"To anyone who lives in the Holy Spirit, the present Christ is experienced as the new and determinative principle of our existence."[22] The teaching of the historical Jesus has made clear what this principle

[20] *DG*, I, p. 58.
[21] *Ibid.*, p. 70.
[22] Harnack, "Der gegenwärtige Christus," *RA*, V, NF, p. 119.

is; his life exemplified it in a person; the effect of that teaching and that life was such that other men experienced this new principle. What is this new and determinative principle which is experienced as the present Christ?

Or, asked differently, what is the nature of Christ's redemption? Is it a gift? Does it relate at all to sacramental or confessional understandings? If not—and certainly the answer to the latter question is "not"—what does "redemption" mean for Harnack?

As a contribution to a symposium on the Atonement, Harnack wrote an article, in 1900, on "Christ as Redeemer." It was originally published in English and eleven years later appeared in German in the *Reden und Aufsätze* series.[23]

This article states his position forthrightly and unambiguously, and it therefore deserves careful attention. Harnack admits that he is attempting to speak to a contemporary situation which has in a variety of ways denied the Christian doctrine of redemption. Today, he declares, "the belief in redemption has lost its certainty, and the desire as well as the search for it is almost extinct."[24] Many still claim to be monotheists, and affirm the ethics of Christianity, but will have nothing to do with the notion of redemption. Particularly, there are those who say they feel no need of redemption, those who call it a weak and debilitating doctrine, and those who hold that though it is valid, the Church is mistaken in claiming that it can have anything to do with someone who lived eighteen centuries ago.

But almost all are more or less agreed that the contemporary *Weltanschauung*, as they call it, makes it impossible to retain the idea. Psychology has given us a new picture of man; investigations of the origins of morals have changed our views of evil and sin; historical science has given us a historical Christ instead of a heavenly one; critical philosophy has indicated the limits of the knowable and the real—where can one therefore find room for a view of redemption and a redeemer?[25]

The belief in inevitable progress is partly responsible for this view, and Harnack denies his own adherence to it. To be sure, the *forms*

[23] "Christus als Erlöser," *RA*, II, NF, pp. 81–93. According to the note in *Aus Wissenschaft und Leben*, Band II, Harnack was one of seventeen theologians who had been asked, in the winter of 1899–1900, to contribute an article to a symposium on "The Atonement in Modern Religious Thought." This was published in 1900 by James Clarke and Company of London, and appeared in German "*zum erstenmal*" in the *RA* volume.

[24] *Ibid.*, p. 81.

[25] *Ibid.*, p. 82.

in which men's views of redemption have been held have been in part destroyed, but the essence remains the same. He reiterates here his conviction that there is a "same mind" at work in history and in us, quoting Goethe's remark, "Mankind is always progressing, and man always remains the same," to prove this constant in humanity; and he declares that on the highest levels of man's life there is a residual restlessness for self-completion, and as long as this obtains, there will be a place for a message of redemption and a redeemer. He then details six points in an attempt "to justify the Christian belief in redemption," and declares that it is not his purpose "to prove one definite standpoint," but rather to "recall definite facts to remembrance."[26]

In the first place, those who say they feel no need for redemption "either deceive themselves, or they are thinking only of one particular kind of redemption"; for this need "to be free from the common run of life, and to win a higher and deeper existence" is universal.[27] That this is true is proved by the number of false gods to which men turn for redemption. Many turn to art and science, which promise such a redemption from triviality, proving thereby that this "noble aspiration" to rise above "the stream of the ordinary" and "to be free from the past" cannot be destroyed.[28] In making this point, the foundation for the rest of Harnack's explication has thus been declared: all men by nature are aspiring creatures, and as such their aspirational nature and their attempt to free themselves from the past never cease to operate.

But one can go further in describing this longing for redemption: "Wherever the Christian religion has come, wherever the faintest ray of its light has penetrated, there the recognition that righteousness is the highest good and guilt the greatest evil has firmly rooted. The desire of all desires is to be pure and to have inner peace."[29] Here Harnack's eloquence pours forth, mixing some anthropology, some biology, a bit of Judaism and of Greek philosophy, a bit of Christianity, all under the aegis of Goethean wisdom:

> It is not true that the great majority of men are so sunk in the ordinary, self-seeking business of life that they have completely lost the pure and the holy, and also the feeling for and the search after it. It is also not true that any science or worldly knowledge can kill this feeling. Certainly

[26] *Ibid.*, p. 83.
[27] *Ibid.*
[28] *Ibid.*, p. 84.
[29] *Ibid.*

we must admit that modern development has come dangerously close to this, and along with this danger has threatened man's inner life, claiming to prove the worthlessness of our ethical feelings by citing their origins. This attempt cannot succeed. It does not matter where our moral sensibilities were acquired . . . today we feel a responsibility with respect to good and evil within ourselves. However we develop our theories, there is this responsibility which lays its claim upon us. What does it matter if we can show a butterfly that it was once a caterpillar, and could only crawl? Now it is a butterfly, and rises above all that which previously restricted it. Mankind has in his successive development experienced a metamorphosis of a higher kind. When this metamorphosis began, no one can say; for its origin lies beyond the ken of history. The result, however, lies before us. . . . We can know by way of history one of the last phases of this development: the epoch of the Israelite prophets and of Socrates and Plato. This epoch was fulfilled within the Graeco-Roman world through Christ and his disciples. They have brought to us a new way of perception, and a new life, which we feel not only as an external duty, but also as the unveiling of our true nature and as an achievable goal.[30]

Furthermore, "every open eye establishes this as true, and the unbiased historian must confirm it."[31] (In the English, published by the Colloquium in 1900, there is an interesting variation: "Goethe remarked it, and the penetrating eye of the historian confirms the fact."[32] The fact that Harnack's "open eye" is here identified with the Goethean wisdom does not lack significance.) But what then is this "new" that has entered history?

The deepest theme of personal life, and the real theme of history, is the struggle between unbelief and belief, the struggle for God and redemption. The individual and humanity, aided by the powers of the ethical and the holy, seek to free themselves from transitory things and to establish a kingdom of love, the Kingdom of God.[33]

Modern historians declare this an illusion, and restrict all history to temporal struggle. But they are wrong. Thousands today would regard this ethical ideal as of greater value than life itself. "This certainty need not be proved by reflection; the ethical, life with God, declares itself with the same gentle power as the laws of nature."[34]

We believe that Harnack has declared his fundamental axiological

[30] *Ibid.*, pp. 84–85.

[31] So reads the German, *ibid.*, p. 85.

[32] Harnack, *et al.*, article with no title in *The Atonement in Modern Religious Thought* (London: James Clarke and Company, 1900), p. 113.

[33] Harnack, "Christus als Erlöser," *RA*, II, NF, p. 86.

[34] *Ibid.*

bias in this identification of the aspirational nature as ethical will. *Because* so much modern thought has challenged the whole conception of an ethical sense, this modern thought must be opposed and overcome. The naive argument of those who threaten ethical feeling, viz., the equating of the origin of a thing with its value, can have no valency—that this feeling is there is a fact, and it lays its claim upon us. We judge only by results, only by present realities. That which is beyond history, as prior to, above, or subsequent to, cannot be examined and should be excluded from consideration; but that there was a "new" which came into history with Jesus Christ is for every impartial historian a fact. This "new" is the ethical ideal which makes necessary a continual struggle as one attempts to actualize the kingdom of love, the Kingdom of God, a kingdom of ethical ends. And this can be actualized because Christ gives us a new way of looking at the world and ourselves, and a new way to live. He who looks so, and lives so, will feel the implicit demands of this new external Ought, but he will, because this new life reveals his true nature, be able to achieve this Ought. The Kingdom of God, which is preeminently a kingdom of love, will be built by men who have discovered in Jesus Christ their true nature.

Since this is true, it follows that redemption "in its highest meaning can only be that power which helps us to live a pure and holy life, a life with God, and fills us with the conviction that we are not dealing here with illusion, but that we save our life by losing it."[35] It further follows that there is no redemption which takes place outside our *personal* situation. Whatever might be revealed outside our experience is of no efficacy to us. Again, if this redemption is to free us from the mundane and the worldly, only God himself can be the redeemer. This the prophets and the psalmists knew and declared; and the experience which they detail in their writings, the search for the living presence of God, is consistent with the experience of everyone who has sought after redemption.

Here a great contradiction arises, for it appears "that a human redeemer is an impossibility. Not only does it appear so, but it is so. Only God is the redeemer. A mysterious bond unites each man with God, and only if he feels this personal bond . . . can he be redeemed."[36] But Christianity refers to Jesus as the redeemer; how is one to deal with this contradiction? Harnack replies that there are some people so religiously disposed that they can find God and live

[35] *Ibid.*
[36] *Ibid.*, p. 87.

in him without the help of others. These persons are rare. The prophets were such, but a part of their experience of God was the resultant demand that they proclaim God to their weaker brethren. The moment God was sought in the experience of holy men rather than in nature was the greatest moment in the history of religion. "Henceforth religion became an integral part of the inner life, bound up with morality."[37] Mankind learned that only in man could the highest revelation of God be given, for God is "the Holy One"; and holiness cannot be revealed in nature. In communicating their experience, these holy men evoked in their hearers a similar experience, and thus in a sense became redeemers themselves.

What is Harnack saying in these latter two points? Redemption can be *only* the power that works for ethical ends, and this power validates itself to us only in its working. This power is a gift of God, but thereby a problem is raised. For Christianity claims Jesus as redeemer, and by Harnack's prescribed limits, Jesus can be understood only as "human." But if only the human can be investigated historically, how can the statement that only God can be the redeemer stand? Harnack introduces a "mysterious bond" to solve this difficulty, but it does not meet the question of the validity of Christianity's claim that Jesus is redeemer. Indeed, one can say that this question is never answered in such a way as to threaten the more fundamental affirmation that God alone is the redeemer. Harnack cannot accept any two-nature doctrine. Jesus remains Jesus, and God remains God, and any unique relation between them is to be seen, presumably, only in a "uniqueness of degree of apprehension" of this mysterious bond on Jesus' part.[38] He was "religiously predisposed" in such a way that, seeking like all others, he could find God and declare to fellow-seekers how to seek. That which leaps the chasm between God's eternity and man's time always remains unknowable. What man can know—all that he can know—exists in his time. That God is holy, that holiness cannot be revealed in nature, that holiness can be revealed in man in man's time, that this revelation takes place in the higher feeling, that it is in essence a moral power—these are the articles of faith within whose limits Harnack *always* works.

Certainly this requires a more precise statement of the role of Christ as redeemer, and Harnack proceeds to outline this role. Jesus was a prophet, and unless one understands the background and meaning of this word he can never understand Jesus. "But Christianity not only calls him a prophet, but distinguishes him from all other prophets,

[37] *Ibid.*, p. 88.
[38] Matt. 11:27.

confessing that he is the redeemer . . . . How is this confession to be understood, and how can it be justified?"[39] One might call in Jesus' own testimony about himself: "It cannot be doubted that he distinguished between himself and all the prophets, and claimed a unique place for himself. But this testimony would remain *ineffectual* if it did not lead us to the conclusion that he was justified in making such a claim. *Blind submission to his claim has no moral worth.*"[40] This is certainly the crux of the matter. The italicized portions[41] make it absolutely clear that the categories are to be brought to Jesus: he is to be held responsible to them, not the obverse. Harnack seems to be specifying here what Jesus *must* mean, and he does this by using his own axiological categories. Any aspect of Jesus' life and work which does not fit into the preconception of utility and the production of worth in this time is to be avoided. Elsewhere, in discussing asceticism, Harnack could declare categorically that Jesus could not have sanctioned anything like this. Why? Because it would not fit the *a priori* of "value-producing activity."[42] Yet on what basis could Harnack do this? Because of the necessity of the givens, which dictated that *value* should be the basic referent, because of Harnack's heritage, which required that this value be related to Jesus, and because of a basic fidelity to historical science in the full sense in which Harnack conceived it. Jesus must be conceived as solely human, and therefore describable by a historical method; he must be regarded as "unique"—but not in any ontological sense; and he must be viewed as the exemplar of a new life, which was oriented basically to "value."

The distinguishing differences between Jesus and the rest of the prophets (though one still retains the term as descriptive of Jesus) are these: Jesus was the last prophet, and those who came after him were either false, or they depended upon him; in the latter case, we are not justified in speaking of men like Paul, Augustine, and Luther as prophets. Further, other prophets drew about them only small groups of men, but Jesus has become the prophet for great numbers from his time till now. Again, "while the other prophets possessed only an imperfect knowledge of God, correcting each other, he has given us the fullest knowledge of God in his preaching that God is the holy and almighty Father, and also merciful love."[43] Finally, the other prophets evidence a truncation between knowledge and act, but no

[39] Harnack, "Christus als Erlöser," *RA*, II, NF, p. 89.
[40] *Ibid.*
[41] The italics are mine.
[42] *WC*, pp. 68–76.
[43] Harnack, "Christus als Erlöser," *RA*, II, NF, pp. 89–90.

one can discern in Jesus any deviation in deed from that which he preached. These are facts, and because of these facts Jesus has been honored, and should be honored, above other prophets.

But now the dénouement! Jesus is a prophet, and must be understood as such. His own affirmations about himself are to be judged, as we have seen, at the bar of ethical efficacy. At this crucial point, Harnack did not overleap his prescribed bounds, but followed through to the conclusions which his announced delimitation made necessary: Jesus also must be judged by "the higher feeling" which is the ethical judgment. And what is the verdict? He must be considered above the others on the basis of the principle, "What did a man actually effect?" He was the *last* prophet, and all who deserve the name subsequent to him have been his heirs. He was the *most influential* prophet, considering the numbers who have attached themselves to his teaching. He was the most *perfect* prophet the world has seen, for his insight into the nature of God and his activity has never been surpassed. And he was the most *consistent* prophet, living out in deed what he declared in word. There is no point at which the limits have been overstepped.

Finally, Harnack considers the content of the confession of the earliest Christianity regarding Christ. In this confession, Christ was called the reconciler, who had died for our sins, and he was regarded as living in the faithful, directing, governing, and fulfilling their existence. On the second point, Harnack declares, one need not dwell, for that he does take inward possession of us is simply a fact, not an illusion or a paradox. But what lies behind this fact, "which is expressed in the confession 'Christ lives in me,' the conviction of the eternal life of Christ, his power and majesty, is a secret of faith which resists all explanation."[44] Of the first point, that Christ died for our sins and reconciled us to God, more needs to be said. Does God require a reconciliation? Is he not love? In the parable of the prodigal, did the father demand expiation before he accepted the son? Did he not grant justification to the publican on the basis of his confession alone? This is the center of Jesus' Gospel, that he has revealed God as eternal love. God has not been turned from wrath to love only on the condition that someone pay him something in order that he might forgive.

Yet this does not completely exhaust the matter. For there is an unbreakable law which compels the sinner either to deny God or to fear and flee him because he is a wrathful judge. "This is the hardest and

[44] *Ibid.*, p. 91.

the most real punishment for sin, that one is alienated from God."[45] Indeed, this alienation is sin itself. This punishment either drains the heart of man of all that is high and holy, or it transforms belief in God into a continual terror, or it does both. "This position is unnatural and false, yet it is not false, because it declares the necessary consequence of this self-willed, perverse relationship."[46] How can man be freed from this perverse relationship? There can be no self-redemption here, but the power must come from without:

> Deeds alone, not words, are really effectual, or rather, words which are at the same time deeds. When the Holy One descends to sinners, when he lives and walks with them, when he does not regard them as so unworthy that he could not accept them as brethren, when he requires nothing of them except that they accept his presence among them, when he serves them and dies for them—then they believe again in the Holy, because they have actually experienced it, and at the same time it dissolves their horror of his judgmental power. They discover that the Holy is actually Mercy, and that there is something more powerful than nature, something more powerful than justice—almighty love.
>
> It is within this framework that man must regard the life, the word, and the death of Christ. Thus it has been regarded, and thus it must be regarded. He creates the conviction that forgiving love is a fact, the highest revelation of all higher life, and that this love is greater than punitive justice, which no longer can appear to be the last word. Whoever believes this is reconciled with God; for God does not need reconciliation, but man must be led back to him. But the reconciler is Christ; for he redeems men from the law of sin under which they had fallen, either to deny God, or to think of him as a terrible judge. How does he redeem? Through this alone, that his word, his life, his death, i.e., he himself enters into the inner experience of the soul, and in his experience frees us from the force of the law of sin, which is an unnatural law of nature.[47]

This, Harnack holds, is the basic form of the Christian affirmation about redemption and the redeemer. He admits that it is not necessary to confess it in precisely this way in order to be a Christian, nor should one hold that God's ways are exhausted in such a statement. But it is true that every Christian to be such must believe that Christ did not call the righteous but the sinners to himself, those who trembled in their search after righteousness. History also teaches that the most profound Christians have been those who not only pro-

[45] *Ibid.*
[46] *Ibid.*
[47] *Ibid.*, p. 92.

claimed Jesus as a prophet, but regarded him as a redeemer and reconciler. And they included in their proclamation not only his words and his work, but also his sorrows and his death. In some way he suffered what sinners should have suffered. But this feeling and this judgment does exhaust the possibilities as to what we can say. Speculation can lead us no further, and to try to state explicitly the way in which this act is a justifying act is to debase it and reduce it to a law of nature. "It is always revealed to us simply as a fact and transcends the limits of the reason. The Cross of Christ, like all crosses which stand in the service of the brother, and likc merciful love itself, is a holy secret."[48]

There is much lacking in this description, as Harnack probably recognized, when one compares it to the confession of the Church. It is significant to note that he sets the concluding point of his article in this framework (i.e., the Church's earliest confession), covertly implying that what he has had to say from his historical standpoint had already been said. Thus he "does not dwell" on the point of the indwelling Christ; he admits that this is a fact—one could wish that the nature of this "indwelling" had been explicated (would it turn out to be the gaining of that higher level of ethical power?)—but it is also "a secret of faith that resists all explanation." The first content-statement of the earliest confession, that Christ died for our sins and reconciled us to God, *is* explicated. There is a definite dissociation of the doctrine of the Atonement from all those theories which stressed the wrath of God or the justice of God. God is not a cosmic ogre who must be appeased before he can love. The alienation that exists in sin is not a part of the divine action—how could it be, if God is love?—but it is "a necessary consequence of self-willed" perversity. Necessary to whom? Not to God, who descends to sinners; but necessary to man, who because of his perversity is alienated, and because of his alienation either denies or misconstrues God's true nature, and flees in terror. This is *unnatural*; this is not man as man should be. Yet, if man is in this condition (and Harnack nowhere that the writer can discover deals with the question as to how or why man came to be so perverse), clearly he cannot save himself. He needs an example, an enlightenment, a great deed and word which will enter his perverse life and dissolve his terror and his denial by making clear to him that this is a result of his own self-imposed alienation. The deed that overcomes the perverse nature is the deed that overcomes justice with love.

[48] *Ibid.*, p. 93.

Christ's work in this action is to "create the conviction" that love is the supreme fact of life. He does this, in the fulness of his work, by entering into the soul's inner experience—which, we may note, Harnack has already described as "a secret of faith which resists all explanation." But one can say of this experience that it frees us from the force of the law of sin, which is, however, an unnatural law. It is admitted that there is no binding necessity to confess the doctrine of the Atonement in precisely this way. It is necessary to affirm that Christ called sinners to himself, and that the greatest Christians have regarded him as redeemer. But there follows a statement with a most significant omission: Harnack says of these great Christians that "they included in this action not only his words and his work, but also his sorrows and his death." Certainly to admit that "in some way he has suffered what sinners should have suffered" is to leave open the possibility of going further than a simple moral interpretation of the death of Christ; but to stop with the death of Christ as the end of his redemptive action—or, rather, to ascribe this as the terminal action in the systems of the "great Christians" is to omit what history *does* attest: that these Christians always went further to say that "God raised him." Nor is it an adequate answer here to hold that the redemptive action ceases with the death, and the indwelling action, this mysterious bond, is begun—which one would reasonably expect to be Harnack's formulation. For this is to truncate the kerygma in a way that no historical method can prove to have been the actual case. It may be that Harnack's father spotted a fateful flaw in his son's system when he challenged him on his omission of the resurrection. There is implied in this challenge the all-important question of the methodological validity of stating limits as to what can be believed or known, or what can happen.

On this matter, Harnack made clear in a letter to Maurenbrecher in 1910 what he believed could be said about the resurrection: "I hope that your further studies . . . will lead you to the conviction that the original estimate of Jesus as the Messiah and the faith that after death he *must* be Lord and ruler, has nothing at all to do with Adonis and Osiris, but *stands solely on the impression which he had evoked within his personal disciples*."[49] To reject the Adonis hypothesis does not mean that one must accept the subjective alternative which Harnack presents. One does not need to deny here that this impression was made; but to say that *all* that can be said "in the light

[49] "Der proletarische Charakter des Urchristentums. Offenes Antwortschreiben an Herrn Dr. Max Maurenbrecher," *RA*, II, NF, p. 182.

of the Cross" is that "in some way he suffered what we should have suffered," that speculation is fruitless (which, if true, is not the only option), that this "feeling and judgment does exhaust the possibilities," is to announce to the Bible in categorical fashion what its limits are. Indeed, though one should not, according to Harnack, demean the Cross by stating the nature of the justifying act there consummated, Harnack proceeds two sentences later to identify this act in his own way by making it "like all crosses which stand in the service of the brother." The holy secret is perhaps thereby made to be not so secret. For one can at least say that this redemptive activity is ethical, that the fact of its effect is historically discernible, that Christ's role in it is limited to his words and work, his life and death, by which, entering into the inner experience of the soul, he leads men back to God. The heart of the mystery—the "mysterious bond" which unites man with God—remains, everything being said, no different from the "mysterious bond" which unites Christ to God. Christ is our exemplar, and beyond that—mystery.

C. CHRISTIANITY AND HISTORY

Harnack's *Christianity and History* provides a ready-made transition from the consideration of Christianity's central personality to the consideration of its course of development. For in this work he identifies and answers three late nineteenth-century challenges to the centrality of Jesus. These challenges, in Harnack's own words, are:

[1] It is just because the Christian religion is a part of history, and consequently of that *development* of which all history consists, that it is no more than a link in that development; and therefore its founder cannot be allowed any peculiar or unique position.[50]

[2] Even though the founder of the Christian religion may have been an incomparable man, he lived many centuries ago; and it is therefore impossible . . . to lay hold of him as the rock of our life; it is not the *person* which we have any longer to consider, but the *doctrine*, the *principle*.[51]

[3] We are told that we may speak of Jesus Christ as we will, and he may have been all that we say, but that we cannot be certain of it; for where our idea of him has not been destroyed by historical criticism, it has been rendered doubtful; and, even though it were more trustworthy than it is, still the facts of history can never be known with a certainty that would entitle us to make them the foundation of our religious belief.[52]

[50] *Christianity and History*, p. 26.
[51] *Ibid.*, pp. 26–27.
[52] *Ibid.*, p. 27.

To the first challenge Harnack responds that there is no longer any doubt that the use of the concept of *Entwickelung* is required: "It is only by this method that a true understanding of history can be attained."[53] This does not necessarily carry with it the view espoused by materialism, however, for even in the political sphere, where the struggle for material existence dominates, factors of a nonmaterial character disturb the pattern. Even more, in the history of intellectual and moral ideas, the simple explanation of cause by environment is inadequate. That environment enters into causation is undeniable, but it is personality that strikes into flame the knowledge that the past has transmitted to us. It is not a question of novelty only, as some would make it, but the question of the living Word, the person, who "has always been a power in history, along with and above the power of circumstance."[54] As this is true in history generally, it is true in the highest sense in religion. Religion has developed, and is in a state of continual development, yielding, changing, overcoming, but this overcoming takes place only through the individual will of a person. Of Jesus, Harnack declares, "It was not what the person said that was new and strange . . . but how he said it; how it became in him the strength and power of a new life; how he transmitted it to his disciples. That was his secret, and that was what was new in him."[55]

The second challenge is more serious: Jesus is lost in the dim mists of antiquity, and therefore all that can remain is the "doctrine" or the "principle"—or, as is sometimes stated, "religion is wholly a matter of relation to God—God and the soul, the soul and God."[56] Harnack admits that the relation of the soul to God *is* the substance of religion. Religion is not, however, simply a recognition of this truth, but the power of this truth must possess one. For "we may recognize and acknowledge the claims of the Christian religion, and the peace and beauty of the religious life, and yet be quite incapable of raising ourselves to its level."[57] There is the goal, but we lack the power to move toward it. We are aware of our bonds, but we are unable to free ourselves from them. "There is no one who has had this feeling, or who has it again and again, and is delivered from it, but knows that he has been delivered because God has spoken to him."[58] Now the voice of God is not bound. But we know that the way in

[53] *Ibid.*, pp. 29–30.
[54] *Ibid.*, p. 33.
[55] *Ibid.*, p. 35.
[56] *Ibid.*, p. 40.
[57] *Ibid.*, p. 42.
[58] *Ibid.*, p. 43.

which this voice has spoken to us has been in the main through human intervention: "one Christian educates another . . . and the strength to will what we approve comes from the mysterious Power by which one life awakens another."[59] And the place of Jesus? "At the end of the series of messengers and agents of God stands Jesus Christ. They point back to him, and it is from him that has sprung the river of life."[60] Yet the objection that Jesus Christ is "a power of the past" is not yet fully answered. And in this further answer Harnack reveals his own personal faith and at the same time the limits beyond which, as we have seen, he was unwilling to go.

His answer is developed as follows: The Christian faith is not a gentle exaltation of our earthly life. It is decision for God and against the world. "It is . . . the recognition that in and above Nature and her changes there is a realm of sanctity and love, a city not built with hand, whose citizens we are to be; and with this message there comes to us the demand that we should cleanse our hearts and deny ourselves."[61] But how can we know that there is such a Reality? "May it not be that we are altogether confined within the sphere of mechanical nature?"[62] The Christian faith resolves this deepest of all doubts by looking to Jesus Christ, and the resolution is accomplished

> not in the form of philosophical demonstration, but by looking with a confident trust to the image of his life. When God and everything that is sacred threatens to disappear in darkness . . . when the mighty forces of inexorable nature threaten to overwhelm us, and the bounds of good and evil to dissolve; when, weak and weary, we despair of finding God at all in this dismal world—it is then that the personality of Christ may save us. Here we have a life that was lived wholly in the fear of God—resolute, unselfish, pure; here there glows and flashes a grandeur, a love, which draws us to itself.[63]

Harnack's essential answer to those who would rule out Jesus' importance by defining religion solely as a relation of God and the soul, is *not* to deny this relation, but to insist on the difference between "knowledge of" and "being possessed by"; he thereby emphasizes the experience of deliverance, which is a work of God, but which is mediated to us through persons; Jesus (*not* Abraham) stands "at the end of the series of messengers and agents of God" (which clearly

[59] *Ibid.*, p. 44.
[60] *Ibid.*
[61] *Ibid.*, pp. 45–46.
[62] *Ibid.*, p. 46.
[63] *Ibid.*, p. 47.

declares Harnack's estimate of the Old Testament); what Jesus mediates is "a recognition that in and above Nature and her changes there is a realm of sanctity and love," which recognition makes demands on us; and finally, and of most importance, Harnack sets the problem squarely within the Ritschlian context of man against Nature, and resolves the problem by looking to "the personality of Christ" and its saving example.

The final challenge questions the possibility of pinning one's faith on a person who has become increasingly remote through historical criticism, and, even more basically, of knowing the historical with such certainty as will permit the structure of faith to be built thereon. Harnack answers the first part of the question by admitting that many of the stories about Jesus have been rendered suspect or completely incredible. Of those which remain, the historical way of proceeding has insisted that Jesus be seen in his time, taking into account the limitations that are a necessary part of historical existence. But the sayings and discourses which are "credible" "lose no particle of their power and validity, unless it can be shown that the main lineaments of the personality of Christ, and the sense and true point of his sayings, have been altered."[64] Historical criticism has not produced any such evidence.

But what of historical certainty? How can faith be built on anything less than great miraculous deeds? Harnack responds that there is no greater fact than that of the new life of the Christian community. And that passionate cry for the rending of the heavens "is not born out of the depth and strength of the faith which the apostle Paul describes," but "readily falls under the utterance of the Lord: *Except you see signs and wonders, ye will not believe*."[65] The ultimate reliance of faith is God the Lord. No historian is capable of demonstrating with evidential certainty enough details that one may construct a faith thereon. In fact, external detail can never certify faith. "But the spiritual purport of a whole life, of a personality, is also an historical fact: it has its reality in the effect which it produces; and it is here that we find the link that binds us to Jesus Christ."[66] Even so, it is not fair to say that such details as have been handed down mean nothing. Many of them, previously ruled out by rationalistic or apologetic exegesis, have been re-established. Further, the didactic value of all that has been written of Jesus should not be overlooked. Much that

[64] *Ibid.*, p. 56.
[65] *Ibid.*, p. 60.
[66] *Ibid.*, pp. 60–62.

the tradition reports has its real significance in the spiritual meaning it contains as in the message of the Ascension, which teaches us that Christ lives and rules with the Father. Again, details can act to faith as a prop to the vine, supporting and guiding, though this may be a mixed blessing. Finally, much in the New Testament which is recorded as history has a symbolical significance, i.e., "the same spirit which unveiled to our eyes the power and the glory of a divine life . . . has also veiled the truth for us with a delicate web of ingenious legend, a poetry that moves the heart, and has thus brought it home in picture and parable."[67] But this kind of interpretation also can be dangerous, encouraging the foisting of one's own mind upon history, confusing the plant and the prop, or deadening "the force of historical facts as real facts, and the personality of Christ as a real personality."[68]

It is not necessary to comment here on Harnack's further insistence on fidelity to historical method. But it should be pointed out that *personality* is the key to his interpretation, and we believe that he thereby flings wide the gate for his axiological presuppositions. His "historical certainty" is, at the root, based on the "historical fact" of the "spiritual purport . . . of a personality"; the reality of this "historical fact" lies "in the effect it produces"—and this is "the link that binds us to Jesus Christ." The central principle is therefore a pragmatic one; everything that goes beyond this must be interpreted by a permissive sort of exegesis which can find value in legend, poetry, picture and parable. But these must never be confused with the real kernel, which is the "real personality."

Another facet of the problem of Christianity and history, and one that Harnack gave attention to in a number of different contexts, was the relation of Christianity as a historical movement to history in its most general sense. As we have seen, he tried to state the case for the historical study of Jesus Christ with great exactitude; and the problem is not dissimilar when the subject of study is the "people" of the New Covenant. Here, as in other cases, Harnack was a fighter on several fronts at once. He could not accept the traditional way of interpreting Christianity as a kind of "specially special" historical movement. He could not agree with those who made it simply one religion alongside others. He strongly opposed those who denigrated it as a worthwhile subject for study. If, as he tried to formulate and defend a theory of church historiography which would refute these positions and positively emphasize his own convictions, he sometimes

[67] *Ibid.*, pp. 65–66.
[68] *Ibid.*, p. 66.

appears to hone the razor's edge too thin, one does well to remember that the task he set for himself was extremely complex.

He stated the main point quite bluntly in an 1895 lecture: "When all history seems to be a ceaseless process of growth and decay, is it possible to pick out a single phenomenon and saddle it with the whole weight of eternity, especially when it is a phenomenon of the past?"[69] Harnack began his answer with a quick glance at the process by which history had come to its present status. The eighteenth century had belittled history, exalted Nature and Reason, and subscribed with a passion to Lessing's principle that "*historical truth, which is accidental in its character, can never become the proof of the truths of Reason, which are necessary*."[70] From this principle it was deduced that all historical religions are in reality only the one true natural religion in disguise, whose content is Reason. This view was overcome, thanks to Herder, the romantic movement, Hegel and Ranke, and to a powerful reaction within Christian faith itself. "In the place of shallow talk about divine nature and profane history, about the 'eternal truths of reason' and casual records, we have arrived at the knowledge of *history*; of the history from which we have received what we possess, and to which we owe what we are."[71] Development and personality have been the two conceptions, apparently opposed, but actually determinative of the work of the historian, which are contained in the meaning of "history." When this came to be understood, religion was rightly seen as a growth that falls within the history of humanity.

In 1904, Harnack further developed this theme in an address at the St. Louis Exposition.[72] Pointing out that ancient and medieval Christian writers regarded the Church's history as different from world history, and that this view has continued to the present among the orthodox church historians, Harnack demurs: "The fact that there is absolutely no criterion by which we can distinguish two kinds of history is enough to destroy it."[73] It was not until this view was given up that any possibility of really understanding the *one* true history of the Church was effected. This view was challenged in the seventeenth century, further weakened in the eighteenth, and finally over-

[69] *Ibid.*, p. 18.
[70] *Ibid.*, pp. 19–20.
[71] *Ibid.*, p. 24.
[72] "Über das Verhältnis der Kirchengeschichte zur Universalgeschichte," *RA*, II, NF, pp. 41–62. Tr. by Thomas Bailey Saunders as "The Relation Between Ecclesiastical and General History," *Contemporary Review*, LXXXVI (Dec. 1904), pp. 846–859. We use Saunders' translation.
[73] *Ibid.*, p. 847.

come in the nineteenth. Now we can say with assurance, "*The history of the Church is part and parcel of universal history, and can be understood only in connection with it.*"[74] But if this is true, one must examine universal history to see how the history of the Church is bound up with it. Harnack then specifies four kinds of history—political history, the history of religion in general, the history of philosophy and of knowledge as a whole, and economic history—and discusses each.

A knowledge of political history is basic to the study of church history, for the Church is a community with a constitution:

In every age the first thing to consider is the constitution of the Church. But in every period of the history of the Church its constitution has been dependent on the general political conditions and ideas of the time; or, to put the matter more accurately, the Church has at all times shown a tendency to copy within itself the constitution of the State in which it lived, or to prescribe to the State the constitution which the State was to have.[75]

In considering the study of religion in its general manifestation, Harnack indicates a hesitancy to accept all the conclusions of the *religionsgeschichtlich* method, remarking that "we are more inclined today to overvalue than to undervalue the influence of alien religions, and we are too ready to assert dependence where all that is in question is a parallel set of phenomena, developing here and there spontaneously."[76] Yet the method has contributed much, and promises still more.[77]

The third requirement for the proper understanding of church history is that it be set in relation to philosophy and knowledge as a whole. This must be done because Christianity is essentially a reasonable religion, and "stands nearer to the highest qualities and activities of the mind than to the lower."[78] However, Harnack takes occasion to make the point that Hegel's conclusion, that philosophy and Christianity in its highest form are identical, does not follow:

But these circumstances must not blind us to the fact that religion and a philosophical theory of the world, so long as the latter keeps to its own ground, are two different things. Religion is a definite state of feeling and will, basing itself on inner experience and on historical facts. This

[74] *Ibid.*
[75] *Ibid.*
[76] *Ibid.*, p. 852.
[77] Cf. *infra*, pp. 206–209.
[78] Harnack, "The Relation between Ecclesiastical . . . ," *Contemporary Review*, p. 854.

it remains even in its higher stages, and hence the intellectual element in it, although an absolutely necessary element, always takes the second place. . . . Religion is . . . an instinct . . . which . . . [in Christianity] is not concerned with the empirical *Ego* and with earthly life, but with the inmost core of this *Ego*, which in another world, the world of Freedom and the Good, sees its true home.[79]

Finally, the history of the Church is closely bound up with economic history. Harnack explicitly disavows the view which holds that intellectual life and higher development can be explained on the hypotheses of the materialists and determinists. Nonetheless, there are phases of church history, e.g., monasticism and the medieval fiscal practices, which require that attention be paid to economic factors.

Harnack then proceeds to warn against underestimating the "*special character* which attaches to the history of the Church."[80] One question must remain central for the church historian: What is the Christian religion? If this is kept central, other matters may be investigated as contributory; but if church history loses this central concern, it will lose the right to be a special subject of study within the science of history. Only if one gives himself completely to this question will the secrets (*Geheimnisse*) become known, and, at the same time, the mysteries (*Heimlichkeiten*) will be seen to remain inviolate. Here Harnack affirms a variant of his "kernel-husk" theme, and of his principle that though Christianity must be studied on the basis of the historical facts, it remains in essence an inner experience which cannot be finally represented in any historical form. Secrets we may know, mysteries, never. Should the latter then be avoided? Certainly not:

In the history of the Church . . . these *Heimlichkeiten* go very deep and are very precious. We have seen that there is no such thing as a double history, and that everything that happens enters into the one stream of events. But there is a single inner experience which everyone can possess; which to everyone who possesses it is like a miracle; and which cannot be simply explained as the product of something else. It is what the Christian religion describes as the *New Birth*—that inner, moral, new creation which transmutes all values, and of the slaves of compulsion makes the children of freedom. Not even in the history of the Church can one get a direct vision of this inner evolution accomplished in the individual, nor by any external facts whatever can anyone be convinced of its possibility and reality. But the light which shines from it throws its rays on what

[79] *Ibid.*, p. 855.
[80] *Ibid.*, p. 859.

happens on the stage, and lets the spectator feel in his heart that the forces of history are not exhausted in the natural forces of the world, or in the powers of head and hand. This is the *Heimlichkeit* of the history of the Church because it is the *Heimlichkeit* of religion.[81]

Ding an sich we cannot know; but the power, the direction, and the purpose of a given epoch can be identified and described in their historical manifestation. This is a history which recognizes itself to be distinct from Nature, and therefore it must be investigated on the basis of a theory of historical causation, as opposed to simple natural causation. It cannot thereby pierce the veil which encompasses Reality, but, remembering its relativity, it can point to the historical effects which emerge from the *Heimlichkeit* of the New Birth.

But if the *Heimlichkeit* of the history of the Church is also the *Heimlichkeit* of religion, and if the Church was influenced both in its origin and development by the religions of the ancient world, why does Harnack oppose or give only qualified approval to the work of the *Religionsgeschichtliche Schule*? A proper answer to this question will entail some consideration of the nature and the puropse of this "school," and of the relationship between Harnack and the *Religionsgeschichtlern's* outstanding thinker, Ernst Troeltsch. In a 1909 essay, discussing the general religious life and thought of Germany, Weinel assesses this movement as representing a great hope for German theology. Protestantism within the churches had counterpoised only a vague, pietistic, anti-intellectualistic orthodoxy to the materialistic science, the utilitarian ethics, the Catholic Ultramontanism, and the rugged Bismarckian "will to rule." Opposed to this orthodox anti-intellectualism, the *Religionsgeschichtliche Schule* was bent upon "extending historical and systematic study beyond the limits set by the earlier isolation of Christianity, and restoring it to its proper place in the study of universal religion."[82] The common purpose of the group was "to apply our studies to the service of life, to rescue Christianity from its state of isolation in regard to the modern world."[83] This could be accomplished only by recognizing that "the ultimate foundations of our modern theory of the universe are to be sought in Nature and History."[84] This means that the old attempts to prove the existence of God, as well as the attempt to build a metaphysical foundation for religion, have been given up. Instead, with Kant and

[81] *Ibid.*
[82] Weinel, *op. cit.*, p. 729.
[83] *Ibid.*, p. 730.
[84] *Ibid.*

Schleiermacher, the basis for faith in God must be sought in other provinces of life:

We believe that God meets us in the persons of those great men who are the active agents of evolution, the creators of ideals, and the prophets of the unknown Deity. The History of Religion has shown us that there are but few ultimate ideals open to the choice of mankind, when once the resolution has been made to find satisfaction in the Higher that speaks in human nature, and not to vegetate.[85]

The words have a familiar ring; certainly there is little here that Harnack would have questioned. Ernst Troeltsch specifically set forth his view of what the *religionsgeschichtlich* approach meant in a brilliant essay entitled "The Dogmatics of the *Religionsgeschichtliche Schule*," published in 1913.[86] He partly disowns the "*Schule*" title, declaring that "method" is a much more accurate descriptive designation. Furthermore, he claims, there is nothing new about the total method, which in its general outlines arose with the collapse of the simply supernaturalist apologetic of the eighteenth century. However, he finds two distinct movements among those of his theological contemporaries who employ this method. The one essays the historical investigation of the development of Christianity itself, and is concerned with concrete problems; the other is more theological in the distinctive sense of that term, seeking to establish the validity of Christianity after the supernatural ground has disappeared. The first movement is much more limited in its concerns, and Troeltsch places Harnack here. Those employing the method in this way simply try to set forth the rise and development of biblical religion in contact with other religions, both in assimilating and in opposing manifestations. The second movement has a much greater problem than the first, for it must try to establish the validity of Christianity *de novo*. These theologians, of whom Troeltsch is one, renounce "all appeal to supernatural communications and foundations, [and] seek to answer the questions that they ask purely on the basis of historical development."[87]

There are important points of agreement between Harnack and the *religionsgeschichtlich* approach, as Troeltsch has pointed out. That this is true is indicated by Harnack's lecture on the relation of church history to general history, where he insists that Christian history is one

[85] *Ibid.*, p. 731.
[86] See Chap. V, note 19.
[87] Troeltsch, "The Dogmatics . . . ," p. 6.

species of a more general genus.[88] The world must be conceived historically, not dogmatically in terms of an absolute revelation. This means also that the method of research will be critical and will admit relativity. Anything new that emerges in the historical process will be viewed, therefore, as born of finitude, and continuous in type and pattern with what has gone before. Harnack, with Troeltsch, abjured supernaturalism. He, too, held that Jesus was to be regarded as the mediator of the Gospel, and not, in his person, a part of the Gospel itself. And, as Troeltsch points out, Harnack was willing to use the method to investigate the history of Christianity.

But the major point of agreement lay in their estimate of the purpose of historical study. In his memorial address for Troeltsch, Harnack quoted as the scientific testament of Troeltsch's life the closing words of his *Historismus und seine Probleme*:

> For the great task of formulating a new philosophy of history, only believing and bold men will suffice—not the skeptics or mystics, nor the rationalistic fanatics or omniscient historians. This cannot be the work of any single individual. It is naturally the work of many, first of all in the solitude of their own personalities, and then in broader circles. . . . The most important contribution would be a great artistic symbol, as were the "Divine Comedy" and "Faust." . . . But the task itself which obtains, consciously or unconsciously, for every period, is particularly demanding in our time. *The idea of this reconstruction means to overcome* history by history and to construct the foundation for new creative activity.[89]

It was in this statement that Harnack discovered his most fundamental point of agreement with Troeltsch. Troeltsch had gone on to explain the statement in conversation: "It means to accept one's fate, to love it, and to turn it into something better; the means and the method are discovered in the process of doing this."[90] Harnack had himself used a similar formula as early as 1888 in a memorandum to the Prussian Ministry of Education, in which he was discussing the importance of church history to the Church:

> I am of the firm conviction that the way in which church history is handled is decisive for the future of the life of the Church, insofar as it depends on faculties and teachers. Not *exegesis alone*, and not *dogmatics* will lead us in progressive ways and give us a clearer knowledge of that which is really valuable, but a better understanding of *history*. Not exegesis and dogmatics, but the results of church historical research . . .

[88] *Supra*, pp. 203–204.
[89] Quoted from Harnack, "Ernst Troeltsch," *RA*, IV, NF, p. 365.
[90] *Ibid.*

will break the burdensome proscriptions and the traditions that bind men's consciences. Cardinal Manning once made the frivolous statement: "One must overcome history by dogma"; but we say the opposite: one must refine dogma by history, and we as Protestants have the complete certainty that we do not thereby destroy, but build.[91]

Yet there were points at which Harnack stood in disagreement with the proponents of the *Religionsgeschichtliche Schule.* The main disagreement lay in the respective estimates of the supremacy of Christianity. Harnack placed himself more deliberately within the context of the Christian community, both by academic interest and by personal conviction. He was interested in studying the religion of those cultures contemporaneous to early Christianity *only* from this standpoint, and to the degree that such study could contribute to the history of the Church. Troeltsch's criticism of the Ritschlians (including Harnack) is valid at this point: there was a type of biblicism inherent in the limits which they set to their work. Harnack was not interested in the kind of philosophical comparison which was part of the method of the *Religionsgeschichtliche Schule*: for, as a part of his antimetaphysical bias, he regarded this as giving no possibility of certainty. Instead, he insisted that one stand squarely on historical investigation, using historically derived wisdom as a basis for action.

The basis of Harnack's lack of enthusiasm for some of the work of this "school" is twofold: in addition to their reduction of Christianity to one religion beside others, they manifested an inordinate concern with nature. Harnack was not, of course, a supernaturalist. He too affirmed that what can be known must be limited to the givens of historical existence within nature, and no double standard of truth is possible. But he had reacted against that type of thought which sought to explain man solely in naturalistic or rationalistic terms. There were "secrets" which only history could discover, and "mysteries" which moral faith must affirm. In his reaction against materialism, he tended to regard any consideration of nature by the historian as subversive of the fundamental task. The *Religionsgeschichtliche Schule* saw this as a fundamental flaw in Harnack's method. They believed that a nonsupernaturalist apologetic, such as Harnack espoused, related to the question of Christianity's uniqueness, implying a genus "religion" of which Christianity was one "species." Therefore all religions must be studied comparatively. It was later to become Troeltsch's obsession to find "the absoluteness

[91] AZH, p. 176.

of Christianity" as one species of the genus. Harnack, as we shall see, refused this procedure: for him, Christianity was *the* religion, not on a supernaturalist basis, but an *ethical* one.

As early as 1901, Harnack challenged this school in an anniversary address at the University of Berlin, and twenty years later he wrote to Vischer "how very desirable it is to show the '*Religionsgeschichtlern*' how subordinate the problems which they shove into the foreground really are. With their romantic obsession with primitivism and their exaggerated '*Formengeschichte*' a whole generation of genuine interest in early church history can go to the devil."[92] The address of 1901 raised a furore among his friends, who felt that he was showing an improper conservatism about the newest method. There had been discussion as to whether the theological faculty should be limited to the investigation of the Christian religion, or whether it should be expanded to include, or even oriented around, the history of religion generally. The reasons against such a change were for Harnack, overbearing. In the first place, the real understanding of any culture, or even the religion of any culture, requires a broad study of the total culture, including its language, literature, philosophy, and social and political history. To study a religion alone would only encourage a hopeless dilettantism. In the second place, though it is probably a prejudice, viewed idealistically, that a theological faculty should become absorbed in a single religion, what kind of a religion is this? "It is that religion which possesses the Bible, whose history encompasses a known, unbroken period of nearly three thousand years, and which still today can be studied as a living religion."[93]

In the third place:

We want the theological faculties to continue to emphasize the investigation of the Christian religion because Christianity in its pure form is not a religion beside others, but it is *the* religion. And it is the religion because Jesus Christ is not one master beside others, but because he is the Master, and because his Gospel corresponds to the innate purpose of humanity as history reveals it. I have said previously that it is the Bible which determines the mid-point of all the studies of theological faculties. I must say still further that this mid-point is Jesus Christ. What the first disciples received from him was much more than the individual words and the preaching which they had heard, and therefore his own self-witness

[92] *Ibid.*, p. 515.

[93] Harnack, "Die Aufgabe der theologischen Fakultäten und die allgemeine Religionsgeschichte nebst einem Nachwort," *RA*, II, p. 168.

surpasses that which they said about him in their representations of him. This could not be otherwise: his disciples were convinced that in Christ they possessed not only a teacher; they brought to full expression and declared an inner position which they had experienced through Christ and received from him. They knew themselves as redeemed, new creatures, redeemed through him. Therefore they preached him as Lord and Savior, and it is in this preaching that Christianity has moved through the centuries.[94]

Though one cannot scientifically demonstrate all of the influences of this religion, and of its founder, as these are confessed by faith or observed by pious speculation, historical knowledge justifies the claim of this religion to be the highest good which mankind possesses. "It is the task of the evangelical-theological faculties, working from a scientific standpoint and using its means, to act as the guardians of this spiritual heritage, to certify it in its purity, to protect it from misunderstanding, and to bring its historically recognized content to ever-clearer understanding."[95]

Finally, the theological faculties should not become *religionsgeschichtlich* faculties for a practical reason. The statutes of the faculties specify that theological faculties, themselves working in the service of the Church, have as their duty to inculcate this dedication to the Church in their students. Though "we cannot and should not in our historical work think of the doctrine and the needs of the Church," inasmuch as "the pure knowledge of the object" ought to dominate us, yet, "that a theologian has no heart for his Church, nor for its confessions and its life, and prefers to correct her rather than to agree with her, is argued against by all experience."[96] Rade and many others took up the challenge of this lecture, and brought forth from Harnack a postscript,[97] where he reiterated his position.

Basically, the locus of disagreement between Harnack and Troeltsch lies at the point of the definition of Christianity. Troeltsch believed that Harnack's definition, "brotherly love founded upon trust in God as the Father of Jesus Christ,"[98] in reality regards Christianity simply "as the preaching of Jesus concerning the Kingdom of God interpreted in terms of Kantian ethics."[99] The difficulty from the *religions-*

[94] *Ibid.*, pp. 172–173.
[95] *Ibid.*, pp. 173–174.
[96] *Ibid.*, p. 176.
[97] Harnack, "Nachwort," *RA*, II, pp. 179–187.
[98] Troeltsch, "The Dogmatics . . . ," p. 12.
[99] *Ibid.*

geschichtlich point of view is that on the basis of such a definition Christianity cannot

be regarded as the actual unity of all the factors in the historical development. The nature of Christianity cannot be determined in this fashion, for a genuinely historical point of view reveals to us such a variety of interpretations, formulations, and syntheses that no single idea or impulse can dominate the whole. Thus the essence of Christianity can be understood only as the productive power of the historical Christian religion to create new interpretations and new adaptations—a power which lies deeper than any historical formulation which it may have produced.[100]

The essence differs in different ages, and this recognition must underlie any modern attempt at a dogmatics; simply to use the Bible or the confessions is not adequate. Descriptively, one may say of this essence that it is the subjective personal interpretation and synthesis which present thinking derives from the entire situation with reference to actual living issues and for the purpose of directing future activities. In other words, Troeltsch challenges Harnack for his procedure in attempting to identify a single "essence"; for him, Christianity has been so multiform, historically, that "no single idea or impulse can dominate the whole."

Troeltsch, secondly, saw Harnack's position as embodying a fateful concession with respect to method. Troeltsch resolved to be true throughout to his method, and in his historical labors evidenced a singular ability to put all presuppositions, including his own, under scrutiny. From the standpoint of an admitted relativism, he sought to combat the destructive effects of a completely skeptical relativism which qualified all values into meaninglessness, and to stem the tide of a reviving mysticism. He fought the interpreters who reduced all history to sociological environmentalism, as well as the positivistic philosophers of history. He regarded the work of Harnack very highly, estimating his *Das Wesen des Christentums* as a "symbolic concatenation which equalled Ranke's *Epochen*."[101] At the same time, he believed Harnack to be under the influence of historicism. Though Harnack's " 'doctrine of humanity' is a conscious counterpoise to his historicism,"[102] though "he went beyond Baur in the painstaking investigation and calculation with which he wrote his-

[100] *Ibid.*
[101] Troeltsch, *Der Historismus . . .* , p. 42.
[102] *Ibid.*, p. 529.

tory,"[103] and though "he understood the meaning of responsibility with respect to the past and the future,"[104] yet, because of his insistence on bringing to history a standard of worth which did not necessarily arise out of the history itself, the result was "an ideological-dogmatic representation of history."[105]

The crux of Troeltsch's charge is this: that Harnack brought to his historical work a "given" which was not itself historically derived. In its broadest terms, this is what we have designated as Harnack's "axiological norm."[106] If the counterpoising of this norm to his historicism was conscious, it is still possible that Harnack derived it in other than historical ways. Troeltsch believed, in other words, that Harnack did work from a particular presuppositional framework, though he disclaimed such. Troeltsch himself sought to be more consistent, and sought to conjoin what he called the "metaphysical-religious" and the "historical-religious" into a unified system. In the working out of this system, Troeltsch admitted a relativism, and sought to be consistent by questioning the absoluteness of Christianity. At this point, Harnack demurred; thereby, he was left with an unresolved dilemma: his attachment to an axiological essence and a historical method which were *not* necessarily complementary. For when religion is defined as "a definite state of feeling and will, basing itself on inner experience and historical facts," a fundamental fissiparity is revealed. On the one hand, there is the involved theory of historical knowledge, demanding a scientific procedure; but on the other hand there is the appeal to an inner experience "which cannot be simply explained as the product of something else." This experience is identified as "that inner, moral, new creation which transmutes all values" but in itself remains an inviolate mystery. On the one hand, "everything that happens enters into one stream of events"; but on the other, there is the claim of a "special character" to church history, which, when identified, involves Harnack immediately in axiological prepossessions.

Further, the controlling question for the church historian, "What is the Christian religion?," innocent though it may appear, is charged with significance. For here a nisus to essence procedure is implied in the way the question is asked, and the answer to the question is stated solely in terms of a moral essence. Christianity, as concerned

[103] *Ibid.*, p. 53.
[104] *Ibid.*, p. 70.
[105] *Ibid.*, p. 369.
[106] *Supra*, p. 14.

with "the inmost core" of the *Ego*—the trans-empirical *Ego*—in the "world of Freedom and the Good," speaks of a *New Birth* which is an inner experience, a mystery unreachable by historical study. "Everyone can possess" this; "it is like a miracle"; yet it is inexplicable in terms of anything else. This is Harnack's Holy of Holies; when *Religionsgeschichte* attempted to make this also one relativity beside others, Harnack demurred: Jesus was *the* Master because he evoked this transmuting experience, and that's an end of it. This is the place where his lauded *Einheit* and *Sicherheit* is joined. But what does this imply with respect to Harnack's stated purpose? "To understand Christianity historically and set it in living relation to all historical event" means to identify the essence of Christianity; but when this is done, the historically multiform phenomenon which is church history is judged by *a* particular moral norm! Harnack is correct, *cum sensu prorsus alieno*: "A single phenomenon [is saddled] with the whole weight of eternity"; but, fatefully, this phenomenon was *not* derived from Harnack's magnificent historical investigation. In the final analysis, it is Harnack's "inner experience," that which constituted his axiological *a priori*, which judges history.

For, finally, the relation between history and this *noli me tangere* is such that history can only lead one to the outer court, probing the *Geheimnisse*. The essence lies deeper, as an inviolate *Heimlichkeit*. Christianity, as concerned with the transempirical *Ego* and the world of freedom and the good, transcends scientific historical processes of understanding. One can, of course, see the effects of the Christian mysteries, and historical procedure can certify these effects. It cannot, however, point in a simple way to the source of these effects. History can destroy too sure interpretations; it can say "not here" and "not there"; but history cannot explain the New Birth, nor describe the process leading to it, nor convince anyone of its possibility and reality. The *most* that history can do is to point to the effects and say, "There is something"; it is religion alone, religion as "a state of feeling and will," *not* first or primarily an intellectual process, which makes it possible for one to "feel in his heart" the morally transforming experience.

Yet even here, we note, the limits within which man lives his life remain firm. Harnack will not say "Er gibt" certainty of faith. He will say "Es gibt" a certainty of faith. The quintessential New Birth is not, finally, given; everyone can possess it as an achievement. The Kantian limit of knowledge holds, and something closely resembling "the moral law within" prevails. Is this, then, "Christianity understood historically and set in living relation to all historical event"? No. It is Christianity understood morally, in terms of a particular axiological essence. Harnack's history can reduce; it is not, *pace* Harnack, history that overcomes. This honor is reserved for inner moral experience.

XIII

The Bible

A. AUTHORITY

IN CONSIDERING Harnack's view on the authority of the Bible, one's position is analogous to the Harnack of 1885, seeking the principle of organization for the *Dogmengeschichte*. Previous *loci* arrangements were, he believed, simply not relevant to the requirements of a new and different time. With regard to his view on the authority of the Bible, it can be said that in one sense this is an irrelevant question. His *way* of investigation—the historical—and the presupposition of that way—"the same mind is in history and in us"—in effect prescribed the answer to the question of "authority" before the question was raised.

That this is true one can easily demonstrate from a series of comments drawn, almost at random, from the seven *New Testament Studies* which Harnack issued from 1906 to 1916 (English translations of the first six volumes, 1907–1922).[1] Thus, in his *Luke, the Physician*, historical circumstance determines the content: "Had not history itself in its inexorable yet providential progress made evident what a writer about the year 80 A.D. must relate and what he had to pass over?"[2] Again, in the same work, familiar Harnackian

[1] See note 142, Chapter XI.
[2] Pp. 134–135.

emphases emerge in the description of Paul's religion: "Because his faith masters his inmost soul, because it pierces to the very depths of his moral consciousness, he ever struggles upward out of the realm of magical rites."[3] Or this: "Of course, it [Luke's history in The Acts] does not satisfy all the requirements of later days, but it abides because that which is excellent is certain to succeed."[4] One can ask, too literally perhaps, how many identifiable principles of Harnack's historiography are present in the following:

History can be narrated in two ways: one can gather together a heap of more or less important and characteristic stories—memorabilia; or one can concentrate everything around a central point of interest. This central point can be a personality or an idea, and the idea can be pictured as fixed or as in development. What has St. Luke done? . . . . He must group his material around an *idea* . . . . It would supply an excellent criterion of selection . . . . A genuine inspiration of genius, which loses nothing of its excellence in that it seems to us now so very natural.[5]

Finally, a fascinating description of Luke's artistry:

The elasticity and play of feeling which we recognize and do not regard as out of place, not only in such authors as Eusebius and Sulpicius Severus, but even in a Livy and Tacitus, we must also allow to St. Luke. Baur's criticism has brought us much that is valuable, but it has not escaped the danger of making the writers of the New Testament, one and all, merely *types*, with the consequence that a less rigid view must appear as wanting in logical accuracy, if not as something worse. As a result, either the authors were driven into exile out of their own period, or their works were condemned to amputation and mutilation. This danger has in essential points been removed through the advance of science; yet there still remains a disposition to conceive of a writer of the New Testament as more of a type and to make more stringent demands upon his consistency—and even upon his conscientiousness, inward integrity, and intellectual constancy—than human nature can bear, and than the circumstances of the times allowed.[6]

In effect, all of these statements illustrate Harnack's principle that the historian is to act as a royal judge, confidently identifying the animating idea of a work or an epoch, representing the facts his source work has unearthed on the basis of a rich wisdom of life.

[3] *Ibid.*, p. 141.
[4] Harnack, *The Acts of the Apostles*, p. xvii.
[5] *Ibid.*, pp. xvii–xviii.
[6] *Ibid.*, p. 27.

Where this principle is operative, what can the authority of an objective *document* mean? Obviously, only so much as the subjective interpreter places in it. And though, consistent with our judgment that the authority of the Bible, for Harnack, is finally irrelevant, there is very little discussion of this category in his writings, there are several places where he briefly deals with it.

First, in his *Bible Reading in the Early Church*, describing the Lessing-Walch controversy, Harnack makes clear what the authority of the Bible *cannot* mean.[7]

This controversy had been set off by Lessing in 1775 when he had developed the not-original view that the New Testament had been preceded by the Christian Church and Christian faith. After an initial exchange with Goeze, a pastor of Hamburg, in which Lessing defended the view that the rule of faith was more ancient than the New Testament, and that the Church at first developed and grew without this portion of the Scripture, Lessing proceeded to challenge all comers. He set forth twenty propositions, unfortunately overstating his case, and Walch of Göttingen, the outstanding patristic scholar of Germany at this time, devastatingly pointed out Lessing's errors. The inordinate glee of the orthodox at Walch's victory overlooked the fact, however, that the crucial part of Lessing's case, which had to do with the priority of the rule of faith to the Scriptures, had not been answered. By declaring the priority of the rule of faith, Harnack avers, Lessing "has earned the immortal glory of having broken the spell of the dogma of the Bible."[8] For

> under this dogma Protestantism suffered in yet higher degree than Catholicism. We can today scarcely imagine with what crushing weight this dogma pressed upon religion, upon the spheres of historical investigation and all other realms of culture, while its spell still prevailed unbroken; indeed, even those theologians who imagine that they still hold fast to this dogma have no suspicion how the bells sounded before they were cracked! In their looser theological arguments they in some places make play with the doctrines of the inspiration, infallibility, clearness, and sufficiency of Holy Scripture; in a hundred other places, they know nothing of these formidable things, and they make use of the freedom which, since Lessing, has pressed forward in irresistible progress. In earlier times theologians were much more logical than their orthodox successors; they knew what it meant to possess an inspired book, and what demands such a possession implied.

[7] Tr. J. R. Wilkinson (New York: G. P. Putnam's Sons, 1912).
[8] *Ibid.*, p. 8.

It is true that even they were not fully conscious of this; even they allowed themselves to make deductions; otherwise sense and reason would have broken down.[9]

Harnack then appends a lengthy footnote, in which he discusses certain of the problems that are involved when one speaks of an "authoritative" book:

They attentuated and in a hundred instances did not draw the conclusions which resulted from the nature of a divine book. In a hundred instances they treated it as an ordinary book because it was simply impossible to draw all the conclusions implied by the character of a divine book. Is, for example, such a book translatable? The Alexandrian Jews were at least logical enough to see that it was impossible . . . for men to do this. They therefore . . . claimed that their translation was also inspired . . . . Moreover, an inspired document is not only untranslatable without the same divine assistance that created it, but it is also uninterpretable . . . . Inspiration and a sacred court of interpretation necessarily hang together. . . . Of course the sacred tribunal of interpretation is also an impossibility if its decisions must admit the control of philology and grammar. The doctrine of inspiration has at all times been taken seriously only as a question of dogmatics and upon paper, and as such has gained simply a kind of phantom existence. In practice, its consequences are either not drawn at all, or only in a half-hearted way, because they simply cannot be drawn; human life could not endure them.[10]

In this footnote we have Harnack's answer to the question of an authority in Scripture, insofar as this means a "divinely inspired" book. If there was present in the Scriptures a doctrine of angels, the angels would have to consider it; as man, one can only say what can be said historically about such matters. Therefore, since any such authoritarian view of Scripture raises problems which are unanswerable from the standpoint of history, the authoritarian view must be abandoned. But what one sees here as the main debility for Harnack is the unendurable strain which *any* view of authority places upon a person. This unendurable situation must be resolved even if, as his later critics charged, in so doing one surrenders that biblical anthropology which gives the Gospel its point. However much, therefore, one may agree with Harnack on the question of a "sacred book," the really significant part of this statement lies in the fact that he sees a threat to "unity and certainty," and to man's "higher life." Since these were the axiological "touch-me-nots"—though, to

[9] *Ibid.*, pp. 8–9.
[10] *Ibid.*, pp. 9–10.

be fair, one must admit that Harnack also dealt with the problem on the historical level—"authority" in the sense of "divinely inspired book" must be irrelevant.

But if this is true, why should Christianity retain the Bible at all? If one cannot speak of a "divinely inspired book," in what sense can one give any preeminence to the Bible? The key to an answer here can be found in a short Christmas meditation entitled "Heilige Schriften."[11] Dealing with the question "How have writings become sacred writings?" Harnack gives the preliminary answer that writings are regarded as sacred either because the persons who wrote them are held to be worthy of veneration, or because the contents of the writings are lofty and sacred. But there is a deeper answer: "Writings also become sacred writings because they evoke holy and noble thoughts in those who read them."[12] The purpose of historical science is to discover the original meaning of ancient writings (here the biblical books are especially mentioned) and "thereby much is revealed to be entirely profane which has been accorded the authority of 'sacredness.' The best example of this is the 'Song of Songs.' "[13] That anyone could still ascribe to this book "sacredness" in the light of the historical knowledge concerning it is unbelievable. What has actually happened in such a case is that, "Without knowing it, they have transformed the original text, have read their own pious thoughts into it, and read in this writing only what they wish to read."[14] And even these pious thoughts do not remain the same; from generation to generation they are transformed. As this is true of total books, so it is true of individual tales within books. Harnack, writing at Christmas, uses the story of the wise men as an example. No one knows how these legends arose or what their original sense was; nor does anyone know what the author of Matthew intended to communicate by including them in his Gospel. Yet the striking fact is that scarcely any other parts of the New Testament have become or remained so consistently beloved as these infancy stories. One can say that these are noble legends, sublime in themselves, however one interprets them; and though this is true, what was meant by their invention is something quite different from that which is seen in them today.

How is one to deal with this fact, once recognized? On the one

[11] Harnack, "Heilige Schriften," *RA*, IV, NF, pp. 65–67.
[12] *Ibid.*, p. 65.
[13] *Ibid.*
[14] *Ibid.*

hand, "there is a kind of intellectual conscientiousness to which, if the unhistorical character of sacred stories can be proved, the stories are thereby spoiled . . . . One cannot quarrel with this conscientiousness; for in a formal sense it is right."[15] *Yet:* "It makes us poor, and it fails to appreciate the law by which such spiritual and sacred things develop and are transmitted."[16] Furthermore, this sort of intellectual conscientiousness is not consistent; for if it were, it would leave us little on which we would still be able to build and to develop. For thought flows swiftly, constantly deepening and extending itself, though the forms and receptacles are transformed very slowly; "many of them appear to be established for eternity."[17] These legends are just such receptacles. Yet it would not be fair to proscribe this intellectual conscientiousness; for it gives us a certain power without which we would stand helpless with respect to every myth. We do not hold every relic as estimable simply because "holy thoughts" were at some time bound up with this relic. True progress is achieved in this respect only out of conflict: a progress which does away with dead forms and purifies thought, by means of a conflict of feeling and knowledge. One must in any case remain true to that which is given to him, in some the sharp sense for the factual, and in others piety and sympathy. But in one thing it is possible to unite these two elements: in the conviction that the most valuable thing in our heritage lies in the stories and thought that have come down to us concerning a personal life, with which time has nothing at all to do. In whatever form and whatever language this story is told, it will be understood today as it has been for centuries.[18]

It is instructive to note that in this short tract the deepest answer which Harnack gives to the question of the formation of "sacred writings" is to be found in their power to evoke "holy thoughts." Harnack is aware of the problem which results from such an answer —that one transforms, reads into, and finds what he wishes to find in the writing. To the charge that was placed against him that he also did precisely this, he has a ready answer: intellectual conscientiousness in historical investigation. By this method one is able to distinguish hull and kernel, and to walk the middle way, albeit one of conflict, between feeling and knowledge. It is our conviction that the former of these human faculties ultimately prevails in Harnack's

[15] *Ibid.*, p. 66.
[16] *Ibid.*
[17] *Ibid.*
[18] *Ibid.*, pp. 66–67.

biblical interpretation. Harnack thought that he escaped the dangers here by employing the historical method. It was the charge of Loisy and others that he, too, found in the Gospel just what he wanted to find, that his "kernel" was not so historically derived as he declared, and that he had been untrue to his "reductionistic" historical method by stopping short of complete annihilation of the Gospel in maintaining that there was a kernel.

In what sense, then, can the Bible be spoken of as authority? In its entirety, not at all; the idea of an authoritative book is simply impossible. Harnack would hold that it is better not to use the word at all with respect to the Bible. But certainly Harnack does exercise *an* authority as he comes to the Bible. This authority resides in the *subject*, in the "holy thoughts" that are evoked when one reads the Bible. Harnack fairly recognizes this as raising a real difficulty: for how can one read the Bible and have these "holy thoughts" evoked —e.g., in the Christmas stories—when his intellectual conscientiousness plainly tells him that so much of the material is unhistorical? For an answer, Harnack goes to that principle which is central in *Das Wesen des Christentums*: to admit the conflict between "feeling and knowledge," to remain true to whatever is demanded of one, be it knowledge or piety, and to unite these two elements into an "inner unity" by the conviction that the greatest *value* in our heritage "lies in the stories and thought that have come down to us concerning a personal life."[19] Insofar as the Bible contributes to this conviction, it can make a contribution to this subjective authority; but it does not possess, in itself, a self-justifying authority.

B. REVELATION

The necessity which Harnack felt to respond to the positions of two of his most eminent contemporaries provides the clearest direct insight into his view of revelation. One of these men, Karl Barth, had been his student; the other was his emperor. A remarkably revealing series of questions which Harnack addressed to Barth in 1923 furnishes a succinct statement of his position, and we quote it in full.[20]

Barth had been Harnack's student in 1906, "listening with great devotion and openness to his lectures, and taking part in his semi-

[19] *Ibid.*, p. 67.
[20] "Fünfzehn Fragen . . . ," see note 21, Chap. VIII.

nar."[21] In 1920, Barth and Harnack were the platform speakers at a student conference at Aarau. The daughter records that "the effect on Harnack was shattering. There was not *one* sentence, not *one* thought, with which he could agree."[22] For two years, Harnack followed the development of the dialectical theology, and then wrote his "Fifteen Questions to the Betrayers of Scientific Theology." Correspondence and published exchanges followed, but no understanding resulted; and the content of Harnack's fifteen questions leaves no doubt as to why such a rapprochement was impossible:

1. Is the religion of the Bible or the revelations in the Bible sufficiently *definite* that one may simply quote the Bible when he would speak about faith, worship, and life? If not, shall one relinquish to subjective individual experience the task of establishing the contents of the Gospel? Is it not necessary, rather, to utilize historical knowledge and critical reflection?

2. Is the religion of the Bible or the revelations in the Bible so *simple and clear* that one needs no historical knowledge and critical reflection in order to understand them correctly? Are they, conversely, something so *incomprehensible and indescribable* that one simply must wait until they stream forth in his heart, since no human spiritual or mental faculty can reach them? On the other hand, are not both of these representations false, and does not man require historical knowledge and critical reflection in addition to an inner openness in order to understand the Bible?

3. Is the *experience of God* distinct from the *awakening of faith*, or identical to it? If it is distinct from this experience, how is the awakening of faith to be distinguished from uncontrollable enthusiasm? If it is identical, how can it be established in any way other than the preaching of the Gospel, and how can the content of this preaching be discovered without historical knowledge and critical reflection?

4. Is the *experience of God contrary to or disparate from all* present experience, so that there is no escape from the necessity of a *radical flight from the world*—and therefore no avoiding of sophistry, inasmuch as one must still remain in the world; for is not the flight from the world also something worldly, inasmuch as it rests upon an individual decision of the will?

5. If God and the world (life in God and earthly life) are simply opposites, how is the close union, indeed the equivalence, of the *love of God and the love of the neighbor*, which comprises the kernel of the Gospel, to be understood? But how is this equivalence possible without the *highest valuation of ethics*?

[21] AZH, p. 532.
[22] *Ibid.*

6. If God and the world (life in God and earthly life) are simply opposites, how is *an education in godliness*, i.e. in *goodness*, possible? But how is education possible without historical knowledge and the *highest valuation of ethics*?

7. If God is simply nothing at all like he has been represented in *cultural development and in its knowledge and ethics*, how can one defend this culture and his own continued existence from atheism?

8. If the pantheism of *Goethe* or the God-concept of *Kant* and all related concepts are absolute opposites to the true declarations about God, how can one avoid turning over these declarations to the *barbarians*?

9. However, if it is conversely correct that, as in all physical and spiritual development, *contrasts are at the same time stages*, and *stages contrasts*, how can one grasp this basic knowledge and build on it without historical knowledge and critical reflection?

10. If the knowledge that "*God is love*" is the highest and final knowledge of God, and love, joy, and peace are his sphere, can one remain suspended forever between the door and the hinge . . . willing to perpetuate this horror?

11. If the emancipating declaration, "*Whatsoever things are true, honorable, just, well spoken of, if there be any virtue, or any praise, think on these things*" still has value, how can one justify the separation of the experience of God from the experience of the good, the true, and the beautiful? Rather, should not these two be bound together through historical knowledge and critical reflection?

12. If all sin is nothing else than the *defect of awe and love*, how can one repair this defect except through the preaching of *God's holy majesty and love*? Can one risk this if he mixes in all possible paradoxes and penchants?

13. If it is certain that there is *within man the unconscious, the realm of feeling, the numinous, the fascinating*, etc., and that these cannot be grasped by the *reason*, understood, purified, and defended in their true form, how can one blame reason or, indeed, completely reject it? And what could one expect if this heroic work were achieved? Does not gnostic occultism immediately raise itself from this wreckage?

14. If the *person of Jesus Christ* stands in the center of the Gospel, can the foundation of dependable and common knowledge about this person be laid other than through *critical-historical studies*—so that one does not substitute an *imagined Christ* for the real one? But who attempts to carry through these studies except the scientific theologians?

15. Is there—admitting the slowness, the short-sightedness, and the countless weaknesses—any other theology than one which stands in a

binding and common relationship *with science generally*? And if there is one such somewhere, what power of conviction and what value comes from it?[23]

There followed after the publication of this article a number of exchanges between Barth and Harnack, with no consensus. The last letter which Barth wrote expressed a regret that there appeared to be no common understanding of the present task of theology; at the same time, Barth paid Harnack the highest compliment with respect to his contribution to historical knowledge. Harnack's last word on the subject of the dialectical theology was contained in a letter to Rade in 1928:

Our present theology is highly motivated and pays attention to main problems—and that is salutary. But how weak it is as science, how narrow and sectarian its horizon, how expressionistic its method, and how short-sighted its representation of history! . . . Ritschl is today the most betrayed, although in my estimation he offers a great deal with which the Barthians could comply. But the sons are still more antagonistic to the fathers than the grandparents were. What especially appears to be lost at the present time is the connection of theology with the *universitas litterarum* and with culture; instead of this what is emerging is a new union of evangelical theology with Catholicism. . . . We hope that this will prove to be only a stage of transformation, and that a real evangelical butterfly will emerge from this cocoon.[24]

Weak as science, sectarian in scope, expressionistic in method, and short-sighted in its view of history—these are cardinal sins for Harnack. Salvation for theology would lie in the opposites: strong as science, universal in scope, rigorous and objective in method, and encompassing the full sweep of history in its purview. What would result constitutively if this latter sequence were adhered to would be the employment of a historical-critical approach to the study of the Bible; the inclusion of all culture, with its contrasts, within one unified *Weltanschauung*; the testing of this *Weltanschauung*, at all stages of its development and in its final form, at the bar of moral value; as corollary to the affirmation of moral value, the affirmation of a dependable and knowledgable structure within life which can be mastered, and from which all occult elements can be purged; and the possibility of arriving at, and the necessity of committing oneself to, that essential Gospel of which Jesus Christ was the human embodiment.

What Barth essentially affirmed against the Harnackian liberalism

[23] "Fünfzehn Fragen . . . ," *RA*, V, NF, pp. 51–54.
[24] AZH, pp. 535–536.

was this: "I distinguish . . . faith as God's work in us (for only God can make audible to us what we are not able to hear, I Cor. 2:9) from all known and unknown human organs and functions, including all our so-called experiences of God!"[25] In the *Römerbrief* he had specified the types of human activity by which man sought—vainly—to come to God: introspection, human knowledge, experience, psychology, and historical thought.[26] Thus man creates culture; but such a humanly created culture has nothing to do with justification before God. Even the study of history cannot mediate to us any picture of Jesus which supplies this justification. "The Word became flesh—God himself became a historical-human reality. The historically recognizable existence of Jesus of Nazareth is not, in any case, this reality."[27]

The second main point of difference between Harnack and Barth has to do with the relation between theology and science. While Barth insisted on the necessity of joining theology and preaching—i.e., any theology to be relevant must be a *declared* theology—it is not the "simple Gospel" of Jesus, but the message of God's holy majesty and love which should be declared. This message is one that is given, *senkrecht von oben.* Knowledge, even scientific knowledge, cannot yield it. Therefore Barth could alter that relationship of science and theology which Harnack considered sacred; for Barth, theology should not primarily seek union with, nor hold itself dependent upon, science. The questions which Harnack puts to Barth in his provocative article make clear the degree of disagreement at this point. Seven times in this list of fifteen questions Harnack lauds "historical knowledge and critical reflection" as the only possible way to proceed. Are we to rely on "subjective personal experience"? Is there a "simple and clear" *or* "incomprehensible and indescribable" content to the revelations in the Bible which either requires no historical knowledge, or dictates a passive attitude? How are we to identify or distinguish "the experience of God" and "the awakening of faith"? How is any "education in godliness" possible without historical knowledge? How can one grasp and build on the knowledge of the contrasts and the different levels in physical and spiritual development without historical knowledge? How can the experience of "the good, the true, and the beautiful" be bound together with the experience of God except through historical knowledge? How can one know anything about Jesus, and thus avoid the danger of substituting "an imagined for a real Christ,"

[25] *Ibid.*, p. 531.
[26] *Ibid.*
[27] *Ibid.*

except by historical knowledge? The concluding, "editorial" question, with which Harnack sums up the position he holds, also emphasizes his high estimate of science: Is there any other theology which can carry conviction and produce value than "that one which stands in a binding and common relationship with science"?

Thirdly, Harnack fastens upon a fundamental difference with respect to human achievement in the realm of culture and ethics. An introductory question inquires whether the experience of God is so disparate from all present experience that we are required to flee the world. Does not the "kernel of the Gospel," which is "the love of God and the love of the neighbor" (note Harnack's equivalence here) require "the highest valuation of ethics"? Does not "education in godliness" presuppose "the highest valuation of ethics"? If cultural development, its knowledge and ethics, can say nothing of God, how is this culture and one's own existence to be defended against atheism? Must beloved Goethe and respected Kant be given up because their central categories "are absolute opposites to the true declarations about God"? Finally, must not the "experience of God" and the experience of "the good, the true, and the beautiful" be bound together? In all of these questions it is clear how important it is to Harnack that Christianity be confessed and defended to the culture. Any challenge to this central commitment, such as Barth has made, brings forth from Harnack the strongest kind of defense of which he is capable.

We may note a fourth difference implicit within this list of questions, that touching upon the doctrine of man. Barth's Kierkegaardian insistence that man's existence is in tenuous suspension "between the door and the hinge" was utterly reprehensible to Harnack. That childlike simplicity which one finds in the statement "God is love" stands in direct contradiction to such a view. This more irenic view of man is expressed in the twelfth question also; here, sin is declared to be "defect," and the remedy for sin the preaching of God's majesty and love. But Harnack accused the dialectical theologians of introducing speculation, philosophical apparatus, and abstract terminology into their preaching, thereby making the simple message of God's love incomprehensible.[28] The daughter quotes the father's motto in this regard: "Not to speak of the common with uncommon words, but to speak of the uncommon with common words."[29] Harnack could not understand what was meant by "anxiety," "the boundary," the "*incognito*"; but what seemed to trouble him even more at Aarau

[28] *Ibid.*, pp. 533–534.
[29] *Ibid.*, p. 534.

and after was the fact that he could not believe that those who used the terms understood what they were talking about either. There is no evidence that he ever altered his view that the dialectical theology was weak as science, irresponsible with respect to culture, and so concerned with speculative abstractions that it could never do justice to history.

There can be no doubt, after a careful reading of these "fifteen questions," as to how Harnack interprets revelation. Certainly it has nothing to do with metaphysical considerations. It is evidenced above all in *persons* who actualize Harnack's *sola fide*, i.e., "subjective holy thoughts." To the question which he had asked of Barth, "Is the experience of God contrary to, or disparate from all present experience?," Harnack would have given a resounding "No"! One could conceivably speak of "inspiration," or of the "Word of God," but, as in the case of the concept "revelation," only *cum sensu prorsus alieno.*

That Harnack's view of revelation is far removed from that of orthodoxy, and that it is consistent with his position on authority is revealed in a fascinating article which he wrote in 1903. Again, we may look backward to the declarations of the Leipzig years, in which he declared himself free from the old orthodoxy, and forward to the controversy with the "betrayers of scientific theology" to demonstrate that this was a position which he held throughout his scholarly life. The article itself is entitled "Der Brief Sr. Majestät des Kaisers an den Admiral von Hollmann."[30] The fascination of the article lies in the facility with which Harnack handles the tendentious relationship which he bore to the Kaiser at this time; we must bypass this matter with regret.[31]

The article was written as a result of the famous Babel/Bibel controversy, set off by a lecture of Friedrich Delitzsch, the orientalist. The Kaiser was in attendance at this lecture, and, egged on by his court preacher, Dryander—so Harnack's daughter reports[32]—came to the conclusion that certain of Delitzsch's views were dangerous to the religious life of Germany. Actually, as Harnack was to point out, "there was no controversy at all, so far as science was concerned.

[30] Harnack, *RA*, II, NF, pp. 65–71.

[31] Cf. AZH, pp. 339–355, in which the relationship is described as changing from one of suspicion to qualified acceptance to the bestowal of a title. Cf. also Prince von Bülow, *The Memoirs of Prince von Bülow*, tr. Geoffrey Dunlop (Boston: Little, Brown & Company, 1932), III, *passim*, for a rabidly critical estimate of this relationship.

[32] AZH, p. 342.

It has long been a matter of common knowledge that it was from Babylon that some of the myths and legends of the Old Testament, as well as other important elements of the ancient Israelite culture, emanated."[33] But the Kaiser, self-professed Defender of the Faith, lacked this common knowledge, discovered in conversation with Delitzsch that he "represented the Person of our Savior in a denatured way,"[34] and, to quell any possible misconception that he agreed with Delitzsch, wrote a letter to his friend von Hollmann setting forth his views. The letter was published, showing that the Kaiser was taking a position diametrically opposed to that of Delitzsch. In the letter, he developed a "double-view" of revelation in human history, and his own views on the person of Christ. He held that there were two levels of revelation in human history: on the one level were to be found such men as Hammurabi, Moses, Abraham, Homer, Luther, Shakespeare, Goethe, Kant, and Frederick the Great (*sic*); on the other level, the "more religious," Christ appears. The formula to describe him runs "Christ is God, God in human form."[35]

Harnack began his article by complimenting Delitzsch for making known "from the house-tops" what had previously been limited to a small circle. This was the recognition of Babylonian influence on the Old Testament, and the consequent untenability of any view of plenary inspiration. The succeeding paragraph is an astounding one, however, and perhaps it can be understood only in terms of "the circumstances of the situation." At the best, we may interpret it in the frame of reference suggested by Harnack's discussion of authority as that which evokes "holy thoughts."[36] One might say further in its defense—it certainly cries out for explanation—that Harnack is evidencing that "mediating" quality which he extolled. At the worst, it becomes a facile verbal solution, framed with a "clear eye" on the "higher regions." In any case, it is enigmatic:

But has he indeed done that? [I.e., set forth a more correct view?] He has undoubtedly dispelled a serious error—that all the sources of the Old Testament are wholly original. But of *how little value* are the sources in the history of religion and of the human intellect! If someone were to come forward today and declare to the public: . . . you have previously believed that Goethe's *Faust* was an original work; but it is a late secondary product; . . . how would one answer him? Everyone would laugh at him, and Delitzsch would join in the laughter. To be sure, he has not

[33] Harnack, "Der Brief . . . ," *RA*, II, NF, p. 65.
[34] AZH, p. 342.
[35] *Ibid*., p. 343.
[36] *Supra*, p. 222.

intended to estimate the worth of the Old Testament religion on the basis of its dependence on Babylon; however, he has not in my estimation done enough to keep his hearers and readers from forming a false impression. For what these hearers and readers allow to Goethe is not extended to the prophets and psalmists. Further: because until now a superhuman idea of the Old Testament has prevailed, the pendulum, according to a well-known psychological law, is swinging to the opposite extreme.[37]

This almost unbelievable paragraph lends presumptive evidence to the claim that Harnack's own view of religion—indeed of the essence of Christianity—was remarkably independent of his own historical investigation, being constructed rather on the ground of his axiological presuppositions. What else can his statement that the sources are of "little value" portend? Here one can see at work that process of which Troeltsch spoke: the counterpoising of a doctrine of humanity to his historical investigation.[38] It is not without significance that it is Goethe who should provide his example, standing favorable comparison to the prophets and the psalmists. If Delitzsch, furthermore, did not intend "to estimate the worth of the Old Testament religion on the basis of its dependence on Babylon," is he to be held responsible for the "false impression" which his listeners and readers formed? Harnack, having suffered the same kind of misinterpretation of his positions, shows little sympathy with his colleague. It as little behooves Harnack later to assert, in a panegyric on the Kaiser's intentions, that "what the Kaiser is desirous of making clear is that Delitzsch's authority as an Assyriologist cannot avail to prop up his theological doctrines; and in that he is quite right."[39] Indeed, the principle is valid; but, as his critics charged, was not Harnack's theological doctrine propped up by his authority as a church historian, and does he not share here, and propound elsewhere, a view very similar to that of Delitzsch on the divinity of Christ, and claim that he arrived at this view on the basis of his historical study?[40] Kettle and pot! And where is there a better documentation of the "well-known psychological law" of the swinging pendulum as it touches Old Testament study than in Harnack's own famous judgment in his work on Marcion?

Harnack prefaces his evaluation of the Kaiser's letter with seven paragraphs of flattery, but then declares that the Kaiser is mistaken

[37] Harnack, "Der Brief . . . ," *RA*, II, NF, p. 66. Italics mine.
[38] *Supra*, p. 104.
[39] "Der Brief . . . ," *RA*, II, NF, p. 67.
[40] Chap. XII, B.

in his two main points: his view of revelation and his view of the divinity of Christ. The word "revelation," he affirms, cannot be admitted by science; to her it is transcendental. Yet faith cannot be deprived of the word, and therefore a cleavage between the two appears to be unavoidable. However, "in the course of development a certain common ground has been reached," for evangelical faith today recognizes "*a revelation in persons only*."[41] All other alleged revelations are thereby set aside as containing no revelatory significance whatever. The Kaiser has recognized this, he thinks, and therefore took as his starting point the fact that God reveals himself in persons, and particularly in persons of preeminence. Because such persons also represent for science a mystery in their individuality and power, a possible *rapprochement* is broached. To be sure, Harnack, by identifying his presupposition, immediately makes it evident that science is limited here: for "that I and others should feel that these personalities are revelations of God is an act of inner experience which no science can either create or deny."[42]

The Kaiser, however, has set forth a theory of a double revelation, and here Harnack demurs, striving to save something from the impending wreckage:

> The imperial letter distinguishes between two kinds of revelation: one general and the other of a more religious character. And in this distinction there is great force; for it brings out in boldest relief the fact that there is no more weighty business for man than his relation to God, and that on the nature of this relation everything depends. On the other hand, however, thoughtful people cannot possibly content themselves with the theory of two kinds of revelation running, so to speak, parallel to each other; indeed, his Majesty's letter itself gave expression to this view . . . . There cannot consequently be two revelations—religion, moral power, and knowledge being most closely interwoven—but only one, the bearers of which were and are in truth wholly different from each other in character, vocation, and mission. If Jesus Christ loses nothing of his individuality and uniqueness when placed in a line with Moses, Isaiah, and the psalmists, neither does he lose anything by being ranged side by side with Socrates, Plato, and the other personages named in the imperial document. The religious contemplation of history can in the last analysis be only one and indivisible—humanity, which God takes from the depths of nature, from error and from sin, and redeems and adopts it by raising it to the relation of sonship.[43]

[41] Harnack, "Der Brief . . . ," *RA*, II, NF, p. 69. Italics mine.
[42] *Ibid.*
[43] *Ibid.*, pp. 69–70.

Having introduced the question of the divinity of Christ in the discussion of revelation, the Kaiser has made it necessary that the two be considered in juxtaposition. Harnack first states his conviction that the Church must repudiate every view of Christ which does not set him apart from other teachers. If this appears to be somewhat illogical after his insistence that the revelation in Christ and the revelation in these other great men stand in the common framework of humanity, his point is somewhat clarified when one sees what he means by Jesus' uniqueness. But though he argues that there ought not to be any question here, in view of the plain speaking which Christ, his disciples, and the world's history have presented, and declares that "in his word he still continues to speak just as plainly to us as formerly to his disciples," this does not mean that the formula, "the Godhead of Christ" is to be used: "He himself did not use it, but chose other designations . . . . The ancient Church did not speak without qualification of the Godhead of Christ . . . . Even in the sense of the old dogma, 'God-manhood' is the only correct formula."[44] And now Harnack touches once again on his familiar themes as he comes to the crucial demonstration:

In it the mystery is almost again restored which, in accordance with the will of Christ himself, must ever enfold this question. He made no secret of the fact that he is the Lord and Savior; and his disciples were to learn and to feel this through his word and work. But how his relation with his Father originated he kept to himself, and hid from us. Viewing it then in the light of my historical insight and perception, I should say that the formula "Man and God" is not wholly free from objection because it tries to enter that realm of mystery into which no insight is possible for us. Still this formula may stand, because in truth it claims to explain nothing, but serves only to shield from profanation that which is unusual, just as the expression "Son of God" does. The Pauline saying "God was in Christ" seems to be the last word which we can venture to utter here, after we have slowly and painfully freed ourselves from the delusion of ancient philosophers, that we can fathom the mysteries of God and nature, humanity and history.[45]

Cultured sycophancy aside, what is Harnack's position here? There is one revelation, and it is in persons. Humanity—in its most sublime reaches—must therefore be the object of religious contemplation insofar as history is concerned; this humanity unites religion, moral power, and knowledge. Of the mystery of Christ's divinity, one can

[44] *Ibid.*, p. 70.
[45] *Ibid.*, pp. 70–71.

only say that it is impenetrable; though Jesus affirmed his own Lordship and Saviorhood, it is only in his word and work that this is known and felt. Thus the event of justification and reconcilation to God cannot be understood; it can only be appropriated on the assumption that Christ had the value of God for us.

It is particularly distressing to find Harnack using his own historical insight as the court of appeal when one observes that what this "historical insight" has revealed to him is that "no insight is possible for us" with respect to "that realm of mystery."[46] The conviction remains firm that there is here a fundamental confusion from which no amount of Attic dexterity can extract Harnack; and that he has substituted "theological insight" and prepossession for historical understanding.

What is revelation for Harnack? It is preeminently the teaching of Jesus, a teaching which in itself pointed to God, but which contained no mention of the special relationship of Jesus to God. Jesus embodied this revelation in the sense that he lived a life consistent with the teachings that he gave, and this constituted his only uniqueness—at least, his only "discussable" uniqueness. For "to be historical is to be limited," and this limitation not only precludes any metaphysic, but practically precludes traditional theological formulations. This was a view which never forgot that man was temporal, and that he could not penetrate to the mysteries of God. Some have interpreted Harnack as asserting the principle that all formulations about God must be subject to radical criticism, and that there must always be a genuine openness when one speaks of deity.[47] Others have gone further to say his position created a vacuum, and into this vacuum flowed the presuppositional structure of nineteenth-century German culture. Hence Harnack was accused of *Kulturprotestantismus*, where the norm was "the Gospel" of this culture. In the latter case, Harnack is charged with defaulting to an anthropocentrism.

It would appear that there is truth in both of these statements, and that Harnack cannot be understood according to one only. If pressed, we would hold that the balance falls with the latter. The basis for this judgment is the double vocation implicit in Harnack's conception. He would "understand Christianity historically"; and he would discover "the inner form." The result is "historical axiology," which, whether anthropocentrically circumscribed or not, is the *necessary* formula to use. From this standpoint, the *locus* of revelation had to

[46] *Ibid.*
[47] Pauck, *op. cit.*, p. 345.

be in persons, for there could be nothing higher *which was knowable*. Yet there was that within which validated itself to one (and here the possibility of *a priori* norms is fairly unlimited), and this became Harnack's "authority." Because there was that in Jesus which fit into these *a priori* categories—but also because Harnack was, *nolens volens*, a son of Lutheran orthodoxy—Jesus was to be regarded as the one who, above all others, had "revealed" God. And, finally, because the Bible remained the only real source for knowledge about Jesus, it must be given at least a provisional priority. But even here, it is all-important for Harnack that "historical axiology" shall specify to the Bible what is husk and what is kernel.

c. LAW AND GOSPEL

If Harnack's daughter and biographer is correct—there is no reason to doubt it—in reporting Harnack's purpose as "finding the truth in the mean rather than in the extreme,"[48] we would expect his position on the relation of the Law and the Gospel to go beyond simple affirmations or denials. We have seen in the article on the Kaiser's letter that Harnack could walk the razor's edge. But we have also seen, in the major judgments of the *Marcion*, that Harnack could take extreme positions. One could use, here also, a Harnackian principle, and find the resolution for this apparent ambiguity in the development which takes place in his own inner life. Before an interpretation of any sort is set forth, however, Harnack's own statements should be examined. Two articles written in 1910 pertain to the question of Law and Gospel: the one entitled "Hat Jesus das alttestamentliche Gesetz Abgeschafft?,"[49] the other "Das doppelte Evangelium im Neuen Testament."[50]

To the question raised in the first article, Harnack admits that within the church there is a widespread view that the answer should be affirmative, but declares that a simple affirmative answer is not possible on the basis of the New Testament evidence. It is not true, as some have declared, that there are many places in the Gospels where Jesus broke with the Law. Most of these alleged instances are places where Jesus was correcting the tradition of the Pharisees, and thus affirming the true sense of the Law.

But it is true that there are places where Jesus' teaching comes

[48] AZH, pp. 487–488.
[49] *RA*, II, NF, pp. 225–236.
[50] See Chap. VI, note 32.

into conflict with the Mosaic Law: he issues a commandment against swearing under any conditions, he contradicts the basic principle of the Law (an eye for an eye) by commanding us not to be angry or to return evil for evil, he tells us to love our enemies, he makes the Sabbath subordinate to man and thus declares a new viewpoint, and by his intercourse with publicans and sinners he declares by deeds that he stands above the Law. It appears then that Jesus took a contradictory position with respect to the Law:

> This contradiction indeed is present and cannot be removed by the assumption that Jesus held the Law to be basically correct and did away with only certain parts of it. The Law is a unity; he who violates it in part, or even in one single small point, thereby destroys it in its entirety. Where could one draw the line? What part did he recognize, and what part did he reject? The attempt at a classification would show how impossible such an attempt is. The contradiction remains in force.[51]

Still there must be some explanation for this contradiction, for Jesus cannot have held a flagrantly contradictory position. The most seemly way to resolve the difficulty is to say that he took one position early in his career, and another at a later time. But the facts of the case give no positive evidence that this was true.

The beginning of the resolution of the difficulty is obtained when it is recalled that the prophets also distinguished between commandments. The prophet speaks in the name of God; when he makes distinctions in the Law between that which is primary and that which is secondary, his distinction is to be accepted as the true sense of the Law. Because the prophet is speaking in the name of God, he does not feel the contrast between the Law and his own words.

But one must go further than this. Jesus was convinced that he was not only a prophet, but was also the Son of God who knew the Father and therefore did not need the Law in order to recognize and to declare the will of God. "This consciousness gave him an absolute inner freedom, and with it an absolute freedom with respect to the Law. It was this consciousness which let him speak the words 'You have heard . . . but I say unto you.' "[52] Indeed, it is his doctrine that his "easy yoke" could be set in contrast to the old, hard yoke because of this certainty of doing God's will; thus he "called tax-collectors and sinners instead of the righteous and thus founded a new community within the old, and a new covenant with God."[53]

[51] Harnack, "*Hat Jesus das . . .* ," *RA*, II, NF, pp. 231–232.
[52] *Ibid.*, p. 233.
[53] *Ibid.*

On this dynamic basis, what is the relationship between the old and the new covenant?

It was God's business to decide this and to make it clear, not Jesus'. It was not necessary that Jesus himself should know the answer to every inner contradiction. Nor was it necessary, while he lived in the fear and the love of God, to practice that hyper-criticism of the scribes, but rather to live creatively as God's Son out of his immediate experience.[54]

But does this explain the contradiction?

Objectively seen, the relation of Jesus to the Law is involved in a contradiction, but subjectively (that means, as seen from his standpoint), he was not conscious of the contradiction, for he saw in the Law the same will of God which he through his own immediate knowledge of God had experienced, and he said and did only what the Spirit of God told him to say and to do.[55]

The contradiction is not, therefore, explained; for Jesus, it is irrelevant. Jesus, like all great spirits, was not a negatively directed, but a positively directed man. It is far more creative to *be* something than to be against something. One does not first destroy and then start something new, but one develops new life in the old plant, and by and by the old will die and a new and nobler shoot will unfold. Jesus' method was precisely this. He did not first destroy the Law, in order to create something new, but he planted his teaching on the Law, stripped off the dead leaves which constricted the little shoot, and thus gave it light and air. The health of the plant lay in this shoot, and by pruning the dead growth, he mediated new life. The old branches, which were no longer able to bring forth fruit, gradually weakened and died. What Jesus stripped off was sin, self-seeking, the service of mammon, self-justification, religious hypocrisy, and the arrogant assertion, "We have Abraham for our father." He left the Law as it was, but he began a strong inner revolution which finally led to its overthrow. Within the Old Covenant he founded the New, without thereby determining what should become of the Old.

The early Church in Jerusalem believed that they could take the same position vis-à-vis the Law which Jesus himself had taken, and cultivate the Old and the New in an equal way. This was a great, though understandable, error. For what Jesus had mediated to them was a new spirit and new life, not something already complete and finished in itself. This new talent must not be buried, but should

[54] *Ibid.*
[55] *Ibid.*, p. 234.

rather let the new spirit work in the creation of new life. "They were not the true disciples of Jesus who slavishly extolled him and were not willing to make any forward step which he had not publicly enjoined; only those who lived their lives in love and freedom were his disciples.[56] The exemplars here are those who first preached the Gospel at Antioch, and Paul, when he declared that "Christ is the end of the Law for everyone who believes." For this eventually must result, that the Law be set aside. The distinction between the Old and the New must be declared; that which Jesus had grafted onto the old Jewish stem would finally bring about the overthrow of Judaism and the advent of a new religion, the religion of Jesus Christ:

"The Law was given by Moses, but grace and truth came through Jesus Christ." This knowledge is the key to the development in the apostolic era. Not through his teaching did Jesus communicate this, but his disciples learned it in his person, in his work, his sorrows and his majesty. But further, the love and the freedom which are so clearly in all the words and parables of Jesus, and which he placed over the Law without weakening it, proved to his disciples what path they must travel, and gave them the courage to break with the Law, which Jesus himself had still allowed to stand.[57]

Harnack's explicit answer to the question of the relation of the Law and the Gospel is clear enough: the Gospel "as Jesus preached it" fulfills the Law rather than destroying it. But this does not mean that Jesus *knew* what the relationship between Law and Gospel was. Living by a creative inner certainty, based on his "immediate experience," he was, objectively, "involved in a contradiction"; but this contradiction was not recognized by him because of his subjective commitment to God. It has only been in the "development," presumably, that the contradictory relation of Law and Gospel has become obvious. And this came about, wonder beyond wonder, in spite of an initial error in attempting to emulate Jesus' attitude toward the Law, through the discovery of a "love and . . . freedom" which was in his "person and work" and "in all the words and parables of Jesus": these things constituting a "grace and truth" which, however, he did *not* teach.

The disciples therefore learned something "through Jesus Christ" which he himself had not taught, and this implies the "gospel of"/ "gospel about" dichotomy which Harnack refers to as "the double

[56] *Ibid.*, p. 235.
[57] *Ibid.*, p. 236.

Gospel." Ever since 1900, when Harnack delivered the famous *Das Wesen des Christentums* lectures at the University of Berlin, he had been under intermittent and sometimes thunderous fire for the statement "the Father alone, and not the Son, belongs in the Gospel as Jesus preached it."[58] His daughter contends that this became such a rock of stumbling only because Harnack was basically misunderstood. Those who criticized him did not see that "Harnack spoke of a double Gospel, the one Gospel '*as Jesus had preached it*' and the other the Gospel '*as Paul and the Evangelists had preached it.*' "[59]

In his article on the double Gospel, the "first Gospel" is detailed in the famous three points of *Das Wesen des Christentums*: the Kingdom of God and its coming, God the Father and the infinite value of the human soul, and the higher righteousness and the commandment of love.[60] "Here the Gospel is a joyous message and is preached to the poor, the meek, the peace-makers, and the pure in heart."[61] The "second Gospel" is what one finds in Paul: "But here it is the preaching that God's Son descended from heaven, became a man, by his death and resurrection brought salvation from sin, death, and the devil to those who believe, and thereby realized the eternal purposes of God."[62] This "second Gospel" took its place alongside the first, and almost overcame it. But it never could quite accomplish this, even in the ages when dogmatics prevailed. "Not only does this 'first' Gospel live in the hearts of all those who take the Christian religion in complete earnestness, but even in dogmatics it does not disappear."[63] Some say that the Gospel is a unity and because certain features of it, its miracles and mythology, can no longer be held, the totality of it must be surrendered. But in such a statement one is denying that the human soul has eternal worth, that there is an ethical good which is the life principle of the spirit, and that there is a living God. If one denies these points, an entirely new ethic must be constructed—if indeed one can speak of an ethic after all the content which is contained in the "first Gospel" is removed. This denial actually has taken place, Harnack declares, and this is why this "first Gospel," the Gospel of Jesus, is today involved in a death struggle for existence. Those of philosophical persuasion give assur-

58 *WC*, p. 125.
59 AZH, pp. 246–247.
60 *WC*, p. 44.
61 Harnack, "*Das doppelte Evangelium . . . ,*" *RA*, II, NF, p. 215.
62 *Ibid.*
63 *Ibid.*, p. 221.

ance that one can construct an "ideal fable" out of the "second Gospel."[64] But in the attempt they eliminate the person of Jesus, and their representation is therefore of little worth.

But is there, then, any value in the "second Gospel"? Harnack declares that there is, and he summarizes his position in this regard in an enlightening paragraph:

> The "second" Gospel cannot be held in the form of the two-nature doctrine; for it not only contradicts the historical, but the very possibility of knowledge. Every statement about Jesus Christ which does not take into consideration the fact that he was a man is unacceptable, because it conflicts with the historical representation of Jesus' life. But with this observation the "second" Gospel is by no means negated. If it is certain that no God appeared and no God died and was resurrected, it is even more certain that we know nothing really about God through our senses and our natural knowledge. Further, it is certain that the only place that we can meet God is in our personal higher life and ethical striving. God is holiness and God is love. If this is true, then God is revealed only in personal life, only in men; he works only through men, redeems only through men, and perfects only through men. And for the human in this sense there is no generic concept; for the human can be represented only as the individual and the singular. But in what measure God fulfills the individual and uses others as his instruments one can learn only from deeds, i.e., from history; no philosophy can give us information here or prescribe limits. The "second" Gospel proclaims that God has made Jesus of Nazareth Lord and Christ for humanity, that his work was God's work, and history has placed its seal upon this proclamation. This seal is not the seal of the Church—for the great extension and actual dominion of Christianity can in themselves prove nothing—but it consists in the fact that for almost nineteen hundred years, and at the present time, faith in Jesus Christ creates children of God who know themselves to be redeemed, who are enabled to overcome the world.[65]

Both Gospels are necessary. In a formula, "the 'first' Gospel contains *the truth*, the 'second' Gospel contains *the way*, and the two together bring *the life*."[66] But it follows from this that "it is unnecessary that one must be fully conscious that Jesus Christ is the way by which one comes to the truth. Christ is also Christ in this way, that a brother becomes a Christ for others. It is always personal life in God which brings others to this experience, and through this alone new life can

[64] Here Harnack probably has in mind the "*neu-Rousseauismus*." Cf. AZH, p. 296.

[65] Harnack, "*Das doppelte Evangelium . . . ,*" *RA*, II, NF, pp. 223–224.

[66] *Ibid.*, p. 224.

be produced."[67] However, this personal life in God will lead one to the ever more certain conviction that Jesus is the Christ.

In this essay, Harnack admits the influence which the "situation" of the time has had on his formulation of this position. The denial of any validity to Christianity by materialism must be challenged because it rests on a false historical view as to what Christianity *really* is, but perhaps more significantly, it denies the worth of the soul, and therefore utterly debilitates man in his ethical striving. What Christianity *really* is for Harnack is Kantian morality dressed up. The three postulates—the existence of God, immortality, and moral freedom—are stated explicitly. This is "the Gospel as Jesus had preached it." Harnack believes that he has arrived at this conclusion "solely" by a historical method, and he insists that any statement about Jesus Christ which "conflicts with the historical representation" must be unacceptable. Philosophy on the one hand, and certain types of dogmatics on the other, *presuppose* what he was in relation to God, and are therefore unacceptable guides. Yet this is impressively curious. For in the facile attempt to distinguish the "first Gospel" from the "second Gospel," Harnack not only ignores those who, by this time, had radically challenged his "historical" portrait of Jesus and his "historical" identification of the essence, but he inserts his own axiology, his own "philosophy," his own "type of dogmatic" in a determinative way. Thus, he holds, revelation can only take place in the uniqueness of "personal life," and in "ethical striving," and only the *result* that issues in history can tell us whether God has so acted through individuals; which, by whatever name, is still a "dogmatic" statement based on certain philosophical assumptions. Again, Jesus Christ is the uniquely unique, not because the Church has so declared in the "second Gospel"—this would be "overcoming history by dogma"—but because history has found in him the efficacy to produce a "personal higher life" which overcomes the world and creates children of God through faith. This statement also represents a strange merging of history and axiology. Finally, in his "formula," Harnack reveals again that facility which would bring together into a unity both "Gospels," but he is hardly convincing, and his final solution to the problem is an appeal to his "personal higher life and ethical striving." This is Harnack's axiological *noli me tangere*; and history thereunto affixes its "seal."

We have arrived at the point where the question must again be asked, this time on the basis of Harnack's explication: In his discus-

[67] *Ibid.*

sion of the relation of Law and Gospel, has he found his truth in the mean or in the extreme? Certainly his resolution is ideologically neat if one grants him his fundamental assumptions on "development" and "the essence of Christianity." If one does grant these assumptions, the answer to the question will be: He finds the truth in the mean. If one does not grant them, the answer will be that the truth he finds is a contrived and extreme truth. No one would disagree with that more historically oriented section at the beginning of the first essay. But from the moment that Harnack declares that "Jesus cannot have held to a flagrantly contradictory position"[68] the development becomes questionable. Everything depends upon what is meant by stating the problem as Harnack has stated it. Is this simply a logical necessity which declares to Harnack that Jesus could not have done thus and so? Many of Harnack's critics, and in particular Schweitzer, would have taken the diverse position that one has no right to bring the categories to Jesus, telling him to fit into them. But more importantly, one is reintroduced at this point to Harnack's "surd." Jesus is "unique"—this is demanded—yet he must be understood and explained. Between this Scylla and Charybdis Harnack tacked, not only in this article, but in his total corpus. He had said at the beginning of his career that the problem which obsessed him was, "How can I become his disciple?" He reaffirms this fundamental orientation here. He had related his vocation as church historian to this problem. Thus, in historical-critical scientific labor, it was never possible to operate simply on the basis of historicist positivism; one must go further and deeper to ask the question of "worth-for-persons," and this question must be related to Jesus.

When he comes to consider the apparently contradictory relation which Jesus held with regard to the Law, he resolves it by an appeal to a higher authority that was resident in Jesus, his consciousness that he was a prophet and "the Son of God who knew the Father." Now this might appear to be circumspect orthodox theology. But Harnack does not develop what he means when he applies this term to Jesus. Elsewhere we have noted this hesitation to speculate about the implications of such a statement. He ascribed the hesitancy to those limitations beyond which his methodology would not allow him to go. He would not indulge in speculation on the relation of God and Jesus in any other than what he called a historical sense.

Is it not fair to point out, however, that by appealing to this higher authority to resolve the contradiction, he removes the question from

[68] Harnack, "*Hat Jesus das . . .*," *RA*, II, NF, p. 232.

the ground of the historical, and places it on the ground of the "dogmatic"? Is there not too strong a resemblance between the "unity and certainty" which Harnack from the beginning held as the aim of his own life, and the quality here discovered in Jesus? This could be interpreted as following from his Christian commitment, the statement of the requirement for one who would truly follow Christ. But such an observation only begs the question which is relevant: Can the picture of Jesus to which historical understanding contributes be so completely drawn as Harnack claims? The eschatological school held that it could not be. Tyrrell judged that Harnack's picture was drawn not from historical knowledge but from psychological self-portraiture.[69] Certain modern scholars have interpreted the Messianic consciousness as a vastly different complex than Harnack here suggests. Perhaps the fact that Harnack had to find an essence, by the logic of his method, the fact that he could find this in the "spiritual heritage" on the basis of his assumption that "the same mind is at work in history and in us," and the fact that he could not admit "dogmatic" characterizations such as are contained in Mark and Paul, shut him up to the necessity of constructing an ideal Jesus from Q and his own consciousness, if Jesus was to be portrayed at all. Perhaps. In any case, it is bitter medicine to have to take Jesus as a "positive thinker."

D. CANON

To the point of weariness, perhaps, we have belabored Harnack for having worked within a structure of presuppositions at the same time that he protested his historical neutrality. He uses the word "presuppositions" himself, as we have seen in discussing the *Dogmengeschichte*, but he does not mean those personal subjective commitments which one brings to any material. Such commitments he regarded as theoretically indefensible; when he uses the word, it might more accurately be designated "suppositions," held on the basis of the impact the material itself makes. In spite of all his caveats and protestations, however, we believe the record itself speaks against him. Nowhere is this more apparent than in his consideration

[69] G. Tyrrell's statement: "The Christ that Harnack sees, looking back through nineteen centuries of Catholic darkness, is only a reflection of a liberal Protestant face seen at the bottom of a deep well." Quoted from *Christianity at the Cross-Roads* (London, 1909), p. 44, in Robert Grant, *The Bible in the Church* (New York: The Macmillan Company, 1948), p. 188.

of the question of the canonicity of the Old and the New Testaments, what it means and how it originated—and declined.

To the degree that the reader is convinced that Harnack's "rich and many-sided wisdom of life" was suffused with a *Lebensideal*, he will find almost incredible this comment on the work of Blass, Ramsay, Weiss, and Zahn:

These scholars are influenced partly by prepossessions in reference to the Canon of the New Testament, partly by the conviction that miracles really happened, partly by both these prejudices. This attitude of theirs has most unfortunately rendered their research and their demonstrations subject to suspicion, even in those points that have nothing to do with the aforesaid prepossessions. In the history of the criticism of the New Testament any Apologetic with a dogmatic bias has always promoted radicalism, or has at least made critics deaf to proofs.[70]

Harnack then characterizes Blass's work as insulting to the critical school, "though at the same time he betrayed a very slight conception of deeper historical questions";[71] Ramsay had a clear eye and great learning, but this was "at the service of a method which seeks to extract from the sources more than is really in them";[72] and Zahn "cannot efface the impression that he conducts historical investigations like a counsel for the defense *à tout prix*."[73] Furthermore, "all these scholars and those allied with them, showed little sense of the debt we owe to Baur and his followers, of the deepening of our insight into historical questions, and the broadening of our outlook that has been brought about by their labors."[74] After such sweeping charges of "prepossession," one might expect to find a great many qualifying phrases attached to one's own judgments. Instead one finds the famous judgment from the *Marcion*: the retention of the Old Testament as a canonical document within Protestantism is indefensible. Regal judging, to be sure. Presuppositionless—never!

The question whether there is any sense in which the Old Testament can be spoken of as canonical Christian Scripture can be answered very simply: No. But Harnack does not thereby deny all value to the Old Testament. It is a book worthy of being read. He would not deny, and indeed did a great deal to clarify the fact of a *historical* continuity of Old and New Testaments. The important

[70] Harnack, *The Acts of the Apostles,* p. 302.
[71] *Ibid.*
[72] *Ibid.*
[73] *Ibid.*
[74] *Ibid.*, p. 303.

question, however, that of canonicity, was answered in his considered judgment of the work on Marcion, and it brought forth replies that made necessary a further explication by Harnack. Karl Holl was one of those to whom Harnack wrote in explication of his meaning:

Speaking of the Old Testament, with respect to its use in the Church, I believe that we generally agree. Neither would I remove it from the covers of the Bible nor cease its instruction: I would like to see it evaluated and handled in the same way that Luther handled the Apocrypha—"good and profitable for reading." I say this emphatically.

I have been able to teach my children (to whom I have, in part, given the first religious instruction) in this way, and without difficulty: I say to them that the Old Testament is obsolete, and is beautiful and of worth only in certain parts; it is the Jewish Law and history; *our* Testament is the New. The same thing can and should be said in the schools.[75]

Now it is clear that Harnack's judgment in the work on Marcion depends on the idea of a progressive development in history. The services which the Old Testament provided at the time of the emerging great Church were real and necessary *in the givens* of the time. The retention of the Old Testament at the time of the Reformation was *inevitable*, because of the lack of historical insight. But the contemporary situation is one vastly different as to givens, and possesses this emancipating historical insight. Therefore the Old Testament should be retained no longer as a part of canonical Christian Scripture. This is a fair statement of Harnack's position, when we append the warning that "historical insight" is always to be seen in that full sense which he had set forth. He would have held that the Old Testament should be read for purposes of understanding the great personalities who are there available in their own works and in the history of Israel. But the Old Testament cannot be efficacious for that which most concerns man in this present time, viz., his achievement of the higher righteousness. This is available in the Gospel alone. Further, a retention of the canonicity of the Old Testament introduces all sorts of contradictions and confusions into the Christian endeavor, and acts, in Harnack's own words, with a "crippling" effect. This was one of the givens which Harnack thought he saw in his own time, and his announced purpose to "confess and defend" his position demanded that he exercise his felt responsibility and declare

[75] AZH, pp. 317–318.

himself. The key, then, is to be seen in the "situation"; Harnack admits that this is true in the Marcion judgment, and we believe that he thereby not only states a historical principle, but declares *what he himself practiced.* And, of course, if he did it here, there is no reason to doubt that he would use this same *modus operandi* with respect to his identification of the essence of Christianity. It is not going too far, with respect to the Marcion judgment, to suggest that the statement is aimed at the recrudescence of an "unscientific theology" which he saw in Barth.

Harnack went further than a simple denial of unity to the Testaments, however. As we have seen in the discussion of the Lessing-Walch controversy, he denied all that was implied in the concept of an "authoritative book," holding the idea to be simply impossible. Thus, not only is the canonicity of the Old Testament denied, but the validity of the concept of any "authoritative" Scripture is challenged. But Harnack clearly held to some view of value for the New Testament which he denied to the Old; and this can be seen if one distinguishes between objective and subjective authority. This distinction is nowhere more evident than in his *Das Wesen des Christentums,* where he is discussing the contribution of Protestantism: "It protested against all formal, external authority in religion; against the authority, therefore, of councils, priests, and the whole tradition of the Church. *That alone is to be authority which shows itself to be such within and effects a deliverance: the thing itself, therefore, the Gospel.*"[76] A fair question is whether this view is consonant with other statements in Harnack's works. To answer this question, we must go beyond a simple reiteration of Harnack's judgment that the Old Testament should be rejected as Christian Scripture and try to trace the considerations involved in the judgment. There is no point on which there would be a wider disagreement between Harnack and contemporary biblical scholars than here. As we have seen, this judgment, contained in his work on Marcion, was unacceptable to many in his own day. But it is a crucial judgment for understanding his biblical interpretation, it is straightforwardly set forth, and, we believe, it is a necessary conclusion from that position which he defended.

The question as to how this "liberating" religion, Christianity, came to be, in any sense, the "religion of a book," cannot help but be a problem. Why did Christianity claim to be the true heir of the Old Testament? Why did it create a New Testament? In his work,

[76] *Ibid.,* p. 239. Italics mine.

The Mission and Expansion of Christianity in the First Three Centuries, Harnack devotes a chapter to the subject "The Religion of a Book and of a History Realized," and declares that "Christianity . . . never was and never came to be the religion of a book in the strict sense of the term."[77] Yet it was on the very verge of this, in the first instance with the Old Testament, and then, after the "canonizing" process of the latter half of the second century, with the New Testament.

With respect to the Old Testament, the process can be quickly described. Marcion and the Gnostics had indignantly repudiated the Old Testament as a Christian book, and they were in turn repudiated by the Church. Paul, "when we read him aright,"[78] was also opposed to casting away the Old Testament, but the position which he took was so complicated that he was not understood at all. The fact that the Church kept the Old Testament is intelligible, for the Church believed that God had authored it. The possibilities of interpreting so rich and comprehensive a literature were well-nigh inexhaustible, and not the least contribution which it could make to the Church was its great aid in Christian propaganda. Christianity, then, simply took over the Old Testament because of its efficacy in providing certain desiderata for any expanding faith. When the New Testament achieved a place of dominant influence, some of these Old Testament contributions fell into the background. Christian morality, for example, was now based on the teaching of Jesus rather than on the Old Testament content. But most of the services which the Old Testament had rendered remained useful. Theoretically, the Old Testament might be "*expunctum*"; practically, it was allegorized to supply evidence for the truth of Christianity. After the conquests of the second century, even less care was manifested in the use of the Old Testament than that exercised by allegorism. For, "as the churches became stocked with every kind of sacred ceremony, and as they carefully developed priestly, sacrificial, and sacramental ideas, . . . the *letter* of the Old Testament ceremonial laws was applied to the arrangements of Christian organization and worship."[79] There was a falling-back to the Law. Only the Gospels ranked with or above the Old Testament; the Epistles did not come into prominence until the time of Augustine.

These are the conclusions at which Harnack arrives with respect to the historical question of the Church's retention of the Old Testa-

[77] I, p. 353.
[78] *Ibid.*
[79] *Ibid.*, p. 362.

ment as a canonical book. We must now consider his investigation of the problem of the origin of the New Testament, and his evaluation of the consequences thereof. For we have seen that this, too, *must* be a problem, not only from the standpoint of historical science, but more importantly because of the theological norm to which he subscribed. The question is deeper than, Why an Old Testament?; it becomes, Why any canon at all? That Harnack recognized this as the real question is a token of his willingness to take on the hardest problems; for certainly the problem of canonicity is ineluctable when one has set forth a theory of the "essence of Christianity" in the way he did. We have argued that this necessity to discover an "essence" lay in the multiform heritage which he enjoyed; and we have held that the "essence" itself was conditioned by the cultural givens within which he lived. We are here in a sense testing these judgments, and going further to state another: that when the "essence of Christianity" is described as Harnack has described it, the concept of a canonical book entirely evaporates.

Harnack's judgments as they relate to the New Testament are to be found in *The Origin of the New Testament and the Most Important Consequences of the New Creation.*[80] In the first section of this work, Harnack lists five questions that must be answered. In answering the first question, "What is the reason, and how did it come about that a second authoritative collection of books arose among Christians?"[81] four motives are given: "the supreme reverence in which the words and teaching of Christ Jesus were held"; "the interest in the death and resurrection of the Messiah Jesus," this being the force of Paul's work; "the conception of the 'New Covenant' necessarily suggested the need of something of *the nature of a document*"; and "the problem presented to the Church since the second century by the presence of a considerable Christian literature."[82] In these motives, Harnack declares, "*the New Testament exists in embryo.*"[83] Where did the authority come from for producing such a work? From the "apostles, prophets, and teachers," who were regarded as having a higher authority than others. How did the New Testament actually come into existence, "supporting the necessity in idea"[84] of it? For motives do not by themselves create, and authority requires practical conditions. These conditions were present,

[80] Tr. J. R. Wilkinson (New York: The Macmillan Company, 1925).
[81] *Ibid.*, pp. 2–3.
[82] *Ibid.*, pp. 7–17, *passim.*
[83] *Ibid.*, p. 20.
[84] *Ibid.*, p. 25.

however: the existence of a body of "candidating" literature, public lection, and the "adversative" influence of various heretical movements. Harnack makes the rather striking speculative statement that "whether apart from the conflict with heresy a New Testament would ever have come into existence is to be answered in the affirmative," and gives as his reason that "the idea of the New Covenant and the tendency to establish and confirm the idea would necessarily have resulted in calling the second sacred collection into being."[85] To the second question, "Why does the New Testament contain other works in addition to the Gospels, and thus appear as a whole with two divisions (Gospel and Apostle)?"[86] the answer can be given in one word: Tradition.

What this means is "the need of the present appealing to the authority of the past."[87] But Harnack does not leave his historical judgment unalloyed here:

> In the New Testament, letters which serve momentary and particular needs are set on a level of equal value with the Gospels; what is merely personal with what is of universal import; the Apostles with Christ; their work with his work! In a compilation which is invested with divine authority we must read: "Drink a little wine for thy stomach's sake," . . . . Side by side with the words of divine mercy and loving-kindness in the Gospels we meet with outbreaks of personal strife in the Epistles; side by side with the stories of the Passion and Resurrection, the dry notes of the diary of a missionary journey.
>
> He who would show how two absolutely disparate entities have yet come together can only solve the problem if he can prove that they form the extreme wings of a complex whole that is governed by an idea. The idea in question here is the idea of *Tradition.* One of the great problems which has silently dominated the inner history of the Church for centuries is the problem, *"Scripture and Tradition." In the compilation of the New Testament this problem already, to a certain extent, found a solution; indeed, properly speaking, the strivings and conflicts that have taken place since this solution, i.e., since the creation of the New Testament, are all of them only of secondary import. The main battle was long since fought and decided in favour of Tradition when the New Testament was compiled and in the very fact of its compilation*; but unfortunately, historians have not yet generally recognized this truth. The New Testament itself, when compared with what Jesus purposed, said, and was, is already

[85] *Ibid.*, p. 31.
[86] *Ibid.*, p. 3.
[87] *Ibid.*, p. 49.

a tradition which overlies and obscures. When then we speak today of the antagonism and conflict between Scripture and Tradition, the tradition in question is a *second* tradition.[88]

Here, we submit, is Harnack's answer to the problem of "canonicity." Here is the test of our previous judgments, and our conclusions are affirmed; and here is the complete evaporation of the idea of "canonicity" in favor of a "canonized essence."

The third question, "Why does the New Testament contain four gospels and not one only?"[89] can be answered in the same way as the second: because of the interest in sure and certain tradition. And the fourth, "Why could only one 'Revelation' keep its place in the New Testament?"[90] can be quickly dealt with by pointing out that apostolicity of authorship had become the canonical norm.

The final question, "Was the New Testament created consciously?"[91] must be given an affirmative answer and the evidence is the inclusion of the book of Acts. That the Gospels should have been regarded as canonical one can understand without employing any notion of "conscious creation"; and that the apostolic epistles should have come to a canonical status can be explained from such evidence as public lection. But "*the placing of this book (the Acts) in the growing Canon shows evidence of reflection, of conscious purpose, of a strong hand acting with authority; and by such conscious action the Canon began to take form as Apostolic-Catholic.*"[92] Furthermore, the fact that "we find in force at the end of the second century" the three criteria of apostolicity, the rule of faith, the canon, and the episcopate, is intelligible "*as the reflection and the expression of the self-consciousness and ecclesiastical character of the leading church.*"[93] It was Rome that gave form to this new collection about 200, thus "*in idea*" creating a closed canon.

When Harnack turns to "the consequences" of the creation of this new book, the value judgments are joined to the historical judgments. That this is true, the eleven-point summary makes clear; though we shall pay particular attention to the second and third points only, the entire summary is included as yet another illustration of this "Tendenz":

[88] *Ibid.*, pp. 42–44.
[89] *Ibid.*, p. 3.
[90] *Ibid.*
[91] *Ibid.*
[92] *Ibid.*, p. 97.
[93] *Ibid.*, p. 105.

(1) The New Testament immediately emancipated itself from the conditions of its origin and claimed to be regarded simply as a gift of the Holy Spirit. . . . It became in principle the final court of appeal for the Christian life.

(2) The New Testament has added to the Revelation in history a second written proclamation of this Revelation, and has given it a position of superior authority.

(3) The New Testament definitely protected the Old Testament as a book of the Church, but thrust it into a subordinate position, and thus introduced a wholesome complication into the conception of the Canon of Scripture.

(4) The New Testament has preserved for us the most valuable portion of primitive Christian literature, yet at the same time it delivered the rest of the earliest works to oblivion and has limited the transmission of later works.

(5) Though the New Testament brought to an end the production of authoritative Christian writings, yet it cleared the way for theological and also for ordinary Christian literary activity.

(6) The New Testament obscured the true origin and the historical significance of the works which it contained, but on the other hand, by impelling men to study them, it brought into existence certain conditions favourable to the critical treatment and correct interpretation of these works.

(7) The New Testament checked the imaginative creation of events in the scheme of Salvation . . . but it called forth, or at least encouraged the intellectual creation of facts in the sphere of theology and of a theological mythology.

(8) The New Testament helped to demark a special period of Christian Revelation, and so in a certain sense to give Christians of later times an inferior status; yet it kept alive the ideals and claims of primitive Christianity.

(9) The New Testament promoted and completed the fatal identification of the Word of the Lord and the Teaching of the Apostles; but because it raised Pauline Christianity to a place of high honour, it has introduced into the history of the Church a ferment rich in blessing.

(10) In the New Testament the Catholic Church forged for herself a new weapon with which to ward off all heresy as un-Christian, but she has also found in it a court of control before which she has appeared ever increasingly in default.

(11) The New Testament has hindered the natural impulse to give to the content of Religion simple, clear, and logical expression, but on the other hand it has preserved Christian doctrine from becoming a mere philosophy of religion.[94]

In discussing the second point, Harnack expounds on the significance of a written proclamation achieving authoritative "revelatory" status alongside the revelation in history:

In Judaism . . . one has long been accustomed to see the revelation of God to his people in a double form: God has revealed himself in a long chain of facts, institutions, persons, etc., and he has deposited the content of this revelation in a book and has thus embodied it permanently for men in written letters. In course of time the book itself became revelation, indeed *the* revelation . . . and . . . revelation itself was regarded as consisting of accounts of events, doctrines, laws, ideas, and so forth.

Scarcely was the New Testament created when here also the same idea makes its appearance. . . . It represents the revelation of God as a literary revelation.

Thus the Christian revelation acquired a quite different, or rather a "higher" nature; it became a complex of ideas . . . because the revelation is given as a revelation in writing. From this point of view the Christian religion became a religion of a book, namely of the book of divine ideas. Then it necessarily followed that the revelation in historic fact, including the historic Christ, of which the book gives the narrative, must fall into the background when compared with the revelation in writing and must become something symbolic. It is merely "Mythos," while in the book the "Logos" bears sway. Hence what really matters about Christ is not that as Christ he had an earthly history, but that as the Logos of the written record he reveals eternal truth.[95]

Harnack, of course, rejects such a cavalier treatment of "events," for when the revelation in history was changed into a revelation in writing, "the whole idea of religion was altered and was fixed in the direction in which, up to this time, it had been developing."[96] When this was conjoined with a similar evaluation of the Old Testament, and its acceptance as canon, religion became "just as much knowledge concerning what happened on the second day of creation as it is knowledge of the loving-kindness of God, of the journeys of the

[94] *Ibid.*, pp. 115–162, *passim.*
[95] *Ibid.*, pp. 121–124.
[96] *Ibid.*, p. 124.

Apostle Paul as of the coming of the Saviour."[97] Revelation for Harnack is clearly not Logos, nor is it Mythos; there is a revelation only in event. But that this is not so simple an answer as it appears to be is evidenced by the necessity to specify, and the content of the specification, of what the event *means*.[98]

The third point emphasizes the brilliancy of the coup brought off by the Church in canonizing the New Testament; for if the Old Testament continued to dominate the Church, there was always the danger of re-Judaizing Christianity; but on the other hand, if it were not held in high esteem, the Church was liable to the attacks of the heretics who rejected it. With the canonization of the New Testament, the Church could anathematize Jewish Christians for their lack of the New Testament, and Gnostics for their failure to accept the Old. But with its coup it introduced difficulties in relating these two Testaments, which could only issue in the subordination of the Old to the New. Actually, the total result was a salutary one, for the fact that the Old Testament contained something "relative" warded off the full biblicism which might have resulted otherwise; and the fact that both Testaments were retained left "the way to the *historical* treatment of the two Testaments . . . open for future ages."[99] One can thus see a dialectical relationship at work, and this is to be found in all of the remaining points.

An analysis of this work might begin with an expression of surprise at Harnack's barely concealed animus against the Pauline material. This is seen particularly in the section of the work relating to origin. In speaking of the Gospels and the content of "divine mercy and loving-kindness" therein, in comparison to "personal strife" and "the dry notes of the diary of a missionary journey," as found in the Epistles and Acts, Harnack finds "two absolutely disparate entities." Such a radical bifurcation is possible only if one has already decided that the essence of Christianity is teaching, and a particular content of teaching, and that everything that will not fit the presupposition as to what this content is should be ruled out. Why not, one might ask, compare "the particular needs" served by I Corinthians 15 with the "universal import" of the genealogy of Matthew? Harnack would doubtless demur; but this is not an invalid use of his own principle.

Second, there is a clear Hegelian influence in the manner in which

[97] *Ibid.*, p. 125.
[98] Cf. *supra*, p. 251.
[99] Harnack, *The Origin of the New Testament . . .*, p. 130.

Harnack finds the development to be under the influence of *ideas*. These "absolutely disparate entities" which one finds in the New Testament "form the extreme wings of a complex whole that is governed by an idea."[100] One could scarcely find a better illustration of thesis-antithesis-synthesis working itself out under the influence of the rational. Further, the New Testament was "necessary in idea,"[101] "the idea of the New Covenant . . . would necessarily have resulted in calling the second sacred collection into being,"[102] tradition is an idea which, in juxtaposition with Scripture, "has silently dominated the inner history of the Church for centuries,"[103] and the creation of a closed canon in idea, and later in actuality, is a product of "the reflection and expression of the self-consciousness . . . of the leading church."[104] Further, the structure and the content of the last nine "consequences of the new creation" are remarkably Hegelian in form.

Third, when one juxtaposes this first and second comment, it becomes quite evident that for all his emphasis on historical event, Harnack is really quite contemptuous of historical particularity. Though he can emphasize the "earthly history" of Christ, the "essence of his teaching" becomes for Harnack an ephemeral "relation." Though the "historical treatment" of the Bible is held to be essential as against the "mythology of ideas" interpretation, this treatment in actuality derogates concrete particulars (like the "dry notes of the diary of a missionary journey," or Paul's prescription for Timothy's stomach—if so it was) in favor of an "essence" which is derived *from* the sources by Harnack's reason. Indeed, in the crucial passage quoted above,[105] it becomes a question of "absolutely disparate entities" (the "merely personal" against "what is of universal import," "outbreaks of personal strife" against "the words of divine mercy," etc.) One can well imagine what would have resulted if Harnack had interpreted the pungent passage in II Kings 18, dealing with the Rabshakeh's threat against Jerusalem's defenders.[106] One cannot

[100] *Supra*, p. 248.
[101] Harnack, *The Origin of the New Testament* . . . , p. 25.
[102] *Ibid.*, p. 31.
[103] *Ibid.*, p. 43.
[104] *Ibid.*, p. 105.
[105] *Supra*, p. 248.
[106] II Kings 18:27 (*RSV*): "But the Rabshakeh said to them, 'Has my master sent me to speak these works to your master and to you, and not to the men sitting on the wall, who are doomed with you to eat their own dung and to drink their own urine?' "

escape the conclusion that there is in Harnack a fundamental abhorrence of the real and dirty stuff to which "historical event" refers in biblical material. Therefore it is the "higher" personal life in which God's revelation is to be found: and this, we maintain, is *Harnack's* "intellectualization" of the Bible.

Fourth, it may be noted that Harnack presupposes a "pure essence" in the *teaching* in his declaration that "the New Testament itself, when compared with what Jesus purposed, said, and was, is already a tradition which overlies and obscures."[107] That what we have in the New Testament is the product of the Church few would deny; but that there is an *identifiable* "essence," purposed, spoken, and lived by Jesus, already submerged and hidden by tradition in the New Testament, can be affirmed only by absent angels, present fools, or the genius caught in the grip of an *a priori*. Finally, it is just this *a priori* which determines that the relation of the Old and the New Testament must be seen as one of radical discontinuity. For Harnack's "essence" is just that relation of the soul and God which emancipates, gives power and direction and the possibility of results, produces value, challenges the authority of every book or creed, and, at the same time, can never surrender the certainty that its object is God as Jesus has shown him to be. This relation is best exemplified in the teaching of Jesus, and shows itself in him and in Christians in value-producing activity. But law means bondage, it cannot give power for life, it imposes authority, it claims attestations which cannot be historically verified. Though the law may have had its justification in its time, and though the historical givens of the early Christian period may have made it necessary to hold onto the Old Testament, there is a *development* operating in the historical process which demands that one must overcome history—by history, so Harnack said. But this latter "history" must be understood as Harnack understood it, in order for the formula to have any meaning. And so understood, it becomes evident that one overcomes history by Harnack's "essential Christianity." The reason the Old Testament must be given up is because it lacks this essence; the *only* reason the New Testament should be kept is because it contains it.

But actually, it is not the entire New Testament that should, according to this logic, and, apparently, according to Harnack's own statements, be conserved: for "the New Testament . . . is . . . a tradition which overlies and obscures."[108] All that should properly

[107] *The Origin of the New Testament . . .*, pp. 43–44.
[108] *Ibid.*

be conserved is the shucked Gospel. This is not to deny the Old Testament its historical value: it "rendered services" to the Church in a crucial time. So did the New Testament and its closed canon, and the rule of faith, and the episcopate. The argument is from utility all the way. The utility of the Old Testament has passed; the utility of dogma has passed; Roman Catholicism—indeed, any "Catholicism"—should pass; and by the same token, that part of the New Testament which is included under "tradition" should pass. Only as the hull to protect the tender essence can it be justified. In short, there is no unity to the Scriptures, no continuity; there is only the one blazing point, preceded by a law that bound, and followed by a tradition that obscured. Whimsy suggests that the discovery of this essence, buried as it was in four millennia of Jewish and Christian dogmatics, is a greater miracle by far than Balaam's loquacious ass or stinking Lazarus' reanimation.

Is Christianity, then, the religion of a book? Harnack's historical answer is in the negative. And his own judgment as to whether it should be the religion of a book is so patently obvious as to require no further explication.

E. HERMENEUTICS

We have seen that Harnack insisted upon historical-critical research, objectively pursued, as the key to understanding the thought of the past. "*Not exegesis alone*, and not dogmatic will lead us to a sound progress, but the results of church historical research . . . will break the power of the traditions now burdening the consciences of men."[109] We have seen, on the other hand, how he emphasized the necessity of making historical judgments; and we have held that these judgments were made on the basis of an axiological norm which had as its purpose the overcoming of nature and the validation of Christianity to the culture. His insistence in the first case was fronted against what he considered to be a jejune orthodoxy; in the second case, the main opposition was materialism. In the first case he was protesting against one form of the Church in the name of the essential teachings of Jesus; in the second, he sought to overcome the baneful effects of a self-professed scientific monism by affirming "science" and "religion" in the same breath.

That Harnack regarded his historical-critical activity and his historical "judging" activity as complementary rather than contradictory

[109] AZH, p. 176.

is certain. It is as though his insistence that life is *something absolutely worthful* provided at the same time a standard of worth won from historical study, and an *a priori* in terms of which the powers, the direction, and the results of a given historical epoch can be evaluated. This standard of worth is not dependent upon religion, though the highest religion, Christianity, declares it; but it is a lesson taught by history itself. History everywhere buttresses the statement of Jesus that "Whoever would save his life must lose it."[110] Not in narrow egotism, but in the freedom of the spirit, communing with other great personalities, will history be overcome and the future served.

Liberare becomes therefore the purpose of Harnack's work. To free the Church from the sterile clutches of orthodoxy; to free his contemporaries from the monism which depersonalized the human being; to free himself from the limits that a particular kind of theology had placed upon him, as well as from presuppositions of a metaphysical sort; to free historical investigation of the early Christian period by a faithful amassing of data in definitive editions; these and many more liberating intentions motivated him, in minor and major areas. His "value-words" and phrases recur hundreds of times: "unprejudiced," "the clear eye," "simple," "enhance our standard," "the summits of our inner life," "an abiding disposition towards the good," and "inner freedom," to suggest only a few. It is fitting, therefore, that Harnack should be regarded as the classic representative of liberalism in theology. There is no word of self-description on which he would have caviled less than the word "freedom." And when Troeltsch remarked that Harnack's *Das Wesen des Christentums* represents a "symbolic concatenation," i.e., that it stands as an almost pure type of liberal thought, he has suggested a valid and fruitful principle for the interpretation of his colleague.[111]

The fact that Harnack was a liberal, even the "representative man" of liberalism, does not *de facto* lend credence to his claim of being free from prepossession. He may tell us, over and over, that "it is not superfluous to declare that the method which is here employed is influenced by no prepossession of any kind."[112] But having seen what we have seen, we will take the gentler advice of Robert Grant and evaluate Harnack's biblical interpretation "on the basis of [his] theological outlook as well as on the basis of the criticism itself."[113]

110 *Ibid.*, p. 552.
111 *Der Historismus . . .*, p. 42.
112 *The Acts of the Apostles*, p. xlii.
113 *The Bible in the Church*, p. 141.

There is the historical-critical research (the criticism itself); and there is the regal activity (the theological outlook). There is the affirmation, "there is no other method for the exegesis of Holy Scripture than the grammatical-historical";[114] and there is, as we shall soon note, *Das Wesen des Christentums.* How do these Siamese twins operate in Harnack's biblical interpretation?

To ask the question in this way may appear to be an unfair juxtaposition; for Harnack was insisting, in the first instance, against those who determined scriptural meanings dogmatically, that these meanings could be determined only via the grammatical-historical approach. In the second instance, he was not dealing primarily with the exegesis of Holy Scripture, but was interpreting it. But it then follows that Harnack has chosen to delimit exegesis to a restricted discipline, as a preparatory function in the broader endeavor to work one's way through to a position, to "construct a whole," to "gain certainty and unity." Exegesis, then, is not identical with interpretation, but is only one part, albeit a necessary part, of this larger task.

What exactly is required in order to carry out this "grammatical-historical" exegesis? Grubbing "scavenger's labor," "close and detailed examination and discussion of vocabularly and style,"[115] "deep and reverent study of the tradition,"[116] a method "influenced by no prepossession of any kind,"[117] the abjuring of "mythological explanations," the requirement "to examine things . . . microscopically,"[118] and the insistence that all questions of fact be "subject to the control of history."[119] As we have noted, *ad nauseam*, one can take almost any volume of Harnack's work—particularly his New Testament studies—and can discover, in each, statements insisting on the inviolability of the historical-critical method.

To detail further an answer to the question as to what Harnack included in his grammatical-historical exegesis would be superfluous after the extended treatment we have given in the previous section on Marcion. However, a glance at his bibliography proves that he kept abreast of the new developments and discoveries in the areas of New Testament and Church history, collecting data and commenting on the data: the 642 published reviews of the works of his contemporaries, the 49 contributions of the *Texte und Untersu-*

[114] AZH, p. 69.
[115] Harnack, *Luke the Physician*, p. viii.
[116] Harnack, *The Sayings of Jesus*, p. vi.
[117] Harnack, *The Acts of the Apostles*, p. xliii.
[118] Harnack, *The Date of the Acts . . .*, p. 144.
[119] Harnack, *Bible Reading in the Early Church*, p. 4.

chungen series, all of a textual nature, and the 38 annual reports on the work of the Commission on the Church Fathers of the Prussian Academy. Two of his more "specialized" productions will indicate that it was not only the "big" questions that engaged his attention: the 1875 article entitled "Über eine in Moskau entdeckte und edirte altbulgarische Version der Schrift Hippolytus *De Antichristo*," and the 1887 article entitled "Über eine in Deutschland bisher unbekannte Falschung des Simonides."[120]

One could play this game indefinitely; but the point is certainly incandescent. It is understandable that Erik Peterson could testify, in the light of the contribution which Harnack made to the understanding of the sources and the tradition of the early Church, that "this same Harnack who declares that a return to Catholicism is not possible for us because of the historical knowledge which we possess, has opened a way for a return to the Catholic tradition as no other person has done."[121]

Harnack's separation of exegesis and interpretation opens the possibility that his norm for interpretation may not be arrived at solely, if at all, from the biblical material which one is considering, but that it may come from some other source. This is a problem which has haunted hermeneutics from the beginning, and never more than at the present time.[122] Harnack was not unaware of this problem, and he solved it for himself in a way which contributed greatly to the formulation of the liberal theology, and brought against him the charge of betraying the Bible. Stöcker contemptuously remarked of the liberals that "the Reformation took its stand on *theses*, modern liberals on *hypotheses*."[123] It should be insisted here that the way in which Harnack solved this problem was carefully thought out. Against those who regard Harnack as naive in his biblical interpretation, it must be objected that he was quite aware of what he was doing.

In summary, we have seen that he insisted that exegesis was based on the foundation of grammatical-philological-historical investigation. The interpretation had a *broader* basis, which was determined by the necessity "to find certainty and unity" in the particular givens

[120] The former article appeared in *Zeitschrift für historische Theologie* (45, pp. 38–61); the latter in *Theologische Literaturzeitung* (12, pp. 147–151).

[121] "Briefwechsel mit Adolf Harnack und ein Epilog," *Theologische Traktate* (Munchen: Kosel, 1951), p. 316.

[122] Cf. Alan Richardson and W. Schweitzer (eds.), *Biblical Authority Today* (Philadelphia: Westminster, 1951), *passim.*

[123] AZH, p. 310.

of late nineteenth- and early twentieth-century culture. Because "one cannot jump out of his skin," and because Harnack's commitment was to a historical method, the result was a characterization of the "essence of Jesus' teaching" which could serve as the standard of worth in the time in which he lived. The old concepts of revelation, authority, and inspiration were no longer viable. Yet the necessity to find certainty and unity always forced one to search for "the tentative absolute." Though Harnack found this in the "essence of Jesus' teaching," we believe that the norm by which this essence was derived was not biblical; rather, it was a compound from his rich heritage, brought into a synthesis by Harnack. The process by which this norm came into being should be described before we turn to the work which, above all, inculcates it.

Ecclesiastical dogma had been increasingly challenged in the eighteenth century by the developing concern for biblically oriented understanding. One facet of this concern, certainly the most striking, was described by Schweitzer in his work on the search for the historical Jesus. By the beginning of the nineteenth century, it was possible to distinguish the question, What do the Scriptures teach? from the question, What is dogmatic truth? The influences which had brought about this situation dated back at least as far as the Deists,[124] and during much of the eighteenth century took the form of a search for the "truths of natural reason." But all rationalistic, anthropocratic attempts to counteract ecclesiastical dogmatic formulations took second place once the "new science" of history came into its own. Even so, the reluctance of the Church to surrender or to qualify its "revealed dogmas" prescribed a curious rear-guard action where every position was surrendered only after it had been defended to the limit.

In the early nineteenth century, the fact that revelation was to be seen *cum sensu prorsus alieno* was made clear in the separation of biblical study into Old Testament study and New Testament study. There followed in Old Testament study the departure from the *Lehrbegriff* method to a method emphasizing the history of Old Testament religion, although *Lehrbegriff* still found its champions. New Testament study centered for a long while in the "quest for the historical Jesus," with Strauss representing a landmark, though Baur was by all odds the outstanding New Testament scholar of the period. Increasingly, the historical point of view was adopted in the inter-

[124] So Hirsch, *Geschichte der neuern . . .*, I, pp. 244 ff.

pretation of the New Testament, as the work of Neander, Beck, and Ritschl attests, but interest was largely confined to the relation of the separate New Testament writings to each other. The last half of the nineteenth century was "the period of bloom"[125] for this biblical interpretation based on historical study, which saw itself as representing the climax of biblical studies. By tracing the historic and genetic development, in which process biblical introduction, historical exegesis, and textual criticism were all presupposed, one could then set forth what biblical theology really was in its essence.

With the rise of *religionsgeschichtlich* investigation in the nineties, the positions held by the liberals were increasingly attacked, as Christianity was set in the broader context of its non-Christian environment. The whole concept of a New Testament theology was called into question, and it was insisted that any attempt at setting forth a New Testament theology represented a uniting of two disparate things; that New Testament theology deals with only a segment of Christian life and thought; and that the treatment of New Testament books apart from their background and environment ignored or minimized their relation to the Jewish and Hellenistic background.[126] Harnack was not liable to some of these charges, but he was liable in the picture of the liberal Jesus which he had drawn. It was this picture which Wrede and Schweitzer attacked, insisting that the strange and in many ways unknown Jew who was hidden behind the Gospel records had nothing in common with the well-adjusted world-affirmer which Harnack portrayed. The historical interest remained dominant, however, during the first two decades of the twentieth century, with increasingly less being said about divine revelation. When the explosion came, as we have noted, it was in violent reaction against the antidogmatic dogmatism of historicist relativism; and the dialectical theology of Barth has fathered many of the forms of "spiritual exegesis" extant.

We have seen that Harnack claimed "to belong to no camp,"[127] and it must be admitted that no set of precise specifications quite fits him. But that he was a liberal, whether one speaks of this as a school or not, is certainly undeniable. Living in a time when historical method was regarded as the key to all secrets, contributing to

[125] Clarence Tucker Craig, "Biblical Theology and the Rise of Historicism," *Journal of Biblical Literature*, LXII (Dec. 1943), p. 284.

[126] *Ibid.*, pp. 287–288.

[127] AZH, p. 87, ". . . his critics were not certain in which 'camp' he belonged —for that anyone might belong to *no* camp would have been unheard of!"

and shaping in major ways the historical investigation of the Church and her documents, he came to express in classical form what is designated as "liberalism." Yet, we would hold, one does not really understand liberalism if one refers to it simply, or mainly, in terms of its content; it is more accurate to regard it as fundamentally a method. As a method, it is not so much concerned to irrigate deserts as to drain swamps. Therefore it always appears to be liable to the charge of "reductionism." But if "man shall not live by method alone," he had best still not live without it, particularly if he claims to be a historian. Harnack claimed not to be able to find "life" in the orthodox theology of his youth, nor in the Barthian formulation which emerged in his old age. In both cases, his fundamental criticism was at the point of method. But he did not thereby deny the validity of the genuine apprehension of meaning which was communicated to those who held these positions, or to those who were Catholic, or even to the radical enthusiasts. He found his own meanings elsewhere, but he would not, even at the insistence of his brother, set forth an alternative to the Apostles' Creed which meant so much to the "silent in the land." He pointedly disclaimed the role of reformer. But against the historical reductionism which fidelity to his method prescribed for him, he counterpoised a doctrine of humanity.[128] Perhaps this fidelity to his method meant that he could never affirm as much in terms of Christian dogmatic content as his critics. But he would not be untrue to this method; and perhaps, as he drained swamps, he destroyed—or at least mutilated—some lilies: but he also killed some quite senile mosquitoes.

But finally, is it the historical criticism or is it the theology which dominates Harnack's biblical interpretation? We are aware that in the preceding pages the answer may not appear to be unequivocal; and we can only repeat our refrain in attempting to explain, if not to justify, whatever seeming disparity is present: that it is unfair to this many-sided man to interpret him in either/or categories—therefore "historical axiology," not simply "history" or "axiology"—but, in the same breath, the value-referent finally dominates. How can one say this, having just affirmed that "fidelity to his method" was his *sine qua non*? Only on this basis: that "fidelity to his method" meant, in operation, a reductionism, a working through to the "essence" or the "inner form"; that the end result of this process is a naked individual standing in splendid undogmatic openness before

128 *Supra*, p. 104.

"God"; that in this stance "the thing itself" shows itself to be authority internally, and "effects a deliverance." *But*—this is our contention—this "thing itself" which flows into the naked individual (because he is *not* naked) is a pragmatic, value-affirming, contemporaneous "Gospel."

XIV

The Reality of Christianity

A. INTRODUCTORY

NO INTERPRETATION of Adolf Harnack can fail to give a central place to *Das Wesen des Christentums*. Harnack's contemporaries regarded this work as the distillate of his position. All subsequent theologians, whatever else they may know about Harnack's life and work, know *Das Wesen des Christentums*. And Harnack himself gave ample evidence that the position he held in 1899–1900, when these lectures were given, represented his hard-won convictions. We will examine this position by noting the structure of the work, summarizing its contents, considering representative criticisms, and finally evaluating this "reality" in the context of Harnack's total theological—or axiological—commitments.

The fact that the book grew out of a series of extemporaneous lectures has significance, since one may assume that the choice of this topic, and not another, already tells us, quite independently of what the book says, how central this category was for Harnack. Further, it is not unfair to assume that the face-to-face lecturer/hearer situation would evoke the most existential statement of which a person was capable.[1]

[1] The critics missed *no* opportunity to find fault. Hermann Schick, for example, criticized Harnack for giving the lectures extemporaneously, pointing out that the importance of the subject and the fact that so many were in attendance should have required more careful preparation. AZH, p. 241.

Beyond its extemporaneous setting, the substance of the book demonstrates with what passion and integrity Harnack held on to that stated purpose of his youth "to confess and defend the independently won position in all sincerity." *Das Wesen des Christentums* is, par excellence, apologetic. The question which burns throughout this work, and throughout this man's life, is at issue: Can one be a Christian today? In order to answer this eternally present question, so Harnack believed, one must identify what Christianity in its reality is. We have referred to this elsewhere as a "nisus to essence" procedure; but by calling it a procedure, we intend to remove nothing of its living character.

It must still be said that though one *cannot* interpret Adolf Harnack adequately by giving attention *only* to *Das Wesen des Christentums* (in which case one would see a "reality" affirmed, without the method and the labor and the cost of that affirmation), one can discover here in its most pristine and symbolic representation the *idea* without which any interpretation will be misleading. In the metaphor of the "watershed," one may say that this work is, indeed, the peak of the range; that one *achieves* this peak after arduous and methodical labor, not by being deposited, *senkrecht von oben*, upon it. "To work *through* the dogmatic to the inner form": for Harnack there is no other way.

And in *this* case, at least, the interpreter who would represent Harnack fairly must follow Harnack's way; for only so will he *see* Harnack's truth. Whether he will accept Harnack's truth is not at issue.

B. THE STRUCTURE AND PRESUPPOSITIONS OF *DAS WESEN DES CHRISTENTUMS*

Broadly, the organization of this small work is similar to the organization of the *Dogmengeschichte*.[2] Following an introductory section, Harnack considers "The Gospel" and "The Gospel in History." The part of the book that deals with "The Gospel" is in turn divided into two parts: "The Main Features of Jesus' Message," where the well-known three features are stated and developed, and "The Gospel in Relation to Certain Problems," where Harnack deals with aceticism, the social question, and the questions of public order, civilization, Christology, and creed. The second major division of the book considers the Christian religion in the Apostolic Age, in its develop-

[2] As Loisy notes, *The Gospel and the Church*, p. 4. Rolffs also made the point, see note 147, this chapter.

ment into Catholicism, and in its Greek Catholic, Roman Catholic, and Protestant forms.

Simply to list these rubrics is to make clear that in these lectures Harnack is providing a synopsis of a life's work. When *Das Wesen* is read in this way, one is constantly impressed with Harnack's power of synthesis. Vignettes of men and positions on which he had already written individual volumes stand out in sententious clarity. As a single example, consider two sentences characterizing the results (*Leistungen*) of the Church's labor at the beginning of the third century:

> Had the Church at the beginning of the third century been asked by way of reproach, "How could you so far forget your beginnings and to what have you come?" it might have answered: "Yes, I have come to this; I have been obliged to discard much and to take up much; I have had to fight—my body is full of scars, and my clothes are covered with dust; but I have won my battles and built my house; I have beaten back polytheism; I have disabled and almost annihilated that monstrous abortion, political religion; I have resisted the enticements of a subtle religious philosophy, and victoriously encountered it with God the almighty Creator of all things; lastly, I have reared a great building, a fortress with towers and bulwarks, where I guard my treasure and protect the weak." This is the answer which the Church might have given, and truthfully given.[3]

A random and incomplete analysis of the contents of the *Reden und Aufsätze* series further illustrates the point that *Das Wesen* is the concatenation of "theology as vocation."[4]

Since this is true, it means that many of the themes dealt with in *Das Wesen* have been covered elsewhere, and need not be reconsidered in detail here. For example, there is the same insistence on the validity of the historical approach;[5] the expected repudiation of "speculation,"[6] the emphasis on sources;[7] the distrust of "apologetics"

[3] *WC*, p. 168.

[4] In the *Reden und Aufsätze* series alone, one can trace "the Gospel in history" through the individual speeches and articles: in Vol. I, Augustine, Monasticism, Luther, Melanchthon, and Neander; in Vol. II, the Reformation, Roman Catholicism, Ritschl, and contemporary Protestantism; in Vol. III, the rise of the Papacy, contemporary Roman Catholicism and Protestantism; in Vol. IV, Jesus, the new Testament, and the early Church Fathers; in Vol. V, Augustine, the Greek Church Fathers, and Protestant culture; in Vol. VI, Jesus, Roman Catholicism, and Protestantism; and Vol. VII, Marcion and the Reformation. Indexes to the entire seven volumes are given in *Aus der Werkstatt des Vollendeten*, pp. 295–302.

[5] *WC*, pp. 5–6.

[6] *Ibid.*, pp. 7–8.

[7] *Ibid.*, pp. 17 ff.

as usually practiced;[8] the emphasis on the centrality of Jesus;[9] the passion to discover the "reality" or the inner form;[10] the insistence that the same mind is at work in history and in us;[11] and the complex process by which Harnack deals with the interrelationships of all of these entities.[12] For the sake of unity, it may be worthwhile to summarize these themes, as *Das Wesen* reveals them, before turning to the main features of Jesus' teaching.

Harnack remarks at the beginning that it is a strange but true fact that everyone from the time of the Gnostics to Tolstoy has been anxious to possess Jesus. The result of this clamor for possession has been confusion. Harnack essays to relieve this confusion by asking a simple question: What is Christianity? To arrive at an answer to this question, he suggests that the historical method must be employed:

> It is solely in its historical sense that we shall try to answer this question here; that is to say, we shall employ the methods of historical science and the exerience of life which is earned by witnessing history. We thus exclude the view of the question taken by the apologist and the religious philosopher.[13]

We shall return in a moment to the "apologetic" question; regarding his comment about the "religious philosopher," Harnack goes on to say that had the lectures been delivered in 1840, one would have sought by speculative reasoning to arrive at some general conception of religion and to define Christianity as a species of the genus. But men have come to see that "life cannot be covered by general conceptions," and though it is going too far to say that religion is a "vacuum which every one fills up in a different fashion" (*rather*, Harnack holds, Augustine is right in his famous "Thou hast made us for Thyself . . ." statement), proving this "is not the task that we shall undertake in what follows. We shall keep to the purely historical theme."[14]

Regarding the emphasis on sources, one half-sentence will suffice: ". . . I feel it is my duty to tell you briefly how matters stand respecting the sources of our knowledge."[15]

[8] *Ibid.*, pp. 6 f.
[9] *Ibid.*, pp. 8–9.
[10] *Ibid.*, pp. 11–12.
[11] *Ibid.*, pp. 10–11.
[12] *Ibid.*, Chap. I and II, pp. 1–32.
[13] *Ibid.*, pp. 5–6.
[14] *Ibid.*, p. 8.
[15] *Ibid.*, p. 17.

Harnack's statement that he will exclude the apologetic view is in direct contradiction to our earlier estimate that *Das Wesen des Christentums* is, par excellence, *apologetic*. To understand the basis of the contradiction, it is necessary to examine his statement about "apologetics" to see what he means. For Harnack, apologetics is essential, and it is "a great and worthy undertaking. *But it is one which must not be confounded with the purely historical question as to the nature of that religion. . . .*"[16] Harnack goes on to say that low standards prevail in this discipline, that the whole subject is in a deplorable state, that both the means of defense and the positions to be defended are unclear, that the procedures are undignified and obtrusive, that every public relations gimmick is used, and that it has been employed as an ecclesiastical utilitarianism. In short, it has been deprived "of its earnest character," reducing the "simple and sublime" Christian religion to a "job-lot at a sale," "a universal remedy for all social ills."[17]

Das Wesen—that is, the *reality* of Christianity—is something so precious to Harnack that such tactics nauseate him. Apologetics as it was being practiced in his time, he must reject; but apologetics as it should be, he was practicing. *He* saw the latter type as being grounded in historical research; indeed, *he held* the historical research to be a discrete discipline. The apparent contradiction is resolved, however, to the degree that one accepts the view that Harnack's historical research also had theological axes to grind. He himself admits this in his statement "we shall employ the methods of historical science *and the experience of life (Lebenserfahrung) which is earned by witnessing history*."[18]

The emphasis on the centrality of Jesus is, perforce, threaded throughout the entire work. In the introduction, the answer as to where we must look for our materials in describing Christianity's reality is "*Jesus Christ and his Gospel*."[19] But since "every great and powerful personality reveals a part of what it is only when seen in those whom it influences," we must look at "the effects which he produced in those whose leader and master he became."[20] The argument here is more complex than this, but the centrality of Jesus is indisputable.

The nisus to essence procedure is explicitly affirmed, over and over.

[16] *Ibid.*, p. 6. Italics mine.
[17] *Ibid.*, pp. 6–7.
[18] *Ibid.*, p. 6. Italics mine.
[19] *Ibid.*, p. 8. Italics mine.
[20] *Ibid.*, p. 9.

". . . to grasp what is *essential* in the phenomena, and to distinguish kernel and husk";[21] "it follows that the historian, whose business and highest duty it is to determine what is of permanent value, is of necessity required not to cleave to words but *to find out what is essential*";[22] ". . . by the very fact that our survey embraces the whole course as well as the inception, we enhance our standard of what is essential and of real value."[23]

This is possible because "the same mind is at work in history and in us." In spite of the fact that the situation of Jesus (and his disciples) in their own time, with all "their feelings, their thoughts, their judgments and their efforts . . . bounded by the horizon and the framework in which their own nation was set and by its condition at the time,"[24] determined that theirs was a "limited and circumscribed mental and spiritual disposition" and "historical environment,"[25] yet: "We shall see that the Gospel in the Gospel is something so simple, something that speaks to us with so much power, that it cannot easily be mistaken. . . . No one who possesses a fresh eye for what is alive, and true feeling for what is really great, can fail to see it and distinguish it from its contemporary integument."[26]

Finally, the entire first two lectures indicate how seriously Harnack took these kinds of questions, and to what great pains he went to make clear the relationships between these methodological and substantive difficulties. This is not the place to estimate his success; but as we shall see in the following development, these are estimable difficulties indeed, to whose negotiation only the great give themselves.

C. THE CONTENT OF *DAS WESEN DES CHRISTENTUMS*

1. The Main Features of Jesus' Teaching

They are three, yet one; for "*each is of such a nature as to contain the whole; . . . the kingdom of God and its coming, . . . God the Father and the infinite value of the human soul, . . . the higher righteousness and the commandment of love.*"[27]

Harnack admits the ambiguity which surrounds the first term, as

[21] *Ibid.*, p. 10. Italics Harnack's.
[22] *Ibid.*, p. 11. Italics Harnack's.
[23] *Ibid.*, p. 12.
[24] *Ibid.*, p. 10.
[25] *Ibid.*, p. 11.
[26] *Ibid.*, p. 12.
[27] *Ibid.*, p. 44. Italics Harnack's.

interpreted sometimes in an eschatological sense, sometimes in an immanent sense; and he conceded that there is no doubt that Jesus shared the eschatological world-view of his contemporaries. However, this did not exhaust the meaning he placed in the term; in some sense, the kingdom of God is already present, and this view was original with Jesus. That there is a fundamental paradox here must be admitted; and the way in which Harnack resolves this paradox is both characteristic and masterful. He suggests that the radical antithesis which we see today between these views did not exist in Jesus' culture. Then he employs his distinction of husk and kernel, and works his way through the difficulties:

Truly the historian's task of distinguishing between what is traditional and what is peculiar, between kernel and husk, in Jesus' message of the kingdom of God, is a difficult and responsible one. How far may we go? We surely cannot want to rob this message of its innate quality and color; we cannot want to change it into a pale scheme of ethics. On the other hand, we cannot want to lost sight of its peculiar character and strength, as we should do were we to side with those who resolve it into the general ideas prevailing at the time. The very way in which Jesus distinguished between the traditional elements—he left out none in which there was a spark of moral force, and he accepted none which encouraged the selfish expectations of his nation—this very discrimination teaches us that it was from a deeper knowledge that he spoke and taught. But we possess testimonies of a much more striking kind. If anyone wants to know what the kingdom of God and the coming of it meant in Jesus' message, he must read and study his parables. He will then see what it is that is meant. The kingdom of God comes by coming to the individual, by entering into his soul and laying hold of it. True, the kingdom of God is the rule of God; but it is the rule of the holy God in the hearts of individuals; *it is God himself in his power.* From this point of view everything that was dramatic in the external and historical sense has vanished; and gone, too, are all the external hopes for the future. Take whatever parable you will, the parable of the sower, of the pearl of great price, of the treasure buried in the field—the word of God, God himself, is the kingdom. It is not a question of angels and devils, thrones and principalities, but of God and the soul, the soul and its God.[28]

The "quality and color" of Jesus' message inhered in its dualistic, eschatological form; the striking metaphors and graphic images Jesus retained. The deeper knowledge which he possessed was not a kind of generalized ethical arcanum; it was a living relational thing, and must therefore, in his teaching, be set in sharp and vivid language.

[28] *Ibid.*, pp. 48–49. Italics Harnack's.

Throughout this entire description on Harnack's part there runs the sense of the kingdom of God as a dynamic, active, gerundial thing, not a static and unchanging structure.

Secondly, Harnack treats the theme which occupies so large a place in his thought: God the Father and (the infinite value of) the human soul. It is significant that in this, as in the preceding "feature" of Jesus' message, these two elements—God the Father and the ennobled soul—are identified with religion itself. Here he particularly stresses the fact that the Gospel contains no particularistic elements. To make his case, he cites four sections from the New Testament: the Lord's Prayer, "Rejoicc not that the spirits are subject unto you, but rather rejoice because your names are written in heaven," "Are not two sparrows sold for a farthing? and one of them shall not fall to the ground without your Father. But the very hairs of your head are all numbered," "What shall it profit a man if he shall gain the whole world and lose his own soul?"[29] The Lord's Prayer is significant because, unlike prayers of a lower order, it does not go into particulars, but leads us to the height where the soul is *alone with its God*. The "Rejoice . . ." saying is interpreted to mean that the all-important element in religion is the consciousness of being *safe in God*. This is further buttressed by the third saying, which declares that "the *assurance that God rules* is to go as far as our fears go, nay, as far as life itself—life down even to its smallest manifestations in the order of nature."[30] Finally, the last saying puts a man's value as high as it can be put, for the whole world is to be regarded as not worth one human soul. This carries with it a stern warning of duty, for it represents the transvaluation of value; one is to evaluate everything according to the degree of its contribution to the increase of value for mankind.

The final feature of Jesus' message, the higher righteousness and the commandment of love, represents the Gospel as ethical, but this in no way depreciates its value. Jesus' view of the ethical can be developed by citing four points: First, "Jesus severed the connection existing in his day between ethics and external forms of religious worship and technical observance."[31] Harnack here cites "Corban" as his evidence.[32] Secondly, "in all questions of morality, he goes

[29] *Ibid.*, pp. 55–56.
[30] *Ibid.*, p. 58. Italics mine.
[31] *Ibid.*, p. 62.
[32] Mark 7:9–13 (*RSV*): "And he said to them, 'You have a fine way of rejecting the commandment of God, in order to keep your tradition! For Moses

straight to the root, that is, to the disposition and the intention."[33] The evidence cited here is the "Ye have heard . . . but I say unto you" passages of the Sermon on the Mount. Thirdly, "what he freed from its connection with self-seeking and ritual elements, and recognized as the moral principle, he reduces to *one* root and to *one* motive—love."[34] Harnack here emphasizes that this "is always the love which *serves*,"[35] and cites the parable of the Good Samaritan as his evidence. And finally, "Jesus made love and humility one."[36] The parable of the Pharisee and the publican is the evidence for this union. The summary of this section of his lectures declares overtly what Harnack believes Jesus meant by religion:

In Jesus' view, this humility, which is the love of God of which we are capable . . . is an abiding disposition towards the good.

It was in this sense that Jesus combined religion and morality, and in this sense religion may be called the soul of morality, and morality the body of religion. We can thus understand how it was that Jesus could place the love of God and the love of one's neighbor side by side; the love of one's neighbor is the only practical proof on earth of that love of God which finds its life in humility.

In thus expressing his message of the higher righteousness and the new commandment of love in these four leading thoughts, Jesus defined the sphere of the ethical in a way in which no one before him had ever defined it. But if ever we are threatened with doubts as to what he meant, we must steep ourselves again and again in the Beatitudes of the Sermon on the Mount. They contain his ethics and his religion, united at the root, and freed from all external and particularistic elements.[37]

This is not the place for a full evaluation of the three features, but one point may be made, visible in Harnack's treatment of each. This is the fact that there is a striking unity in all of Harnack's identifications and explications. Of course, this is just to state the problem: was this unity really there, identified by a presuppositionless method—or

---

said, "Honor your father and your mother"; . . . but you say, "If a man tells his father or his mother, What you would have gained from me is Corban" (that is, given to God)—then you no longer permit him to do anything for his father or mother, thus making void the word of God through your tradition which you hand on. And many such things you do.' "

33 *WC*, p. 62.

34 *Ibid.*, p. 63.

35 *Ibid.*

36 *Ibid.*

37 *Ibid.*, pp. 63–64.

did *he* put it there? In the first instance, is the equivalence which he declares to exist between God and the kingdom, whereby everything historical, external, or particularistic is relegated to "husk," and all that remains is "God . . . coming to the individual"—is this equivalence truly the center of Jesus' message? When Harnack admits that it is never expressed as such, being inexpressible, and must therefore be discovered in that "deeper knowledge which he spoke and taught," has he not made possible the reconstruction of the "kernel" according to the norm to which he gave fealty? In the description of the second feature, has he not transvalued the theocentric ethic of the Bible (this is an arguable point, certainly) by placing together God and the Father *and* the infinite value of the human soul? Particularly when his nisus to essence method requires that ultimately this shall become one thing, and his abnegation of speculation into "mystery" leaves, perhaps, only the soul? And in the case of the third feature, where the higher righteousness is identified as *one* thing only, love, has his norm not been operating determinatively to *create* problems when the time comes to consider other qualities? The answers are not, certainly, self-evident, for the "reality of Christianity" is not, it may be, as self-evident as Harnack believed. Everything depends upon the validity of his identification of that "reality."

2. *The Gospel in relation to . . .*

In the second part of the first section of *Das Wesen*, Harnack deals with six specific problems and their relation to the Gospel. These are:

> (1) The Gospel and the world, or the question of asceticism; (2) the Gospel and the poor, or the social question; (3) the Gospel and the law, or the question of public order; (4) the Gospel and work, or the question of civilization; (5) the Gospel and the Son of God, or the Christological question; (6) the Gospel and doctrine, or the question of creed.[38]

Regarding the question of asceticism, Harnack affirms that it "has no place in the Gospel at all; what it asks is that we should struggle against mammon, against care, against selfishness; what it demands and disengages is *love*; the love that serves and is self-sacrificing."[39] To demonstrate his conclusion against a prevalent opinion that the Gospel is world-denying, Harnack cites the charge made against Jesus that he was a wine-bibber, the fact that the disciples did not understand Jesus to be an ascetic, and "Jesus' leading thoughts":

[38] *Ibid.*, pp. 67–68.
[39] *Ibid.*, p. 76. Italics Harnack's.

The man who associates any ascetic practice with the words "Take no thought," "Be merciful, even as your Father in heaven is merciful," and so on . . . does not understand the sublime character of these sayings, and has either lost or has never attained the feeling that there is a union with God in which all such questions as shunning the world and asceticism are left far behind.[40]

On the relation of the Gospel to the poor, Harnack bases his case on the second commandment, "Love your neighbor as yourself." By these words "Jesus turned a light upon all the concrete relations of life, upon the world of hunger, poverty and misery;" and he spoke these words not as *a* religious maxim but as "*the* religious maxim."[41] Harnack then demonstrates, in a moving passage, his own commitments on the "social gospel." There may have been astonishment in the lecture hall at Berlin at such forthright statements as "People ought not to speak of loving their neighbors if they can allow men beside them to starve and die in misery";[42] or "As has been truly said, its [the Gospel's] object is to transform the socialism which rests on the basis of conflicting interests into the socialism which rests on the consciousness of a spiritual unity";[43] and "The fallacious principle of the free play of forces, of the 'live and let live' principle—a better name for it would be 'live and let die'—is entirely opposed to the Gospel."[44]

The relation of the Gospel to the law is discussed under two aspects: as related to constituted authority, and to legal ordinances generally. On the first matter, Jesus was no revolutionary, and "he laid down no political program."[45] The other question is more complicated, and Harnack cites Sohm's work and that of Tolstoy to make one side of the point: "that it is in contradiction with the character of the Gospel and the community founded thereon that the Church has developed any legal ordinances at all."[46] Alternatively, there are those who "contend that the Gospel takes law and legal relations under its protection."[47] Harnack finds the latter view "a mockery of the Gospel,"[48] as though all things presenting themselves as law at a certain moment

[40] *Ibid.*, pp. 72–73.
[41] *Ibid.*, p. 85. Italics Harnack's.
[42] *Ibid.*, p. 86.
[43] *Ibid.*, p. 87.
[44] *Ibid.*
[45] *Ibid.*, p. 89.
[46] *Ibid.*, p. 93.
[47] *Ibid.*
[48] *Ibid.*

were to be sanctified; but he does not thereby agree with Sohm or Tolstoy. In fact, Harnack's argument here has elements of curiosity in it, for he argues on the one hand that just as God is profligate in sending his rain and sun on just and unjust alike, the Christian is to show love to the enemy and disarm by gentleness; while on the other hand he seems to present the Gospel as irrelevant to questions of public order: "Then let us fight, let us struggle, let us get justice for the oppressed, let us order the circumstances of the world as we with a clear conscience can, and as we may think best for our neighbor; but do not let us expect the Gospel to afford us any direct help . . ."[49] For "the Gospel is above all questions of mundane development; it is concerned not with material things but with the souls of men."[50] We may say that Harnack's "simplicity" here is complex.

The question of the relation of the Gospel to civilization is prefaced by a reference to David Friedrich Strauss's estimate that there is a defect in the Gospel because it is not concerned with art, science, and progress.[51] Harnack's answer provides some fascination. In the first place, if the Gospel had not possessed this "defect," it would have become "entangled" with civilization—probably, as in Roman Catholicism, with a particular period of civilization.[52] Second, work and the progress of civilization is not the highest ideal, and "there is a great deal of hypocritical twaddle"[53] talked about it. The highest ideal is to make oneself "a native of the kingdom of God, the kingdom of the Eternal, the kingdom of Love."[54] For, finally, though Jesus saw "a kingdom of justice, of love, and of peace,"[55] he knew that our labor must not be for the progress of civilization, but "placed at the service of God and neighbor."[56]

On the Christological question, which is a question of a different order, we need say only that here Harnack summarizes the position we have already noted, and to which we will return in considering the charge of one of his critics.[57] It is here that one of the most "inciting" of Harnack's judgments is given: that "*The Gospel, as Jesus proclaimed it, has to do with the Father only and not with the Son.*"[58]

[49] *Ibid.*, pp. 100–101.
[50] *Ibid.*, p. 101.
[51] *Ibid.*, p. 102.
[52] *Ibid.*, p. 103.
[53] *Ibid.*, p. 104.
[54] *Ibid.*, p. 105.
[55] *Ibid.*, p. 106.
[56] *Ibid.*, p. 107.
[57] We refer to Hermann Cremer. See *infra*, pp. 290–292.
[58] *WC*, p. 125.

The last question dealt with in this section, the relation of the Gospel and doctrine, receives short shrift indeed. Although "on the essential points everything that it is necessary to say has already been said,"[59] there is a more substantive reason for brevity. The Gospel is *not* a theoretical system of doctrine; to confess a creed means to do the will of God in the certainty that he is the Father, to do as Jesus did, evidencing in feeling and action that one's confession is genuine.

In concluding this section of the book, Harnack adverts to the objection that the Gospel *Weltanschauung* has been overcome, and since the Gospel was "indissolubly" bound up with this *Weltanschauung*, it must, regrettably, be given up. Harnack denies the indissolubility of the bond, declaring that the Gospel is timeless, for it directs itself to "man who is always the same."[60] But further:

> the Gospel is based—and this is the all-important element in the view which it takes of the world and history—upon the antithesis between Spirit and flesh, God and the world, good and evil. Now, in spite of ardent efforts, thinkers have not yet succeeded in elaborating on a monistic basis any theory of ethics that is satisfactory and answers to the deepest needs of man. Nor will they succeed.[61]

This would appear to be an absolutely debilitating view. The Gospel is based on the antithesis of Spirit and flesh. The life of the Spirit is what we must seek. But no theory which answers our needs has been, or can be, elaborated on the basis of the withdrawal which seems to be demanded by this dualism. Therefore, we are trapped.

Harnack does not deny this dualism; he does deny the necessity of withdrawal. On what basis? This: "That there is a unity underlying this opposition is a conviction which can be gained *by experience*; the one realm can be subordinated to the other; but it is only by a struggle that this unity can be attained, and when it is attained it takes the form of a problem that is infinite and only approximately soluble."[62] On the basis of this analysis Harnack declares that the tyranny of matter can be broken only by self-conquest. For we must pay attention to that which we can know and deal with, living by a faith which is not open to demonstration:

> We have to do with a dualism which arose we know not how; but as moral beings we are convinced that, as it has been given us in order that we

[59] *Ibid.*, p. 127.
[60] *Ibid.*, p. 129.
[61] *Ibid.*, p. 130.
[62] *Ibid.*

may overcome it in ourselves and bring it to a unity, so also it goes back to an original unity, and will at last find its reconciliation in the great far-off event, the realised dominion of the Good.[63]

Harnack admits the limits of finitude, which means that all such efforts can be only patchwork, "for we are unable to bring our knowledge in space and time, together with the contents of our inner life, into the unity of a philosophic theory of the world. It is only in the peace of God which passeth all understanding that this unity dawns upon us."[64]

We shall return to this important formulation presently, after we have completed the summary and considered several of the challenges to Harnack's interpretation. Before we leave this, however, two points, also to be developed later, should be mentioned. First, this is the most pointed explicit confession of that axiological *noli me tangere* which characterizes Harnack's work. Second, we believe that this confession is based on assumptions which are more "Greek" than biblical. We are not primarily concerned here with the "dualism" which is affirmed to be basic, nor with Harnack's envisioning of the "realised dominion of the Good," though one might argue that the use of these particular categories has significance. We are primarily concerned with the fact that Harnack's statement of the problem is sated with anthropocentrism. He sees men—all men, including Jesus—as involved in a battle with a hostile and tyrannous nature, possessing only their own "personal higher life and ethical striving" as guide and power. Man experiences, he aspires, he "opens himself," he overcomes, he attains unity. And man does all of this vis-à-vis the world. This is, we maintain, a magnificent ethic, one that can stand without shame in the courts of the Stoics. But from this standpoint the biblical declaration that "the Word became flesh and dwelt among us, full of grace and truth; we have beheld his glory" and "he has made . . . known [the Father]"[65] cannot be made. For man's vis-à-vis according to the biblical view is not primarily a hostile and tyrannous nature, but a sovereign God. And man's duty, seen from this point of view, is not to overcome the world, but to be faithful.

3. *The Gospel in History*

In the second major division of *Das Wesen*, the historical course of this Gospel is traced by Harnack through its main transitions and

[63] *Ibid.*, p. 131.
[64] *Ibid.*
[65] John 1:14, 18.

in its main manifestations from the time of Jesus to the present. He begins with "The Christian Religion in the Apostolic Age," and identifies the three characteristic features of the new community: it recognized Jesus as the living Lord; religion was regarded as an actual experience, a living union with God; and it emphasized the leading of a holy life in the expectation of the Lord's return. Harnack concentrates on the *results* of each of these beliefs as they were implemented in the community. Thus, the idea of Jesus' death as a sacrifice "put an end to all blood-sacrifices."[66] Again, "Whatever may have happened at the grave . . . '*this grave was the birthplace of the indestructible belief that death is vanquished, that there is a life eternal.*' "[67] On union with God, the book of Acts makes clear that the joining of "a full obedient subjection to the Lord with freedom in the Spirit is the most important feature"[68] of Christianity. And the leading of a holy life is everywhere regarded, in the New Testament, as required. "Where," Harnack asks, "have we another example in history of a religion coming in with such a robust supernatural consciousness, and at the same time laying the moral foundations of the earthly life of the community so firmly?"[69] The expectation of the Lord's return Harnack regards as providing a powerful motive, or "lever," for the leading of a holy life, but in itself it is an adjunct. Harnack remains true to his nisus to essence procedure in suggesting: "What we are thus taught is that the most inward of all possessions, religion, does not struggle up into life free and isolated, but is clothed in bark, so to speak, and cannot grow without this."[70] The conviction of Jesus' appearances after death, he believes, "may also be regarded in the same light."[71]

In his discussion of Paul, "who delivered the Christian religion from Judaism"[72] by "conceiving the Gospel as the message of redemption already effected and of salvation now present,"[73] by regarding it "as a new force abolishing the religion of the law,"[74] by perceiving "that religion in its new phase pertains to the individual,"[75] by placing the

[66] *WC*, p. 136.
[67] *Ibid.*, p. 140. Italics Harnack's.
[68] *Ibid.*, p. 143.
[69] *Ibid.*, p. 148.
[70] *Ibid.*, p. 149.
[71] *Ibid.*
[72] *Ibid.*, p. 152.
[73] *Ibid.*
[74] *Ibid.*, p. 153.
[75] *Ibid.*

Gospel "in the great category of spirit *versus* flesh, inner *versus* outer existence,"[76] Harnack agrees with Wellhausen that he transformed "the Gospel of the kingdom into the Gospel of Jesus Christ."[77] It is he who thus lays the foundation for the great Church which is to emerge. However great he must be regarded, it is through him that "*the formation of a correct theory of and about Christ threatens to assume the position of chief importance, and to pervert the majesty and simplicity of the Gospel.*"[78]

In the second transition period, "The Christian Religion in its Development into Catholicism," new forms were developed and these forms "meant limitation and encumbrance."[79] Harnack turns aside from his account long enough to drive home the essential point for the historian: that "the Gospel did not come into the world as a statutory religion, and therefore none of the forms in which it assumed intellectual and social expression . . . can be regarded as possessing a classical and permanent character. The historian must always keep this guiding idea before him when he undertakes to trace the course of the Christian religion . . ."[80] The significance of this period in the history of Christianity has already been detailed in our discussion of the *Dogmengeschichte*. We shall not repeat it here, but we simply note Harnack's judgment that it is in this second period that "the greatest transformation which the new religion ever experienced" took place.[81] True, in this Old Catholicism, the power of the Gospel retained some of its power: "the hope of an eternal life, the full confidence in Christ, a readiness to make sacrifices, and a purity of morals";[82] but a husk and a covering had developed. To penetrate through this to "the thing itself" had become harder; in short, "it had . . . lost much of its original life."[83]

As the Christian religion manifests itself in Greek Catholicism, its two achievements, the overcoming of polytheism and the fusion of religion and nation, were attained at a great cost. The hypostatizing of tradition, the highly refined intellectualization of Christianity, and the emphasis on ritualism turned "the Christian religion from a worship of God in spirit and in truth into a worship of God in signs,

[76] *Ibid.*
[77] *Ibid.*
[78] *Ibid.*, p. 158.
[79] *Ibid.*, p. 164.
[80] *Ibid.*, pp. 164–165.
[81] *Ibid.*, p. 165.
[82] *Ibid.*, p. 187.
[83] *Ibid.*

formulas, and idols."[84] Harnack reserves his strongest scorn for this denigration of "the thing itself": "*It was to destroy this sort of religion that Jesus Christ suffered himself to be nailed to the cross,* and now we find it re-established under his name and authority."[85]

Roman Catholicism's achievements are two: in its role as leader and educator, and in its insistence on independence from state domination. Its character has been shaped by three elements: Catholicism (which it shares with the Greek church), the Latin spirit, and Augustinianism. The Augustinianism has kept alive an "*inward and vivid religious fervor,*"[86] but by its claim to a divine dignity, visibly expressed in an institution, the Roman Church has secularized the Gospel.

The Gospel says, "Christ's kingdom is not of this world," but the Church has set up an earthly kingdom; Christ demands that his ministers shall not rule but serve, but here the priests govern the world; Christ leads his disciples away from political and ceremonious religion and places every man face to face with God—God and the soul, the soul and its God—but here, on the contrary, man is bound to an earthly institution with chains that cannot be broken, and he must obey; it is only when he obeys that he approaches God.[87]

As against this representation which obscures the Gospel, the Protestant Reformation stands for "a spiritual religion,"[88] a movement in which "religion was brought back again to itself, insofar as the Gospel and the corresponding religious experience were put into the foreground and freed of all alien accretions."[89] Religion here—Harnack unabashedly proclaims it—"was *reduced* to its essential factors, to the Word of God and to faith."[90] This Word of God did not mean, for Luther, "Church doctrine, it did not even mean the Bible; it meant the message of the free grace of God in Christ which makes guilty and despairing men happy and blessed; and the 'experience' was just the certainty of this grace."[91] In this understanding, Luther recovered "the thing itself." And what this thing is in its reality is "*something so simple, so divine, and therefore so truly human, as to*

[84] *Ibid.*, p. 204.
[85] *Ibid.*, p. 205. Italics Harnack's.
[86] *Ibid.*, p. 223.
[87] *Ibid.*, p. 226.
[88] *Ibid.*, p. 230.
[89] *Ibid.*, p. 231.
[90] *Ibid.*, p. 232. Italics Harnack's.
[91] *Ibid.*

be most certain of being understood when it is left entirely free, and also as to produce essentially the same experiences and convictions in individual souls."[92]

D. THE CRITICS

Several rubrics occur over and over in the critiques of *Das Wesen*. There are four which are particularly evident: *Kulturprotestantismus*, Harnack's essence of Christianity, his proclaimed method, and his view of Jesus and the Christological problem. It would be an impossibility to call up *all* of the critics. As his daughter records, "There was no pastor's conference or synod, and scarcely a periodical or daily, which did not take sides."[93] The criticisms, as one might expect, ran the gamut from responsible analysis to personal calumniation. One tract opposing his representation bore the title, "Judas, do you betray the Son of Man with a kiss?"[94] And a conference in Mecklenburg entertained a formal proposal to cite Harnack as falling under the curse of Galatians 1:7–9.[95]

We shall pay attention to five of the critics, three contemporary with Harnack, the other two of a later generation. The five are the famous Roman Catholic modernist, Loisy; an American who stood in the Reformed tradition, Richard Niebuhr; a prominent leader of the United Free Church of Scotland, James Orr; a German Lutheran who opposed Harnack's position, Hermann Cremer; and a former student of Harnack who supported his position, Ernst Rolffs.

In 1902, Alfred Loisy published his *L'evangile et L'église* as an answer to Harnack's *Das Wesen des Christentums*. This is by far the most thorough and thoughtful analysis of *Das Wesen* extant. This book set in process a development that was to end with Loisy's excommunication in 1908, in spite of the fact that he believed he was defending the faith of the Roman Church against Protestant rationalism.

He notes initially that Harnack has declared as his aim "just to catch the point of view of history,"[96] and agrees to discuss his work on the basis of the data of history. But at the very beginning, this raises a difficult problem; for Harnack had claimed that on such a

[92] *Ibid.*, pp. 236–237. Italics Harnack's.
[93] AZH, p. 245.
[94] *Ibid.*
[95] *Ibid.*, pp. 245–246.
[96] Loisy, *The Gospel and the Church*, p. 2.

basis one could extract a single principle from the Gospel and use it as the touchstone for all the subsequent development of Christianity. Everything in Harnack's book, Loisy—rightly—declares, is based on this fundamental "essence" which is the Gospel. Further, because this is true, the value of every judgment contained in this book, as in the *Dogmengeschichte*, which is written from the same point of view, depends upon the validity of this principle. Loisy expresses anxiety with such a procedure:

> Is this really the definition of a historical reality, or merely a systematic method of consideration? Can a religion that has filled such a place in history, and renewed, so to speak, the conscience of humanity, take its origin and derive its whole value from a single thought? Can this great force be made up of one element?[97]

Rather, must not one ask whether such a fact can fail to be complex? Indeed, "is the definition of Christianity, put forth by Herr Harnack, that of a historian or merely that of a theologian who takes from history as much as suits his theology? . . . . Is the theory actually deduced from history? Is not history rather interpreted by the light of the theory?"[98]

Loisy believes that Harnack *has* oversimplified the problem and interpreted Christianity in the light of his own theology. And he has done this because, basically, he has "wished to reconcile Christian faith with the claims of science and the scientific spirit of our time."[99] This reconciliation is accomplished by the reduction of Christianity to a filial sentiment which suits our needs; but to deal with a historical question in this way is inexcusable. For it means that Christianity is reconciled with science by giving up everything in Christianity which might embarrass the reconciliaton. The only valid procedure, if one is to try to discover historically what the essence of the Gospel is, would be to rule out at the beginning the question of utility for today, and to "seek the dominant preoccupation of the early Christians, and all that their religion lived by."[100] This search should be conducted by "a critical discussion of the gospel texts, the most sure and clearly expressed texts, and not those whose authenticity or whose meaning may be doubtful."[101]

At this point, Loisy holds, Harnack has been something less than

[97] *Ibid.*, p. 4.
[98] *Ibid.*
[99] *Ibid.*, p. 6.
[100] *Ibid.*, p. 8.
[101] *Ibid.*, p. 11.

true to a sound method: "His definition of the essence of Christianity is not based on the totality of authentic texts, but rests, when analyzed, on a very small number of texts, practically indeed on two passages:—'No man knoweth the Son, but the Father: neither knoweth any man the Father, save the Son.' and 'The kingdom of God is within you.' "[102] Loisy twists the critical dagger by declaring that both of these passages "might well have been influenced, if not produced, by the theology of the early times. This critical prepossession might thus have exposed the author to the misfortune, supreme for a Protestant theologian, of having founded the essence of Christianity upon data supplied by the Christian tradition."[103]

The point is certainly well taken; and Loisy goes on to develop it in a way that must have been avidly read by Cardinal Richard's committee. For though he finds this method of Harnack to be faulty, in that he selects certain texts to the exclusion of others equally well authenticated, Loisy admits that it is difficult to distinguish "between the thought of the Master and the interpretations of apostolic tradition."[104] For Christ drew up no systematic statement of his own doctrine, he wrote no treatise on his work; what we have in the Gospels is a weakened and confused echo of his teaching, "the general impression He produced upon hearers well disposed toward Him, with some of the more striking of His sentences, as they were understood and interpreted; and finally there remains the movement which He initiated."[105] Loisy then declares the basic point of difference between himself and Harnack:

> Whatever we think, theologically, of tradition, whether we trust it or regard it with suspicion, we know Christ only by the tradition, across the tradition, and in the tradition of the primitive Christians. . . . The attempt to define the essence of Christianity according to the pure gospel of Jesus, apart from tradition, cannot succeed.[106]

Turning to the "essence" itself, Loisy remarks the strangeness of the fact that Harnack could even use the word, with its metaphysical connotations; and, furthermore, that in using it he will admit no movement and development in the essence itself. Rather, Harnack's essence is a sentiment, identical in Jesus and in all Christians, thus constituting itself continuous and unchangeable. But is such a view

[102] *Ibid.*, p. 12.
[103] *Ibid.*
[104] *Ibid.*
[105] *Ibid.*, p. 13.
[106] *Ibid.*

historically defensible? "Has the Divine mercy been understood in absolutely the same way by the apostles and by Herr Harnack?"[107] Loisy thinks not:

What, for instance, of the hope of an eternal kingdom, constantly preached by Christ, and never allowed to perish by the Christian Church? . . . . What of Christ Himself, Whose place as Messiah belongs to the Primitive Church, and has never ceased to occupy the thought of the Church from the beginning? What of all the different themes of evangelical teaching, of which not one has been regarded during the Christian centuries as accessory? All of these elements of Christianity, . . . why should they not be the essence of Christianity? Why not find the essence of Christianity in the fullness and totality of its life. . . ?[108]

Loisy uses the analogy which Harnack mentioned and rejected in his work, that of the "peeling off" of the various layers of a fruit, to charge him with a reductionism which peels with such perseverance that little remains at the end. This process he holds to be indefensible in a historian, particularly in one who announces beforehand that he has no prepossessions, and is looking at the question solely from the historical point of view.

Finally, Loisy alludes to the anthropocentric bias which Harnack possessed, even in his consideration of God: "The God of Herr Harnack, driven from the domain of Nature, driven also from history, insofar as history is made of facts and play of thoughts, has taken refuge on the heights of human conscience, and is now only to be seen there by those who have keen perception."[109] Perhaps this criticism, so stated, is too strong, but the location of Harnack's point-of-revelation in the conscience, and the specification of the necessity of the "clear eye" to apprehend this God, simply fits "the facts of the case."[110]

In many ways Niebuhr's *Christ and Culture* is one resounding Barmen Declaration whose central note is "theocentricity." It is in

[107] *Ibid.*, p. 15.
[108] *Ibid.*, pp. 15–16.
[109] *Ibid.*, p. 21.
[110] Loisy's critique is the most careful and complete of the many written. In *The Gospel and the Church*, there are six main sections, each dealing with a fundamental theme which Harnack has developed. These are: "The Sources of the Gospels," "The Kingdom of Heaven," "The Son of God," "The Church," "The Christian Dogma," and "The Catholic Worship." Loisy first gives a summary statement of the position which Harnack has defended and then discusses it from his own historical and ecclesiastical point of view.

this work that he presents a profound criticism of Harnack with respect to the essence of Christianity.

Niebuhr rightly points out that "the virtue of Christ which religious liberalism has magnified beyond all others is love."[111] He does not deny, of course, that this is an important virtue as taught by Christ and all those who have followed him. But when one goes so far as to say that what Jesus "freed from its connexion with self-seeking and ritual elements, and recognized as the moral principle, he reduces to *one* root and to *one* motive—love,"[112] Niebuhr demurs. Why is such a reductionism necessary? Why must one specify *one* root and *one* motive? And if this is done, is it accurate to say, on the basis of historical-critical study, that "love itself, whether it takes the form of love of one's neighbor or of one's enemy, or the love of the Samaritan, is of one kind only.?"[113] Is this truly the religion of Jesus?

Actually, Niebuhr holds, to speak of the moral principle as "love itself," "of one kind only," as something that "must completely fill the soul," is "to command love for its own sake,"[114] and this Jesus nowhere does: "The virtue of love in Jesus' character and demand is the virtue of the *love of God and of the neighbor in God*, not the virtue of the love of love. The unity of this person lies in the simplicity and completeness of his direction toward God, whether the relation be one of love or of faith or of fear."[115]

From this it follows (since this is a truly theocentric stance, Jesus always submitting himself to God's unqualified sovereignty, and to this alone) that all human relations toward God are to be valued with reference to his absolutely "love-worthy" character as the only "ultimate object of devotion."[116]

Niebuhr believes that those who describe the ethic of Jesus solely in terms of love do so on the basis of a misinterpretation of his theology. God for Jesus, they declare, is the Father; "fatherhood is regarded as almost the sole attribute of God, so that when God is loved it is the principle of fatherhood that is loved."[117] But this is to misinterpret Jesus' theology, for

> Though God is love, love is not God for him; though God is one, oneness is not his God. God whom Christ loves is the "Lord of heaven and

[111] *Christ and Culture*, p. 15.
[112] Quoted from Harnack by Niebuhr, *ibid.*
[113] Quoted from Harnack by Niebuhr, *ibid.*
[114] *Ibid.*, pp. 15–16.
[115] *Ibid.*, p. 16.
[116] *Ibid.*
[117] *Ibid.*, pp. 16–17.

earth"; He is the God of Abraham, Isaac, and Jacob; . . . . The greatness and the strangeness of Jesus' love of God does not appear in his love of cosmic love, but in his loyalty to the transcendent power that to all men of little faith seems anything but fatherlike.[118]

The liberals, Niebuhr believes, have been so impassioned in their attempt to reduce the Gospel to a single principle of unity that they have not accurately represented the full dimensions of that which is found in the accounts of Jesus' teaching and action.

But what of the rejoinder of the liberals that Jesus in reality taught a double love, a love of God and of the neighbor? What of Harnack's insistence that the ethic of Jesus has two foci, "God the Father, and the infinite value of the human soul"? Niebuhr answers that "such statements forget that the double commandment . . . by no means places God and neighbor on a level, as though complete devotion were due to each."[119] Now it may not be completely fair to Harnack to suggest that he placed God and the neighbor on the same level. Harnack would not have disagreed with Niebuhr's succeeding statement that "it is only God who is to be loved with heart, soul, mind and strength,"[120] though, if our interpretation is valid, his anthropocentric point of view would prescribe a quite different treatment of this text than that which Niebuhr gives.

In his estimate of man as possessing "infinite value," however, Harnack has clearly deviated from the thought of the New Testament, at least if this value is interpreted as being intrinsic to man as man. For, as Niebuhr suggests, Jesus "does not speak of worth apart from God. The value of man . . . is his value to God. . . . His love of God and his love of neighbor are two distinct virtues that have no common quality but only a common source."[121] Niebuhr believes that Harnack's interpretation of the essence of the Gospel focused to a single point, and on the basis of this evaluation he is justified in regarding Harnack's position as inadequate.

But though we believe that Niebuhr's conclusions are valid, we do not believe that he has been completely fair to Harnack in the way he has stated the case. Furthermore, since there would appear to be some contradiction in holding at the same time that "Harnack would have agreed that 'only God is to be loved with heart, soul, mind and strength,'" and claiming that Niebuhr's conclusions are basically valid, we must attempt to explain our position on this

118 *Ibid.*, p. 17.
119 *Ibid.*
120 *Ibid.*
121 *Ibid.*, p. 18.

matter. Niebuhr claims that it is the liberals' passion for discovering a single principle of unity that brings on their fundamental difficulty. This we agree with, but it must also be noted that for Harnack, at least, there is a diversity even within this unity. This diversity roots in his fundamental anthropocentrism, and issues in the position that there is a "proximate" unity which is achievable by men, and a final unity, "the realised dominion of the Good," which man cannot achieve. In achieving this proximate unity, it is the love of the neighbor which will be efficacious; God, who will achieve the final unity, is to be loved because he is good.

To Niebuhr's claim that the double commandment does not place God and neighbor on the same level, Harnack would therefore agree: "only God is to be loved with heart, soul, mind and strength." But: because of the binding limits within which man lives, and which have not and cannot be broken from either side, it is pointless to speculate about the Being of God or the nature of that final unity which he will ultimately bring about. What man can know on the basis of his inner experience and his ethical striving, what he feels must be true, is that he has been given this context of struggle in order that he may achieve the proximate unity; in the process of "overcoming" he is given "the consciousness of being safe in God." With this consciousness is bound up the conviction that the soul has an infinite value. Therefore, Harnack does not *deny* the final unity, nor does he deny that "the value of man . . . is his value to God." But, because *there has been, finally, no revelation in the sense that God has disclosed himself*, but only in the sense that man—preeminently Jesus—has "opened himself," the practical result is to place *man* at the zenith, to "put a man's value as high as it can be put," and to evaluate everything according to the degree of its contribution to the increase of value for mankind.

As Harnack put it, "the love of one's neighbor is the only practical proof on earth of that love of God."[122] Harnack had to affirm the "infinite value" of man against the rampant materialism of his time; but he could not say that God has made himself known in Jesus Christ in any sense except that set forth above. The limits of man's temporality are never broken, and for Harnack this means that man must be faithful to his own highest nature, striving to overcome the blind and relentless Nature that is about him. God remains *absconditus*, and revelation means, essentially, ethical discovery.

---

[122] *WC*, p. 64.

Orr's essay entitled "Professor Harnack on Christ and His Gospel" was contained in a 1903 collection of essays on Ritschlianism.[123] Orr begins by setting forth a description of the "situation" out of which Harnack worked; this was a scientific and critical age which was faced with the necessity to give up Christianity or to interpret it in such a way as to make it viable to the modern man. Harnack's *Das Wesen des Christentums* is an attempt to give a positive answer to this dilemma. In this work, Orr holds, Christianity is interpreted as having an abiding value, but at the same time there is "the fullest acceptance of the results of modern science, culture, and historical criticism."[124] In these lectures, Orr admits, one cannot help feeling "a depth . . . of religious feeling, an overmastering conviction of the worth of Christ's religion, intense devotion to Christ himself."[125] But at the point of Harnack's "modernity," Orr finds an important qualification in Harnack's position "that Christianity has nothing to do with philosophy or theories of nature."[126] For though he is almost completely a modern "man of culture," though he finds no place for real miracles, yet "he calls a halt . . . when the view of the world becomes monistic—when the thinker would break down the oppositions between 'God and the World, the Here and the Beyond, the visible and the invisible, matter and spirit, the life of impulse and the life of freedom, physics and ethics.' "[127]

Orr can speak with appreciation of the legitimate emphases which Harnack makes; what he finds in the Gospel is indeed there, and in his attempt to relate the Gospel to the problems of today, he has rendered a signal service. However, he believes that Harnack, though emphasizing elements that are truly Christian, has left out elements that are even more essential; and he has thereby taken away the proper basis for that Christianity which he acknowledges. For even that Christianity which he acknowledges cannot live—to say nothing of Christianity as the churches have known it—unless "more is conceded to Christianity than he allows."[128] Certainly there is no question but that churchly Christianity—"as embodied not merely in the dogmatic structure of the creeds, but in liturgies, hymns,

[123] James Orr, *Ritschlianism: Expository and Critical Essays* (New York: A. C. Armstrong and Son, 1903).
[124] *Ibid.*, p. 118.
[125] *Ibid.*, pp. 118–119.
[126] *Ibid.*, p. 119.
[127] *Ibid.*
[128] *Ibid.*, p. 121.

prayers, preaching, in our whole Church worship and profession"[129] —must disappear if Harnack's Christianity is accepted. For it cannot be doubted that

> a . . . Christianity which allows no room for miracles; which rejects all doctrine save that of God the Father; which scouts Christology; which concedes to Jesus no substantial place in His own Gospel; which does not admit the resurrection; which has no atonement for sin . . . is not the Gospel as any historical Church today professes or practices it.[130]

Is this a fair criticism? Does not Harnack speak of Jesus as the Son of God in a unique sense? Does he not speak of the Easter faith, of the hope of immortality, of the forgiveness of sins?

> He does speak of these things, and that is the trouble of it, when we seek to weave his thoughts into some kind of unity. For, not only does he not speak of them consistently, or in terms that convey clear ideas to the mind,—not only do his utterances swim in a tantalizing vagueness, —not only are they not brought together in coherency (this might involve doctrine), and have not an adequate basis for them,—but it is Harnack's most energetic contention that these things do not belong to the essence of the Gospel as Jesus Himself taught it.[131]

We agree that "that is the trouble of it," indeed. For even if we were to proceed on Harnack's "energizing principle" that we must work through the historical *Stoff*, and combine with the knowledge there gained a rich *Lebenserfahrung* in order that we may arrive at "certainty and unity," we find any final certainty and unity forever blocked in Harnack by his fundamental stance. This, we may suggest, can be regarded as a great strength or a great weakness—and in either case, it is "necessary" for Harnack within his givens. It is a strength if one means thereby that man must always remain conscious of his finitude and his relativity, and never claim to "know as God knows." It is a weakness if one implies thereby that man can place limits on the freedom of God, or if he claims that this principle can be employed as a presuppositionless *a priori* by which one extricates oneself from the necessity to take a position.

Specifically, this would mean that Harnack was bound *not* to regard as essential to the Gospel that which the Church had historically regarded as essential: else he could not speak to his "situation"—an

[129] *Ibid.*, p. 122.
[130] *Ibid.*
[131] *Ibid.*, p. 123.

absolute requirement—but would be swallowed up by a "dogmatic" orthodoxy. On the other hand, he was bound to regard Christianity as "the absolute religion," at least in part because he was the son of Erlangen. In this awful tension he lived and worked. He had to gain certainty and unity, yet this could not be so dogmatic as to render one ineffectual in the culture. His solution of this impossible "living between Erlangen and Goethe" was *Das Wesen des Christentums.* To hold such an essence as identifiable from the plethora of *Kirchengeschichte* must be regarded as a problematical assumption. But Harnack solves this, we suggest, in agreement with Orr, by making of his "essence" such a will-o'-the-wisp that he could hold to the "absoluteness of Christianity" on the one hand, and demur on any systematic dogmatic formulation on the other. Truly, truly, as his daughter said, "his critics were not certain in which 'camp' he belonged—for that anyone could belong to *no* camp was unheard of."[132]

Orr, in the remainder of his essay, concentrates on the question, Does Jesus belong in his Gospel as an integral part of it? He notes that in the correspondence with Cremer, Harnack emphasized the latter part of his famous statement, "as Jesus Himself taught it," suggesting that Cremer overlooked this. But Cremer (so said Orr), "with great justice, answers that it had not occurred to him to regard this as a qualification of the statement."[133] The point is well taken. For in the section in which this statement occurs, Harnack is making the point that it is from Christ's teaching that the Gospel essence is to be discovered. He declares that there is nothing provisional in it, that Christ's Gospel is in truth the whole Gospel, and this must be kept free from alien intrusions. Orr concludes: "The proposition, then, truly represents Harnack's contention; yet, in defending it, he is, we venture to think (1) unjust to himself; (2) inconsistent with his own later statements; and (3), what is most important of all, untrue to the facts of the case."[134] For to defend this proposition would mean to regress from the understanding of Schleiermacher and Ritschl that Jesus was a part of his own Gospel; it would mean to admit inconsistency, for Harnack in the "tracing of the Gospel in history" clearly affirms that Christ became a part of his Gospel, and that this was a proper development; and it would mean simply to deny the view of Paul and Augustine and Luther, for whom Jesus

[132] AZH, p. 87.
[133] Orr, *Ritschlianism . . .*, p. 124.
[134] *Ibid.*, p. 125.

was indubitably a part of the Gospel. Orr's conclusion is that "it seems impossible to clear Harnack's view of . . . self-contradiction."[135]

In 1901, Hermann Cremer gave a series of lectures at the University of Greifswald in answer to Harnack's interpretation of the essence of Christianity. This work is distinguished by the fact that it was the only criticism of his position which Harnack answered.

Cremer's point of view is that of a pietistic orthodoxy, for which Christianity is a continual paean of praise to the Christ who has redeemed sinners. His central criticism of Harnack is therefore based on the inadequacy of the "Gospel" which Harnack set forth to speak to the sinner. Cremer states his unwillingness to enter into disputation over the validity of Harnack's suppositions about religion and what it *must* be. Rather,

> in the controversy with Harnack the question is, whether the Christianity of the apostolic message is right, or whether it must be replaced by a Christianity of modern reflection and still more modern enthusiasm. The Christianity of the apostolic message applies to the lost sinner, to whom it offers salvation through the wondrous grace of God. . . . Harnack's Christianity applies to the modern man who feels himself vexed, not by the moral but by the intellectual problem, because the moral problem, How is the sinner saved? does not exist for him.[136]

In setting forth the deficiency of the "Christianity of modern reflection," Cremer goes straight to the Christological question. For this modern Christianity, Christ is a

> natural phenomenon of history, appearing in the normal course of history, who worked and still works like every other important man, only that He surpasses all others in power; who . . . has put His gifts and the knowledge of God . . . into such relations with motives and objects that He alone solves the mysteries of our life.[137]

He is to be regarded as a man, "nothing else, only distinguished by His very prominent . . . moral gifts, whereby he worked himself up to a perfect communion with God, and showed himself to be in full and blessed independence of the world."[138] Cremer then places

[135] *Ibid.*, p. 129.

[136] *A Reply to Harnack on the Essence of Christianity*, 3rd ed., tr. Bernhard Pick (New York: Funk and Wagnalls Company, 1903), p. xiii.

[137] *Ibid.*, p. 3.

[138] *Ibid.*, p. 4.

alongside this "modern Christianity" which Harnack represents that which he considers to be the true statement of the matter:

The other religion regards Christ as an entirely irregular appearance in history. . . . The meaning of His life and nature is unique. . . . He is the God-man, whose incarnation and humanity is a humiliation continuing itself unto death and down into the realm of the dead, that in the deepest depths of our misery we should not be deprived of the sympathizing Man of Pity and Savior.[139]

This is the central question for Cremer, but he does not regard it as answerable solely by a historical method. Here is a basic disagreement with Harnack also. To approach the question of the meaning of Christ as Harnack does, saying, "This is an historical question . . . and as an historical question it can only be solved by way and with the means of historical inquiry,"[140] is for Cremer an oversimplification. To be sure, it is "from one aspect an historical question . . . but it is questionable whether it is *merely* an historical question, and whether it is to be answered by the ordinary means of other historical inquiry."[141] For Christianity is not simply "the religion which Christ Himself . . . practiced," but "the principal thing . . . is . . . that which He does for us."[142] Or, put in another way, "*He is not, like ourselves, a subject of religion; on the contrary, He is the object of the religion, the object of Christianity.*"[143]

In addition to the problem of Christology, Cremer deals with one other main point, that relating to Harnack's attempt to make Christianity relevant to his culture. He charges Harnack with an interpretation of Christianity which is open only to those critically trained in historical science and exegesis, i.e., the "cultured." In the Preface, he compares Harnack's *Das Wesen des Christentums* with Schleiermacher's *Reden*:

Schleiermacher had to deal with an estrangement from the Gospel through the fault of rationalism; Harnack, with an estrangement from Christianity through the fault of the attestation of the Gospel itself. . . . For not only the doctrines developed by theology . . . but the most essential traits of the New Testament Gospel, are the causes he assigns for unbelief among the cultured.[144]

139 *Ibid.*, pp. 4–5.
140 *Ibid.*, p. 6.
141 *Ibid.*
142 *Ibid.*, pp. 7–8.
143 *Ibid.*, p. 8.
144 *Ibid.*, p. xi.

Thus, because he was more aware of the "situation" within which he lived, and the impossibility of making the New Testament picture of Christ communicant with this situation, than he was of the historical givens as they lie open to the view of history, he constructed from the Gospels an "essence" which would speak to his time.

But when one interprets Christianity in this way, a more serious problem is raised than that for which Harnack's interpretation attempts an answer. For then one must distinguish between "cultured" and "common" Christianity: "Harnack has distinguished between 'powers' and 'props' in this matter of comprehending truth. This distinction is especially flattering to the semiculture of our times. We, the cultured ones, have the 'powers'; the remainder of mankind reach up to it only by means of the 'props.' "[145] For Cremer, there is no defense for this position: "We need to have this contrast only uttered to feel it as the frivolous boasting of a so-called aristocracy of culture."[146]

Ernst Rolffs's article entitled "Harnack's 'What Is Christianity?' and the Religious Currents of the Present" was originally published in *Christliche Welt*. To indicate the interest which Harnack's lectures aroused, Rolffs lists the literature which had been produced in barely two years, representing every facet of theological concern.[147]

Rolffs himself is strongly sympathetic to the point of view set forth by Harnack. He admits that Harnack "presents a modern type of Christianity,"[148] and indicates the extent to which he believes such a modern type is necessary by declaring that Harnack

> here offers to the present age a Christianity which is elastic enough to take up into itself the new ideas won for modern culture by the labors of Lessing and Kant, of Goethe and Schiller, of Hegel and Schleiermacher, and by the exact sciences of the nineteenth century, without thereby losing any of its religious warmth and moral strictness. Such a fusion of the Christian religion and modern culture is simply a necessity for the health of the spiritual life of Germany.[149]

Rolffs compares Harnack to Schleiermacher in two decisive par-

[145] *Ibid.*, p. 14.

[146] *Ibid.*, pp. 14–15.

[147] *Harnack's Wesen des Christentums und die religiösen Strömungen der Gegenwart* (Leipzig: Hinrichs, 1902). Listed are 11 books from German Protestants, 49 articles in periodicals, 14 newspaper reviews, 14 Catholic "answers," 21 foreign productions, and translations into 6 languages of the work itself.

[148] *Ibid.*, p. 3.

[149] *Ibid.*, pp. 3–4.

ticulars: as Schleiermacher's early development stood under the influence of the *Brüdergemeinde*, so Harnack stood under the influence of orthodox Lutheranism; and as Schleiermacher in his maturity became a religious philosopher of independent strength, so Harnack became a scientific historian of the first rank. In the combination of these two strengths Rolffs sees the great contribution of Harnack to his contemporaries; he represents science at its best, and he would imbue it with a faith. This judgment, shared by Delbrück, Troeltsch, and, latterly, by Bultmann, saw the great merit of *Das Wesen des Christentums* in the fact that it was a "symbolic concatenation" (as Troeltsch stated it) of the work of the nineteenth-century historical-critical movement, joined with a positive statement of a faith by which a modern man can live.[150]

But Rolffs admits that "a personality can never be a pure type."[151] This applies also to Harnack. He is, above all, a man of science; as a scholar, he conceives it to be his duty to declare what is true about his subject, religion. This is more important to him than an intellectually defensible Christian *Weltanschauung*. Rolffs cites Naumann's criticism of Harnack, that he had set forth a view of Christianity which was "too abstract,"[152] but Naumann did not see that it was Harnack's own vocation as a scientific historian which determined for him the direction which his explication had to take, and the limits that were thereby set for him.

In fact, the picture of Harnack which emerges from Rolffs's characterization is a fascinating one for this very reason, that he regards Harnack as one who, on the basis of his intense and undoubtedly deep personal faith *would have liked* to say much more on many of the crucial points at issue than he did say. But it was his fidelity to his vocation as a scientific historian which set the limits beyond which he would not go. Of particular significance as a case in point is Harnack's method of dealing with the Resurrection. Rolffs admits that he finds this the most unsatisfying part of the entire work; but he believes that one can explain Harnack's reticence to go further than he does on the basis of his methodological limitation. Always the historian, he would not violate the limits of that which was his-

[150] For Bultmann's judgment, see his Introduction in the Harper Torchbook edition of Harnack, *What is Christianity?* (New York: Harper & Row, 1957). The Introduction was originally written by Bultmann for a fiftieth anniversary edition of *Das Wesen des Christentums* (Stuttgart: Ehrenfried Klotz Verlag, 1950), and was translated by Salvator Attanasio and Ephraim Fishoff.

[151] *Harnack's Wesen* . . . , p. 5.

[152] *Ibid.*

torically discoverable; but always, at the same time, a deeply religious person, he would not dispute the right of others to believe what they were impelled to believe. Or, in Rolffs's fine sentence, "I can well understand Harnack's point of view; though he believed he was bound to investigate that which was investigable (*Erforschliches*), he extended to others the privilege to reverse that which was not investigable."[153]

Certainly Rolffs's interpretation would go far toward explaining the fact that Harnack would not regard himself as a "reformer"; he was first of all a historian. Nor would he prepare a "substitute" for the Apostles' Creed, as his brother requested him to do. Nor would he enter into disputatious argument with those who heaped journalistic vitriol on his work almost from the beginning of his literary activity. Such a position as Rolffs suggests would not be without difficulties, however. If it makes Harnack out as a sort of latter-day Origen, who believed in one standard for the "wise" and one for the "simple," one for the "scientific historians" and one for those who were impelled to "believe more," it falls under the judgment of Cremer that this is the "boasting of a so-called aristocracy of culture." Furthermore, and perhaps more important from Harnack's own point of view, it is open to question on the basis of *Das Wesen des Christentums* whether Harnack did not really believe that there was truly only *one* Christian Gospel, that which "Jesus had preached," available alike to the simple and the wise. If this solution of Rolffs does justice to that deep and pervasive religious dimension which one cannot but observe in Harnack, it leaves him an essentially schizoid man, lacking that "certainty and unity" which he everywhere extols. But it cannot be denied, however one may deal with the resolution of the difficulty, that there are in truth these two facets to the man, as we have insisted from the outset.

The problem which Rolffs has raised, "How can one do full justice to *history* and to *faith*, avoiding some real or covert bifurcation?" is an important one. Harnack's problem is even more complicated than this, however, for by renouncing "philosophical-theological speculation," he was not only trying to steer between Scylla and Charybdis, no easy task in itself, but he was trying to do so with a locked rudder.

It is evident from these descriptions of the various critiques of Harnack that there are wide areas of agreement. On the charge of

[153] *Ibid.*, p. 10.

Kulturprotestantismus, there is agreement that Harnack is determinatively influenced by the inner necessity to speak to the situation in which he lived. This situation demanded a reinterpretation of Christianity (Orr), in which Christianity and science would be reconciled (Loisy); the result was a "modern type" of Christianity (Rolffs) which, however, sets up an impossible bifurcation. With respect to the "essence of Christianity," Loisy holds that Harnack's nisus to essence procedure is invalid, and that what he discovers thereby is only a "sentiment"; Niebuhr maintains that to reduce the essence of Christianity to a single quality, love, is invalid; Orr charges that this essence remains deliberately vague; and Cremer denies that this essence deals with the central point of Christianity, redemption. As to the method manifested in the *Wesen*, Loisy finds it to be reductionistic and unfair to the very canons of historical criticism which Harnack espoused; Rolffs holds that Harnack must be understood primarily as a scientific historian; and Cremer believes that the essence of Christianity is more than a historical question, and to try to answer it "just from the standpoint of history" must end in failure. Finally, on the matter of Christology, Cremer radically disagrees that "Christ is a natural phenomenon," as Harnack had made him out to be; and Orr declares that any Christianity which "scouts Christology" does not represent Christianity as it has been historically.

What is the legitimacy of these "charges"? And what do the charges of the critics contribute to an understanding of Harnack's estimate of the reality of Christianity?

The first charge is that of Harnack's *Kulturprotestantismus*. Harnack has been flogged with this *word*, and sometimes with that which it signifies, as perhaps no other liberal. There is a double explanation of this. In the first place, Harnack did attempt to speak to the problems of the culture of his time, for which purpose he had to employ terms which would communicate to "the cultured despisers." The second—and much less justifiable—reason for this flogging lies in the fact that Harnack was identified with "Harnackians." Whereas Harnack had come to his achieved position by contending with his orthodox heritage, many liberals, lacking this heritage and lacking the struggle to overcome it, therefore succumbed to a *Kulturprotestantismus* interpretation with very little understanding of the "*Protestantismus*."

Perhaps it is inevitable that any great man should be misinterpreted just because his greatness makes of him an *ipse dixit* authority; certainly "history shows" this to have been the case in many instances.

The point is that Harnack's conclusions were based on the faithful and prodigious labor that characterized his life, and these conclusions were arrived at by the employment of that multidimensional method which has been described; but many of the camp followers took his conclusions without themselves wrestling through the struggle for unity and certainty out of which his method was born. As an example, Harnack declared that the Gospel had little to do with dogma *only after he knew dogma*, and he did know it. Whether his judgment was justified or not, he would never have made it if he had not mastered dogma; dilettantism was a cardinal sin for him. Indeed, one sees a covert operation of this dread of "taking anyone's word as authority" in the way in which he interpreted the growth of dogma; for he held that this authoritative stance which the great Church increasingly came to assume obscured the process of the free operation of the Spirit. Yet perhaps a great many of Harnack's followers made this very mistake. Harnack became the authority, Harnack's *conclusions*, not his *method*. Harnack had demolished "speculative" theology; therefore one does not need even to be introduced to it anymore. Harnack recovered the kernel of the Christian religion from the husks of dogma; therefore one can burn the barn and live in the granary. Harnack had rejected traditional Christology in favor of the simple Gospel of Jesus; therefore one can bypass orthodoxy. Certainly it must be emphasized that Harnack would have categorically rejected such a procedure.

But there can be no doubt, of course, that Harnack was concerned to conserve for and synthesize into Christianity the scientific and cultural achievements of his and previous times. He would doubtless have agreed with Rolffs that "such a fusion of the Christian religion and modern culture is simply a necessity for the health of the spiritual life of Germany."[154] But clearly it was his concern for the "health of the spiritual life of Germany," *not* the deliberate intention to adjust Christianity to a point of cultural acceptability, which motivated Harnack. Perhaps his fundamental passion, to "confess and defend" Christianity against the threats of materialism and its "debunking" of man, led him to an overstatement of the debilities of confessionalism, which he saw as inutile, to an overoptimistic appraisal of human possibility, and, consequently, to a neglect of those aspects of Christian faith which emphasize man's creatureliness with respect to God.

However, though it was Harnack's intention to penetrate the cul-

[154] *Ibid.*, p. 4.

ture with Christian truth "as he saw it," the fundamental problem is whether he did not, by his optimistic anthropology and his anti-speculative bias, joined with his confidence in historical method, bring to "Christian truth" a standard that conformed more to the cultural norm than to the historical givens of Christianity. For example, is Harnack's "God" the sovereign, acting deity of Abraham, Isaac, and Jacob, of the prophets and Jesus? Or is he more like the Greek Absolute, who embodies the Good, the True, and the Beautiful, but remains *absconditus* in history? The latter, a much more palatable deity for a scientific culture, is not unlike the deity described in Harnack's works. The same intrusion of a cultural norm obtains in Harnack's interpretation of Jesus, of "man," and of Nature.

On the criticism relating to the "essence," we believe Loisy is correct in challenging Harnack's nisus to essence procedure in dealing with Christianity, but inaccurate in identifying it simply as a "sentiment"; that Niebuhr does not state Harnack's best case, for he fails to set Harnack's reduction of this essence to one root and one motive in the context of the total position; that Orr has a right to feel exasperated at the "vagueness of the essence," but thereby implies that he does not see it as "simple," which is laudable; and that Cremer's judgment that this essence fails to deal with the central point of Christianity, redemption, is valid or not depending on whether one defines redemption as he does or as Harnack does.

Harnack's definition of the essence of Christianity and his procedure in arriving at it show clear Kantian and, in its Goethean form, romantic influences. There are evidences of Kant's influence in Harnack's description of the limits within which man exists and reasons. We have already observed the identities between the main features of Jesus' teaching and the Kantian postulates. The category of Duty, though discoverable in the form of a circumlocution (the responsibility of the person to overcome history by history, to seek certainty and unity), is central in Harnack's thought. With respect to romanticism, and particularly Goethe, Harnack often uses the "great man" in a "scissors and paste" way, taking some striking aphorism as a *bon mot* for a particular situation (e.g., "Mankind is always progressing, but man always remains the same"). But he agrees, substantitively, with Goethe on such matters as the individual struggling within himself to overcome his fate, to be free, or to realize life; or, the individual struggling with a tyrannous nature in order to overcome it (which stance is perhaps the main Goethean influence). One must qualify here by pointing out that in spite of these important areas of agreement, Harnack remained a servant of the Church to the degree that he never surrendered the centrality of Jesus (as he saw him), and he always qualified his conception of "love" to make it more than a mere human sentiment.

This is the point where Niebuhr is inadequate, for he fails to do justice to the context. To be sure, Harnack speaks of "*one* root and *one* motive—love"—but a few lines later, he indicates that this love is not so simple by declaring that "Jesus made love and humility one." True, he can say that "this humility . . . is the love of God of which we are capable." But add to this the basic affirmation, "It is only in the peace of God which passes all understanding that this (final) unity dawns on us," and the pattern that results is not so unequivocally simple as Niebuhr makes it. Harnack's "God" may not be the "God" some find in biblical faith; his statement that "it is certain that the only place that we can meet God is in our personal higher life and ethical striving" may indeed place restrictions upon the deity which, from a biblical standpoint, is indefensible (and surrenders his history to his axiology in the process); but Harnack's "love" cannot be described *apart from* its relation to his "God," nor can it be called only a sentiment. Only by an inadequate assessment of the total context can one make such judgments.

To engage Harnack at the point of method is to grapple with a titan. Only a historian of the caliber of Loisy, who elsewhere had confessed the great contribution which Harnack had made to the understanding of Christian tradition, could demand attention by making the charge of inadequacy.[155] And it is to be noted that Loisy's charge is directed here to the "reductionism" of the method employed in the discovery of the "essence," not to Harnack's method in general. Actually, Loisy is accusing Harnack of inconsistency. Rolffs's and Cremer's criticisms, taken together, provide a documentation of the "inconsistency," for both make statements which can be supported from *Das Wesen des Christentums*. This is, of course, the problem. To Rolffs's statement that Harnack must be understood primarily as a scientific historian, the overt introductory declaration that "it is solely in its historical sense that we shall try to answer this question"[156] may be cited as support. To document Cremer's position

[155] Loisy, in obliterating a bizarre theory of Couchoud, who had questioned Harnack's historical competence, pays tribute to Harnack's erudition. See his article on "Marcion's Gospel," *The Hibbert Journal*, XXXIV (1935–36), pp. 378–387.

[156] *WC*, pp. 5–6.

that the question of the essence of Christianity is much more than a historical question, one may cite Harnack's own most significant confession, to the effect that judgments of value finally are not obtainable from history, but are the creation of feeling and will. Harnack elsewhere claims that the process of discovering what is essential, for all of its dependence upon historical investigation, is, *finally*, answerable to another norm. "The thing itself reveals it," he states, and proceeds to explicate this in terms of "a fresh eye" and "true feeling." And, in a succeeding passage, discussing "the historian's task of distinguishing . . . kernel and husk" he emphasizes in a very unhistorical way that "we cannot want" to do this or that—which is hardly a valid approach for one who claimed to hold no prepossessions where "understanding Christianity historically" was concerned.

It can be demonstrated from Harnack's own mouth, therefore, that axiology is ultimately victorious over history. But it is important to emphasize that this discovered domination of history by axiology does not give one the license to "reduce" Harnack's thought to a single, simple essence. We have insisted throughout this book that Harnack's axiology is not as simple as it is sometimes made out to be, and his historical method, whatever its limits, was so many-sided that it yielded a real increment to the understanding of Christian institutions and thought. Loisy, Peterson, and Barth, to name a few of those who regarded his constructive formulation as inadequate, nevertheless recognized the tremendous contribution which Harnack had made to the understanding of Christian history. It is unfortunate, and it is inexcusable, that Harnack has been understood and interpreted by so many on the basis of his theological liberalism alone.

The final charge of the critics, concerning Harnack's Christology—or the lack of it—is closely related, at its central point, to his method. Neither Cremer nor Orr, who, respectively, challenge Harnack for making Christ a natural phenomenon and for scouting Christology, gets to this central point. For Harnack would not say more than his limits permitted about Jesus as the "Christ," and therefore he and Cremer simply stood on different ground. Harnack, furthermore, could have agreed with Orr that Christianity has been concerned, in the course of its history, with Christology; but Harnack's question was that of Christianity's "essence," and he simply did not believe that this Christology was a part of that essence. Even if one agrees with Orr—and many others—that the Christological discussions are misrepresented if they are made to be "intellectualizations" only—as Harnack seems to have believed—the point that must be considered here is whether Harnack really read back a nineteenth-century axiological norm into a first-century man. Is "the Christ that Harnack sees, looking back through nineteen centuries of Catholic darkness, . . . only a reflection of a liberal Protestant face seen at the bottom of a deep well"?[157] Or, stated more generally, is the essence which Harnack finds in Christianity Jesus' "Gospel" or is it Harnack's "gospel"?

To Tyrrell's charge, we suggest that, so stated, it is inaccurate. If he means that Harnack sought to make of Jesus a modern man, the charge is simply insupportable. Jesus was a man of his time, Harnack held, and that time is past. The *Weltanschauung* of Jesus was that of a first-century Jew, with its angels and demons, its heaven and hell. This *Weltanschauung* must be given up, but it can be, because this was only the "contemporary integument" within which the "essence" was carried. But this "essence" of Jesus' teaching—"the treasure which the soul possesses in the eternal and merciful God"—transcends all times and places and *Weltanschauungen*. In this sense alone Jesus was the eternal contemporary.

The question then becomes (and, to be charitable, it should be admitted that this may be what Tyrrell meant), "Is the *kernel* of Jesus' teaching which Harnack finds in fact *Harnack's* kernel?" And here, the answer must be affirmative. In order to make this crucial point, we shall attempt, with the aid of an explication by Richard Niebuhr, to set forth a text and interpret it. The text:

The concepts of God and man in biblical faith differ from the concepts of God and man set forth by Harnack. Biblical faith is theocentric: Harnack's interpretation of biblical faith, though it contains certain theocentric aspects, is, finally, curved back toward man. The resultant interpretation of God, of man, and of Jesus Christ is thereby altered.

To interpret this text, we refer to Niebuhr's *best* critique of theological liberalism, particularly as it relates to Ritschl; but we believe the criticisms are alike applicable to Harnack. Niebuhr charges that though the liberal theology was concerned to reaffirm the understanding of Luther that "God and faith belong together,"[158]

[157] Tyrrell, quoted in Grant, *Bible in the Church*, p. 188.
[158] Niebuhr, *The Meaning of Revelation*, p. 23.

Ritschl . . . began to analyze God's nature simply from the point of view of a member of the human community confronting nature. Having said that Christian judgments are value-judgments he proceeded to set forth a value-scale which was not that of Christian faith, for which God is the highest value and could not be God were he not absolute in worth, but was rather the value-scale of civilized man.[159]

When this is done, God becomes instrumental, man becomes the measure, and what one has, ironically enough, is a Hellenization and secularization of the Gospel in a completely disparate sense than that which Harnack suggests.

Now the Bible can be interpreted from this point of view, for it does speak of man's dominion over nature, and of his value above that of all other creatures; but prior to this is the affirmation that he is a creature under God. Being the sort of creature that he is, he lives by some sort of faith. In this sense, the anthropocentric stance would seem to be inevitable; it is always *man* who is doing the believing.[160] Theocentricity would appear from this point of view to be an arrogance, a sort of metaphysical irrelevance. But Luther and his true (*sic!*) interpreters were never so simple as to believe that man looks at himself from God's point of view, an obvious absurdity. Theocentricity means rather that the object of the faith which man is always exercising is God who is, *nolens volens*, the Alpha and Omega, the God of Abraham, Isaac, and Jacob, the Father of Jesus Christ; he is the only ultimately love-worthy object. But does this mean that Harnack is to be charged with leaving God on the periphery, and pursuing independent human ends? Can one maintain this in the light of his pages in *Das Wesen des Christentums* where he is dealing with God and the soul? "God"—no. The God who is attested in biblical faith, the God who is the object of theocentric faith—this is *the* question. And we admit that we approach this question with the greatest trepidation.

"God" is at the center of Harnack's thought, surely enough. But, because of the "limits" within which Harnack saw man to be confined, he had to give a particular interpretation to Christology—which indeed can be for him no more than a "Jesusology." For Jesus was confined in nature as we are, and that which he possessed was what all men possess; and because this is true, we can "open ourselves" as he "opened himself" to God; the "fresh eye" and "true feeling" which we have, he had; and that which came to him must be there-

159 *Ibid.*, p. 29.

160 See Harnack, "Fünfzehn Fragen . . . ," *RA*, V, NF, pp. 51–54.

fore that same "thing itself" which comes to us. Man ought properly to say nothing about Jesus which goes beyond this; and yet, we may ask, is this not to deviate from the biblical position? For is it not clear that for Jesus God was the God of the Covenant, a God who had his own distinctive purposes, an active God who creates and shatters and rebuilds, a God who lays his inalienable claim upon man by making him to stand in the divine image?

Such a theocentric position, as Niebuhr points out, is most difficult to hold consistently. For the men who try to hold it always live in a world of rival faiths, in which they seek to demonstrate the superiority of their faith to that of others. But when this demonstration is attempted in any other way than that which "makes the God of Jesus Christ the measure of all things,"[161] theocentricity has been given up. This is the substance of the charge that Niebuhr makes against the liberals. They sought to prove the worth of Christianity by comparing its estimate of, and contribution to, man and his self-realization, with other faiths—in other words, they reduced it to that which it held in common with other faiths. But Christianity had from the beginning claimed to be not one faith among others, but *the* faith. And it had not based this claim upon Harnack's "given" that "it is *the* religion because Jesus Christ is not one master beside others, but because he is the Master, and because his Gospel corresponds to the innate purpose of humanity as history reveals it,"[162] but it had made this claim on the ground that "God who spoke to our fathers by the prophets has in these last days spoken to us by a Son."[163] This is the theocentric faith which was confessed by the Church in history; and whether or not this form is used, *all* biblical forms, and most historic forms of Christian confession affirm the priority and the sovereignty of Jesus' God. To say that Jesus was the Master because "his Gospel corresponds to the innate purpose of humanity" is to take another position.

E. THE PROBLEM OF THE "REALLY REAL"

1. Leading Themes and Context

Paul Tillich is reported to have responded, when someone asked the question as to whether the Resurrection was "really real": "Stop!

[161] Niebuhr, *The Meaning of Revelation*, p. 32.
[162] Harnack, "Die Aufgabe der . . . ," *RA*, II, pp. 172–173.
[163] Hebrews 1: 1–2.

You have committed the unpardonable metaphysical sin."[164] With all necessary cautions expressed, we will rush in, in the following summation, where metaphysicians fear to tread. For the "reality of Christianity" was Harnack's problem and he meant thereby the "real reality," whether he calls it "the inner form of Christian truth," "the independently won position," or uses some other euphemism.

There is only one way, according to his constant insistence, to identify this reality. The 1903 edition of *Das Wesen*,[165] in a special preface, takes account of the critics' charges that his method claimed more than it could deliver; and he reiterated, with passion, that "historical understanding begins when one frees the essential and the unique . . . from the contemporary husks."[166] He admits that much must be sacrificed in such a method, "but the attempt must be made. For neither the antiquarian, nor the philosopher, nor the enthusiast (*Schwärmer*) can have the last word here, but the historian; for it is a purely historical problem to establish the essential character of an historical phenomenon."[167] And if it is true, as it certainly is for Harnack, that *Lebenserfahrung*, the experience of life, is conjoined with the methods of historical science to make up "historical sense," we shall have to make the most of it.

The standard is "the reality": Harnack never wearies of proclaiming it. He had said to Althoff, in a memorandum of 1888, that if theological faculties could have only one church historian, this must be an *early* church historian. "The center of gravity of church historical study lies in the history of the church and of dogma in the first six centuries. . . . Here he gets the standard which he must apply to the later history, and if he is not well-grounded by independent study in this period, he will be led by a will-o'-the-wisp in his estimate of later history. . ."[168] But even more specifically, beyond the early centuries, one must go to the *fons et origo*. In the 1903 edition of *Das Wesen*, answering those who argue for a "Das Ganze" approach rather than a "Das Wesen" approach,[169] Harnack unambiguously announces his position: "If we do not learn to develop the essence and

[164] This was reported to me as having taken place in one of Tillich's classes at the Union Theological Seminary. It is a nice story, and should be true, even if the quotation may not be precisely correct!

[165] Harnack, *Das Wesen des Christentums*, 45 bis 50 Tausend ed. (Leipzig: Hinrichs, 1903).

[166] *Ibid.*, p. vi.

[167] *Ibid.*

[168] AZH, pp. 174–175.

[169] Cf. Loisy, *The Gospel and the Church*, p. 4.

the kernel of our religion, and to value our confessional or personal individuality solely as a branch on a great tree, how shall we attain to unity in religion, which must be the purpose of all our work?"[170]

Harnack held that it is in Jesus Christ that this unity is to be attained; here only one finds the answer to the search for a way to overcome the world. Because this is true (and history has established the truth of this value-judgment), he is *the* Master, and Christianity is *the* religion. When the problem is stated in this way—i.e., how to overcome the world—all those dogmatic concerns which exercised the Church for so large a part of its history become irrelevant. When one asks, "How can I overcome the world?" the only adequate answer can be one in which practical utility is provided, and all "metaphysical concerns," because they raise unanswerable and inutile questions, must be rejected as irrelevant.

The orthodox, of course, rejected Harnack's statement of the problem. On the basis of the converse declaration that "the world *has been* overcome by God in Christ," their question became, "How can I be faithful to this deed of God, and declare in my works that the Grace of God has been shed abroad in our hearts?" Yet it may be argued that this latter "Gospel," like the "Gospel" which Harnack espoused, has had in history, because of men, a similar career of synthesis and diastasis. When its declaration is made as though one possessed it in forms and dogmas, the only task then being the celebration of the form and the conceptual adherence to the dogma, its own internal judgmental principle rises up to shatter its pretense. That Harnack thought he saw this in the ecclesiasticism of his day is not open to doubt. This was the one front on which he fought.

There was another front which represented even more of a danger, for the opposition not only denied the forms and the dogma, but also Harnack's corrective. Here we mean such positions as the monism of Haeckel, the atheism of Feuerbach, and the materialism of Marx and his German interpreters.[171] These avowedly autonomous positions posed even more of a threat than that of arid orthodoxy. Harnack's "war on two fronts" was thus determined in its plan and execution by the necessities imposed by these givens. Particularly with respect to

[170] *Das Wesen* . . . (1903 ed.), p. v.

[171] Eduard von Hartmann, for example, commented: "Not only is the person who would lead us back to the sixteenth century a reactionary; to a greater degree, the one who would lead us back to the world-view of the eleventh century, or the sixth, is reactionary . . . But most reactionary of all is the one who would place us again in the first century, in the time of the primitive Christian community." AZH, p. 246.

the latter case it may be held that, if Harnack's statement of the problem as "How can I overcome the world?" transferred the basis of argument from biblical to modern grounds, the provocation was extreme.

In any case, it is always with respect to this situation that Harnack's work proceeds. He must ask, on the one hand, how one can affirm the value of human existence against the varieties of materialism which were increasingly threatening man's sense of worth. He must ask, on the other hand, how one can avoid that pretension which claims to probe behind the human phenomenological realm to declare the very secrets of God. This value is affirmed, and this pretension avoided, by making the central datum the person of Jesus. It is he who personifies the Gospel. The pretension is avoided because he was a human being, with a "solely human nature." But the value is affirmed because in this person, and no other, we actually meet that "inner certainty and unity" which we seek, and which gives us that knowledge of God and of ourselves which enables us to overcome the world. In saying that Jesus had a "solely human nature," Harnack did not mean that one could explain him completely by a historical and psychological analysis. This statement must be taken in counterpoise to those docetic or two-nature theories which sought to deal with metaphysical essences; Harnack would not have said "merely" human, for to him humanity was a deep and mysterious realm. In making the person of Jesus the central datum *because* here alone we confront that which "gives certainty and unity" (i.e., the Gospel), however, Harnack opened himself to the charge of apriorism. This is not meliorated when the similarity of "the Gospel" to the three Kantian moral postulates is noted.

Bearing in mind this situation out of which he worked, we can understand the way in which Harnack portrayed Jesus. Because it is true that Harnack did his work under this necessity to affirm value, the questions with which he dealt had to be stated in this form: what must be the relation of the historical Jesus to "the Gospel," and what must be the nature of the essence which is discovered in the New Testament? To state the questions in this way may appear to be a gross injustice to a historian who himself claimed that he never came to the study of a historical question with presuppositions. Actually, he seems to have meant by this claim that the rudimentary steps in his method were always taken with the strictest fidelity to the canon of objectivity. One can substantiate the judgment that the further one progresses through the stages of scientific knowledge, the more determinatively do Harnack's presuppositions operate. Therefore, one expects to find in *Das Wesen des Christentums* a veritable mob of presuppositions; for the Christian religion is the reality which constitutes the very center of his vocation.

The Christian religion is something simple and sublime; it means one thing and one thing only: Eternal life in the midst of time, by the strength and under the eyes of God. It is no ethical or social *arcanum* for the preservation or improvement of things generally. To make what it has done for civilization and human progress the main question, and to determine its value by the answer, is to do it violence at the start.[172]

At the risk of "reading into," one can insist on "reading out of" this statement what is present; and what Harnack here appears to be defending is the conception of a timeless "reality" in the Christian religion which cannot be challenged because it cannot be specified. Thus the derogation of "ethical" activity is more apparent than real; for everything depends upon the *purpose* to which ethical activity is directed. The Gospel is not only "eternal life in the midst of time," but, because it deals primarily with God, it is above the relative goods of the world and of culture. Had it been otherwise, the Gospel might have been relevant to first-century Palestine, but it would not have been an eternally relevant Gospel.

As this relates to Jesus, he was situated in his day as we are situated in ours; he was a man, and as such was shaped by his situation. There was nothing within him which was not also possessed by other humans: else he would not have been "truly human." But there was an opening of the human consciousness which he possessed in a way which no one else has ever achieved; out of this consciousness he declared the Gospel, and with the declaration he personified it in himself. Therefore it is the task of the historian to discover *that* which is of permanent validity beneath all the transitory features which came to be associated with Jesus as the Church reasoned about him. *That*, which is the essence, may not be identifiable, according to Harnack; but the only option to making the attempt at identification is to admit that the Gospel is identical with its earliest form, that it came with its time, departed with its time, and must be rejected in a different time. This Harnack will not say. He will not make the Gospel simply an "ethical *arcanum*" for the improvement of things generally, for to do so would be to deny its eternal relevance. The Gospel transcends all forms in which it has been, is, or will be cast.

[172] *WC*, p. 7.

Harnack further emphasizes this timelessness of the Gospel in a discussion which clearly reveals his commitment to a developmental hypothesis:

The Gospel . . . contains something which, under differing historical forms, is of permanent validity. . . . The history of the Church shows us in its very commencement that "primitive Christianity" had to disappear in order that "Christianity" might remain; and in the same way in later ages one metamorphosis followed upon another. From the beginning it was a question of getting rid of formulas, correcting expectations, altering ways of feeling, and this is a process to which there is no end. But by the very fact that our survey embraces the whole course as well as the inception, we enhance our standard of what is essential and of real value.[173]

Not only is development present in the history of the Church as one metamorphosis follows another, but the "standard of what is essential and of real value" has been enhanced. Obviously, Harnack is referring here to the increment of knowledge made possible by the historical approach; and yet he can affirm, with all of his confidence in historical method, that there is "a more excellent way" to discover what is essential:

The thing itself reveals it. We shall see that the Gospel in the Gospel is something so simple, something that speaks to us with so much power, that it cannot easily be mistaken. Comprehensive and methodical directions and general introductions are unnecessary to enable us to find the way to it. No one who possesses a fresh eye for what is alive, and true feeling for what is really great, can fail to see it and distinguish it from its contemporary integument.[174]

One may be permitted some doubt here as to whether Harnack really meant that the discovery of this essential quality of the Gospel was as simple a process as he made it out to be. And one may refer to his own protracted struggle in order to make the point. He declares that anyone "who possesses a fresh eye" and "true feeling" cannot fail to distinguish the kernel from the husk. Yet how does one get this "fresh eye" and "true feeling"? Certainly Harnack made it eminently clear in his correspondence in the seventies and the eighties that gaining this unity and certainty was neither simple nor easy. Indeed, we would argue, it is only on the basis of his particular full-fledged method that his particular conclusions about the reality of Christianity,

[173] *Ibid.*, p. 12.
[174] *Ibid.*

and his particular views on the "fresh eye" could have developed. Which is to say, obliquely, that there is a real involvement of his history and his axiology.

It is important that we note his statement that "Jesus Christ's teaching will at once bring us . . . to a height where its connection with Judaism will appear only a loose one."[175] This follows necessarily from his "kernel" principle, as he quite well realized in his criticism of the eschatological school. But here, against Harnack's judgment that the connection between Jesus' teaching and Judaism was a "loose" one, we may front the judgment of Weiss, one of the pioneers of the eschatological school. In his *Christus: Die Anfänge des Dogmas*, Weiss remarks upon the rapidity with which the Christological doctrine solidified, declaring that "already in the New Testament the principal conceptions of the later dogma are essentially present."[176] How did this come about? "The answer of recent theology is as follows: the speedy development of the Christology . . . was due to the fact that *before* the appearance of Jesus there was a Christology, i.e., a doctrine of the Messiah, . . . already in existence, . . . among the Jews."[177]

Weiss then goes on to comment, "This conception broadly taken is undoubtedly correct, and its full significance ought to be realized."[178] He does not deny the uniqueness of Jesus; indeed,

> the Jewish doctrine . . . could never have turned the longing . . . into joyful certainty that the hope was now fulfilled. . . . This radical change . . . presupposes a power of attraction the strength of which it is impossible to overestimate. . . . Thus at the foundation of the doctrine of Christ, and in every stage of its development, there is a belief in Jesus.[179]

But what he does deny is Harnack's near-Marcionite "Jesus" with his "loose" relation to the historical Judaism of his time. For Weiss believed that even if there were such a "kernel" as Harnack described, it could never be separated out, inasmuch as Jesus was from the beginning regarded as the Messiah, and every record we have was written from that standpoint. The difference in the judgments on this point, when explicated, gives a radically different view of Jesus' place within the Gospel, of his relation to that which preceded him, and of the further development of dogma.

175 *Ibid.*, p. 14.
176 Johannes Weiss, *Christ: The Beginnings of Dogma*, tr. V. D. Davis (London: Philip Green, 1911), p. 12.
177 *Ibid.*
178 *Ibid.*, p. 13.
179 *Ibid.*, pp. 13–14.

A further statement which needs to be examined is one which deals with the relation of "history" and "value"; for it makes abundantly clear the contextual nature of Harnack's approach:

History can only show how things have been; and even where we can throw light upon the past, and understand and criticize it, we must not presume to think that by any process of abstraction, absolute judgments as to the value to be assigned to past events can be obtained from the results of a purely historical survey. Such judgments are the creation only of feeling and of will; they are a subjective act. The false notion that the understanding can produce them is a heritage of that protracted epoch in which knowing and knowledge were expected to accomplish everything; in which it was believed that they could be stretched so as to be capable of covering and satisfying all the needs of the mind and the heart. That they cannot do. This is a truth which, in many an hour of ardent work, falls heavily upon our soul, and yet—what a hopeless thing it would be for mankind if the higher peace to which it aspires, and the clearness, the certainty and the strength for which it strives, were dependent on the measure of its learning and its knowledge.[180]

If one were inclined to employ the proof-text technique, this is the passage to which he would point to make the case that, in the final analysis, Harnack's axiology dominates his history. Yet, from a contextual approach, it is clear that Harnack is here drawing together those emphases which are recurrent throughout his work. The limits of knowledge are respected, even where history is involved; speculation is implicitly rejected; man's voluntary capacity is emphasized above the intellective; the need of men is made determinative; the ethics of aspiration dominate; and "peace," "certainty," "clearness," and "strength" are the ends to which the aspiring man commits himself.

This pressing of all apparent ambiguities into a contextual whole is evident in Harnack's characterization of Jesus. To employ a single example, that dealing with the silence of the sources on Jesus' development till the age of thirty, Harnack turns the *e silentio* argument to good account by declaring what the "negative information" thereby communicated means. It means, first, that it is highly improbable that Jesus went through the rabbinical schools, for he does not speak of technical theological culture, learned in scholarly exegesis; it means, secondly, that he could have had no relations with the Essenes, for his teaching and his action is in many ways the explicit opposite of theirs; and thirdly, it means that Jesus could not have had within his life any stormy crisis or radical breach with the past:

[180] *WC*, p. 16.

In none of his sayings or discourses, whether he is threatening and punishing or drawing and calling people to him with kindness, whether he is speaking of his relation to the Father or to the world, can we discover the signs of inner revolutions overcome, or the scars of any terrible conflict. Everything seems to pour from him naturally, as though it could not do otherwise, like a spring from the depths of the earth, clear and unchecked in its flow.[181]

To all of this, it must be asked how Harnack can possibly *know* this. Or, when he describes Jesus in this way, "He is possessed of a quiet, uniform, collected demeanor, with everything directed to one goal. He never uses ecstatic language, and the tone of stirring prophecy is rare. Entrusted with the greatest of all missions, his eye and ear are open to every impression of the life around him—a proof of intense calm and absolute certainty,"[182] we again want to ask how Harnack can possibly know this. Two answers are possible: either he does not know it, or he has deliberately extruded all elements which conflict with his axiological necessities, and has chosen, with value-explications, those elements which fit these necessities. The answers are not contradictory, and we believe that both are true.

---

2. *Harnack's "Reality"*

It is customary to regard *Das Wesen des Christentums* as the key to Harnack's position. This is valid if the interpretation which follows from it is based on a broader assessment of his work, particularly his method. Often this is not done, and the resultant interpretation runs somewhat as follows: Harnack held to the necessity of subjective interpretation; inasmuch as the Old Testament does not contribute to the present needs which dominate man, according to Harnack, it therefore could have nothing essential to say; the Christian must reject the Old Testament as canon and hold onto the New Testament only; the center of the New Testament is the teaching of Jesus; this teaching can be reduced to three essential statements; when these statements are examined, they all reduce themselves to one basic theme, love. These six propositions are not an unfair summary of the usual "reductive" interpretation of Harnack, and one can, of course, provide documentation for these points from many pages of the lectures.

The interpreters then begin to explicate these interpretations; some

181 *Ibid.*, p. 29.
182 *Ibid.*, p. 31.

have said that Harnack is guilty of *Kulturprotestantismus*, some have said he eviscerated all Christology and regarded Jesus as a nineteenth-century liberal, some have challenged his method, holding that he was simply a "reductive historicist," and most have held that his "essence" must be challenged. We are attempting no grand vindication of Harnack. However, there are clues in Harnack's famous lectures which, when brought to the total corpus of Harnack's work, to the above characterization of his position, and to the listed criticisms, provide a much-needed clarification.

The first clue is to be found in the section which deals with the "proximate" and "final" unity, to which reference has already been made.[183] We quote the relevant portions in more complete form:

That there is a unity underlying this opposition between God and the world is a conviction which can be gained *by experience*; the one realm can be subordinated to the other; but it is only by a struggle that this unity can be attained, and when it is attained it takes the form of a problem that is infinite and only approximately soluble. . . . It is by self-conquest that a man is freed from the tyranny of matter. . . .

We have to do with a dualism which arose we know not how; but as moral beings we are convinced that, as it has been given to us in order that we may overcome it in ourselves and bring it to a unity, so also it goes back to an original unity, and will at last find its reconciliation in the great far-off event, the realised dominion of the Good.

Dreams, it may be said; for what we see before our eyes is something very different. No! not dreams—after all it is here that our true life has its root—but patchwork certainly, for we are unable to bring our knowledge in space and time, together with the contents of our inner life, into the unity of a philosophic theory of the world. It is only in the peace of God which passeth all understanding that this unity dawns upon us.[184]

If one tried to compress this into a single statement, it would emerge somewhat as follows: Man is a moral being who finds himself confronted with two opposing realities, God and the world; he is convinced that there must be an ultimate unity underlying these opposites, and this conviction is buttressed by the experience of struggle by which he seeks to overcome this duality *in* himself; he can overcome the lower of the two realities, the world, and subordinate it to God, achieving a "proximate" inner unity; but this inner unity, when at-

[183] *Supra*, p. 275.
[184] *WC*, pp. 130–131.

tained, does not answer the ultimate problem of the original or the final unity, which remains hidden; only God can bestow the thing itself, the certainty of the final unity, though this is in no sense propositional and cannot therefore unite our space-time knowledge and our achieved inner unity into a philosophically unified theory of the world.

If this is a fair summary of Harnack's quintessential position, it follows: (1) that *love* is not the final category *for man*, but *duty*, love being God's gift of himself; (2) that man's duty is (a) to give himself in unreserved effort to overcome the tyranny of the world as it affects him, and (b) to open himself to the God who is Love, who gives the certainty of final unity; (3) that this duty (2a) can only be fulfilled by knowing history (space-time knowledge) and overcoming it (thus achieving "proximate" unity), but always opposing every too-certain claim that God's gift ("final" unity) can be controlled by man; and finally, (4) that the implications of being "such-and-such" as a man, and not otherwise, are (a) that *Jesus* himself, being a man, could experience the "thing-in-itself" as God's gift, and could personify it, but could not state it in binding propositional formulas, and (b) that the Gospel *for man* is sheer gift (1) in the givens of our moral nature and (2) in that "final" unity which dawns upon us. It follows from this that any faith which synthesizes into itself the necessity to criticize all systems—which the Gospel faith does, being dynamic rather than static—threatens the very existence of any acclaimed once-for-all dogmatic formulation.

Placing this over against the usual characterization of Harnack's position, what are the tenable conclusions at which one may arrive? One could say of these six steps of the hypothetical characterization that none of them is totally false, but, standing naked, they are misleading. On subjectivism: yes, but this must be seen as a reaction against propositional Christianity, as the only pragmatic point of view in a post-Kantian period, and as the necessary corollary of being human. On rejecting the Old Testament: yes, but because it has been superseded by the New, and then only after one has mastered its contents and seen its historical contribution, albeit in the form of husks which initially enclosed the Gospel kernel. On the authority of the New Testament: yes, but not in the orthodox sense of authority, which made too-certain claims about its knowledge, and did not distinguish between the kernel and the husk in the New Testament. On the centrality of the teaching of Jesus: yes, but this does not exclude the fact that one sees in his person the manifestation of the saving element in history, nor that he did not state in propositional form the contents of his experience with God; his teaching then comprises "all that man can say," but in the teaching itself, God remains the giver of unity. On the reduction of Jesus' teaching to three essential statements, and the final reduction to one theme, Love:—

But here, at the crux, we must pause to consider and evaluate just what *Harnack* is saying in this famous identification of the content of Jesus' teaching: this is the second important clue for the understanding of *Des Wesen des Christentums*. We would argue here that Harnack's interpreters did precisely what he had insisted over and over must not be done: they made content-propositions out of these statements, intellectualized them, took them to be the three "ideas"—or the one "idea," Love, if the identification is further distilled—which comprised the Gospel, and thus transformed them into something completely different from that which Harnack had in mind. The question to be asked, therefore, is "How does Harnack develop these three statements"?

First, the kingdom of God and its coming. The very form of statement here is significant. The kingdom of God is not some static substantive entity; it is gerundial. One does not say, "Lo, here," or "Lo, there," of the kingdom. One says, rather, "The kingdom of God comes by *coming* to the individual, by entering into his soul and laying hold of it. . . . Everything that was dramatic in the external or historical sense has vanished. . . . It is not a question of . . . thrones and principalities, but of God and the soul, the soul and God."[185] "Take whatever parable you will . . . God himself is the kingdom."[186] If Harnack is not saying here that God gives *himself* (to men, to be sure), and that this *giving* is the kingdom, then language is deception. If he is saying this, then to make his "kingdom of God" a man-produced entity is grossly inaccurate.

Secondly, God the Father and the infinite value of the human soul. Both of these things—God and the soul—have already been emphasized in the explication which Harnack gives to the first point. Harnack here further indicates that it is in this *relation* that the essence of Christianity is to be "discovered"—if, indeed, "discovered" is an apt word at all. Thus, "the Gospel is in no wise a *positive religion* like the rest; . . . it contains *no statutory or particularistic elements*. . . . To no sphere of earthly life is it confined or necessarily tied down."[187]

[185] *Ibid.*, p. 49. Italics mine.
[186] *Ibid.*
[187] *Ibid.*, p. 54. Italics mine.

What a difference there is between this and the interpreters who made Harnack's "essence" to be "all good work in all good causes." This work is implied, of course; but it is never identified as the Gospel simply because Harnack's "essence" is never related solely to the soul, but is always seen *in relation to* God. The four examples which Harnack gives in this connection all confirm this point.[188]

Thirdly, the higher righteousness and the commandment of love. Again, the form of the statement must be noted, for too often the latter part is taken as an independent entity standing on its own. For Harnack, it is impossible to speak of the actualization of the second commandment, the love of the neighbor, unless this is done in terms of that which has preceded. We do not mean simply the first commandment here, though that is involved, for "to love God" is not possible unless there be a prior dying of the self. Indeed, love is defined as "what remains when the soul dies to itself . . . the new life already begun."[189] This is no mere willed act: it is the *commandment* of love. And this can be actualized only by that attitude of humility which combines religion and morality: "Humility is not a virtue by itself; *it is a purely receptive attitude* . . . in a word, the opening up of the heart to God."[190] It is only after this prior relation has been experienced by the soul, vis-à-vis God, that anything that is good can emerge. To define the ethical in this way is a vastly different thing than to define it as those before Jesus had—and one might add that it is to define it in a different way than most of Harnack's interpreters did.

Does Harnack then "reduce" Jesus' teaching to three essential statements, with a final reduction to one thing, love? If these are made to be three content-statements, no. If these are seen as all emphasizing the central matter with which religion deals, God and the soul, and describing that ultimate and final unity which God is and gives, love, yes.

To employ an analogy which will make clear Harnack's point, we suggest the following: Man is the kind of being who finds himself confronted with a wilderness (the world), but in this situation he is inalienably certain that there is a transcendent power which made both himself and the wilderness. This inalienable certainty (his moral nature) that there is a power within whom there is unity finds substantiation in his own struggles as he attempts to "tame the wilderness." He can "chart the wilderness" (space-time knowledge) and

[188] *Supra*, p. 270.
[189] *WC*, p. 63.
[190] *Ibid.* Italics mine.

achieve a certain conquest over it (overcome the world), thus achieving a proximate level of inner unity. But after he has achieved this preliminary unity, the more fundamental problem—the relation of the "wilderness" and himself in it to the ultimate unity of all things—remains hidden. Only God can give this certainty that there is such a unity, only he can give the unity, and when he does it is not cast in the form of propositional knowledge. Thus "man's taming the wilderness" does *not* provide the categories by which this unity can be described; nor does the coterminous recognition of the power of God, joined with man's moral effort, provide such categories. In short, there are no such categories; the "peace of God" truly passes all understanding. One can say "the wind blows as it will" but he cannot say from whence it comes or whither it goes.

Is this all of Harnack's "Gospel"? What about his statement that in *persons*, preeminently in Jesus, the Gospel is "embodied"? Yet this is just the point for Harnack! For when one looks at the teaching of Jesus, over and over there is this assertion that the kingdom of God is indeed under the law of the spirit; it is God's kingdom, given to those who, *like Jesus*, open themselves to it; it cannot be bound into propositions or dogmas by men who would "help God!" For truly to "help God" and to participate in the "building of the kingdom" would mean to remain open always to the "facts of humanity," on the one hand, and to the certainty that the ultimate transforming unity which is God is unbound, on the other.

What about the assertion which Harnack makes that there *is* a "kernel" and that this kernel is a simple thing? One may communicate here what Harnack is trying to say by pointing out that Einstein held that his theory of relativity was a simple thing, in fact the essence of simplicity. In terms of our analogy, Harnack the forester discovered in the wilderness which is the world that the Gospel "as Jesus preached it" was a "new" thing, coming down from God, and placing upon man an absolute claim not only to show up all other trees as temporal, but to declare just this, that there is a "tree of life." To live in the presence of this "essence" is to find joy, unity, and certainty, but it is also to find that all the trees of the temporal wilderness are exactly that and no more: spatial, temporal constructs. These must be endured, but man's final duty is to that pure and simple "essence." Behold: "The three spheres which we have distinguished . . . coalesce; for *ultimately the kingdom is nothing but the treasure which the soul possesses in the eternal and merciful God.*"[191] This—nothing else—is Harnack's "simple Gospel." For those who want content-statements

[191] *Ibid.*, p. 67.

about the Gospel, this can only be interpreted as "reductionism." For those who hold to the New Testament accounts as "inspired" in some verbal fashion, this can only be seen as "reductionism." For those who have some confidence in the historical reliability of the Gospels, this can only be interpreted as "reductionism." It is understandable in the light of Harnack's statement that he could be charged with "peeling the Gospel" until there was nothing left. But he would certainly answer, "Is 'God and the soul, the soul and God' nothing?"

It is understandable that biblical fundamentalism could rail at this evisceration of all content from the Gospel. But Harnack would inquire, "What can 'inspiration' mean in addition to the relation of God and the soul?" It is understandable that any form of confessionalism would see this "simple" statement as totally destructive of the tradition. But Harnack would answer, "If one leaves 'God and the soul' out of consideration in the forming of Christian tradition, nothing is left." For Harnack did not deny the necessity of historical constructs; he simply insisted that the power which brings forth tradition must be given priority to the tradition itself, else form overcomes faith. It may be objected that this is not fair, that one can take these Augustinian categories as central and still go further to specify what is meant in terms of content and dogmatic statement. Harnack would have held that this is precisely what did happen, and that such a process of encystation is not only the fact, *wie es eigentlich gewesen ist*, but necessary. (At least, it *was* necessary; whether Harnack held that it no longer *is* necessary, or that there were no "husks" in his own formulation is a real problem.)

But one final point needs to be noted here. After declaring what this "simple Gospel" is, Harnack goes on to remark that "it needs only a very little trouble to develop this thought into everything that Christendom has known and strives to maintain."[192] So that this "Barmen Declaration" could be, and was, developed in the history of the Church into those great systems of thought, the philosophies of history, the *Summas*, the creedal statements, the abjuring of creedal statements; around this kernel clustered Christologies, monasticism (intra- and extra-worldly), Papacy and Spirit-mysticism, holy wars and pacifism, Catholicisms Greek, Roman, and Reformed, predestinarians and pealeists; ecumenical conferences met from Jerusalem to Evanston; and the kernel was Romanized, Hellenized, feudalized, Anglicized, Germanized, Americanized, and syncretized, withal. All this from the single simple kernel, "God and the soul, the soul and

[192] *Ibid.*

God"? That is Harnack's thesis. And the demand that man finds to be present within himself as a moral creature is, if he is a historian of Christianity, that he work through every layer, assess every document, evaluate every movement. Only then can an understanding of this "reality"—or, rather, *that* there was and is such a reality which defies all such encystation by asserting itself again and again in a judgmental way upon the husks—be achieved.

We respectfully submit that this is not simple.

We furthermore respectfully submit that the recognition that this is not simple is basic to an evaluation of Adolf Harnack. Generally, this recognition is not accorded him.

PART FIVE

SUMMATION

XV

"Wie mache ich es, sein Jünger zu werden?"

CAN ONE be a Christian (meaning, subjectively, "to be a disciple," and objectively, to be a mediator) in the givens of the nineteenth and twentieth centuries? This is a theological question, to be answered historically. Was the answer "historicist" in presupposition, its unity derived from an individually justified *Humanitätsideal*? What happened to Harnack's symbolic concatenation in succeeding decades, and what is its present valency?

These are the "end" questions. As they are engaged, one assertion must be set forth as dominating the interpretation. Stating this assertion smacks of redundancy, for the attempt to be both fair and accurate in what has preceded has illustrated it literally hundreds of times. But it cannot be too strongly declared that *any attempt to interpret Harnack must resist a unilineal pattern*. The technique of the taxidermist must be rejected, for too many Harnackian "straw-men" have already been constructed. The century was too rich in points of view, and Harnack was too much a man of the century, to declare of him "Lo, here, and lo, there." Out of all the particulars thus far presented, there emerges a picture of many shades and colors. One cannot single out a sole feature by which to interpret Harnack, as Rolffs understood when he made his simple statement that "a personality can never be a pure type."[1]

One may be permitted the expression of a regret that the purposes of this work do not allow as much attention to "Harnack the human being" as one would like, subjectively, to accord him. The biography of his daughter, however personally oriented, reveals a man of strong and warm sympathy and understanding, one to whom the imitation of Christ, as he apprehended him, was a steady and dominant passion. Harnack's "humanity" may be briefly indicated here by citing three vignettes. Holl wrote this personal tribute, after the publication of *Das Wesen des Christentums*:

> It does me good that I have once again been confronted, in your lectures, with that form. In the last few years I have stood in dread of coming to terms . . . with Jesus. . . . There above all I have traced the power which is not of the world or of time . . . . I thank you for more than the gift of a book, and I hope that these lectures will find many hearers who will recover, through them, the simple joy and the simple sense of the glory of Christianity.[2]

The second vignette, set late in 1918, after the armistice had been signed, shows Harnack in a well-nigh unique character: playing solitaire in the evening, his existence so troubled and so impersonal that he wished to end the day without thought and without feeling.[3] And finally, a touch of his humanity from 1923, when he was seventy-one years old: surprised by Archbishop Söderblom, in whose home he was visiting, playing with the children and conversing with them "in a way such as only the reality and the simplicity of genius . . . knows how to do."[4]

This was "the man," on the personal level. It would be untrue to him and to the purpose for which this book has been written, to dwell on these and other personal qualities.[5] For he himself resisted spying into the motives of children, friends, and opponents alike, believing

[1] *Harnack's Wesen* . . . , p. 5.

[2] AZH, pp. 243–244.

[3] AZH, p. 509.

[4] *Ibid.*, p. 505.

[5] One further moving tribute, that of Dietrich Bonhoeffer, spoken at Harnack's grave: "Harnack was concerned with the veracity of the answers given. We learned from him that truth will only be born out of freedom. We saw in him the protagonist for freely expressing what was once perceived truly. We saw in him the man who shaped his judgment anew again and again, and gave expression to it most clearly notwithstanding the anxious narrowness of the multitudes." *Gesammelte Schriften*, III, p. 60, in The Chicago Theological Seminary *Register*, LI, 2 (Feb. 1961), p. 5.

that this was a violation of independence and freedom; and, on the other hand, this work is not biography, and he knew as well as any historian the difference between biography and history.

But, as is true elsewhere, so here: rubrics harden easily and quickly, and they falsify. To interpret this man as a kind of "scholarly computer," from whom over sixteen hundred objective items flowed during the course of his life, is to miss the naïveté, the poignancy, and the rich humanity of him. It is to forget, possibly, that with an astounding singleness of purpose and dedication he pursued *the* question of his youth throughout those sixteen hundred productions and through his multiform activities. It is to pass by the fact, so very clear in the daughter's biography, that there was a higher unity in this life which transcended the dichotomies suggested in the separations which have been methodologically necessary in describing his role as a maker of modern theology.

But we must reluctantly turn to a consideration of this role, and we begin by adverting to the legacy he left to a country more open, on the whole, to his interpretation of Christianity, than was his adopted homeland. Few American Christians who were born in the first three decades of the twentieth century have failed to be influenced, in small or great ways, by the theological interpretations which he represented. From his first American disciple, Arthur Cushman McGiffert, who studied with him at Berlin and returned to disseminate, through the influential presidency of the Union Theological Seminary in New York, his point of view, to the other hundreds of Americans who took the pilgrimage, a steady and impressive influence manifested itself on American thought. Without ascribing the entire influence of "liberal" theological thought to him, he was its representative man, and the categories in which thousands of American Christians view their faith are the categories which he set forth in a most trenchant expression. "The Jesus of history and the Christ of faith," "all crosses which stand in the service of the brother," the subordination of theology to an ethic of life, and "the essence of Christianity"—all of these, in differing emphasis and cadence, to be sure, became the shibboleths of a second and third generation of legatees.

If we judge that the heritage is ambiguous; if we point out that there were fateful consequences for a pragmatically oriented American theological tradition in this rich Germanic infusion; if it is certain that later emphases of a "neo-orthodox" variety challenged and in part overcame the liberalism he represented, this is not to "answer" or to derogate the position he represented. It is simply to say that his influence and genius is demonstrated, whatever the epigons may have made of him, by the fact that it was *his* position that had to be dealt with.

Subjectively, that position was dominated by the question which heads this chapter. The question was fateful—in no pejorative sense whatever—in that it was answerable, in his givens, only by a particular method. The method was "historical"; but the question was "theological," ultimately. The attempt to separate history and theology into two discrete compartments proved to be, by the nature of the subsuming question, unfulfilled. For the moment that the boundary between historical investigation, on the one hand, and Christian affirmation (for oneself) and witness (in the culture) on the other hand, is approached, commitments of a substantive kind dominate and overcome. The historical method, in the latter years, took this into account by introducing the concept of a "regal, judging" function. It was never absent from the beginning, though covert: for the existential question was never absent. Can one be a Christian in the givens of the nineteenth and twentieth centuries? As Bach was reported to have superscribed on every page of composition "*Ad majorem gloriam Dei*," so this man can be truly read if one sees as the superscription on every page, "Wie mache ich es, sein Jünger zu werden?"

The attempt to answer the question by a "nisus to essence" procedure has been declared a failure by many modern theologians. Several comments may be made thereto. There is a widespread misconception regarding the attempt because of plain semantic confusion. Loisy and Tillich, among the giants, chide Harnack for employing a philosophical category—essence—at the same time that he generally rejects philosophical language and analysis. The criticism is little and carping. "Wesen" must be represented as meaning what the total corpus reveals it to mean; *not* philosophical "essence," but living reality. Furthermore, it is instructive that a nineteenth-century contemporary, *au courant* in contemporary theological fashions, *also* took this question of "being a Christian" as his most existential question. He took a vastly different approach, and he found the "one thing" that must be willed to be a different thing. Perhaps "givens" and "presuppositions" were controlling there also.[6] And finally, one may

[6] "One is to suffer; the other is to become a professor of the fact that another suffered.

The first is 'the way'; the second goes round about (the proposition 'about' is so aptly used for lectures and sermons) and perhaps it ends by going down." *The Journals of Søren Kierkegaard*, a selection edited and translated by Alexander Dru (London: Oxford University Press, 1938), p. 528.

comment that "the moderns" betray more dependence on the "nisus to essence" procedure than they fittingly should, hammering Harnack as they do. Thus "the liberal theologians succeeded in restating the kerygma only at the cost of eliminating or at least obscuring *its very center*."[7] Particularly, when one recalls that incredibly full examination of the sources, the question of the validity of a historical approach (intersticed with theological presuppositions) against a theological approach (intersticed with historical presuppositions) should give any modern substantial pause.

Vantage points differ; what may appear patently obvious to a succeeding generation may have been, in truth, completely absent from a former view. That this is true, liberalism's "representative man" illustrates by his own charge, in the early years of this century, that the critics who were his contemporaries were destroying the substance of the Gospel by reductionism: "By this method [*hysteron-proteron*] of destructive analysis we are left at last with only the critic himself; for, considering the likeness which naturally existed between the circumstances of the first disciples and of the later community, it is possible with very little trouble to object to everything . . ."[8] The fact that he could make this charge is proof-positive that in his own identification of "the reality of Christianity" he did *not* regard his method as reductionistic. And we have tried to suggest (in the chapter on "The Reality of Christianity") that the "essence" or "reality" applies much more to the *procedure* than to that which it discovers; for when discovered, this "reality" is revealed to be a dynamic life principle rather than a static substance.

Finally, on this matter of "being a Christian" and discovering what that means by a nisus to essence procedure (the two are inextricably intertwined for Harnack), it is fair to ask what the vantage point of the interpreter sees as the resolution. In short, we believe the key term is "context." To illustrate: John Burnaby, in his magnificent study of St. Augustine's teaching on the love of God, concludes his work with this relevant statement:

> We may either attempt to reduce the complexity and vagueness of the term to a single "clear and distinct idea," by analyzing, isolating, defining: this and this and this is called love, is confused with love, but Love itself, Auto-Agape, is none of these, it is That and That alone. Or we may, provisionally, acquiesce in the multiplicity, the apparent hotch-potch of dissimilarities which strive to cover themselves with Love's mantle, and

[7] Schubert Ogden, *Christ without Myth* (New York: Harper & Row, 1961), p. 41.

[8] Harnack, *Sayings of Jesus*, p. 205.

ask whether after all they may be parts of an organic whole, aspects of a single spiritual reality.[9]

Simply put, Harnack attempted the first procedure described by Burnaby; he thereby arrived at a reality—"the treasure which the soul possesses in the eternal and merciful God"—which, as he described it, turned out to be not only a "multiplicity" in itself but pregnant of other "realities." To say, for example, "the thing itself, therefore the Gospel," is to utter a contradiction. Troeltsch quite correctly understood this in evaluating, along with other claimed "essences," Harnack's "the biblical preaching concerning the kingdom of God interpreted in terms of Kantian ethics"[10]:

In none of these cases can the idea of Christianity be regarded as the actual unity of all the factors in the historical development. The nature of Christianity cannot be determined in this fashion, for a genuinely historical point of view reveals to us such a variety of interpretations, formulations, and syntheses that no single idea or impulse can dominate the whole.[11]

This, we believe, is correct.

But such a confession—at ground it is that—ought not to be too proud to admit its own possibility of error, and in particular it ought not to blind one to the solid results that emerged from the Harnackian alternative. Harnack's fate is not dissimilar to that of Hegel: the principle of his own system ultimately overcame his system. To say that subsequent history overcame his history is to say that his "real Christianity" was judged as one relativity beside others—but it is to say it on the basis of his principle. One may illustrate this point by referring to the "Guiding Principles for the Interpretation of the Bible" compiled by the Ecumenical Study Conference held at Oxford in 1949.[12] As at Aarau, with Karl Barth, there would have been few points where Harnack would have agreed with the biblical scholars assembled at Oxford. Though they may have been standing upon his shoulders, the climate for understanding the Bible had radically shifted. Not only is the "unity of the Old and the New Testaments" clearly asserted,[13] but the "necessary theological presuppositions" set forth (which, in itself, Harnack would hardly have sanctioned)

[9] John Burnaby, *Amor Dei. A Study of the Religion of St. Augustine* (London: Hodder and Stoughton, 1938), p. 301.

[10] Troeltsch, "The Dogmatics . . . ," p. 12.

[11] *Ibid.*

[12] Richardson and Schweitzer, *op. cit.*, pp. 240–243.

[13] *Ibid.*, p. 241.

speak of "an authoritative claim,"[14] of interpreting the Old Testament in the light of "the Incarnate Word of God, from which arises the full Trinitarian faith of the Church,"[15] and of the recognition of a "divinely established . . . correspondence between some events and teachings of the Old and of the New Testament."[16] The point is, of course, that Harnack's kind of historically oriented understanding of the Bible has been accepted, assimilated, diastasized in part, and superseded by "theological" interpretation. And no matter how much one may try to rid himself of the influence of contemporary interpretation, it is impossible to accomplish this completely. Certainly Harnack's own work continually reminds us to what an extent we are prisoners of a *Geist*.

His work also reminds us of the dangers of any contemporary self-proclaimed absolute standpoint, however strong its claim to be true to "*the* biblical kerygma." We agree as we must with this or that "demythologized" Gospel; and if the Christ that we see is neither the "modernized Jesus" of liberalism nor the "archaized Jesus" (if so it be) of the eschatological school, nor the "demythologized Jesus" of the Bultmannian school, it will be Jesus as seen *sub specie temporis*. The grand coup of those who announce that "we must be faithful to the biblical kerygma," as valid as the principle is, also does not escape this judgment. For is it not, on its own admission, an attempt to identify the essential, the real? Does it not seek the kernel behind the husk, demythologizing in order to remythologize? Is it not an attempt to mediate to "a world come of age" the eternally relevant? And is its question, then, other than the question "Can one be a Christian?" or, more subjectively stated, "Wie mache *ich* es, sein Jünger zu werden?"

On the objective side, the existential question requires of a person that he should be an apologist to those who misunderstand or maintain an attitude of neutrality toward Christianity. This "mediatory" role is a double one in the case of Harnack, for in his "working through to the inner form" he first sought to speak to those within the Church. It is not unfair to say that he judged that he failed, though the extent to which his own views became *de rigueur* in a later time suggest that he underestimated his role here. The second part of his "mediatory" role, involving the culture, set as its purpose the transformation of that culture by bringing it into a living relation—through

[14] *Ibid.*, p. 240.
[15] *Ibid.*, p. 241.
[16] *Ibid.*

persons—with the Gospel. We have tried to make clear how wide-ranging this urge to transformation was by paying extended attention to the milieu within which Harnack developed and worked. This, indeed, was a part of the method which he himself employed in the interpretation of the rise and development of Christianity: to master the cultural givens of an epoch. A cataloguing of Harnack's activities can hardly convey the breadth of this cultural participation. It is almost a case of applying the "You name it, he did it" motto.

But the catalogue or the motto may leave an uncomfortable suspicion of dilettantism: vocation, historian; "second vocation," librarian; "third vocation," president of the Kaiser-Wilhelm Gesellschaft; Rector of the University of Berlin; president of the Evangelical-Social Congress; privy counselor to the Kaiser; editor; lecturer on everything; etc., etc. From the two offers to a chair at Harvard—when the mediation within the Church was not going well—to the offer in 1921 of the ambassadorship to the United States—when Harnack embodied the Germanic culture in his own person—the evidence of his attempt to bring knowledge and life into a Christian synthesis is overwhelming. "A suspicion of dilettantism"—but that only. There is no word *less* appropriate to apply to him. One may fault him if one so desires for his multidirectional attempts at mediation; but a careful reading of the seven volumes of the *Reden und Aufsätze* is a humbling experience, and any trace of suspicion of shallowness disappears.[17]

The apologetic, to be sure, is never blatantly proclaimed; indeed, insofar as the formal definition of that theological discipline is concerned, Harnack rightly disclaims his role as apologist for Christianity. But this is to restrict the term too narrowly. If one defines the purpose of apologetic as von Engelhardt did (to demonstrate "the uniqueness of Christianity . . . over against the common qualities of all other modes of thought," to show "the inner consistency of Christianity over against the contradictions . . . of all other systems," and to

[17] There are thirteen categories of articles in the index to the series. The numbers in parentheses after each category will indicate how many articles are in that category for the entire series: I. On general theory of knowledge and cultural history (18); II. Academy, University and Library (20); III. School (4); IV. On general scientific questions concerning history, religion and the Church (18); V. Primitive Christianity and early church history (33); VI. Medieval and modern church history and church policy (15); VII. The Catholic Church (12); VIII. The social question (12); IX. Politics and the World War (17); X. Congratulations (4); XI. In memoriam (23); XII. Holiday meditations and sermons (13); and XII. Autobiographical (8).

demonstrate "the universality of Christianity . . . by showing that the religious and ethical ideals of the non-Christian world are realized in Christianity")[18] it is clear that in this regard also Engelhardt was the master.

Set, as he was, in a century rich in points of view, Harnack was bequeathed a number of problems of theological, philosophical, and historical character. Harnack's elemental problem was set (was not this true of every Christian thinker after 1800?) by the particular issue of the battle that raged around Immanuel Kant. Materialism was the *bête noir*, that view of life which threatened, with its naturalistic monism, any "*geistige*" interpretation of life. Kant had raised "the problem of the continuity between the Ego and the World,"[19] but he had not answered it. The Idealists took it up, seeking "to affirm the primacy of *Geist* in human life,"[20] thereby fronting their own monism to that of the ever more powerful materialistic monists. William James has summarized, sparely but classically, the results of such an approach when applied to the theological task.[21] What theology should have done, after Kant, was to reorient "the task and content of theology by new reference to the centrality of faith rather than of reason."[22] What it did was to seek in philosophical reasoning an answer to the naturalistic challenge. Harnack, however unwillingly, is to be placed here in the stream of the Idealists and the romantics, seeking to defend monistic "spirit" against monistic "nature."

To be sure, his was not an affirmed philosophical position; nor was it, even, centrally an affirmed theological position. The commitments

[18] A. H. Newman, "Engelhardt, Gustav Moritz Konstantin von," *The New Schaff-Herzog Encyclopedia of Religious Knowledge* (Grand Rapids: Baker Book House, 1958), IV, p. 130.

[19] Pelikan, *From Luther . . .*, p. 101.

[20] *Ibid.*

[21] "First, there is a healthy faith that the world must be rational and self-consistent. . . . Next, we find a loyal clinging to the rationalist belief that sense-date and their associations are incoherent, and that only in substituting a conceptual order for their order can truth be found. Third, the substituted conceptions are treated intellectualistically, as mutually exclusive and discontinuous, so that the first innocent continuity of the flow of sense-experience is shattered for us without any higher conceptual continuity taking its place. Finally, since this broken state of things is intolerable, the absolute *deus ex machina* is called on to mend it in his own way, since we cannot mend it in ours." Quoted by Pelikan in *From Luther . . .*, p. 102, from Willliam James, *A Pluralistic Universe* (New York: Longmans, Green & Co., 1943), p. 72.

[22] Pelikan, *From Luther . . .*, p. 99.

are covert, but the evidence of their presence throughout Harnack's work is indisputable. How often does he evoke the spirit as the realm of true unity, breaking the power of that stark and near-Buddhist nature which is about us! And how assiduously does he insist, in his theology, that *Lebenserfahrung*, the ethical *Humanitätsideal*, is the true content, the reality of Christianity. This he "received" from Ritschl; but this he developed, on his own terms, as the way to overcome the world. And the world that is to be overcome is the "natural" spiritless world of the materialists.

Where the antimony of nature and spirit is dominant as problem, and where unity is to be sought in the higher realm of spirit, any crassly historical "event"—such as "Jesus of Nazareth"—*must* be endowed with whatever particular qualities of *Geist* are required. That *Geist*, for Harnack, was ethical: that is the theological presupposition, and the criterion. Fatefully, in such a circumstance, no document from the past can serve as norm; nothing can serve as norm save inner experience. After the publication of the first volume of the *Dogmengeschichte*, Adolf Lasson criticized the "modern school" for using the New Testament only as source, but not as norm for the determination of its view of Christianity. Harnack annotated his copy of Lasson's criticism, at the point where he referred to "the one-sided and confused conceptions in Paul and John" and "the authentic words of the Lord as transmitted by the Synoptists"[23] with a "Yes" and triple exclamation points.[24] His claim to find a norm in "the authentic words" is misleading, as Loisy understood, and as two generations of New Testament scholarship since Harnack have not been reticent to point out. Loofs, indeed, wrote to him after the publication of the *Marcion*, making the point: "Whoever knows as well as you do the heavy weight of tradition cannot really mean that the demand [which you have made for the twentieth century] is feasible."[25] Loofs referred to Harnack's judgment on the canonicity of the Old Testament; but the point of his comment is that tradition has been underestimated by Harnack, and this is as true in its shaping power as in its binding power. For what the tradition, *nolens volens*, had taken as fundamental, were two other categories than those which Harnack took as fundamental. For the tradition, the categories were God and Man. For Harnack the categories were nature and spirit. The tradition was, of course, ambiguous in its development. But it pointed to a kerygma

[23] AZH, p. 142.
[24] *Ibid.*, p. 143.
[25] *Ibid.*, p. 513.

for which Jesus *was* a part of his own Gospel, as the revelation of God to man.

This kerygma, with *its* fundamental categories, presupposed the exercise of faith, and the explication of this faith in many ways—of which reason was only one. But it did not separate the problem of faith and reason. The kerygma is the judge of the church and its cultus, its dogma, its organization. If, in the process of exercising its regal function, particular postures and contingent formulations are revealed as temporal, it still maintains its "I am" character, being what it is. As Ogden has put it, "the theology of the last forty years has . . . sought to find its way back to a simple acceptance of the New Testament message."[26]

Contrariwise, Harnack's basic categories, as we have remarked, were nature and spirit. Where this is so, reason takes preeminence, and faith is treated, if at all, as an inviolate realm of mystery into which one cannot enter. To speak of Jesus as the kerygma spoke, "God has made him both Lord and Christ," "God raised him," or, as the later tradition was to declare, "Very God of Very God, Very Light of Very Light, begotten, not created," was to violate the silence which Harnack thought appropriate where mystery was involved. Faith and reason, as Theodosius Harnack saw, were thereby separated. And on the ground of what was a consistent antispeculative position, Harnack made the case for the uniqueness of Christianity and the centrality of Jesus by giving this faith and its great prophet preeminent status above all men as a unique religious and ethical teacher.

Thus, for Harnack, the Kantian problem of the continuity between the Ego and the world is accepted as *the* problem. The answer to the problem reiterates the presupposition bound within it: that there is, at every level, continuity. "The same mind is at work in history and in us." Between heaven and earth, not an absolute qualitative distinction, but connections and developments and interrelationships. But it is not even "between heaven and earth," or "between God and man"—it is "between nature and spirit." In effect God's ontal status is set aside as mystery; his value is his value for men, as judged by "the clear eye." But it does not matter, truly, what the judging faculty is; for it is not, ever, a faculty "judged" and "redeemed" *von oben*, ἐν χριστῷ. That would be mystery.

What the setting of the century gave him, beyond the philosophical problem and the theological attempts to overcome it (either by rejecting it, as in the case of the orthodox, or attacking it from a dif-

[26] Ogden, *op. cit.*, p. 42.

ferent direction, as with Schleiermacher and his followers on the one hand, or Baur and his followers on the other) was a relatively new and shining weapon with which to fight: the weapon of history. Harnack's commitment to a historical method, when the conditions are set as we have described them, and when one is studying "Christianity," inevitably brings forth complications. No matter what the disagreements with Harnack as to point of view and interpretation, it should first be emphasized that with a consummate and single skill and devotion he gave himself to this task. In a lecture on education, a subject which at all levels occupied much of his attention, he quotes Mommsen's character-portrayal of Kaiser Wilhelm I, a portrayal which is alike applicable to him:

> The Emperor William was, as all true men should be, a man with a profession. He completely mastered the duties belonging to it, and, as his high calling as a soldier demanded, he spent his life in the theory and practice of military science. There are not many who have as seriously devoted the years of youth and manhood alike to the art of war as he did. Consequently he was amateurish in nothing.[27]

But having attended to his genius, it is still necessary to raise the question as to the suitability of his particular approach to the subject he would study.

If Harnack was a man of his time, a "representative man" insofar as theological liberalism is concerned, he was also a man of his time with respect to the historical method he employed. Adolf Keller has called this method "reductive historicism."[28] Troeltsch has agreed to the "historicist" label for Harnack, but insisted that one must go beyond this in order to understand the full richness of Harnack's position. A true heir of the more defensible contributions of historicism, Harnack led a great army of trained philologists in the recovery and editing of important ancient texts. His insistence on the inviolability of the canons of historical-critical methodology made possible an understanding of the historical character of Christianity which had been previously impossible. This is, without any doubt, his great contribution, and the great contribution of liberalism. Though his concept of history was less Hebraic than is demanded if one is to understand the biblical emphasis on particularity—thereby making possible the addition of a non-Hebraic anthropocentric norm—yet his

[27] Harnack and Herrmann, *Essays on the Social Gospel*, p. 132.

[28] In Review of *Adolf von Harnack*, by Agnes von Zahn-Harnack, *Review of Religion*, I (Jan. 1937), p. 184.

absolute fidelity to *historical* givenness made possible the alternative theological interpretations which have flowered in recent decades. Whatever one may think of the determinative principle of interpretation employed in the *Dogmengeschichte*, for example, it is simply undebatable that this is a monument of historical scholarship.[29] No contemporary biblical theologian, therefore, can with good conscience impugn Harnack's importance.

We believe that it may be argued that after the turn of the century, Harnack became increasingly concerned to synthesize all that his historical labor had achieved into a unity. Troeltsch suggests that an increasing Hegelian passion for a penetration to the *Geist* characterizes Harnack in this latter period. Yet it must be insisted here that what was present in the latter years, this passion for unity, was never entirely absent. Harnack from the beginning bore within himself a tension which may be as near the key to his riddle as one will ever come: the tension between historicist method on the one hand, and his doctrine of humanity, in which his axiological norm was embedded, on the other.

One of the most suggestive criticisms that can be brought against Harnack is contained in the statement that "he should have recognized the inevitability of theological formulation, and deliberately sought to bring his method and his historical studies into rapport with a definite theological base."[30] Lacking this recognition—or at least regarding it in his time as subversive of the historian's vocation, a covert norm filled the vacuum. This became his "theological position," claimed or not. The result may not have been the unmixed curse it is usually represented to be. For when one considers the contribution which Harnack made in his time on the basis of this separation of history and "speculative theology," a much fairer evaluation results. Yet, whereas many of those who shared this "liberal" outlook with Harnack in the seventies and eighties were, increasingly after 1900, and in a flood-tide in the latter years of his life, recognizing the necessity to make one's method comport with the theological base, as well as with the data one hopes to interpret, Harnack adamantly insisted on the separation of one's own beliefs from the "scientific-historical" task. Thus, as we have seen, he could preface

[29] Might it not be accurate to say that Harnack's *Lehrbuch der Dogmengeschichte*, in its conception and development, is a work of the nineteenth-century historical spirit on the ground of Harnack's *Lebensideal*?

[30] I owe this felicitous statement to Professor J. C. Rylaarsdam of the University of Chicago Divinity School faculty.

his study of dogma, written in the eighties, with the assertion, speaking of the "standpoint of the author," that "in a historical work there is no room for such enquiry."[31] And near the end of his life his open letter to Barth and the dialectical theologians indicated that he had not changed his position.

Finally, how far would Harnack admit that his own formulation was under the judgment of his own principle of judgment? If it is true, as Pauck puts it, that "one cannot say anything at all about the nature of Christianity except in terms of historical evidence," can it then be said "in terms of historical evidence," that "no historical form can fully or definitely represent it"?[32] Or does this latter statement indicate a very real and important Kantian presupposition? Is there then a covert norm operating, not only in terms of his practical work, but also to some degree with respect to his historical work? And, most fatefully, is this norm of such a nature that it actually determines the way in which historical evidence will be interpreted? Specifically, does not "overcome history by history" imply as the fundamental problem "man against nature" rather than "man under God" as in biblical faith? And if the problem is stated in this way, must not the nineteenth-century situation demand the answer of *Kulturprotestantismus*? Another form for the "reality," relative as are all others? But perhaps "reductive historicism" will not see that it also is relative, under God. Certainly this would account for Harnack's confession that the theology expressed by Karl Barth communicated nothing to him: "I would never have believed," he wrote to Rade in 1929, "that any speculation could arise among us for which I possess no antenna."[33]

Yet having said all one can say about "covert norms," it is still true that the Christian theologian must be a historian, for the revelation to which Christianity points, however interpreted, is a historical person. With that sentence no theologian would disagree; on the precise definitions of the various terms, and the relative weightings, however, few theologians would agree. Harnack and Loisy would agree on the centrality of Jesus of Nazareth; but for Harnack the centrality is found in the "reality" of the Christianity he preached, for Loisy in the redemption he effected as God's incarnate Word. Both appealed to history. For Loisy the history was borne by the tradition, and inevitably it must be understood through the tradition. Harnack

[31] Harnack, *History of Dogma*, English translation, I, p. vii.
[32] Pauck, *op. cit.*, p. 345.
[33] AZH, p. 534.

described this as "overcoming history by dogma." For Harnack the history was hidden behind the tradition, as kernel is hidden by husk. Loisy characterized this as a systematic method of investigation, but not the definition of a historical reality. Barth and Harnack would agree on the centrality of Jesus of Nazareth for theological vocation; but for Barth, theology is *ministerium verbi divini*—the service of the Word of God.[34] This means that "the theologian is not there in his own right to judge the message preached by the Church, as though in his private philosophy he possessed the supreme norm of truth."[35] For Harnack, the *sola fide* principle, as understood in the light of the teaching of Jesus, *is* quintessentially the message that the Church should preach, and must be so proclaimed by the faithful theologian though he speak it, in any given circumstance, against the Church.

Are we then at double-checkmate? It would indeed appear so, and yet, without attempting a Harnackian mediation, certain points may be gently set forth. In the first place, there is common agreement among these three theologians, and all Christian theologians, that it is "this history and not another" to which the theologian is responsible. In itself, that location of revelation is an act of faith. Second, there is agreement that this responsibility to the revelation is to be exercised "for the Church and for the world." That is implicit in the revelation itself. Third, there is agreement that this cultural responsibility is not to be exercised in such a way as to compromise or to corrupt the content of the revelation. Within these three agreements, particular interpretations vary widely, and bring forth charges of betrayal, inconsistency, and contradiction. Yet no historically oriented theologian will deny the "cutting" effect of Barth's witness in the early years of the 1930's;[36] and no systematically oriented theologian can deny the contribution of Harnack the historian.[37] Finally, the "enfolding into a single party"[38] is not a work of man.

But a further complication regarding Harnack's history must be considered. Is he liable to the same charge placed against some of his most eminent contemporaries—Burckhardt, Croce, Dilthey, and Troeltsch, for example—the charge of historicism?

[34] Mackintosh, *op. cit.*, p. 272.
[35] *Ibid.*, pp. 273–274.
[36] Daniel Day Williams, *What Present-Day Theologians Are Thinking*, (New York: Harper & Row, 1952), p. 21.
[37] See Chap. XIV, note 155.
[38] See Chap. XI, note 135.

There is a trap here which we hope to avoid. Thus far, we have sought to interpret Harnack on the basis of fairly explicit texts and statements which he made, i.e., inductively. To "define" historicism is in itself a difficulty, and any definition will then force us to deductive model building. Let it be. Yet there is a larger purpose for asking the question here, and it is that a final estimate of Harnack's approach must risk a judgment as to the prognosis for revival. There are evidences in contemporary theological circles that such a revival may be in the offing. If so, it is important to assess Harnack's historical understanding and method from the standpoint of the question: has it, at points, elements which are inimical to Christian theological understanding?

In a brilliant introduction to a translation of portions of the seventh volume of Dilthey's collected works, H. P. Rickman distinguishes between the method of the historicists and historicism as a *Weltanschauung*.[39] *Qua* method, "historicists claimed that everything human beings have done, thought, believed and produced is accessible to historical treatment and that the field of historical study is, therefore, the whole of human reality in time."[40] In taking this position, they claimed that objectivity was possible. Further, the historicists rejected "all rigid unhistorical concepts, all fixed starting points outside history."[41] But what of the charge that the point of view of the historian is itself conditioned by time and circumstance? The historicist of course believes what he believes, and holds certain moral, political and religious convictions. Recognizing this, he seeks always to extrude them; Rickman believes (I do not) that this is *de facto* possible. Historicism as a method is, then, "an empirical and undogmatic approach to the multiplicity of factors and their varied interrelations in history."[42]

Historicism as *Weltanschauung* is a different matter: here the historicists "interpret their methodological principles as ultimate metaphysical truths about reality."[43] Relativism thereby rears its head, and nihilism follows soon after, for where is the constant of "independent moral conviction"? Is one not "condemned to sceptical inactivity, or, worse still, are we not tempted into a type of higher

[39] Wilhelm Dilthey, *Pattern and Meaning in History*, (New York: Harper & Row, 1962). Introduction by Rickman, pp. 11–63.

[40] *Ibid.*, pp. 53–54.

[41] *Ibid.*, p. 54.

[42] *Ibid.*, p. 56.

[43] *Ibid.*, pp. 56–57.

opportunism, into bowing down before the forces which seem to be carried vigorously by the tendencies of history?"[44] Dilthey's counterattack on this point affirms on the one hand that "respect for individuality is the anchorage of moral judgments and is not subject to historical relativity,"[45] and on the other that "the relativity of values is only the reverse of the coin of man's creative freedom."[46]

It is evident from this brief characterization that Harnack would not have accepted unreservedly either the historicist method or the historicist *Weltanschauung*. Certainly on the latter there is little reason to pause, although it is of interest to note that, rejecting the relativism of the historicist view, he yet emphasized the two desiderata of Dilthey's counterattack. On the method, there is more to be said. We are too familiar with Harnack's continuous insistence on looking at questions "solely from the standpoint of history" to declare him innocent. He could have and would have agreed with every one of the statements just made on method, except one: that the historian must be self-consciously aware of his own point of view and extrude it from his historiography. One aches for such a statement from Harnack—and does not find it.

Yet perhaps one final comment is needed here. The matter is not so simple as accepting Rickman's characterization, finding Harnack mainly innocent, and acquitting him. Others—Popper, for example[47]—have found historicism to contain other elements, and of these a word needs to be said. Insofar as historicism—on either level—is concerned with development, with purpose, with a necessary continuity, Harnack verges. Insofar as it affirms an immanent meaning within history itself, a progress in realizing this meaning and a predictive capacity, Harnack can be, formally, judged "not guilty." But the formal judgment is possible *because* he intruded into his history that which he himself would not have held should be intruded into his history—his axiological norm, and the judgments that emerge from the employment of this norm. We are saying, then, that had he been consistent with his own professed objectivity, he would be a poor guide. Too many qualities are there—perhaps they are there as a result of the Dorpat-Erlangen influences—which wreak havoc with a simple historicist approach.

[44] *Ibid.*, p. 57.
[45] *Ibid.*, p. 58.
[46] *Ibid.*, p. 59.
[47] Karl R. Popper, *The Poverty of Historicism* (New York: Harper & Row, 1964).

So we return to the union of history and theology through the *Humanitätsideal*, to raise a series of questions. If "overcoming history by history" involves, in the latter sense of "history," a *Lebensweisheit*, is this "rich, deep, and many-sided wisdom" as much a prepossession as that of which he accused the orthodox? Certainly. In his definition of "historical" is there any *a priori* assertion which is itself not historically validated; or—differently expressed—when one says "*Homo sum*," is not a "committing" faculty as well as an intellective faculty assumed? We believe the answer is "yes" to both questions. To what degree were the cultural givens of nineteenth-century Germany determinative of the judgments which Harnack made, first as to fact, and second as to value? We have suggested elsewhere that a high degree of influence was exercised by these givens. To what degree was Harnack a pragmatist? Obviously, as is indicated by his assertion, "That alone is true which is fruitful,"[48] to a high degree. Was his "standard of value" won from history itself, as he claimed, independently of religion? We agree with Troeltsch that it was not, and that Harnack counterpoised a contemporary norm. Can he, as he claims, get at the "reality of Christianity"? He can get at "a" reality, surely enough. But the fact that he *assumes* that there is a reality is at least as instructive as his attempt to isolate it.

For it is in the assumption, operating at the presuppositional and therefore not evocable level, that the Kantian-Goethean-Ritschlian norm works and sways and determines. The Kantian influence lies mainly in the emphasis on *value-for-man*, in the identification of religion as almost entirely ethical. The Goethean influence is especially fateful because it is here, apparently, that Harnack's "anthropocentric quest" finds its immediate source. Harnack can, in his crucial essay on "Christ as Redeemer," identify the "struggle for God and redemption" with the Goethean "struggle between belief and unbelief," and refer to this as "the real theme of history," remarked by Goethe, and confirmed by "the penetrating eye of the historian."[49]

Yet there is a transmutation here; Kantian moralism and Goethean romanticism, unbaptized, cannot provide the efficacy for contemporary Christianity which is demanded. And that the discovery of this efficacy constituted Harnack's central purpose cannot be denied. It is here that Ritschl's influence must be emphasized. Harnack remained knowledgably a Ritschlian in his emphasis on the necessity of one's participation in the Christian fellowship as a condition for understanding the history of Christianity and contributing to a contemporary

[48] AZH, p. 547.
[49] Harnack, *et al., The Atonement in Modern . . .*, p. 113.

repristination of genuine "kernel" Christianity. To be sure, the Church gave him little opportunity to implement this conviction by action, and he had to make his impact felt through his writings. One must, of course, say the same thing with respect to Harnack's many-sided cultural activity, for here also he believed that man could overcome the contemporary threats to Christianity and the higher life only by transmuting the values of the culture and rejecting the nihilistic elements. The question becomes again, therefore, that of the fundamental norm from which all endeavor proceeds. That Harnack held that this norm in his case was the Gospel, and his vocation therefore to baptize culture into the service of a repristinated Christianity cannot be gainsaid.

But perhaps the outstanding contribution which Ritschl made to Harnack was that touching the doctrine of man. Harnack's essential anthropology is to be found in his description of the final stage of truly scientific knowledge. This stage deals with the categories of "norms" and "worth" as we encounter these in the study of men. What is encountered in men which gives rise to these "norms" is conscious spirit. Unless this conscious spirit is wrestled with and made the basis of any interpretation, the interpretation will be worthless. But if this process does take place, "the gloomy depths of nature" are vanquished and man is "led forth" to the pinnacle of historical knowledge. But that which lures man to this higher life "is the conviction that we are not mere fragments of nature, but also bear within ourselves an eternal life as the citizens and creators of a spiritual kingdom."[50]

This would appear to be an extremely high view of man. Yet the possibility that man may not leave the "gloomy depths of nature" is clearly present. It is much more a Kantian ethical striving; and it is instructive that just prior to this statement Harnack had declared that there were only three psychological compulsions which bear upon us: the intellective, the aesthetic, and the religious. The *ethical* is not included, but is identified with the religious. That this identification is intended here is obvious; and elsewhere, in his disparaging remarks about those attempts to identify some religious "compulsion," apart from the ethical, Harnack makes it clear that he stands on this ethicoreligious identification. Indeed, Christianity as he interpreted it is, as Troeltsch remarked, "the preaching of Jesus concerning the kingdom of God interpreted in terms of Kantian ethics."[51]

The referent with respect to which the higher life of man is realized

[50] Harnack, "Über wissenschaftliche Erkenntnis," *RA*, III, NF, p. 194.
[51] "The Dogmatics . . . ," p. 12.

is, then, the conviction that man stands above *nature*. This conviction, we have argued, was born out of the necessities of the last half of the nineteenth century, where Harnack was contending against a variety of naturalistic monisms which sought to reduce man to a thing among things. It is all the more striking, then, that Harnack, holding firmly to this Ritschlian apologetic principle, will not break over and desert his basic methodological principle which asserts that all of man's knowledge is relative. Perhaps Overbeck's stinging criticism has not been evaluated sufficiently highly here. For his charge that the believing theologians "risked nothing" made an indelible mark on Harnack, and he would not desert the canons of his historical methodology even to combat the positions which devalued man.

Turning now to a final assessment of Harnack's axiological norm, we may summarize by suggesting that, however one accounts for Harnack's nisus to essence motivation, the fact is that he did assume such an essence, that he identified it in a particular way, and that he applied it to Jesus.

In assuming such an essence, we suggest, Harnack departs from the essentially Hebraic-Christian presupposition in favor of another. For biblical religion is sated with historical particularity. The interpretation of both the Old and the New Covenant begins with the scandalous affirmation that "in this our *history*" God has acted. For Harnack to reduce the reality of Christianity to a *principle*, therefore, to try to free "the characteristic and unique substance of the Christian religion from its temporal forms and expressions,"[52] is to attempt to interpret biblical faith by a norm which is alien to its very historical character. This is not to say that it is completely false to interpret Christianity as emphasizing the virtues of which Harnack spoke; but when one speaks of *a* reality, and categorically holds that this must be an ethical reality, this result is false. Richard Niebuhr is certainly right in his insistence that

> for the purpose of . . . description a moralist may be permitted to choose the somewhat arbitrary device of pointing out and defining the virtues of Jesus Christ; though it will be evident that the resultant portrait needs to be complemented by other interpretations of the same subject, and that a moral description cannot claim to come closer to the essence than do metaphysical or historical descriptions.[53]

In short, if one is to use the term, then one should speak of "essences," not of a single "essence." But even to do this would be to

[52] Pauck, *op. cit.*, p. 345.
[53] *Christ and Culture*, p. 14.

court constant dangers that historical event would be sacrificed to some ideological scheme.

Not only is the procedure questionable, however; we believe that the *content* of the identified reality is derived culturally rather than biblically. This idea has been so omnipresent in this work that it would be sheer redundancy to re-argue it here. But we may communicate our conclusion as to the referent which determined the nature of this content by juxtaposing two quotations which make clear the difference between a genuinely theocentric and an anthropocentric stance. The one is from Harnack's daughter, describing his purpose as he undertook a new study of Augustine:

"God and the soul I want to know; nothing else!" was his confession as it was also Augustine's. He wanted to make Augustine comprehensible for contemporary men, both as a *man* and as a *Christian*; thereby he would raise the question as to the ways in which our achieved civilization could progress and come nearer the kingdom of God.[54]

The other quotation is from Augustine's "Of the Morals of the Catholic Church," where Harnack's hero is describing the conversion of the Greek virtues in a statement that is flooded with theocentricity:

As to virtue leading us to a happy life, I hold virtue to be nothing else than perfect love of God. For the fourfold division of virtue I regard as taken from four forms of love. For these four virtues (would that all felt their influence in their minds as they have their names in their mouths!), I should have no hesitation in defining them: that temperance is love giving itself entirely to that which is loved; fortitude is love readily bearing all things for the sake of the loved object; justice is love serving only the loved object, and therefore ruling rightly; prudence is love distinguishing with sagacity between what hinders it and what helps it. The object of this love is not anything, but only God, the chief good, the highest wisdom, the perfect harmony. So we may express the definition thus: that temperance is love keeping itself entire and incorrupt for God; fortitude is love bearing everything readily for the sake of God; justice is love serving God only, and therefore ruling well all else, as subject to man; prudence is love making a right distinction between what helps it toward God and what might hinder it.[55]

What is the difference? Harnack "would raise the question as to the ways in which our achieved civilization could progress"—i.e., man's basic orientation is toward culture; for Augustine, conversely,

[54] AZH, pp. 516–517.

[55] Quoted from Waldo Beach and Richard Niebuhr, eds., *Christian Ethics: Sources of the Living Tradition* (New York: The Ronald Press Company, 1955), p. 115.

"the object of this love is . . . only God"—i.e., man is oriented toward God, and is bound to fidelity.

Finally, we have argued that Harnack has interpreted Jesus in terms of his axiological norm. Again, it is not necessary here to re-argue the case. We may say simply that Harnack was shut up to this course by the limits which his methodology (to understand Christianity historically) prescribed; that the nisus to essence procedure (to work beyond the dogmatic to the inner form of Christian truth) provided the only way to break these limits; that the contemporary situation made demands (to confess and defend the independently won position), and rendered inutile any "metaphysical" Christ; and therefore the portrait of Jesus which emerges is that of a value-affirming teacher, solely human, and forced by this humanity to encase his "essence" in the husks that were available.

One can indicate the "fate of Harnack" from 1920 to 1950 with a story, source unknown. According to the story, an English theologian, in the middle of the twenties, had asked a German colleague what influence Harnack was then exerting on German theology. He was given the answer, "We have conducted Professor Harnack to Mount Olympus from which he looks down on a world that knows him no more." It may be that, as in the case of the medieval synthesis represented in Thomas' *Summa*, the hypostatizing of a position in a "symbolic concatenation" marked the moment of the beginning of decline. One could document this amply from church history.

Whatever the "causes" of this decline—one could cite the cultural shock of the war, the emergence of the dialectic theology, or the implicit position-transcending principle within Harnack's own historical point of view (for example, Holl, his pupil, using his method, became instrumental in a revival of Luther studies, and Schweitzer, likewise using a modification of Harnack's method, found a point of view in the Gospels which nullified Harnack's axiological interpretation)—its reality is not in dispute. Increasingly, a way of thinking came into vogue which, without giving up Harnack's historical achievements, reversed, in effect, his procedure. Instead of presupposing a theological position and working at the historical task, this way of thinking presupposed the historical studies and gave its attention to the theological explication. It would be much too simple to regard this only as a case of the swinging pendulum; but this is not the place to hypothesize about historical causation. Suffice it to say that history "surprises" us; and therefore Barth is correct when he points out that "we cannot anticipate which of our fellow-workers from out of the past are or are not welcome to us in our own work. It is always possible that we may in some sense have an especial need of a completely unexpected and at first wholly unwelcome voice."[56] The corridors of history are indeed filled with unanticipated voices.

Because this is true, it is possible that the spate of voices predicting a Harnack renascence (or at least, a renewal of concern with the problems with which the liberal theology grappled) may be engaging in unjustified predictive whistling. Harnack himself was remarkably wary of making predictions, and there is a laudable relevance here to his principle that what one must do is to "overcome history by *history*," that is, to work at one's task of assessing the past with fidelity. That work is coterminous, for Harnack, with "preparing for the future in a responsible way." Such preparation must be distinguished, quite sharply, from *planning* for the future. One works, and a part of this work is the exercise of the "regal, judging" function; but this judgment is based on the study of the past, and even though, as we maintain, Harnack did *not* see that the judgment was based also on an axiological norm of present value, he did not project this norm into the indeterminate future. His "great man" theory is illustrative of the point: great men do not come when they *must* come; they come when they come.

Having said this, we must go on to make a further related point. We believe that Harnack here evidenced an unusual sophistication and humility in the description of the historian's task. His ken was the *past* and the *present*; and there he stopped. Whatever *implications* there may be from this work for the future, however deeply he held that there were desiderata for the church and the culture, whatever hopes he personally held, he did not claim to be a prophet. Those who say that he should have been such by the logic of his own position would do well to ponder the truism that the genius—Aquinas and Schleiermacher, for example—puts together things that do not logically belong together, and in this way opens the future in a new and unexpected way. But we would also suggest that those predicting a renascence of interest in the way of thinking which Harnack exemplified and in the interpretation of Christianity which resulted would do well to follow Harnack's advice and avoid prediction. Those who are convinced of the validity of his position, and

[56] Quoted from Ogden, *op. cit.*, p. 14.

would convince others of it, best serve the present by practicing it. But clearly, emulating Harnack here means going beyond him rather than repristinating him, and certain contemporary theologies give evidence of taking the correct road. Thus, as characterized by one of the younger theologians, two drives now dominate theology: "the renewed determination to pursue theological work in obedience to the kerygma and in critical openness to the entire Christian past and also by the concern to do justice to liberal theology and, in particular, to face in all seriousness the fundamental problem with which the liberal theologians sought to deal."[57] This presupposes no acceptance of liberalism's specific theological content—Harnack's "reality of Christianity," for example—but it does presuppose the legitimacy of liberalism's—and Harnack's—question: *wie mache ich es, sein Jünger zu werden*, in a modern world, a world come of age?

The fateful question here would seem to be whether *both* drives are pursued with the same seriousness. Pursuing theological work "in obedience to the kerygma and in critical openness to the entire Christian past" is a catholic principle with which few would find fault; facing "in all seriousness the fundamental problem with which the liberal theologians sought to deal"—the problem of "Christ and culture" is presumably meant—*can* presuppose a position which is neither obedient to the kerygma nor critically open. One may hazard the judgment that a good deal of contemporary "popular theology" lacks circumspect adherence to both principles, and from a "death of God" or "honest to God" or "back to God" viewpoint effectively scuttles one or the other principle. In this connection it is not irrelevant to pay tribute to Adolf Harnack's greatness. Criticially open to the entire Christian past he certainly was, impassioned to confess and defend Christianity, as he understood it, within and to the culture —who can doubt it? But it was "as he understood it." And even if this is applicable alike to *every* theologian, the fact is that *few* of these theologians control the first requirement as Harnack did. The method which the liberals employed—the historical-critical method —is indispensable if this double task is to be effected. And if Harnack intruded a *Humanitätsideal* in his identification of "the reality of Christianity" (his kerygma), controlling the historical materials as he did, the modern who views this intrusion as a mistake and substitutes his culturally efficacious "biblical kerygma" would be well advised to hold the mirror to his own viewpoint. One cannot escape

[57] *Ibid.*, p. 16.

the conviction that a good deal of "culturally relevant" theology is not only loaded with its own *Humanitätsideal*, but lacks the historical sophistication which Harnack possessed.

In addition to those who view the theological situation in the way just described, there are others on the contemporary scene who represent new and old varieties of theology. Fundamentalism remains as a curious but lively anachronism. Here and there an "old liberal" still raises his voice. The ecumenical movement has gathered together many strains and varieties of orthodoxy, neo-orthodoxy, and liberalism. There is scarcely a single ecclesiastical community which has not experienced in its own context a renewal of theological interest. And certainly it is not a transgression of the bounds of historical judgment to ascribe a significant role in this total renewal to Karl Barth and his work.

Barth's influence may indeed turn out to be as ambiguous as some contemporary theologians claim; perhaps, as he said of Ritschl, it will one day be said of him that he marks "an episode" but not "an epoch" in the history of Christian theology.[58] Indeed, it has been said, in effect.[59] But this kind of speculation seems to be premature, at the least; certainly it represents a kind of guessing that Harnack would not have indulged. And since the fact is that it was Barth's alternative interpretation which most radically challenged the interpretation of liberalism, and, as a fact, prevailed over it, this position cannot be regarded—not yet, at least—as overcome.

Barth did not believe that Harnack, no matter how great his contribution to the historical understanding of Christian origins, had spoken to the primary problem, that of revelation (the Word of God). The distinction between the two men with respect to this problem may be stated in this way: for Barth, God is the "wholly Other," who cannot be approached by any natural faculty which man possesses. There is no preparatory revelation in nature or in the thought of great men. For Harnack, "God is Love," and this is the highest and final statement that one can make about God. There are many stages of preparatory development for the apprehension of this truth, such as Goethean romanticism and Kantian rationalism. For Barth, it is God himself who breaks this impasse, revealing his Word in Jesus Christ, which then becomes a "written Word" in the Bible, and the "proclaimed Word" in preaching. For Harnack, there is no impasse, but a gradual apprehension on the part of man, abetted

[58] See Chapter V, note 32.

[59] See Pauck, *op. cit.*, pp. 357–358.

by the "great men"—the prophets, Jesus—of the nature of God as love. For Barth, the Word that became flesh as a human-historical reality is *not* historically recognizable when one looks at the first-century Jew, Jesus of Nazareth. For Harnack, since God is absolute and remains so, and we are relative and remain so, Jesus must be seen as one man among men, though one may say that his life contains elements for which we do not possess historical analogues. But it is on the basis of historical-critical study, not metaphysical speculation, that we should make our statements. To say that "the Word became flesh" can only mean that in the pure human life of Jesus we are taught that highest and final knowledge about God, that he is love.

There are differences at almost every point of the theological compass. For Harnack, the theological enterprise is marked by the attempt to bring scientific knowledge and judgments of value into a unity, which unity can in turn be productive of value. To this Barth answers that scientific knowledge cannot yield that which is of transcendent importance, faith, which is God's work in us and is not prepared for by any "natural revelation." "There is (*Es gibt*) no certainty of faith. He gives (*Er gibt*) certainty of faith."[60] Harnack's position with respect to the relation of theology to the total ethicocultural achievement of man is clearly one of synthesis and interpenetration. To deny this is to make necessary a flight from the world and an abandonment of cultural gains ("stages" only, to be sure) to the barbarians. Barth would reject the option here presented; to say that theology must not make the culture its primary referent (Harnack of course denied that he did this, holding that his referent was "the Gospel as Jesus preached it") does not mean that culture is an unmitigated evil.[61] It does mean that in matters of ultimate concern, ethical and cultural achievement cannot "act as tutors to bring us to Christ." It is God who comes to us. Harnack viewed man's nature as good, marred only by certain removable defects; man is made to love God and the neighbor, to strive toward those "good, true and beautiful" virtues, to achieve "certainty and unity" (which is in part a gift of God, but only after man has himself pushed to the outer courts). Barth sees man's nature as more ambiguous, man's sin being interpreted as the rebellious lack of trust which results in abortive attempts to overcome his anxious and

[60] Quoted in A. L. Drummond, *German Protestantism since Luther* (London: The Epworth Press, 1951), Chapter 7.

[61] Cf. Barth's own interest in Mozart, as evidenced in *Die protestantische Theologie . . . , passim.*

precarious situation. His problem is only stated when it is declared to him that "God so loved . . . that whosoever believes on him might not perish"; for "to do the truth" is not only, or mainly, a problem of knowing the truth, but a problem of faith, trust, and obedience to the one in whom alone "his deeds are wrought." The Gospel becomes then not the giving of a new truth to man (or even the "husking" of an old encumbered truth), but the active "coming" of a gracious God, "vertical from above," which creates faith. Goethe's Eros and Kant's *Vernunft* are not stages on the way; but just because they are essentially anthropocentric "quests," they can lead only to horizontal goals.

The disparity of these points of view are a truism in theology today. In many ways, the particulars of "the liberal system" and "the Barthian system" illustrate perennial themes of dispute in Christian history. It is a remarkable fact, therefore, to find certain respected voices proclaiming an either/or principle in the attempt, presumably, to do justice to Harnack. Certainly one can go as far as to admit that he has been neglected, misinterpreted, and, on occasion, calumniated. Any attempt to correct this kind of unjustified treatment must be welcomed. But whether the use of an either/or is the appropriate corrective may be strongly doubted. For Harnack does not need protection; he needs to be read. And further, is not the Christian theologian, in the very definition of his call, placed under the order of catholicity? Is it not in this context that the question of the present valency of Adolf Harnack's position must be raised?

From the "spate of voices" to which we have referred, two stand out as unequivocally certain that Harnack's position not only is relevant to the contemporary theological situation, but indispensable to it. Wilhelm Pauck puts it as bluntly as it can be put:

> Today, the human situation, including that of the churches, must be handled by critical anthropological thinking and by means of decisions derived from clear, judicious historical thinking. Barth says that church history is merely an auxiliary theological discipline, because he believes that the church must be guided by dogmatic theology oriented to the Bible. But dogmatic speculation, even if it is based on the Bible cannot help us. What we need most is historical understanding and not theosophy. The churches have more need of a Harnack than of a Barth.[62]

Elsewhere, Pauck judges:

> The importance of Harnack's work and outlook will be more fully recognized in the coming years than it is now. The historical interpretation of

[62] *Op. cit.*, p. 358.

Christianity cannot, in the long run, be neglected by the churches and denominations. The time will come when, on the continent of Europe, theological scholarship and church policy will effect a return to the manner of thinking which Harnack represented. He and Troeltsch will be rediscovered, and their leadership will again be recognized as promising a true and truthful understanding and interpretation of the Christian gospel in the modern world.[63]

The other voice is that of Bultmann: "this 'liberal' understanding, at the very least, contains active impulses which though now obscured nonetheless preserve their legitimacy and will recover their validity."[64] And, speaking of *Das Wesen des Christentums*, "[this work] is to be read not only as a historic document, but also as a contribution to contemporary theological discussion. This would be the case even if the effective themes of this book were devoid of immediate import and even if they were not on the verge of coming into their own."[65]

Interpreting both of these judgments to mean approbation of Harnack's interpretation of Christianity (Pauck: "a true and truthful understanding and interpretation of the Christian gospel in the modern world"; Bultmann: "this 'liberal' understanding . . . contains active impulses" and "the effective themes of this book [are] on the verge of coming into their own"), and not solely of his historical method—with which there can be little cavil—this interpreter, in all appropriate deference, must sum up, with Harnack: the truth is in the mean. It may be theologically astute and humanly courageous, and even historically necessary to "take sides." Very well. We take sides with Harnack in his emphasis on historical understanding, in his identification of *the* controlling question for the Christian, in his apologetic purpose, and in his insistence that it is the gospel that judges the world, not the reverse. We take sides against him in his acceptance of nature and spirit as the poles which set man's theological problem, in his nisus to essence procedure, in his specific identification of the gospel according to his *Humanitätsideal*, and in his refusal to see that he departed from his own self-professed historical canons in identifying this reality of the gospel. Perhaps "refusal" is too strong a word; Bultmann puts his finger squarely on the dilemma when he comments that Harnack "seemed not to realize . . . that he could not deal adequately with precisely these features because of his exclusive reliance on the inductive

[63] *Ibid.*, p. 350.
[64] In "Introduction" to Harper Torchbook, *op. cit.*, p. viii.
[65] *Ibid.*, p. ix.

method that he thought he was following."[66] Perhaps, then, the word should be "unawareness." But the fact is there, and it is the most important single fact for understanding Harnack. At that still point of the turning world, where historical science has had its last word, and the reality is to be unmasked, *there* Harnack becomes a theologian, a nineteenth-century theologian, a richly endowed and many-sided son of Theodosius, Engelhardt, Ritschl, with a pinch of Baur and Hegel; and the kerygma he finds is the *Humanitätsideal*—rich and impressive, to be sure—of his own German genius.

[66] *Ibid.*, p. xiii.

Bibliography

Books

Aulén, Gustav. *Christus Victor: An Historical Study of the Three Main Types of the Idea of the Atonement.* Translated by A. G. Hebert. London: S. P. C. K., 1931.

Barth, Karl. *Die protestantische Theologie im 19. Jahrhundert. Ihre Vorgeschichte und ihre Geschichte.* Zweite Auflage, verbesserte. Zurich: Zollikon, 1952.

Baur, F. C. *Geschichte der christlichen Kirche.* Vol. V: *Kirchengeschichte des neunzehnten Jahrhundert.* Herausgegeben von Eduard Zeller. Tübingen: L. F. Fues, 1862.

Beach, Waldo, and Niebuhr, H. Richard. *Christian Ethics: Sources of the Living Tradition.* New York: The Ronald Press Company, 1955.

Bolman, Frederick deWolfe, Jr. *Schelling. The Ages of the World.* New York: Columbia University Press, 1942.

Bülow, Bernhard Fürst. *The Memoirs of Prince von Bülow.* 3 vols. Translated by Geoffrey Dunlop. Boston: Little, Brown & Company, 1932.

Creed, J. M. *The Divinity of Jesus Christ.* Cambridge: At the University Press, 1938.

Cremer, Hermann. *A Reply to Harnack on the Essence of Christianity.* Translated from the third edition by Bernhard Pick. New York: Funk and Wagnalls Company, 1903.

Drummond, A. L. *German Protestantism since Luther.* London: The Epworth Press, 1951.

Elert, Werner. *Der Kampf um das Christentum seit Schleiermacher und Hegel.* München: Beck, 1921.

Foakes-Jackson, F. J. *Christian Difficulties in the Second and Twentieth Centuries*. Cambridge: W. Heffer and Sons, 1903.

Garvie, A. E. *The Ritschlian Theology*. Edinburgh: T. and T. Clark, 1899.

Gerhardt, Martin. *Ein Jahrhundert innere Mission. Die Geschichte des Central-Ausschusses für die innere Mission der deutschen evangelischen Kirche*. 2 vols. Gütersloh: C. Bertelsmann, 1948.

Grant, Robert. *The Bible in the Church*. New York: The Macmillan Company, 1948.

Harnack, Adolf. *The Acts of the Apostles*. Translated by J. R. Wilkinson. New York: G. P. Putnam's Sons, 1909.

———. *Bible Reading in the Early Church*. Translated by J. R. Wilkinson. New York: G. P. Putnam's Sons, 1912.

———. *Christianity and History*. Translated by Thomas Bailey Saunders. London: A. and C. Black, 1896.

———. *The Constitution and Law of the Church in the First Two Centuries*. Translated by F. L. Pogson, edited by H. D. A. Major. New York: G. P. Putnam's Sons, 1910.

———. *Dogmengeschichte*. Vierte Auflage, verbesserte und bereicherte. Tübingen: Mohr, 1905.

———. *The Date of the Acts and of the Synoptic Gospels*. Translated by J. R. Wilkinson. New York: G. P. Putnam's Sons, 1911.

———. *The Expansion of Christianity in the First Three Centuries*. 2 vols. Translated by James Moffatt. New York: G. P. Putnam's Sons, 1904.

———. *Lehrbuch der Dogmengeschichte*. Drei Bände. Dritte Auflage, ausgearbeitete. Leipzig: Mohr, 1894.

———. *Luke the Physician*. Translated by J. R. Wilkinson. New York: G. P. Putnam's Sons, 1923.

———. *Marcion, das Evangelium vom fremden Gott*. Leipzig: Hinrichs, 1921.

———. *Neue Studien zu Marcion*. Leipzig: Hinrichs, 1923.

———. *The Origin of the New Testament and the Most Important Consequences of the New Creation*. Translated by J. R. Wilkinson. New York: The Macmillan Company, 1925.

———. *Reden und Aufsätze*. Zwei Bände. Giessen: Töpelmann, 1904.

———. *Reden und Aufsätze*, Neue Folge. Bände I and II: *Aus Wissenschaft und Leben*, 1911. Band III: *Aus der Friedens- und Kriegsarbeit*, 1916. Band IV: *Erforschtes und Erlebtes*, 1923. Band V: *Aus der Werkstatt des Vollendeten*, 1930, herausgegeben von Axel Harnack. Giessen: Töpelmann.

———. *The Sayings of Jesus*. Translated by J. R. Wilkinson. New York: G. P. Putnam's Sons, 1908.

———. *Thoughts on the Present Position of Protestantism*. Translated by Thomas Bailey Saunders. London: A. and C. Black, 1899.

———. *Das Wesen des Christentums*. Leipzig: Hinrichs, 1900.

———. *What Is Christianity?* 4th ed. Translated by Thomas Bailey Saunders. New York: G. P. Putnam's Sons, 1923.

Harnack, Adolf, *et al. The Atonement in Modern Religious Thought.* London: James Clarke and Company, 1900.

Harnack, Adolf, and Herrmann, Wilhelm. *Essays on the Social Gospel.* Translated by G. M. Craik and edited by Maurice A. Canney. New York: G. P. Putnam's Sons, 1907.

Harnack, Agnes von Zahn-. *Adolf von Harnack.* Berlin: Hans Bott, 1936.

Kattenbusch, Ferdinand. *Die deutsche evangelische Theologie seit Schleiermacher: Ihre Leistungen und ihre Schäden.* Vierte Auflage, umgearbeitete. Giessen: Töpelmann, 1924.

Loisy, Alfred. *The Gospel and the Church.* Translated by Christopher Home. New York: Charles Scribner's Sons, 1909.

Loofs, Friedrich. *Leitfaden zum Studium der Dogmengeschichte.* Dritte Auflage. Halle: Max Niemeyer, 1893.

Mackintosh, H. R. *Types of Modern Theology: Schleiermacher to Barth.* London: Nisbet and Company, 1937.

Niebuhr, H. Richard. *Christ and Culture.* New York: Harper & Row, 1951.

———. *The Meaning of Revelation.* New York: The Macmillan Company, 1941.

Orr, James. *Ritschlianism: Expository and Critical Essays.* New York: A. C. Armstrong and Son, 1903.

Pauck, Wilhelm. *Karl Barth: Prophet of a New Christianity?* New York: Harper & Brothers, 1931.

Peterson, Erik. *Theologische Traktate.* München: Kösel, 1951.

Richardson, Alan, and Schweitzer, Wolfgang (eds.). *Biblical Authority Today.* Philadelphia: The Westminster Press, 1951.

Ritschl, Albrecht. *Die Entstehung der altkatholischen Kirche.* Zweite Auflage, ausgearbeitete. Bonn: Marcus, 1857.

Rolffs, Ernst, *Harnack's Wesen des Christentums und die religiösen Strömungen der Gegenwart.* Leipzig: Hinrichs, 1902.

Schnabel, Franz. *Deutsche Geschichte im neunzehnten Jahrhundert.* Vol. IV: *Die religiösen Kräfte.* Zweite Auflage. Freiburg: Herder, 1951.

Schweitzer, Albert. *The Quest of the Historical Jesus: A Critical Study of Its Progress from Reimarus to Wrede.* Translated by W. Montgomery. London: A. and C. Black, 1911.

Smend, Friedrich. *Adolf von Harnack. Verzeichnis seiner Schriften.* Leipzig: Hinrichs, 1931.

Smith, Harold. *Ante-Nicene Exegesis of the Gospels.* Vol. I. London: S. P. C. K., 1925.

Tillich, Paul. *Systematic Theology.* Vol. I. Chicago: The University of Chicago Press, 1951.

Troeltsch, Ernst. *Gesammelte Schriften.* Vol. III: *Der Historismus und seine Probleme.* Tübingen: Mohr, 1922.

Weiss, Johannes. *Christ: The Beginnings of Dogma.* Translated by V. D. Davis. London: Philip Green, 1911.

Articles and Periodicals

Craig, Clarence Tucker. "Biblical Theology and the Rise of Historicism," *Journal of Biblical Literature*, LXII (December, 1943), 281–94.

Harnack, Adolf. "Martin Luther, the Prophet of the Reformation," *The Prophets of the Christian Faith.* Edited by Lyman Abbott. New York: The Macmillan Company, 1896, 107–22.

———. "The Relation between Ecclesiastical and General History," translated by Thomas Bailey Saunders, *Contemporary Review,* LXXXVI (December, 1904), 846–59.

Jenkins, Finley DuBois. "Is Harnack's *History of Dogma* a History of Harnack's Dogma?" *Princeton Theological Review,* XXI (July and October, 1923), 389–428 and 585–620.

Loisy, Alfred. "Marcion's Gospel," *The Hibbert Journal,* XXXIV (1935–36), 378–87.

Löwith, Karl. "L'achèvement de la philosophie classique par Hegel et sa dissolution chez Marx et Kierkegaard," *Recherches Philosophiques,* IV (1934–35), 232–67.

Lyman, Eugene W. "Ritschl's Theory of Value-Judgments," *Journal of Religion,* V (October, 1925), 500–18.

Niebuhr, H. Richard. "Religious Realism and the Twentieth Century," *Religious Realism.* Edited by D. C. Macintosh. New York: The Macmillan Company, 1931, 413–28.

Pauck, Wilhelm. "The Significance of Adolf von Harnack's Interpretation of Church History," *Union Seminary Quarterly Review*, Special Issue (January, 1954), 13–24.

Richards, George W. "The Place of Adolf von Harnack among Church Historians," *Journal of Religion,* XI (July, 1931), 333–45.

Troeltsch, Ernst. "The Dogmatics of the *Religionsgeschichtliche Schule,*" American Journal of Theology, XVII (January, 1913), 1–21.

Weinel, Heinrich. "Religious Life and Thought in Germany Today," *The Hibbert Journal*, VII (1908–09), 721–45.

———. "The Present State of Religious Life in Germany and Its Most Important Tendencies," *The Hibbert Journal,* XXII (1923–24), 260–78.

Index of Names

Format by Lydia Link
Set in Linotype Times Roman
Composed, printed and bound by The Haddon Craftsmen, Inc.
HARPER & ROW, PUBLISHERS, INCORPORATED